YALE LAW LIBRARY SERIES
IN LEGAL HISTORY AND REFERENCE

JONATHAN GIENAPP

Against Constitutional Originalism

A HISTORICAL CRITIQUE

Yale

UNIVERSITY PRESS

NEW HAVEN AND LONDON

Published with support from the Lillian Goldman Law Library,
Yale Law School.

Yale University Press books may be purchased in quantity
for educational, business, or promotional use. For information,
please email sales.press@yale.edu (U.S. office) or
sales@yaleup.co.uk (U.K. office).

Set in type by IDS Infotech, Ltd.
Printed in the United States of America.

Library of Congress Control Number: 2024937386
ISBN 978-0-300-26585-9 (hardcover : alk. paper)

A catalogue record for this book is available from the British Library.

This paper meets the requirements of ANSI/NISO Z39.48-1992
(Permanence of Paper).

10 9 8 7 6 5 4 3

For My Parents

CONTENTS

AGAINST CONSTITUTIONAL ORIGINALISM

Introduction: History and Originalism

> The infant periods of most nations are buried in silence or veiled in fable. . . . The origin & outset of the American Republic contain lessons of which posterity ought not to be deprived.
>
> — James Madison to William Eustis, July 6, 1819

CONSTITUTIONAL ORIGINALISM IS inextricably wedded to history. Ever since the provocative theory of interpretation emerged several decades ago, its core commitment—that the United States Constitution should be interpreted today in accordance with its original meaning at the time of its inception—has inescapably implicated historical inquiry.[1] To know what the Constitution means, originalists claim, demands that we look to the past. Sometimes that leads inquirers to the more recent past, especially in the case of the enormously important Reconstruction amendments that were added to the Constitution following the end of the Civil War. But more often than not, it requires a deep dive into the distant eighteenth-century past—a return to the American Founding, when the Constitution was created. While history has always mattered to American constitutional interpretation, the marked emphasis that originalism places on the past sets it apart.[2] Nowhere else do the study of history and the practice of constitutionalism and law so directly and consequentially collide. Nowhere in contemporary American life is history more relevant or important.

Originalism has taken on heightened significance of late. Thanks to the vicissitudes of recent American politics, the United States judiciary is now stacked with self-identified originalists, and for the first time in its history, the Supreme Court boasts an originalist majority. And we have already begun to see how an originalist Court is liable to draw on constitutional history to radically remake modern law. Its recent appeal to the standard of "history and tradition" to decide a slew of landmark cases is only one of the clearest signals.[3] In the coming years, those with the power to determine the content of fundamental American rights—to freely speak and worship, to keep and bear arms, to enjoy equal protection before the law—as well as the powers of the presidency, the legitimacy of the administrative state, and the scope of the national government's power to reform healthcare, address climate change, and protect voting rights, will increasingly do so by reference to history and what the Constitution purportedly meant at the time of its creation. The growing sway of originalist judges, meanwhile, has coincided with the steady entrenchment of originalism in the legal academy. Each year the body of originalist scholarship grows—scholarship originalist judges rely on to justify their decisions. Never, therefore, has it been more important to scrutinize originalism's use of history.

Originalism's engagement with history is often deeply problematic. Despite claiming to recover the constitutional past as it was, most of the time originalists create an alternative past based on the assumptions of the present. Worse, they are seldom even aware that they've done so. They confidently appeal to the early history of the United States to overturn a long-standing precedent, nullify a popular law, or protect a newfangled right, assured that they are getting things right—that they are humbly following the law as originally laid down. But they are not. They distort the very history from which they derive authority. It is past time to confront originalism's use and abuse of history.

To meet this moment, this book mounts a comprehensive historical critique of constitutional originalism. It does so by approaching originalism anew. The debate over originalism has been too narrowly focused. As a result, it has skated over many of the fundamental issues implicated by the theory, issues that raise the most urgent questions about originalists' engagement with the constitutional past. In what follows, I attempt to bring these dimly appreciated issues to the surface to formulate a new critique of originalism. It is not only a critique based in history but one that is intended to show that no critique of originalism is more fundamental than the historical one that cuts right to the theory's foundations. For too long, originalists have bypassed many of the central questions raised by their theory. For too long, they have failed to truly reckon with the history of the American Founding. When we recover Founding-era constitutionalism on its own terms, we discover how deeply at odds originalism is with the history it claims to recover and enforce as our fundamental law. We see how un-originalist originalism turns out to be.

Originalism's Enduring Focus

Among the biggest problems with originalism is the narrowness of its vision. This flaw is not rooted in what its advocates explicitly defend but instead in what they often take for granted and leave unexplored. Most especially, when originalists probe the constitutional past in search of original meaning, their historical investigation is often strikingly narrow and limited. It is typically focused on linguistic meaning—on what the words of different constitutional provisions originally meant—and almost never on the instrument in which those words are found: the Constitution itself. What do important constitutional phrases such as "executive power," "freedom of speech," "the right of the people to keep and bear arms," "equal protection of the laws," or "Full Faith and Credit" mean? In asking these questions, originalists usually assume that the Constitution's essential nature is clear and obvious; that there is little reason to worry if the Constitution as we habitually perceive, describe, and delimit it today is different from the Constitution as it was once perceived, described, and delimited back when it appeared. The Constitution simply *is* the Constitution—the same now and always, from 1787 to the present day. Originalists at least strive to historicize the Constitution's meaning— the entire originalist enterprise is based on the assumption that original and contemporary constitutional meaning might be different.[4] But originalists give little thought to the prospect of historicizing the Constitution itself. They seldom wonder whether, as with the meaning of particular words and phrases, the Constitution was once understood to be a different kind of thing.

Originalism's narrow focus has been one of its hallmarks, but neither its proponents nor its antagonists have much paused to examine it. This is perhaps unsurprising. It is, after all, not hard to understand why there's been relatively little attention paid to the nature of the original Constitution. The Constitution *feels* familiar. When we confront it, we do so with over two centuries of practice, precedent, and experience to draw on. We have been deeply socialized in a set of enduring interpretive traditions that shape our intuitions, organize our conversations, and channel our disagreements. Each new Supreme Court term reinforces these practices, igniting more rounds of public debate shaped by the familiar forms of argumentation and tacit assumptions that have long structured our constitutional culture. It is natural to begin where everyone else seems to—to start where our historical experience and collective socialization suggest we should. It is hardly surprising that people have intuitively fixated on what particular words, phrases, or clauses might mean or have sought to trace the chain of Supreme Court precedent and doctrine, especially when most interlocutors are eager to pose the questions in those very terms. It keeps things focused and concrete while coordinating conversation and study. It is what our evolved constitutional tradition has given us: a shared language of constitutional debate.[5]

Originalism itself emerged from debates within this particular tradition—at a specific moment in time and in response to a specific challenge. Although originalists have subsequently asserted that their theory of constitutional interpretation has been around since the Founding, in its recognizable modern form it only emerged in a much later age, during the ascendance of a liberal Supreme Court in the decades following the Second World War.[6] Under Chief Justice Earl Warren, and later Chief Justice Warren Burger, the Court dramatically expanded the scope of constitutional rights—particularly in core areas such as civil rights, reproductive rights, and the rights of criminal defendants through controversial landmark rulings such as *Brown v. Board of Education*, *Griswold v. Connecticut*, *Miranda v. Arizona*, and *Roe v. Wade*. The Warren and Burger Courts' jurisprudence was celebrated on the political left but criticized by political conservatives angry that the Court was inventing rights nowhere enumerated in the Constitution and, in so doing, exceeding its judicial mandate. Rather than interpreting the Constitution, as was their solemn charge, the justices were accused of legislating from the bench—privileging their subjective values and policy preferences over democratically enacted laws.

Originalism materialized from these charged complaints about judicial activism. The term itself was not coined until 1980, and it was not until later

that decade—when Attorney General Edwin Meese, in a famous speech before the American Bar Association in 1985, defended a "jurisprudence of
original intent," and then a self-described originalist, Antonin Scalia, was appointed to the Supreme Court in 1986—that originalism cohered into a pub-
licly identifiable theory of constitutional interpretation.[7] But its key intellectual
ingredients were forged in the preceding decades.[8] Responding directly to the
Warren and Burger Courts' controversial rulings, early originalists denigrated
the idea of a living Constitution—something political liberals had long
defended—insisting that the Constitution did not change unless formally
amended.[9] It was unlawful, originalists claimed, for judges to supersede the
sovereign people and update the Constitution's meaning, to decide for themselves when society had sufficiently evolved that the Constitution meant
something different than it had before. Instead, originalists argued, judges
ought to treat the Constitution as "dead," its meaning as fixed until lawfully
changed, and focus their interpretive efforts on recovering the original intent
of the Constitution's drafters. The point was less to celebrate the achieve-
ments of the Constitution's authors—even if the theory's political and rhetorical success assuredly was staked to the veneration of the American
Founders—than to constrain rogue judges by ensuring that constitutional interpretation would be structured by putatively neutral principles.[10] Even if the
motivations behind originalism were no doubt as political as anything its
champions sought to displace, the theory was nonetheless sold as a way to
take politics out of constitutional interpretation.[11] It promised to transform a
Constitution that had come to be heralded for its flexibility and "majestic
generalities" back into a set of binding rules.[12] In the process, it would turn
judges back into judges.

   If that was the constitutional and political moment in which originalism
emerged, then the challenge the theory was devised to counter was the threat
of unmoored, open-ended interpretation. Within law, originalism responded
to the challenge posed by legal realism, which had first reared its head
around the turn of the twentieth century. Realists claimed that law was more
than abstract rules judges formally applied to cases that came before them.
Embedded in a set of political, social, and economic contexts, law was invariably shaped by social interests and public policy. Judges, therefore, necessarily made law as much as they interpreted it.[13] Beyond law, however,
originalism was also, more indirectly, responding to the challenge posed by

the specter of radical interpretive indeterminacy, which, in the second half of the twentieth century, was sweeping through several corners of intellectual life as a rising chorus of philosophers, literary critics, anthropologists, historians, and many others were emphasizing the constructed nature of meaning and interpretation.[14] It little mattered that early originalists—like too many critics of pragmatism, poststructuralism, postmodernism, and the various other isms that unsettled them—often had only passing familiarity with the wider intellectual currents they claimed to be swimming against. Against these storms of relativism, originalism promised a formalist stronghold. As an entry in the burgeoning intellectual culture wars of the late twentieth century, it vowed objectivity and neutrality in a legal and intellectual world that had purportedly lost interest in those values.[15]

For early originalists, bringing the Constitution back down to size—to combat living constitutionalism, legal realism, the threat of semantic indeterminacy, and the like—entailed emphasizing its written text and the individual provisions found within. What better way to make the Constitution rule-like than to demand that people stick to the Constitution's explicit textual commands? What better way to tame the boundless readings of the First and Fourteenth Amendments or Congress's power to regulate interstate commerce than to transform interpretation of those clauses into an exercise in parsing semantics and grammar and chasing after historical definitions and concrete usages? American constitutional culture had long taken written constitutionalism seriously, but originalism dramatically heightened the emphasis.[16]

As originalism evolved, the emphasis on textual provisions only deepened. For decades now, the dominant version of the theory has been public meaning originalism. Defended most conspicuously by Justice Antonin Scalia during his lengthy tenure on the Supreme Court, this form of originalism stipulates that modern interpreters are bound only by the Constitution's original public meaning—what its words would have communicated to an average reader at the time they were written—and are thus not beholden to the original authorial intentions that lay behind those words, the original purposes that might have undergirded them, or the original expected applications that were presumed to follow from them.[17] In privileging public meaning over all else, this brand of originalism trained virtually all attention on the meaning of particular constitutional provisions. Eventually, this narrow focus came to seem obvious and natural, leaving few to wonder about the object of interpretation itself—to ask whether the Constitution, as much as the meaning of its discrete provisions, has also changed over time.

Prior Critiques

Ever since it first appeared, originalism has been subjected to penetrating critiques. These criticisms—many of them historical in character, others normative and jurisprudential—have tended to wage battle on originalism's terms, focused primarily on the narrower category of constitutional meaning. They go something like this.

The Constitution had no single original intent or meaning, so trying to divine one is a fool's errand. The Founders were as divided as we are today. Those who wrote the Constitution did not share the same goals or expect it to mean the same thing in practice. The same was true of the ratifiers who approved the Constitution in special conventions throughout the states, not to mention the vastly larger political community for whom they spoke. James Madison thought one thing, Alexander Hamilton another, Thomas Jefferson something different still. All interpreters can do is sift through and pick and choose between the multiple intents and meanings fairly contained in the historical record.[18] In many cases, moreover, original meaning is simply unknowable. The historical evidence is insufficient, or the documentary record is silent, often because the issue at hand was never raised.[19]

In those instances in which original meaning is knowable and can be pinpointed, meanwhile, it is often impossible to apply that meaning to modern circumstances unknown to the Framers without updating, and even changing, the Constitution in the process.[20] In many instances, this is because the Constitution's most important provisions were written in broad, general language precisely so that they could be applied to novel circumstances in the future.[21] This is to say nothing of the frequent complaints that originalists simplify or distort the past in their haste to find a usable past to reach their ideologically favored results.[22] That is, that even when the original meaning— of "executive power," "necessary and proper," "freedom of speech, or of the press," "the right to keep and bear arms," or broader principles such as the enumeration of congressional power, state sovereign immunity, or Congress's authority to delegate rulemaking to the executive branch—can be deciphered, originalists get it wrong.[23]

Beyond originalism's historical mistakes, every bit as problematic is its core commitment that original meaning be binding today. Originalism is illegitimate because it privileges the "dead hand" of the past—the understandings and agreements of generations that have long since left the scene—over those forced to live under that law today. Modern Americans are thus subject to a binding authority to which none of them agreed.[24] To make matters worse, those earlier generations we are asked to follow tolerated, even embraced, slavery, formally excluded scores of Americans (including virtually all women) from political life, defended property requirements for voting, and violently expropriated Indigenous lands. This unsavory reality severely soils the supreme democratic foundation upon which the original Constitution is said to be based. The "people" who breathed life into the Constitution were a woefully inadequate version of that democratic concept. We "the people" of today are not beholden to flawed eighteenth-century values and, instead, should embrace a vision of the Constitution that looks forward as much as backward.[25] On top of all of this, adhering to originalism would mean dismantling much of our current law, which would not only be impractical and detrimental but would abandon hard-won progress and send us back to a benighted time of discrimination and suffering.[26] For these reasons, the nation is better served by alternative approaches to constitutional interpretation that take constitutional growth, practice, and change as seriously as original meaning.[27]

These criticisms continue to raise vital issues, but as potent as they remain, they tend to accept originalism's narrow focus on the Constitution's discrete textual provisions. According to these criticisms, originalists are mistaken either about what is entailed in recovering the original meaning of those provisions or whether we are bound by those meanings today. But the focus remains squarely on the meanings of specific constitutional words and phrases.

It is worth pressing deeper. If we look more closely at originalism, what matters most is not how its defenders think about meaning or specifically interpret the Constitution (crucial though that is) but rather how they conceive of the Constitution itself. In focusing almost exclusively on the Constitution's meaning, originalists glide past the most vital steps in their theory—those that contemplate what it *is* that we are even interpreting and ask whether that interpretive object, as we perceive it today, indeed has the same essence, identity, boundaries, and content as the one created back in 1787. We must look beneath original meaning to the original Constitution.

Originalists' Constitution

When we focus on the Constitution itself, we find the bulk of the originalist argument. What originalists often presuppose about the Constitution itself, while usually obscured and seldom defended, is essential to their theory. Among themselves, originalists disagree on plenty.[28] But by and large, they reference the Constitution and its core attributes in shared matter-of-fact ways. They often assume that the Constitution at the center of modern jurisprudence—the one that currently is debated in federal court and studied in law schools—is identical in kind to the Constitution that was created back in the eighteenth century. At bottom, they presume that the Constitution is a text (that its content is derived from its words), that its meaning is fixed (that the meaning of its words cannot change unless it is formally amended), and that it is a species of conventional law (that it is to be understood and interpreted like other kinds of law). The Constitution, originalists often assume, self-evidently is all of these things. What you see is what you get. The real argumentative action lies elsewhere.

While originalists might not treat their assumptions about the Constitution as especially controversial, these assumptions perform foundational work. For one, originalists' arguments often depend on their just-so descriptions of the Constitution. By seeing the Constitution in a certain kind of way, originalists enable originalism to seem an intuitive way to interpret it. By emphasizing the Constitution's textual character, they make it easier to reduce interpretation to questions of linguistic meaning. By emphasizing the Constitution's legal character, they make it easier to reduce interpretation to questions of legal principle and doctrine.

For another, originalists especially depend on the necessity of their assumptions about the Constitution. Originalists don't supply these assumptions; the Constitution does. They are, in originalists' eyes, *given*. This belief is crucial. Beneath the various normative theories that are often layered on top of it, originalism has long relied on one consistent defense: that, as an interpretive approach, it does not *make* a constitution but merely *finds* and *interprets* one.[29] This was what originalists promised the world from the beginning: a neutral theory of interpretation.[30] Originalists have long insisted that competing theories of constitutional interpretation, especially the many variants of living constitutionalism that have long predominated, impose subjective political and moral values on the Constitution, enabling judges to pick and choose what the law ought to be on the basis of their own preferences or sense of the polity's shifting mood.[31] Originalism, by contrast, claims merely to recover the Constitution as it is, allowing it to speak for itself.[32] This promise is why originalism is, as one acolyte has claimed, the "single, 'true' method of constitutional interpretation."[33] Whereas other theories get caught up in what the Constitution *ought* to be, originalism alone respects the Constitution for what it *is*. One must then still explain why any of us owe fidelity to that Constitution, but it is far easier to make that case if you have already laid claim to the one, true Constitution that there is. If you establish a sharp dichotomy between judges interpreting the Constitution according to what it originally meant and judges interpreting it according to what they think is desirable for it to mean, you have already done the work of equating originalism to fidelity.[34] It is no exaggeration to claim that originalism's success (rhetorical and substantive) rests principally on its purported claim to merely recover the Constitution *as it is*.

This desire to claim the mantle of objectivity best explains originalism's defining shift from original intent to original public meaning as the target of constitutional interpretation. Public meaning originalism—for several decades now the dominant version of the theory—has proved so attractive precisely because it has seemed capable of making originalism properly objective, and thus securing the theory's long-standing aim.[35] Earlier forms of originalism, which tended to speak of recovering the Founders' original intent, were vulnerable to the fact of original disagreement and thus the problem of subjective selection.[36] Like us, the Founders disagreed, so choosing a single interpretation meant choosing one set of Founders over another. But public meaning originalism seemed to offer a solution. By focusing strictly on the text of the Constitution—not what anyone thought it meant but what its words objectively communicated at the time they were written— originalists could disaggregate the Constitution from the quirks and prejudices of its creators.[37] No longer would originalists have to worry about adjudicating the Founders' intramural squabbles. They could simply decipher the Founders' objective creation: the text that had been ratified by the sovereign people. In approving the Constitution, the Founding generation was, as one originalist has put it, "adopting a text" with "an objective public meaning."[38] Which means that "the content of the law," as another pair of originalists has explained, is "embodied in the objective social meaning of its text rather than in the unknowable intentions of those who voted for it."[39] Originalists could now brush the Founders' opinions to the side and tackle the supposedly straightforward empirical matter of discovering what the words of the Constitution originally meant to a hypothetical average reader at the time of enactment.[40] By isolating the Constitution from the cacophony of Founding-era voices that originally surrounded it, public meaning originalism has promised to provide the objective grounding on which the theory has always relied and claimed constitutionalism so essentially needs.

Most everything originalists argue thus rests on their presumed belief that the Constitution *is* as they describe it—that these descriptions offer a neutral starting place for interpretation. Originalism does not—*cannot*—stipulate an optional conception of the Constitution. By its own premises, it needs to unearth and restore the real Constitution—the one that has existed as a matter of brute, undeniable fact. Were they to admit otherwise, originalists would lose claim to their most vital arguments and with that the basic impetus for their theory.

It is for this reason that looking at Founding-era history anew raises such profound questions for originalism, questions that its advocates have thus far proved unwilling or unable to grasp. The cardinal justification for originalism is that it simply recovers the Constitution *as it is*. If, however, the original Constitution was not understood and conceived as originalists assume it must have been, then their essentialist, *just-so* argument collapses under its own weight.

Historicizing the Constitution

That is precisely what happens when we turn to history. The Constitution—never mind its meaning, the Constitution itself—is not just so. The Constitution that is so intuitive to originalists is different from the Constitution that instinctively sprang to Founding-era Americans' minds—certainly the minds of those who participated in and commented on the initial project of constitutional creation.[41] If we return to the Founding and allow the period to speak for itself, reconstructing its constitutionalism on its own terms and charting its dramatic early development, we find that the original Constitution neither presupposed nor necessitated the assumptions upon which originalism so essentially depends.

We find, in particular, different ways of thinking about constitutional writtenness, fixity, and law that amounted to a distinct brand of constitutionalism. Or we find sharp disagreement over the character of written constitutions, the ways in which the Constitution was fixed, or whether the Constitution was in any way comparable to conventional forms of law. The Founding generation committed their constitutions to writing, but because of how they understood both constitutions and fundamental law, they did not assume that writing constitutional principles down automatically erected sharp textual boundaries around those constitutions. To their minds, constitutions consisted of both textual provisions and the preexisting principles of fundamental law. Only later would that change. Meanwhile, steeped as they were in social contract theory, Founding-era American constitutionalists believed that the federal Constitution's content could not be divorced from the kind of union the Constitution represented. They believed that the national government's powers, as specified by the Constitution's text, depended upon whether the instrument spoke for a nation, a union of autonomous states, or something in between. The meaning of the written Constitution thus rested on an underlying socio-historical account of union and sovereignty that could never be wholly derived from the text itself. Because they thought differently about written constitutionalism, moreover, Founding-era constitutionalists often understood constitutional fixity in non-textual terms, which allowed them to believe that constitutional principles were at once fixed and evolving. Finally, even if the Constitution was law of some kind, the Founding generation did not immediately assume that it was alike in kind to other forms of law and thus susceptible to conventional legal interpretation. It took a long time, and a series of crucial transformations along the way, before that idea took hold, and even then, it continued to face challenges. At first and for years to come, many believed that the Constitution was a people's document, not a lawyer's document.

In bringing these differences between originalist and Founding-era constitutionalism into sharp relief, and recognizing the extent to which familiar constitutional assumptions emerged only later—unexpectedly and contingently—we can see just how tenuous originalism's most foundational assumptions truly are.[42] In failing to appreciate the original uncertainty that engulfed the Constitution, and thus the contingent origins of many of their core presuppositions, originalists fail to appreciate how optional their conception of the Constitution is. Indeed, they fail to see that it is a *conception* at all. Nothing about the original Constitution, or fidelity to it, requires describing it as originalists do. Historicizing the Constitution illustrates that originalism's most vital, unspoken assumptions—all those preliminary steps in the theory that are foundational to originalism yet too often ignored—are neither as essential nor as originalist as originalists confidently presume. They are unfounded.

Consequently, when originalists talk about the original Constitution, they engage in subtle yet far-reaching anachronism, distorting the Founding they claim to recover. Rather than recapturing the original Constitution as it existed, originalism wrenches it into the present, transforming it into something decidedly modern and decidedly different from what it once was.

Even though they fail to realize it, then, originalists are, in fact, no less committed to informal constitutional change and evolution than their intellectual opponents. The Constitution that originalists interpret is not the one that existed at the Founding, but one that has slowly emerged over time, as assumptions about constitutionalism, law, liberty, and governance have quietly evolved and interpreters have been socialized to approach constitutional questions in accordance with certain modern orthodoxies. These orthodoxies help erase the discontinuities between our constitutional vocabulary and the one the Founders spoke, making it seem as though our constitutionalism was theirs and the Constitution we habitually see and interpret is alike in kind to the one they created all those years ago. Modern jurisprudence depends on this perceived continuity. But this perceived continuity is a mirage. Our Constitution—the one at the center of modern American legal life—is predicated on assumptions that were largely unknown at the Founding.

Historicizing the original Constitution thus poses a foundational challenge to originalism as it has long been conceived. Because the originalism debate has been narrowly focused, this particular failing, though fundamental, has never received the attention that it deserves. This book is an attempt to remedy that oversight—to bring this historical critique to the center of the originalism debate where it properly belongs.

The argument proceeds in three parts. Part I examines the architecture of originalist arguments—the tacit assumptions upon which the theory tends to rely and the conception of the Constitution that emerges from them. It details, in particular, the implicit conceptions of writtenness, fixity, and law that undergird most originalist argument. With the originalist Constitution in view, part II turns to the eighteenth century—to the Founding generation—to demonstrate the often radically different ways in which people back then conceived of constitutionalism and law. It ranges widely over the terrain of Founding-era constitutionalism, exploring the nature of law, the character of rights, habits of judicial reasoning, ideas of popular constitutionalism, and debates over the character of the federal union to show, first, how differently the Founding generation thought about constitutional writtenness, fixity, and law than we do today and, second, how deeply divided members of that earlier generation were among themselves over how to understand those concepts. Part III then brings this historical evidence into direct conversation with originalist theory to explain why doctrinaire originalists—no matter their long-standing tendency to assume otherwise—can't escape the implications of this evidence, at least not without abandoning the essential features of originalism. Originalists need to either confront this evidence directly or revise their theory in substantial, self-defeating ways. But either way, they can't continue, as has long been their wont, to ignore this history.

A brief word is also in order on what is not discussed in this book. In considering originalists' reliance on historical argument, I focus exclusively on Founding-era history—on the broad period that runs from the mid-eighteenth to the early nineteenth century, during which time the United States earned its independence and constructed the nation's constitutional order. While originalists have always primarily focused on the Founding, it is not the only period they have concentrated on.

Originalists have devoted considerable attention, especially recently, to the Reconstruction amendments that so dramatically remade constitutional life following the Civil War.[43] Even though originalist judges still too often ignore these amendments, originalist scholars do not.[44] They take seriously the Thirteenth, Fourteenth, and Fifteenth Amendments—which ended slavery; enshrined birthright citizenship, equal protection before the law, and the privileges and immunities of citizenship; and forbade disenfranchisement on the basis of race—rightfully recognizing that many fundamental constitutional rights are properly traced to the original meaning of these amendments.[45] That said, while originalists have certainly emphasized the importance of the Reconstruction amendments, they have never contended that those amendments fundamentally remade the Constitution *itself* as an object in the world. The amendments, to be sure, added transformative content to the document—content that unquestionably touched on numerous aspects of law and society, modified the system of federalism that the original Constitution had established, and altered yet other parts of the constitutional order. But the amendments did not, in turn, change the kind of document the Constitution was, the character or boundaries of its content, or its broader relationship to fundamental law. It is not as if originalists have argued, let alone even so much as hinted, that the Constitution was initially something other than a written text or a conventional legal instrument and only became one thanks to the Reconstruction amendments. They have never contended that the amendments remade the Constitution's very essence.

On the contrary, originalists often stress how limited and lawful the so-called second founding was—emphasizing that these changes ran through the document's own prescribed method for lawful amendment and concluding that the Constitution survived the process intact.[46] They bristle at the suggestion that anything genuinely revolutionary, extralegal, or even illegal accompanied the change.[47] They certainly do not accept Thurgood Marshall's famous proclamation at the bicentennial that "[w]hile the Union survived the civil war, the Constitution did not."[48] The dominant constitutional story of Reconstruction that originalists tell is one of continuity and survival. The Founders' Constitution, in essential form, endured. The amendments took the form of new text simply appended to the old. Meanwhile, the Constitution itself—the interpretive object to which those amendments had been added—remained almost entirely unchanged.

While certain critiques of originalism would need to focus in-depth on originalists' understandings of the Reconstruction amendments, that is not true of the critique mounted here. Given that this book's critique is focused on the nature of the Constitution itself, and given originalists' firm belief that the nature of the Constitution has been largely unchanged from 1787 to the present, to develop the particular critique of originalism that follows, our focus needs to be squarely on the Founding era—when the United States Constitution came into the world.

In probing originalism's use of history, this book ultimately hopes, in some small way, to remake our modern constitutional consciousness and to clarify history's value to our constitutional understanding. In appreciating the sharp discontinuities that separate past from present, in seeing the myriad ways in which our appeals to the constitutional past are really ways of arguing over the constitutional present, we ought to see, at last, that *our* Constitution is invariably the product of now.

We can assuredly recover the original Constitution on its own terms—this book is deeply committed to that very proposition. There is, moreover, tremendous historical *and* contemporary value in doing so. But it comes at the cost of finding ready answers to most of the questions that course through our contemporary legal lives. If we historicize our constitutional past, what becomes clear is that the Founding era does not neatly interface with our modern one. We can recover the past largely as it was, or, to make it speak legibly to the present, we can pound it into a new shape. In most instances, those are our choices. In this regard, rightfully understood, history rarely guides us to the Constitution's true, elusive original meaning. Rather, it awakens us to the realization that the Constitution we have come to debate, enforce, and venerate is one of our own making. In this particular context, therefore, history's value lies less in revealing what the Constitution truly means than in revealing what the Constitution most fundamentally *is*. History does not just show us how to be better originalists; it shows us why we ought to move on from originalism as it has long been understood—why our own constitutionalism, as we implicitly practice it, demands something different and far richer.

What we discover, in short, is the historicist character of our Constitution: that there is no separating the history of how Americans have thought about the Constitution from its purported nature. There is no accounting for the Constitution in time without appreciating the ways in which we have been molded to see it. Our Constitution is inescapably the product of history—it is constituted *by* that history. If we come to appreciate that, we can begin to reckon more deeply with the constitutional project in which we Americans are collectively engaged.

PART ONE

THE ORIGINALIST CONSTITUTION

1

Originalist Assumptions

The aspects of things that are most important for us are hidden because of their simplicity and familiarity.
— Ludwig Wittgenstein, 1953

ORIGINALISTS OFTEN TAKE the constitution's nature for granted. With precious few exceptions, their underlying assumptions about what kind of thing the Constitution is and what sorts of properties define it tend to be implied rather than stated, and assumed rather than defended.[1] Yet while these assumptions often remain unexamined, it is no exaggeration to say that most of what originalists argue rests on them.

Despite their importance, the argumentative action usually lies elsewhere. It is often said that originalism coheres around two fundamental commitments: the so-called fixation thesis and the constraint principle.[2] The fixation thesis contends that the Constitution's meaning was fixed when the Constitution was ratified.[3] The constraint principle maintains that the Constitution's original fixed meaning ought to guide and constrain constitutional interpretation today.[4] These twin commitments are what supposedly unites the family of diverse originalist theories and are said to form originalism's theoretical foundation. That is mistaken. The more important, and interesting, premises precede these. The fixation thesis, and by extension the constraint principle, is a claim about constitutional meaning, but each presupposes a robust conception of the Constitution itself. That underlying conception of the Constitution does most of the foundational work.

It's also broadly held. Despite their disagreements, most originalists hold a common image of the Constitution in their mind. There are now several distinct brands of originalism, each with its own emphases and priorities. As noted in the introduction, most originalists in the academy and on the federal bench subscribe to public meaning originalism, which seeks to recover simply what the words of the Constitution meant to a representative original reader.[5] But not all subscribe to this label. Some originalists continue to defend original intentions originalism and attempt to grasp what the Constitution originally meant by understanding what its framers and ratifiers intended it to mean.[6] Some originalists who often claim to be public meaning originalists, meanwhile, take a more historical approach to the endeavor, prioritizing the particular understandings of concrete Founding-era interpreters.[7] Still other originalists defend what they call original methods originalism (discussed at length in chapter 7).[8] And there are other variations still.[9] Even if in practice, the differences between originalists often melt away,[10] within their theoretical debates those differences can produce sufficiently sharp disagreements that observers fairly wonder whether the label "originalism" even describes a single theory with common commitments.[11] It feels, at times, as though originalism has entered a baroque stage in its life cycle, marked by excessive and increasingly esoteric theorizing—a veritable latter-day equivalent of medieval scholasticism, defined by a density of argumentation and theoretical distinctions that would have baffled earlier American constitutionalists.[12] Add to that, originalist academics often seem to be peddling a much different theory from the one defended by practicing jurists, especially those on the Supreme Court, let alone those politicians and public commentators who lend vital support to the originalist mission.[13]

Whatever is to be made of the ever-diversifying originalist landscape, however, what is striking is that most versions of the theory begin from a common understanding of the Constitution itself. Despite their purported and sometimes real differences, originalists often describe the Constitution in the same matter-of-fact sorts of ways, tacitly agreeing on the kind of thing it is. They might not quite agree on the details or emphasize things in quite the same way. There is, in fact, at least one important brand of originalism— original law originalism, most closely associated with William Baude and Stephen Sachs—that breaks with the orthodoxy in notable ways. (This alternative theory is discussed in detail in chapter 10.) But the overwhelming majority of originalists in both the legal academy and on the Supreme Court—from the late Justice Antonin Scalia to current members Justices Clarence Thomas, Neil Gorsuch, and Amy Coney Barrett—are broadly aligned in how they envision and describe the Constitution.

By and large, leading originalists believe that the Constitution is exclusively written, that its meaning is fixed, and that it is essentially lawlike. Each of these beliefs is predicated on underlying conceptions of constitutional writtenness, fixity, and law that form the foundational assumptions upon which the originalist Constitution ultimately depends.[14] These assumptions, and the image of the Constitution that they form, are what matter most. The true originalism debate resides there.

Writtenness

To virtually all originalists, the Constitution's defining feature is that it is a written text.[15] That is what it just *is*. Of the various elements that make up the orthodox originalist conception of the Constitution, none is more prevalent or essential. Every other originalist assumption seems to depend on it. Hear any originalist speak today about the Constitution, and you are likely to see them reach into their pocket to retrieve a thumbed-through copy. As Steven Calabresi and Saikrishna Prakash, leading champions of the theory, have explained, "[t]he central premise of originalism . . . is that the text of the Constitution is *law*."[16] Fixating on the Constitution's writtenness is what makes it easy to focus on just the Constitution itself. The Constitution is not some mysterious brooding omnipresence, some amorphous jumble of customs and norms, or some guiding spirit that morphs with the times; it is a tangible thing that everyone can look at and reference. You can hold the Constitution in your hands, carry it around in pocket form, or see its physical instantiation behind glass at the National Archives. It is a physical document, neatly circumscribed in space.[17] Precisely because the Constitution is written, precisely because it is a concrete object in the universe with clear boundaries, it is an identifiable, objective thing.

Because the Constitution is a written document, originalists reason, its content is distinctively textual in nature.[18] To interpret the Constitution is to interpret its language. As the originalist Stephen Sachs has explained of an orthodoxy he hopes to challenge, "to be an originalist is to read words in a particular way—to take a particular approach to divining the meaning of the Constitution's language."[19] "What does the Constitution mean?" is another way of asking, "What do the Constitution's words mean?" Or more specifically in an originalist vein, "What did this provision originally mean?" is another way of asking, "What did the words of this provision originally mean?" As public meaning originalists repeatedly note, constitutional interpretation is focused on deciphering the communicative content of the constitutional text.[20] That means discovering "the meaning actually communicated . . . by the words on the page."[21] Of course, the Constitution's words can imply more than they narrowly express depending on context, and they might be written at a high level of generality.[22] Some of the document's provisions, moreover, might be ambiguous and vague, even to the point of indeterminacy, requiring what originalists call construction.[23] And sources beyond the written Constitution undoubtedly shape interpretation of its meaning.[24] But none of this changes the basic fact that constitutional interpretation begins with and runs through the text. As the prominent originalist Randy Barnett reminds (adapting Chief Justice John Marshall's famous adage), *"we must never forget it is a text we are expounding."*[25] The text is the sole point of entry—all constitutional content ultimately derives from it. And the text is exclusive—it is the only Constitution in town. "The text," quite simply, "is the sole object of constitutional interpretation."[26] The text is the locus, the foundation, the ultimate source of constitutional substance.[27] According to orthodox originalists, "the meaning of the Constitution" can thus effectively be reduced to "the meaning of the constitutional text."[28]

The ascendance of public meaning originalism, for many years now the theory's dominant form, has only enhanced the importance of constitutional text. Champions of this brand of originalism contend that modern interpreters are ultimately bound by the Constitution's original public meaning—or what the words of the document originally communicated to an average reader.[29] The subjective expectations of the framers, ratifiers, or broader public can certainly be relevant to originalist interpretation, but only the meanings of the words are binding today. In privileging the Constitution's words over other possible sources of historical evidence or influence, this obsessive focus on public meaning has especially stressed the textual nature of the Constitution and fueled the rise of an avowedly linguistic form of originalism, one that treats the Constitution primarily as a form of linguistic communication and relies heavily on insights gleaned from the philosophy of language and linguistics, often more than law or history, to decipher it. This obsessive turn toward language and its uses explains the new growing fascination in originalist circles with corpus linguistics—the big-data approach to language use that allows interpreters to see how particular constitutional phrases, such as "bear arms" or "due process of law," were used across a large corpus of surviving period texts.[30]

Even if public meaning originalism has placed particular emphasis on the Constitution's text, this shift has marked only a change in degree. Earlier originalists, who preceded the rise of public meaning originalism, tended to define the Constitution in avowedly textual terms as well.[31] The same is broadly true of those contemporary originalists who either resist the singular focus on public meaning by continuing to emphasize the importance of original intentions or simply refuse to join in the obsessive originalist fixation on linguistic theory.[32] These rival originalists no doubt advocate a broader historical approach to interpreting the Constitution, one that looks beyond mere linguistic usage at the Founding to the concrete debates in which the Constitution was implicated.[33] But even they nonetheless often share public meaning originalists' view of the repository of the Constitution's content. Originalists inclined to focus on original intent tend to try to decipher what the framers intended particular textual provisions to mean; originalists inclined to focus on original understandings tend to try to decipher what people at the Founding understood those textual provisions to mean; and originalists inclined to use original methods do so in hopes of deciphering what those textual provisions originally meant.[34] Most originalists agree that they are trying to figure out what a *text* means. And with few exceptions, they readily accept that the Constitution's words are the fixed object of constitutional interpretation.[35]

The same commitment even applies to that minority of originalists who have tethered the theory to natural law. Given the enduring dispute that has shaped so much modern legal theory between legal positivists and their critics, natural lawyers chief among them, it might seem that natural law originalists would conceive of the Constitution differently than do conventional originalists. Those who champion natural law usually claim that law is not simply a product of social facts but moral facts as well, and thus disagree with those legal thinkers, mainstream originalists included, who define law as positive enactment through authoritative legal texts. To be sure, there have been those conservative critics of originalism who have raised just these objections, complaining that originalists have decoupled the Constitution from its supposed natural law foundations.[36] These natural law critics of originalism often seem to be defending a different conception of the Constitution than that of those originalists they are criticizing. But that is not true of natural law originalists—those who, perhaps moved by the criticism heaped on originalism by champions of natural law, have sought to marry the two by grounding an originalist interpretation of the Constitution on a natural law account of human flourishing.[37] These self-described originalists appeal to natural law not to offer a competing account of the Constitution but rather to offer an independent moral account of why the stipulated positive law of the original written Constitution ought to be followed.[38] It is a justification for being an originalist rather than a rival account of the Constitution's putative character or content.[39] In that regard, even those originalists who stress the importance of natural law and non-posited morality see the Constitution's identity and content predominantly in terms of its text.

This foundational commitment to the Constitution's writtenness, common to almost all originalists, betrays perhaps the most crucial assumption of all: by virtue of being written, the Constitution automatically provides an account of its own content and how that content is communicated. The Constitution comes hardwired with a model of constitutional communication, one that assumes that the Constitution acquires and communicates content solely through text. What content does the Constitution have? Whatever content is expressed by its text. How does the Constitution communicate that content? According to the principles of linguistic communication. The Constitution's content is thus the set of propositions communicated by its text—its textually expressed sense. Perhaps, on account of context or the particular language in which it is written, some of that content will not be immediately clear from reading the text. But no matter how broadly the Constitution's words are interpreted, or how extensively they are contextualized, or how much they are believed to imply, under this model of constitutional communication, there is no room left for constitutional content that might exist before and independent of constitutional text—content that is acquired and communicated in a different manner altogether. As originalists tend to see things, the Constitution *acquires* content only through words and, in turn, *communicates* that content only through words. As the leading originalist theorist Lawrence Solum puts it, "Originalism is a thesis about the meaning of the text of the Constitution of the United States that was adopted by the Philadelphia Convention—the text as it was written in ink on sheets of parchment at a particular place and time."[40] If the Constitution has content, that is because those who had formal authority to make it put that content there by adopting text that communicated that content.[41]

To make matters concrete: As most originalists see it, delegates to the Constitutional Convention of 1787 created potential constitutional content by writing out the seven articles found in the original Constitution, and then ratifiers in the states subsequently turned that content into fundamental law by formally accepting it. Before the delegates in Philadelphia drafted anything, the proposed federal Constitution had no content; there was only a blank page on which to begin writing. The Constitution acquired content only as the delegates added words to the page, and its content was finalized when they finished writing—and would remain in that state until another body, with requisite authority, added further content by formally amending what the original delegates had written. The Constitution's content is distinctively textual because it is distinctively posited (and vice versa). The force of these assumptions explains why originalists tend to see the Constitution on the model of a statute (a super-statute) and originalism as analogous to textualism.[42] As Justice Antonin Scalia wrote, "What I look for in the Constitution is precisely what I look for in a statute: the original meaning of the text."[43]

For originalists, calling attention to the Constitution's writtenness thus brings on board a comprehensive understanding of constitutional content—how the Constitution acquires and possesses it. Here, in its essentials, is the dominant originalist conception of constitutional writtenness.

Fixity

At the heart of originalism is the concept of fixity—the premise that the Constitution's meaning was fixed at the time of its inception. The principal reason originalist interpretation is necessary is that the Constitution's meaning was locked in place when the Constitution became authoritative law (the fixation thesis). This core commitment creates the key fault line that separates originalists from living constitutionalists—those who believe that the Constitution's meaning is not fixed but evolves over time in response to social change.[44]

For doctrinaire originalists, fixity is inextricably intertwined with writtenness. The two march in lockstep. The Constitution's meaning is fixed because the Constitution is written, and the Constitution is written to ensure that its meaning is fixed. When we write something down—be it a constitution or anything else—we fix its meaning.[45] That is just how things work, originalists contend. But in addition to that, they argue, the Constitution was written to ensure that its meaning would be fixed. Sometimes this claim rests on a historical proposition: the Founding generation opted to reduce fundamental law to writing in order to fix governing principles in place.[46] But more often this argument is based on a thought experiment. Why would people write a constitution down? Clearly, the thinking goes, to ensure that its meaning is fixed.[47] Orthodox originalists fixate on the written Constitution to explain why its meaning is fixed; they also fixate on the reasons for fixing constitutional meaning to explain why the Constitution is written.

As with writtenness, though, originalists' *conception* of fixity is what matters most. What is most striking is not simply that originalists think that the Constitution's meaning is fixed, but the *way* in which they assume constitutional fixity must work and the fact that they assume there is *only* one way in which a constitution could be fixed. The Constitution is fixed, originalists believe, because the *meanings of its words* are fixed.[48] Given that orthodox originalists uncritically conceive of the Constitution as a written text, it is only logical that they conceive of fixation in expressly linguistic terms.[49] "The Fixation Thesis," declare Randy Barnett and Lawrence Solum, two of the thesis's most outspoken defenders, "is an empirical claim about meaning; it describes how language actually works."[50] Constitutional fixation is about linguistic fixation. Nothing originalists write suggest that it comes—or *could* come—in any other form.[51]

Because they see fixation in these terms, originalists assume that constitutional fixity and evolutionary change are necessarily opposed. The Constitution's meaning is either fixed or it evolves as circumstances change—it can't be both. This is simply a matter of definition, a byproduct of what they see as the only conceivable way to comprehend fixation. Of course, originalists often distinguish the Constitution's original textual meaning (variously referred to as its public meaning, communicative content, semantic meaning, or expressed sense) from its original expected application (how certain constitutional provisions would originally have been applied to concrete circumstances).[52] In this regard, many originalists stress that the Constitution's meaning can remain the same even if the application of that meaning to new facts changes over time. This is how originalism and living constitutionalism might even be synthesized.[53] But this ever more popular claim otherwise presupposes the originalist conception of fixation. Applying the Constitution's meaning over time might lead to novel results, but, according to originalists, the meaning itself does not evolve. "Commerce" means now what it meant back then; as does "migration," "executive power," "necessary and proper," or "republican form of government." Only formal amendments to the Constitution's words, originalists suggest, can alter any of that. Because fixation is understood in terms of text, and because fixed meaning equates to fixed word meanings, a constitution whose meaning is fixed is not a constitution whose meaning can evolve. That would be a logical contradiction.

Law

A related but different reason it is so easy to grasp what the Constitution is and originally was, is that, in the eyes of most originalists, the Constitution is so obviously lawlike. This conviction, while prominent, is less central to originalist orthodoxy. Many originalists are happy to treat the Constitution as merely a generic form of written communication rather than as a distinct kind of legal communication.[54] Yet a healthy share of originalists stress the Constitution's putative legal identity. And even those who purport not to, often approach the Constitution from a decidedly legal perspective—from the perspective of a judge or litigant operating according to the familiar logic of jurisprudence. The Constitution might be supreme, fundamental law, but it is still *just* law. Whatever ways it might vary from certain forms of ordinary law, those are differences of degree not kind.[55]

Thanks to its avowedly legal character, the Constitution is subject to familiar forms of legal reasoning and canons of legal interpretation.[56] The "Constitution, though it has an effect superior to other laws," Justice Antonin Scalia once asserted, "is in its nature the sort of 'law' that is the business of the courts—an enactment that has a fixed meaning ascertainable through the usual devices familiar to those learned in the law."[57] This was true at the time of the Founding, many originalists maintain. To construe the Constitution, eighteenth-century interpreters could confidently appeal to well-established methods of legal interpretation.[58] While many of these existent rules applied to different forms of written law, usually they applied to constitutions as well.[59] And this has remained true ever since. Making sense of the Constitution, Gary Lawson and Guy Seidman have claimed, is "an act of legal construction, based on a legal document, using legal language, in a legal context." It is "a legal enterprise."[60]

There are stronger and weaker forms of this argument among originalists. Some stress that the Constitution is written in the "language of the law," a technical idiom requiring distinctive methods of legal interpretation to decipher.[61] Others, meanwhile, insist that the Constitution ought to be treated as though it was written for the general public.[62] Despite these differences, most originalists agree that the original Constitution was a kind of law familiar to legal practitioners today and that making sense of it invites ordinary lawyers' work. They presume that the brand of constitutionalism long dominant in the United States, which has afforded a central role to courts and judges, called forth the various canons of legal interpretation, and followed the recognizable genre of constitutional law, emerged seamlessly from the Constitution's inner logic.[63] "The original Constitution," John Manning has asserted, "is a lawyer's document."[64] Confidence in this fact immediately narrows the focus, brings on board a range of interpretive tools, and allows the concentrated work of interpretation to commence.

Originalist interpretation thus owes as much to its underlying conception of constitutional law-ness as it does to its conception of constitutional writtenness. The two are often conjoined into a common, authoritative descriptor: written constitutional law. Add fixity to the equation—fixed, written law based on an exclusive conception of writtenness, a linguistic conception of fixity, and a law-is-law conception of law—and, in all its essentials, we have the prevailing originalist conception of the Constitution, the one most common among leading originalist academics and jurists alike.

2

Originalist Justifications

Our argument is not flatly circular, but something like it.

— W. V. O. Quine, 1953

WE NOW SEE HOW ORIGINALISTS TEND to conceive of the Constitution. But how do they justify it? Originalists are not shy about defending most of their commitments. They often insist that, because reducing a constitution to writing fixes its meaning, originalism is necessitated by the very nature of a written constitution.[1] Or they claim that originalism is simply the default method for interpreting legal texts.[2] They also stress that only a fixed constitution preserves certain cherished values, such as majority rule, individual rights, and the rule of law, or promotes certain important goods, such as judicial restraint, the predictability of law, or human flourishing.[3]

But none of these arguments, whatever their merits, actually justify the underlying conception of the Constitution upon which they rely. What happens when, rather than asking why originalism follows from writtenness or the making of law, we pose a more basic question: What kind of thing is the Constitution in the first place? Or better yet: What kind of thing was the *original* Constitution when it first appeared? Such inquiries lead to others, namely: Why must the answer be that the Constitution is an exclusively written and distinctively legal text? Why, if the Constitution's meaning is to be treated as fixed, must we understand fixed meaning just as originalists insist? What justifies these descriptions of the Constitution?

What You See Is What You Get

Answering these questions is tricky since originalists' dominant conviction, as revealed through so many tacit assumptions and bare stipulations, is
that these things are just so. In most instances, the argument derives from
straightforward logical inference: that the Constitution is definitively written, fixed, and legal because—channeling a version of *what you see is what
you get*—that is just the kind of thing it obviously is.

Nowhere is this more evident than when originalists describe the Constitution as written. Look at it, and its identity is self-evident. "The central feature of the document—the first thing one notices about it, if not a dolt or a
mystic," Michael Stokes Paulsen has proclaimed, "is its written-ness."[4]
While they are less colorfully expressed, there are countless originalist statements to this effect: "any project of constitutional interpretation . . . must
reckon with the fact that [the Constitution] is a written text"; "the text of the
Constitution . . . is the fundamental law of the land"; "*we must never forget it
is a text we are expounding*"; or, most simply, "the Constitution of the United
States is a text."[5] Sometimes, such assertions are delivered with particular
ontological gusto. "[T]he public meaning (or conventional semantic meaning) of the words, phrases, and clauses," writes Lawrence Solum, "constitute
the Constitution."[6] Or, as Christopher Green has declared of the Fourteenth
Amendment, and by implication the Constitution as a whole, "Textually-ex-
pressed meaning is just what [it] *is*."[7] Most of the time, however, originalists
do not even offer this much, instead describing the Constitution *as* the "constitutional text" as though the two descriptions—the "Constitution" and the
"constitutional text"—obviously pick out the identical object.[8]

No doubt such blithe confidence is explained, to a significant degree, by
the broader workings of our constitutional culture—as much sanctioned by
non-originalists as by originalists—and particularly the central role afforded
the written Constitution *as distinctively written* therein.[9] Though that only
deepens the suspicion that what we are witnessing is a function of socialization and settled habit rather than the requirements of brute constitutional
necessity.

Regardless, the prevalence of such shared premises can't provide a
complete explanation, for there is still sufficient disagreement about the Constitution's relationship to text that originalists have felt motivated to press

deeper. In so doing, many of them have claimed that the Constitution self-referentially announces its own textuality. Here they fixate on two words: "this Constitution"—a phrase that appears twelve times in the document, most notably in the Preamble and the Supremacy Clause of Article VI. The Constitution identifies that "*this* Constitution"—not some other Constitution—is the supreme law of the land.[10] And "this Constitution" is what officeholders take an oath to defend, making it an especially critical reference.[11] But the next inference is the crucial one: according to originalists, "this Constitution" simply means "this *written* Constitution." This clause, Michael Stokes Paulsen and Vasan Kesavan have contended, "establishes the text of the document—'this Constitution,' a written document—as that which purports to be authoritative."[12] And through this phrase, "the Constitution's text prescribes fidelity to a specific, exclusive, defined, determinate written text." This inference is merely assumed to be true—it is just the "painfully obvious answer" to the question, To what does "this Constitution" refer?[13]

"This Constitution" tautologically identifies "this Constitution" as authoritative, but why "this Constitution" necessarily means "this *written* Constitution" is decidedly less clear. One would already have to assume that the Constitution has solely taken written form to jump so effortlessly from one to the next. Nothing, meanwhile, about the fact that officeholders swear an oath to "this Constitution" tells us what it actually is. Such practices can recognize a common reference—and even suggest perceived continuity over time—without identifying a specific object, much less revealing anything essential about the referent itself.[14] They can signal that, from an anthropological perspective, we care about "this Constitution," without proving that we mean the same thing when invoking it, let alone mean anything especially concrete.

Some analysis has probed deeper. While most originalists take the Constitution's nature for granted, a few have more systematically analyzed the matter and defended the proposition that the Constitution is just the text sitting in your pocket. Christopher Green, recently joined by Evan Bernick, marries the Constitution's use of the phrase "this Constitution" to its use of indexicals—words like "here" and "now," whose references change depending on context—to contend that the Constitution "embodies . . . a theory of its own nature" and "presents itself as a historically situated text."[15] But this linguistic analysis focuses on why the Constitution's meaning might have been locked at the moment of adoption, not why that meaning is already exclusively textual and thus spatially bounded by its words.[16] By using the Constitution's formal language to limn its nature, these originalists already presuppose essential aspects of that nature. The analysis thus does not establish that the Constitution is its textual meaning so much as presumes that it must be. While facially more substantial, the self-presentation argument proves no less question-begging, with the key argumentation unfolding between the lines.[17]

This kind of argumentation also crops up when originalists defend the Constitution's putatively legal character. Those most eager to defend this characterization often resort to the *what you see is what you get* argument. The Constitution's form and language, they argue, tells the tale. The Constitution resembles conventional law—it has the telltale features of familiar legal instruments. And it is written, John McGinnis and Michael Rappaport have contended, in the language of law, featuring several technical legal phrases—such as "ex post facto," "bill of attainder," "Corruption of Blood," or "Letters of Marque and Reprisal"—as well as distinctive legal forms such as preambles and prefatory clauses.[18] If that is not enough, the Constitution declares itself the "supreme Law of the Land." By its own presentation, Gary Lawson and Guy Seidman declare, "[t]he Constitution is a legal document—and a legal document of considerable sophistication."[19] As such, its language "assumes the application of legal interpretive rules."[20] As William Baude and Stephen Sachs assert, "[t]he Constitution was a legal document, adopted in a world with legal rules of interpretation already in place."[21] The Constitution's use of legalese, in other words, carries with it instructions for its own legal use. Like other originalist claims about the Constitution's nature, these kinds of arguments confidently jump from the Constitution's language to robust conclusions about the kind of thing the Constitution is and the content it must contain.

The Founders Made It This Way

These kinds of arguments dominate originalist terrain, but sometimes originalists appeal to history rather than logical description and inference. The Constitution is exclusively written with fixed textual meaning, they argue, because Founding-era constitutionalists consciously created a novel brand of constitutionalism rooted in the written word. As Keith Whittington has argued, "the perceived need to fix the inherited fundamental principles of government in a clear and permanent text" drove Founding-era Americans.[22] They wrote constitutions with the express intention of fixing constitutional rules in place. And they did so because they had a precise purpose in mind: to break from Britain's unwritten customary constitutionalism and inaugurate a distinct kind of constitutionalism grounded in certain text.[23]

Originalists have thus been fond of invoking Chief Justice John Marshall's own account of this process in the Supreme Court's celebrated ruling in *Marbury v. Madison* in 1803:

> The powers of the legislature are defined, and limited; and that those limits may not be mistaken or forgotten, the Constitution is written. . . . Certainly all those who have framed written Constitutions contemplate them as forming the fundamental and paramount law of the nation, and consequently the theory of every such government must be that an act of the Legislature repugnant to the Constitution is void. This theory is essentially attached to a written Constitution, and is consequently to be considered . . . as one of the fundamental principles of our society.

Marshall claimed that judicial review was required by the American Revolution's signature innovation: "the greatest improvement on political institutions—a written Constitution."[24] Originalists often claim merely to be channeling Marshall and, by extension, the Founding generation's own understanding of their constitutional order.[25]

Among those originalists who emphasize that the Constitution is a legal document, history too plays a role, if a far more modest one than logical inference is presumed to yield. While most attention is lavished on the Constitution's use of legal terms, we are also told that the Constitution's framers consciously made it a legal text. As most of them were well-trained lawyers and legal draftsmen, they instinctively wrote the Constitution with familiar forms of law and interpretation in mind.[26] We ought not be surprised, then, that the Constitution is written like a legal document, because its chief authors constructed it with that aim in mind.

Logic vs. History

Originalists seldom distinguish between their logical and historical arguments, but what if those arguments pointed in competing directions? What if originalists' historical account of the original Constitution turned out to be unfounded? What if Founding-era constitutionalists thought that writing a constitution did not change or settle its essence, or fix its meaning, in the ways that originalists now assume? What if Founding-era constitutionalists were less sure about its precise relationship to existing forms of law? What if they conceived of their Constitution differently than originalists have?

One potential response would be to deny that Founding-era views about these issues matter any more than historical views about engineering should determine how we assess the safety of old buildings. If a written constitution just *is* a particular way—regardless of what anyone thought at the Founding or since—then historical views about the topic perhaps would not matter. But it would have to be explained *why* one could even, in principle, disaggregate the original Constitution from the understandings of those who made it—how it is possible, conceptually, to speak about an eighteenth-century object divorced from the eighteenth-century intellectual world that breathed life into it. It would have to be explained how the Constitution's logical essence could be neatly disaggregated from its historical character.

These positions have not been developed, let alone systematically worked out, because originalists have yet to directly consider what it would mean if originalist logic and history pointed in competing directions—if what they instinctively take the Constitution to be somehow diverged from Founding-era intuitions. Orthodox originalists, of course, have invested enormous effort discounting the original intentions of the Constitution's framers. But distinguishing between different kinds of original meaning should not be confused with competing ways of justifying the Constitution's core character: why the Constitution—the thing *containing* the meaning—is necessarily defined by one set of characteristics and not another. In this case, we are not talking about the Founders' intentions, but rather the relationship between their constitutional assumptions and the Constitution's essential properties: Is the Constitution the way it is because the Founders *made it so* or because it *just is that way* regardless of what they tried to do and thought they had done?

At times, originalists seem to suggest that the Constitution simply is what it is, no matter what anyone at the Founding thought about it. It is just the thing you put in your pocket. We look to the object, not the Founders, to understand its nature. It could well be that few members of the Founding generation grasped what they had created. They might have misunderstood the nature of language or simply how constitutional communication works. Originalists today, supposedly armed with better understandings of these things, can apprehend what the Founders wrought better than people back then could. Despite often pushing in this direction, however, originalists steadfastly refuse to ever see the argument through to completion. No matter how confident they might be in the Constitution's inherent nature, they are never willing to fully decouple it from the views of the Founding generation.[27] When pressed, they won't entertain the notion that the Founders viewed the Constitution differently than they do. Eighteenth-century framers, ratifiers, or interpreters might not have viewed the Constitution exactly as we moderns do, but on balance, and in all the ways that matter, originalists suggest, they surely did. They did not have a radically different object in mind when they looked upon the Constitution. They too treated it as a document, a thing, a legal text—the thing right there made of words.

Rather than pondering the differences between arguments predicated on the logical nature of a constitution and those grounded in history, originalists instead seem to take comfort in the following kind of reasoning: The Founding generation meant to fix the Constitution as supreme law by reducing it to writing; and if they did not mean to do so, then no matter, because it is simply how things work that writing a constitution down fixes authoritative law in durable language. Committing a constitution to writing necessarily transforms constitutional content into linguistic content and fixes its meaning. Writing a constitution that is to serve as fundamental law necessarily turns it into a legal text. This is just in the nature of things. Unsurprisingly, then, the Founders recognized that they had done just this. It is thus unnecessary to carefully work out *why* the Constitution is just the legal text written in 1787 and amended thereafter, because it is obviously so. Logic, history, common sense, and seemingly anything else one might appeal to all point toward this conclusion. The Constitution is what it is, providing originalists the neutral and objective starting place from which to interpret it.

But this will not do. The Founding generation had their own views on constitutionalism. It is time for originalists to awaken from their dogmatic slumber.

PART TWO

THE FOUNDERS' CONSTITUTION

3

A Foreign Country

The past is a foreign country: they do things differently there.

— L. P. Hartley, 1953

IF WE LOOK CLOSER AT THE FOUNDING era on its own terms, we don't find support for originalists' just-so account of the Constitution and its defining characteristics. We instead find different ways of imagining constitutions and, in the cauldron of revolutionary debate, intense disagreement over the appropriate way to do so. We find distinctive ways of understanding constitutional writtenness, fixity, and law shaping unfamiliar debates. We find that the Founders' Constitution bears little resemblance to the originalist Constitution.

To begin to see the original Constitution on its own terms, we must start with a vital truth: the past is a foreign country.[1] Assuredly, connections between past and present are deep and real. It's only natural for human beings to place themselves in this steady stream of existence and to find the past in the present and the present in the past. But the veneer of continuity can be misleading, obscuring the reality, Sam Wineburg observes, that the past does not often speak to us "without intermediary or translation."[2] This might sound exaggerated, uncompromising, extreme—historians' familiar bromide that all times and places are ineluctably different and demanding contextualization. But it is an important general lesson that repeatedly proves its worth.

The insistence that, to understand the original Constitution, one must contend with the remote character of the past, however, owes less to any general axiom about historical thinking than to the particularities of the specific historical period in question. Assuredly, some periods of history, certainly American history, converge more easily with our own. The continuities are genuine, the similarities well founded, the links substantive. In studying such epochs, we find people whose modes of thought, core assumptions, and orientations toward problems of political and social life map more easily, if always imperfectly, onto our own. But then there are those past epochs where things deviate in more fundamental ways; where the differences are more striking and more significant; where not simply the assumptions shaping thought and debate but the logic stitching them together runs orthogonally to what we find natural or familiar; where, in short, people spoke a markedly different language from our own.[3] It is in these instances that the lesson proves essential: taking the *differences* between then and now seriously is the key to unlocking understanding. Of few historical periods is this as true as the American Founding.

An Unfamiliar Founding

In studying Founding-era America, it is imperative to appreciate how deeply its mental universe diverged from ours. That is hardly because the American Founding is unparalleled in its peculiarity. Obviously, from the vantage of modern America, periods more distant and more geographically far-flung are often considerably more alien than what we find in eighteenth-century British North America and later the United States. But that is just the point. The Founding is so easily distorted and misunderstood not simply because it was different but because it is so easy to assume that it was not.

It is natural to believe that the Founding generation thought as we Americans do today. After all, it is their constitutional order that we still inhabit; their system of government that we still operate, debate, and strive to refine; their political institutions and rights guarantees that we still celebrate and critique. We see ourselves as consciously inhabiting and continuing their tradition. They invoked, moreover, many of the exact concepts we still consider so important—from liberty, sovereignty, and the separation of powers to freedom of speech, the free exercise of religion, and the right to a jury trial.

It can appear as though inhabitants of that eighteenth-century world debated the same things that animate us today—as though they asked the same questions, relied on the same distinctions, and reasoned with resort to the same conceptual categories. It can all seem so familiar, as if the distance between us and them is easily bridged.

Yet presuming this much would be gravely mistaken. As historians of the period have repeatedly demonstrated, the inhabitants of Revolutionary America did not think like us.[4] Stanley Elkins and Eric McKitrick spoke for a wide, diverse collection of scholars when they noted that "the mind and sensibility of the founding generation—more inclusively the Revolutionary generation—has been exceedingly difficult to recover: substantial portions of that mentality have long since ceased to strike echoes and resonances."[5] Immersing oneself in the period's sources and studying them in non-superficial ways, Gordon Wood stressed long ago, instills a "sense of the irretrievability and differentness of the eighteenth-century world."[6] No doubt, many continuities run between now and then, and broadly speaking, the overlap is substantial.[7] But if we put aside the pedestrian and focus instead on the complex areas of thought and culture, such as politics, law, science, or philosophy, the differences stand out. That is especially true of constitutionalism. Eighteenth-century Americans, armed with a different conceptual vocabulary, different presuppositions, and a different understanding of how things hang together, approached that subject much differently than we do today.

It is this contingent combination—profound differences lurking beneath prominent surface similarities—rather than any general feature of historical inquiry that makes it so necessary to approach the Founding with fresh eyes and to historicize it on its own terms, making sure not to impose our habits of mind onto people who did not rely on them. If eighteenth-century American constitutionalists happened to have thought like us or happened to have created and practiced a brand of constitutionalism largely in line with our own, we would not have to worry so much about historicizing them. If, on the other hand, their constitutional ideas and debates did not seem so similar to ours, we would not have to worry about failing to historicize them. From the perspective of modern America, the Founding lands right in the sweet spot. It would be hard, from our vantage, to find any swath of history that seems so familiar yet in reality is so different. And that is why it is so imperative that we historicize it.

The stakes are high. Only if we appreciate that Founding-era constitutionalists thought differently than we do today and we learn how to think the way
they once did can we get much else right about the constitutional world *they*
built and inhabited. There is simply no understanding the American Founding and the Constitution it produced—*as it was originally conceived and understood*—without historicizing both.

This lesson is essential to originalism. Yet too often, originalists fail to
understand it, let alone take it to heart. Originalists tend to approach the
Founding confident in its familiarity, convinced that the eighteenth century
speaks immediately to modern legal concepts and concerns.[8] Consequently,
originalists unthinkingly impose familiar terms, doctrines, and questions on
a past that might not have shared them. In certain respects, this inclination
is not surprising. In looking at the past, people are drawn to the familiar.
Historical thinking is, as Sam Wineburg has argued, an "unnatural act," one
that cuts "against the grain of how we ordinarily think."[9] It's a habit of mind
that must be cultivated, a form of knowing *how* rather than a form of knowing *that*—a skill one learns how to do rather than a body of discrete information one masters.[10] This know-how is often acquired only through dogged
study of the past. One spends enough time immersed in the period's sources
that the peculiarities of that intellectual world begin to come into relief.[11]
One begins to hear the music. At that point, one stops naturally fixating on
the familiar, unable to see or simply ignoring all those bits that fail to align
with one's own understandings and expectations, and instead begins dwell-
ing on those unfamiliar pieces of thought that, it becomes increasingly clear,
pervade so much else.[12] Eventually it becomes obvious that genuinely understanding historical artifacts requires recognizing the degree of incommensurability separating past and present—that comprehending the past means
grasping it on its own peculiar terms. Thomas Kuhn, who forever changed
our understanding of the history of scientific revolutions, once described a
kind of inner transformation that led him to formulate his famous argument. Only by immersing himself in the logic and concepts of Aristotle's
account of physics, so flawed from the perspective of later science, could he
make sense of it.[13] Many leading historians of the American Founding have
come to emphasize the period's foreign conceptual universe through a comparable experience.[14] Knowing how to think historically is thus the product
of, rather than the initial guide to, inquiry.

Sometimes when historians make these points, people worry that they mean to imply that the past is unknowable or unrecoverable.[15] Lest I be misunderstood, let me be emphatic: that is not my point. Far from it. The claim is simply that it takes more work to understand the past on its own terms than is often appreciated. Today, we can immerse ourselves in a foreign culture and slowly habituate ourselves to it. The gulf is not unbridgeable even if conquering it can be arduous and difficult. It requires immersion and the knowledge it imparts—the slow cultivation of new habits of mind and new sorts of know-how. The same is true when studying the past, especially an unfamiliar period like the American Founding. The past is knowable, the Founding is knowable—but getting there requires more work than many are willing to acknowledge or undertake.

Originalists have generally rejected the notion that the eighteenth-century past is so very foreign or so difficult to recover. Like many in law, they are often in a bigger hurry when exploring history. They are not trying to understand the eighteenth century generally but to answer specific legal questions that bear on it. That leads them to train their focus on narrow aspects of history.[16] But in racing so quickly through the past, they fail to immerse themselves in the period's sources for long enough to notice that those particular aspects might not fit their preconceived assumptions. They fail to linger because they don't see the need. From a modern legal perspective, those parts of Founding-era constitutional history seem familiar. Why historicize something that is already legible? Ironically, only the immersion they consider unnecessary could lead them to see otherwise. Thinking historically is unnatural after all—it requires a willingness to dwell on the strange rather than look the other way.

Yet it's not as though historians of the Founding have failed to delineate their methodologies or substantiate their intellectual benefits. After all this time, one might have expected originalists to engage this historicist approach on its own merits. But most of them still ignore historians' pleas, confident that these suggestions aren't at odds with the narrower approach originalists favor. Even though historians have emphasized that the Founding will seem accessible only until one digs deep enough to see otherwise, originalists still assume that the period can be easily understood on the familiar terms of the present.[17] Originalist investigations are often so narrowly conceived—fixated on deciphering the original meaning of certain constitutional words and phrases through narrow semantic and legal parsing—precisely because it is assumed that almost everything else structuring that inquiry was the same then as it is now.

To better see how originalists fail to historicize the original Constitution, it helps to start where they are often narrowly preoccupied: the Constitution's original meaning. In turn, understanding how they fail to historicize constitutional meaning helps illuminate why we must historicize the Constitution itself.

Historicizing Original Meaning

We begin where originalists so often set their sights. Suppose we want to decode something specific and textual in the Constitution: perhaps what the First or Second Amendment originally meant, or maybe the original meaning of a particular word or phrase, such as "commerce," "due process of law," or "cruel and unusual." Even if we adopt such a relatively narrow aim, we still need a much broader approach than is often assumed.

That's because of the particular interpretive challenge we face: the problem of historical distance.[18] We need to figure out how to interpret something not immediately accessible to us because it's the artifact of an unfamiliar past. This is *the* crucial issue confronting any form of originalist interpretation. Yet originalists often fail to grasp this truth. They mistakenly assume that the central interpretive problems raised by their theory are linguistic or legal in character, not historical. For them, recovering the Constitution's original meaning requires getting clear on the nature of language and communication, or perhaps how legal texts in particular communicate meaning. It does not require grappling with potential historical differences germane to the nature of constitutionalism itself.

But that gets things backward. In confronting the eighteenth-century Constitution, the first step in properly framing the inquiry should not be trying to understand how a written text generically communicates via language—how semantics and pragmatics operate in tandem, how contextual disambiguation works generally, or the difference between things like speaker's meaning and expression meaning. Nor is the first step trying to understand the generic interpretive problems produced by legal texts—how judges ought to construe such instruments or navigate the problem of ordinary linguistic ambiguity.[19] Rather, the initial difficulty is trying to understand how to make sense of something written a long time ago by people who thought much differently than we do now. Originalists often think the primary challenge they must surmount is linguistic drift—that key words and phrases found in the Constitution are used differently now than when the Constitution was written.[20] But the principal issue is more fundamental than that: not *linguistic* drift but *conceptual* drift. As, over time, we've come to think differently about various core constitutional concepts, we've drifted from the conceptual scheme in which the Constitution was originally embedded. Bringing the original Constitution back into focus requires reconstructing that original scheme.

That engages us in a particular brand of interpretation, one whose primary objective is bridging the gap between a familiar present and an alien past: of *translating* the unfamiliar into something more legible.[21] The techniques we rely on in our daily lives to help us decipher the meaning of something written relatively recently or something said by a conversation partner are of limited help. The same goes for most of the insights we might glean from the philosophy of language or theoretical linguistics, on which originalists have trained so much of their attention.[22] For all their value, tools from those disciplines by and large were built to solve different problems and don't teach us as much about how interpreters might surmount the distinctive problem of historical distance. Knowing how people living at the same time sharing the same conceptual universe successfully communicate with one another tells us precious little about how to decode an artifact written over two centuries ago by people who did not share our conceptual universe.[23] If we are going to range across other disciplines in search of methodological tools, we ought to know what we are looking for. Unless theorists of language happened to speak to the problem of historicism, their ideas are not especially pertinent to our task.[24]

Bringing the central problem of historical distance into focus recalibrates how we should think about historical meaning and its translation. Constitutional meaning is *thick*. It's predicated on understanding and context, not merely linguistic context but conceptual context.[25] To put matters simply: To grasp what the Constitution's words originally meant, we first need to understand how the people who wrote and first read those words originally thought. If they happened to think the way we do now, originalist work might be straightforward enough. Interpreters today could confront the Constitution confident that their own tacit assumptions and prejudgments had prepared them to intuitively read its provisions just as eighteenth-century readers would have. Taking for granted this kind of overlap, the inquiry could then focus primarily on word definitions, rules of grammar, and patterns of linguistic usage, plugging in bits of linguistic data here and there in order to bridge the modest semantic differences between then and now. But the Founding generation did not think like us. They spoke a different constitutional language marked by (at times profoundly) different understandings of core constitutional concepts—among them liberty, rights, state power, separation of powers, republican governance—as well as the relationship of those concepts to one another.[26] Their understandings of those concepts are not easily rendered on the terms of our thought. It's like trying to fit a square peg in a round hole: the fit is close enough that applying sufficient pressure can force the issue, but not without distorting either the peg or the hole.[27] For this reason, we can't focus narrowly on the semantics and pragmatics of words or merely place those words in their strictly linguistic context, as though they were written by people who thought like us.[28] The same constitutional words, strung together in the same way, with most of the same individual word meanings, can take on an entirely different meaning depending on how one thinks about the web of concepts implicated by them. Disaggregating word meanings from underlying constitutional thinking—meaning from understanding—does not isolate the Constitution's original meaning but quietly wrenches it into the present, filtering an eighteenth-century document through twenty-first-century thinking. If we think like us, rather than like them, we will misread much of what they said and wrote, distorting the meaning their Constitution originally communicated.

It takes far more to bridge the historical distance separating us from the Founding than merely substituting word meanings here and there in the Constitution's text, relying on commonplace techniques of disambiguation or contextual enrichment, or scrutinizing patterns of linguistic usage.[29] We need to push deeper. We need to hear the music. Recovering the meaning of the original Constitution entails learning how to think as members of the Founding generation once did. Learning to think in alien ways is difficult and unnatural. It demands shedding our own interpretive prejudgments and intuitions and conducting the hard work of replacing them with those that guided eighteenth-century inhabitants. It is not a matter of merely familiarizing ourselves with *what* those people thought but more crucially absorbing *how* they thought.[30] That requires spending enough time with Founding-era thought and arguments that it becomes clear how the people who made and debated those arguments connected ideas to one another, identified premises and drew inferences from those premises, and imbued their surroundings with meaning.[31] As Bernard Bailyn aptly put it, the task is "to penetrate into the substructures of thought and behavior" that permeated the Founding, to get at "the silent assumptions" and grasp "the perceptual universes of the participants." Only then can we "identify with that other distant way of thinking."[32]

Standard originalist techniques are no substitute for understanding how people in the past thought about the myriad interconnected ideas that intersected with and undergirded constitutionalism. And originalists struggle to see why because so many of them have been hung up on the wrong distinction, between original meaning and original intent—the classic distinction that supposedly set apart the "new originalism" focused on original public meaning from its defective predecessor that had privileged original intentions.[33] To get at original constitutional meaning, new originalists often privilege what they call "*prevailing* linguistic practice," which, as Randy Barnett and Evan Bernick have put it, is "independent of the contents of the minds of *individual* speakers and interpreters."[34] Here, they aim to distinguish between public linguistic conventions and the potentially idiosyncratic views of particular people—or original public meaning on the one hand and original intent, understanding, or expected application on the other. They wish to know what the words meant to the public, not what particular people read into the words in light of what they thought motivated their construction or was most likely to follow from their implementation. But that's not the crucial distinction. The crucial consideration is not whether we follow meaning or intent but instead whether we treat historical meaning as relatively thick or thin. The key question is not, Does an author's intent or a ratifier's expected application control the meaning of a text? But instead, How broadly and deeply must we contextualize a complex historical speech act (such as a constitutional provision) in order to decipher its original meaning? That becomes a debate over the character and scope of context, which often impinges on the vital relationship between public speech and authorial intent but does not reduce to it and need not turn on it. Public meaning originalists often justify a narrower approach to historical meaning by bracketing original intent, underlying purposes, or expectations—implying that a thicker contextualization would be needed to recover those kinds of things, but not original public meaning, as if one follows from the other. But nothing about devaluing the framers' intents, goals, or aspirations automatically narrows interpretation in that fashion. The context necessary to elucidate public meaning might still be broad and deep (and in the case of early U.S. constitutional history, quite often is).[35]

The reason that context is often so extensive is because meaning is tethered to mind. Maybe, as Barnett and Bernick suggest, linguistic practice can be severed from the contents of specific minds; but linguistic practice cannot be severed from the content of mind more generally. Whichever kind of original meaning we're trying to recover, that meaning is a function of how original readers thought about the world. Complex constitutional provisions necessarily presuppose a thick network of conceptual understandings. The meaning of those provisions was originally *embedded* in a mode of thought and the conceptual universe that structured it. Whatever "freedom of speech" originally meant depended on how people fit together more basic concepts such as republican liberty and governance. We can understand historical linguistic practice in the first place, then, only if we already understand how the people who engaged in that linguistic practice understood a broader cluster of complex interlocking concepts—if we absorb how they thought. Otherwise, we're just going to interpret their linguistic practice *as if they thought like us*—thinking *for* them and *through* them, fleshing out meaning by way of our intuitions rather than theirs—which is a recipe for misreading their practice rather than decoding its objective content. To recover original meanings, we must first recover original minds.

Originalists' persistent failure to appreciate the need for deeper historical translation is among the reasons the recent originalist embrace of corpus linguistics has only tended to compound the problem.[36] Broad text mining aimed at deciphering patterns of linguistic usage in the past can be powerfully revealing, but only ever as a supplement to deeper historical immersion, never a substitute for it.[37] If you haven't first done the work of learning to think as people in the past once did, by immersing yourself in their conceptual universe and acquainting yourself with alternative constitutional thinking, then you're liable to impose your own mental habits on the patterns of linguistic usage you find—as if those words were spoken or written by people who think like you, not them. How else could you read or analyze those words? If the only way available for thinking about law, constitutionalism, and its related concepts is the one you know, you won't be able to make sense of eighteenth-century linguistic practice except from the lone perspective you've internalized—even though that perspective and the myriad assumptions woven into it will distort the very linguistic practice you're trying to comprehend.

Or briefly ponder a much different eighteenth-century legal context: Qing dynasty China. To understand a particular legal text or the meaning of a particular legal concept from that intellectual world, would it be sufficient to merely trace prevailing linguistic practice that had been translated for us? That would be woefully inadequate. We couldn't make much sense of what we were reading or what those legal texts were really saying or doing without first acquiring something like the mindsets of period language users—without first learning a lot about how people in Qing legal culture made sense of law and its attendant concepts. It's no different for the American Founding, even if the conceptual overlap is surely more substantial. Only a false sense of familiarity could lead interpreters to think that they could focus on linguistic usage and practice without first spending most of their time trying to understand what undergirded that usage and practice: a different way of thinking about core concepts that defined law and constitutionalism.

That is the most important context in which the Constitution's language first appeared: the unspoken set of constitutional understandings that were subtly interwoven into everything. Comprehending what a complex constitutional provision originally expressed in 1787 entails first recovering that kind of understanding and, with it, the broader cluster of constitutional assumptions and conceptual formulations that once defined it.

Just take the concept of liberty, which runs through the entire Constitution. At the heart of modern constitutional culture—and certainly modern Supreme Court jurisprudence—is the liberal theory of rights, which tends to define liberty as non-interference. To be free, to enjoy the liberty to exercise a fundamental right, is to be free from outside coercion. The pervasiveness of this thinking helps explain why the Court focuses so obsessively on balancing the trade-offs between respecting individual liberty and permitting the government to act—

how much can the government, acting on a compelling interest, interfere with some people's rights without crossing a line and abridging those rights beyond an acceptable level? Governmental power and individual liberty are at odds. The latter is preserved where the former is prohibited.

Founding-era constitutionalists, however, thought about liberty in a radically different way.[38] To them, liberty was not synonymous with non-interference—it was not a measurement of whether or how much one had been coerced. Indeed, one could be heavily coerced and free, or conversely, lightly coerced and unfree. What mattered—what distinguished those who were free from those who were not—was whether one was subject to an alien will or a will of one's own. Liberty, therefore, could be realized only under a truly representative government, a government that embodied one's consent and thus could be said to be acting in accordance with one's will. This was the reason why representation was so obsessively debated in eighteenth-century British North America—where chants of "no taxation without representation" spurred revolution. This was the reason why representation drove debates over the making of new governments in the newly independent United States. This was the reason why representation was the master concept of the era's constitutionalism.[39] Liberty hinged on it. "Representation," as Moses Mather declared in 1775, "is the feet on which a free government stands."[40] Liberty could not be measured by coercion. If the government represented the people, then by *being* the people—by *re-presenting* them in a legislative assembly—the government could regulate their affairs, even extensively, without infringing their liberty. In contrast, if a government did not represent the people at large, no matter whether or how much it might interfere in anyone's affairs, it was necessarily tyrannical.[41] As Levi Hart declared on the eve of independence, "civil liberty doth not consist in a freedom from all law and government,—but in a freedom from unjust law and tyrannical government:—In freedom, to act for the general good."[42]

At the Founding, therefore, rights were rarely thought of as the inverse of governmental powers.[43] Liberty was not measured by the absence of governmental coercion.[44] Those perceived relationships, so standard today, were mostly out of place in the eighteenth century.[45] They did not structure how people thought about the conditions of political freedom or the basis of government tyranny. Which is why, throughout the early republic, we find a staggering degree of legal regulation and governance devoted to the general welfare taken to be not only wholly consistent with, but essential to, the preservation of liberty, both individual and collective.[46]

If our goal, therefore, is to recover original meaning, we will fail at that task if we simply read the Constitution's words as if they stand on their own, without first coming to terms with the much different understandings of liberty on which those constitutional expressions necessarily depended. We will merely import, unwittingly, our own modern understandings of the concept, as well as all others it implicates, including state power, representation, constitutionalism, and much else, quietly imposing them on an unsuspecting past. We will substitute our own prejudgments for those of the time. That is not a recipe for recovering original meaning; that is a recipe for historical ventriloquism. Eighteenth-century language attached to non-eighteenth-century conceptual thinking does not originalism make.

These mistakes were on conspicuous display in *District of Columbia v. Heller*, the landmark Second Amendment case that remains the most thoroughly originalist ruling issued by the modern Supreme Court.[47] Both the majority opinion and principal dissent based their conclusions primarily on Founding-era history. To make sense of that history, the Court posed three questions predicated on three core distinctions, each of which eighteenth-century American constitutionalists would have found strange: When originally enacted, did the Second Amendment protect an individual or a collective right to bear arms? What initially was the relationship between the amendment's so-called prefatory clause and its so-called operative clause? And did the "people" identified in the amendment originally refer to a collective or to individuals?[48] What defenders of *Heller* fail to understand is that the problem rests not with their answers but with the questions they are asking. Each of these questions, by its formulation, presupposes an anachronistic approach to rights that the Founding generation did not share. If we grasp how liberty was actually understood at the Founding, it's difficult to pose any of these questions in the first place. The Supreme Court built on these mistakes in its most important Second Amendment decision since *Heller*: *New York State Rifle & Pistol Association v. Bruen*, which struck down a New York law restricting the public carry of concealed firearms for violating the right to keep and bear arms.[49] As Jud Campbell has astutely noted, the Court's analysis in *Bruen*, as in *Heller* before it, was "framed by implicit assumptions about the nature of constitutional rights" that diverge from those that undergirded the amendment when it was originally enacted.[50]

The only remedy is to ask different questions and approach the amendment as an inhabitant of the eighteenth century would have. Recovering that alternative perspective requires starting, not with the words of the Second Amendment, but by asking how people understood the concept of liberty and the nature of rights. Most of the work needed to decode the original Second Amendment comes before reading any of its words. Like the justices in *Heller*, few originalists appreciate this insight. Instead, they often dive into the textual analysis, eager to make sense of the amendment's sentence structure and the meanings of its individual words without first contemplating the ways an alternative conception of liberty fundamentally shaped it. The results, predictably, have been deeply ahistorical. Unless we "recover eighteenth-century views about the nature of fundamental rights *before* considering the original meaning of particular rights, such as the right to keep and bear arms," Campbell rightfully cautions, "the 'original meaning' inquiry might be misconceived before even getting off the ground."[51] Imagine trying to interpret the words of the Second Amendment without first reckoning with how the people who wrote and ratified it understood the concept of liberty. No wonder so much Second Amendment scholarship is off track.[52]

On the basis of how eighteenth-century Americans conceptualized liberty and rights, at the time it was created the Second Amendment protected an individual and collective right (for there was effectively no difference) to live in a state that boasted a well-regulated militia, composed of the "people themselves" as a body politic, because living in such a state dramatically increased the likelihood that that state would be free—a "free state" in which public power was subject to the will of the people rather than an agent beyond their consent or control. It wouldn't be an exaggeration to suggest that the phrase "free state" was the most important feature of the original amendment. It means little to us anymore, but it was a potent concept in the eighteenth century, one that packaged a comprehensive view of liberty and public power that undergirded republican freedom. That is to say nothing of the additional, no less important, assumption that the right enshrined in the Second Amendment, like all fundamental rights at the time, would have been determined and enforced primarily outside courts of law.[53] This provision was not written for judges or with legal remedies in mind. It was written for the people and their governance.[54] It was written in a foreign idiom. As a result, the rights originally protected by it don't easily translate into our modern constitutional vocabularies and jurisprudence.[55] If we don't recognize that, we won't understand it.

We must translate a lot more than the meanings of words to begin to make sense of this eighteenth-century provision. And we need to look to a lot more than patterns of linguistic practice. We first need to come to terms with a different way of thinking and habituate ourselves to an alternative conceptual universe. Vital lessons follow from that realization.

Default Interpretive Habits

Given what it entails, recovering original meaning can be a tricky and demanding activity, especially if the text in question was written a long time ago. Because they tend to overlook the gulf between past and present, originalists often defend their methodology on the grounds that it is simply the default way to interpret any historical expression—be it a legal document, a constitution, a letter, a speech, or anything else.[56] It is common to hear that "originalism remains the normal, natural approach to understanding anything that has been said or written in the past."[57] But here they are sorely mistaken. Beyond the various ways the U.S. Constitution is fundamentally distinct from most other interpretive objects we tend to encounter,[58] originalism is *not* the default approach to reading historical texts. On the contrary, it is an unusual and unnatural way to read them. And, indeed, when originalists read historical texts other than the U.S. Constitution, they usually do so in un-originalist ways.

Originalism is an atypical approach to understanding older texts. We still read the Declaration of Independence, John Locke's *Second Treatise on Government*, Shakespeare's plays, or Plato's *Republic* today. But when we do, we rarely read these texts in accordance with their original meaning. That is, we do not typically aim to read them as an original reader would have. That form of reading requires considerable abstraction, the cultivation of which entails substantial labor. Modern readers would need to systematically replace so many of the working intuitions, assumptions, and inferential techniques that guide their reading of a complex text with different habits of mind to cultivate a new kind of interpretive know-how. Few undertake this arduous effort. Instead, when most of us read older texts, we rely on our own tacit assumptions and filter what we read through the terms of our own thought. The standard way to read any historical text is thus to wrench it into the present and make sense of it in light of what we think and care about today—to quietly impose on it the categories of thought that govern our own debates about the world and to unsuspectingly make it speak to things we understand and deem significant. Modern readers do not usually historicize the texts they read. When they do, that's the exception.[59] Only somebody who has not seriously studied the past could think otherwise.

This point steers us to another one: interpretive method is determined not by the object we interpret but by the questions we ask of it. Depending on what we are trying to understand of them, there are various ways to interpret historical texts. Nothing about the simple fact that we happen to find ourselves interpreting *The Prince, Hamlet, Uncle Tom's Cabin, The Federalist, The Souls of Black Folk*, or the United States Constitution requires us to fixate on their original meanings.[60] We might be interested in what these texts have meant across time, how they speak to contemporary problems in political theory or law, or how they fit into literary or philosophical traditions. Answering those questions will only sometimes require thinking historically. If, by contrast, we pose a distinctively historical question, then a certain kind of historical method necessarily follows. Suppose our question takes the following form: What did this particular text mean at the time it was conceived *to people living back then?* Because of the *question* we have asked, rather than the *object* we are interpreting, we are forced to adopt a particular approach, one than enables us to read the text from the perspective, not of somebody today, but of a reader when that text was originally written. Adopting this approach entails the sometimes-arduous work of learning *how to think* in an unfamiliar manner, arming ourselves with different logics in order to see what those original readers would likely have seen when they read the text. No one today is required to read the Constitution as an eighteenth-century American once did. But if one purports to be an originalist and is thus motivated to answer a *particular* question about the Constitution's meaning—the question that has long been at the heart of originalist theory—then one must conduct precisely this kind of historical work.

The Originalist Escape from History

With these insights in mind, we can begin to appreciate why originalists' familiar rejoinders to historians so often miss the point. In one form or another, originalists have attempted to escape history: to claim that the past as historians study it is of limited relevance to originalist inquiry.[61]

Rather than drawing on historians' methods, originalists have increasingly distinguished originalist methods from them. An important minority of originalists, such as Michael McConnell, have resisted this trend, maintaining that originalism must be properly historical if it is to succeed.[62] But most originalists are fond of insisting that they can recover the Constitution's original meaning without replicating what historians themselves do.[63] The two groups, originalists insist, simply do different things: they ask different questions, look at different sources, and utilize different methods.[64] Historians do history; they don't aim to recover—nor know how to recover—legal meaning. Originalists, meanwhile, don't try to do history; they simply conduct ordinary lawyers' work—seeking to understand the legal content of past legal texts. Historians are focused on things like historical motivations, ideologies, and ideas, whereas lawyers are focused on what the law was, what it communicated, and who had the better legal arguments.[65] Law, originalists often claim, is just distinct from the study of history. Historians' complaints about how originalists interpret the past, therefore, are little more than a mark of historians' confusion.[66]

These popular originalist distinctions are beside the point. It is no revelation that the study of law differs in numerous respects from the study of history—who has ever claimed otherwise? That is not at issue. What is at issue is how, given originalists' particular claims about law and the past, the two subject matters intersect. Originalists have made law *about* the past. In so doing, they have posed an empirical and methodological question that is historical in nature. *Given* what they claim the law to be, they require themselves to recover eighteenth-century constitutional meaning as it once existed. Here is where historians enter. If originalists would prefer for law to remain largely separate from history, then they shouldn't have made law a matter of recovering the past *as originally understood*. In a related vein, to defend a distinctively legal approach to the past, the originalists William Baude and Stephen Sachs have asserted that history does not have any authority to determine modern law—that lawyers consult the past because law, not history, requires them to.[67] But this too seems beside the point. Historians have not claimed authority over law. When historians and originalists squabble over how to recover the past, the question at issue is not, What is the law? The question is, *If* modern law, for whatever non-historical reasons, hinges on the original meaning of eighteenth-century law, then how do we in fact recover the eighteenth-century artifacts we've identified as important?

Once venturing back to that past, meanwhile, it makes little difference if originalists happen to target a different kind of original meaning than historians do—that they are after what they call communicative content, legal meaning, or something else. Whatever meaning they might target will be embedded in an eighteenth-century constitutional context, the recovery of which does not differ in kind from what historians do. Originalists, as noted, often act as though they can merely focus on the Constitution's linguistic facts without reckoning with the fact that the people who laid down those words thought about a whole host of things in different ways. If historians claim otherwise, originalists often suggest, it is likely because they are ignorant, not of the past, but of the dictates of modern linguistic and legal theory. They simply don't understand what communicative content *is*, how it relates to legal effect, or how it differs from the kinds of things intellectual historians tend to study. But, as we have seen, it's impossible to disaggregate what the Constitution's words originally communicated from the broader constitutional assumptions that undergirded them. If an eighteenth-century constitutional provision identified and protected a certain right, then doing so necessarily presupposed some concept of liberty and rights. It makes no sense, therefore, to suggest that the meaning of the First, Second, or Fourth Amendment somehow swung free of eighteenth-century conceptual thinking. Those meanings were embedded in that framework. There's no reason, then, to believe that recovering the communicative content of an eighteenth-century text requires any less historicism than any other kind of historical interpretation. Modern legal theory, whatever it might stipulate or require, certainly can't change the nature of historical meaning. It can ask interpreters to construe historical evidence anachronistically, but surely at the cost of recovering anything truly historical. Perhaps originalists are after a different sort of historical meaning than historians tend to target, but that meaning is no less embedded in the past, and thus no less *historical* in nature.

The same goes for the recovery of original law. The originalists William Baude and Stephen Sachs have contended that recovering internal legal sources from the past, and especially what those sources conclude about the substance of law, requires a circumscribed form of historical excavation, something well short of the kind of work historians do.[68] The Supreme Court recently endorsed their argument in the Second Amendment case *New York State Rifle & Pistol Association v. Bruen,* in an opinion by Justice Clar-

ence Thomas, one of the court's arch-originalists.[69] For the "restrictive" lawyers' endeavor, Baude and Sachs say they don't need "the tools of modern
intellectual history" or to adopt the broader approaches championed by legal
historians.[70] The "relevant legal doctrines" they are after "represent an ex-
traordinarily narrow slice of any society's intellectual life."[71] That might be
true of some doctrines, but surely few that implicate questions of national
legislative authority, free speech, state sovereign immunity, executive removal, the privileges and immunities of citizenship, and a host of other constitutional issues central to debates among originalists and their opponents.
Given how many aspects of the Constitution turned on underlying interconnected conceptions of, among other things, representation, liberty, and state
power, it's hard to see how one could adequately reconstruct even the most
internalist of legal doctrines without broader immersion in the period's constitutional culture and thinking. Most doctrines, however narrow they might
appear, were hardly disconnected from the broader paradigms through
which eighteenth-century people oriented their constitutional understanding. No doubt, as today, there were technical differences between ordinary
and legal meaning, political dispute and legal doctrine, but all these categories were surely entangled with the core concepts that defined them, so it
takes equivalent historical work to get at that meaning.[72] How could one
think otherwise? Are we really to believe that every other domain of intellectual life at the Founding demands significant intellectual reconstruction but
somehow not law and constitutionalism? That's tough to swallow.

If originalists have decided, for their own reasons, that the Constitution's
original meaning is the law, then they will need to either use historical methods to recover that meaning or explain why historians are mistaken about
the necessity of those methods. It will not do to insist that different historical
methods somehow follow different historical objects—to claim that historical methods are necessary to recover most kinds of original meanings, just
not the original meanings of legal artifacts. The investigations are not obviously different in kind, certainly not to sustain the kind of sharp categorical
distinctions that originalists often rely on. Historical methods are necessary
to recover historical meaning, no matter the artifact in question—no matter
if it happens to have been written in a technical idiom (philosophical, scientific, theological, or legal); no matter if it takes the form of the communicative content of a speech act as opposed to the complex workings of an

ideology. Unless, that is, originalists can explain why not. Simply claiming that history can't decide what the law is, or that legal interpretation is different from the study of history, will not suffice. Those familiar rhetorical points tell us little about whether a particular kind of method is needed to recover something concretely identifiable in the past. As long as originalists make claims on the past, they will be vulnerable to historical critiques.

This is also why originalists, and a great many lawyers, get into trouble when they insist, as they often do, that they are up to something distinct from historians because they are not simply trying to understand the past on its own terms, as a historian would, but instead trying to figure out the content of past law. Akhil Reed Amar has neatly captured this common lawyers' directive. He laments that historians have often "shied away from offering anything that might resemble an emphatic authorial opinion on a once contested legal issue," suspecting that "[t]his hesitation may reflect the fact that most historians lack formal training in legal analysis." Instead, "many historians today would say they simply seek to understand the past on its own terms. These scholars do not wish to opine on who was legally 'right' and who was legally 'wrong' in days gone by, or what the 'lessons' of the past are for today's law and politics." In contrast, he notes, "[l]awyers, judges, and lawmakers approach the past differently. Constitutional principles and judicial precedents from long ago carry weight today, even though the world has undoubtedly changed in the interim."[73] It is thus the job of the lawyer, Amar implies, to construct a "usable past" that instructs today's decision-makers on who had the better legal argument in the past in order to help them correctly decide cases today.

Amar is right, as far as it goes, about the distinct kinds of questions that historians and lawyers tend to pose to the past, but he is mistaken about what historians are focused on and why. Historians are focused on recovering the past on its own terms because they believe there is no distinguishing good and bad legal arguments until we have first understood how those arguments worked in their original context. We *first* need to reconstruct eighteenth-century legal arguments as they were originally understood, according to terms of constitutional debate that might have since disappeared, *before* judging those arguments. If we jump to the latter step, we'll warp the argument before judging it. The main reason historians are largely uninterested in cataloguing whose legal arguments were better or worse in the past is not due to diffidence or lack of legal expertise. Instead, they believe that what counts as a good legal argument today, on the basis of our familiar argumentative frameworks, tells us little about what counted as a good legal argument in 1787, 1800, or 1825, or why. When modern lawyers judge past legal arguments, they tend to lionize people who sound like themselves and frown upon those who don't. If we take a different approach and reconstruct early constitutional argument by its own lights, what often proves most interesting is the number of claims that were once vital yet would get little traction today. Confronted with this kind of evidence, it is not surprising that historians focus most of their attention on understanding how constitutionalism developed and transformed between past and present; how, among other things, constitutional arguments that were once logical lost their potency. If we dismiss these unfamiliar eighteenth-century arguments on the basis that they were "wrong" by the anachronistic standards of modern constitutional logic, we simply distort the very past we hope to make usable. We don't bring that past into conversation with the present; we mold the past according to the judgment of the present. We *change* eighteenth-century arguments into something they never were.

We can then restate Amar's question into a rhetorical one that answers itself: Why do historians elect not to distort the past? Perhaps lawyers do indeed ask different questions of the past and seek to judge earlier legal arguments in ways historians do not. But nothing about that difference means that lawyers don't need to historicize the past—that is, assuming lawyers ultimately care about the arguments eighteenth-century American constitutionalists made and not the shadows those arguments become when forced to perform for us today.

These various originalist ripostes each betray a common flaw—the one with which we began. They each presuppose a false sense of commensurability with the Founding, an unfounded sense that because eighteenth-century American constitutionalists possessed our habits of mind, their constitutionalism is written in something resembling our terms. If originalists are justified in ignoring historical context, it is certainly not because they ask different questions than historians do or because they focus primarily on law. It could only be because historians are badly mistaken in believing, in the words of Bernard Bailyn, that "[t]he past is a different world."[74] The *only* justification originalists could have for insisting that they can *just* study Founding-era law without knowing a whole lot more about Founding-era thinking would be if the Founders in fact thought as we do today—if our legal paradigms and those of the Founders squarely aligned. That could well be so; perhaps over a half century of historical work on the Founding is profoundly mistaken and predicated on erroneous assumptions. But until originalists establish that point on the basis of sympathetic engagement with historians' methods—something they have yet to do—there is no reason to take their word for it. There will continue to be every reason to believe that law was no less touched by the conceptual orientations of the day than were any other aspect of Founding-era thought and that original textual meaning (no matter which kind) can't be disentangled from the broader conceptual vocabularies in which it was embedded. There is no understanding eighteenth-century constitutional *meaning* (linguistic, legal, or anything else) without understanding eighteenth-century constitutional *thinking*—and, thus, the broader conceptual universe that eighteenth-century constitutionalists occupied.

Originalists' categorical distinctions and varied attempts to bracket law from history cannot resolve their difficulties. In each instance, they assume the very issue in question: that the conceptual premises of eighteenth-century constitutionalism align with modern paradigms. Either historians are right about the need to historicize the Founding, or they're wrong. Either they are right about the differences in conceptual thinking between now and then, or they're wrong. The notion that historicism is somehow pertinent to intellectual history but not legal interpretation aimed at recovering intrinsically historical evidence is implausible. Originalists may ask distinct questions, target distinct kinds of historical meaning, and respond to distinct imperatives of law. So be it. None of that changes the basic methodological point. If originalists are trying to recover the *original* meaning of the Constitution—the content that the Constitution in fact communicated to actual eighteenth-century people, who thought like people in the eighteenth century did—then originalists need to historicize that constitutional past on its own terms, untainted by modern legal and jurisprudential assumptions. Only a false sense of familiarity with the Founding could lead one to believe otherwise.

Broadening Our Historicist Vision

These historicist lessons, so essential to deciphering original constitutional meaning, encourage us to broaden our historical vision still further. If people at the Founding thought so differently than we do today, then surely

they thought differently about the Constitution as well. If our goal is to recover eighteenth-century constitutional content, why would we assume that
the original Constitution can be read, unproblematically, like any modern
legal text?

Appreciating the foreign character of our Founding, in other words, en-
courages us to think still more broadly about the Constitution and the myriad ways in which eighteenth-century constitutionalism might have deviated
from the kind of constitutionalism we have come to know. The Constitution's original meaning was entangled in a thick conceptual web. The same
was true of the original Constitution itself. What ails originalists' search for
original meaning ails originalism generally. Before contemplating what any
individual textual provision in the Constitution originally meant, we should
first ask two questions: How was the Constitution itself originally conceived?
How did people understand the nature of constitutionalism at the Founding? When we ask those questions, we can begin to see the rupture between
then and now, and just how significantly originalists' Constitution and the
Founders' Constitution diverge.

Continuity and Change

To begin to bring these anachronisms into relief, we need to see two things
at once: how so much about Founding-era constitutionalism was strange
and different within a context in which so much was unsettled, up for grabs,
and changing. No account of early United States constitutionalism is complete that fails to emphasize each of these defining features. Members of the
late-eighteenth-century constitutional public shared a general approach to
constitutionalism that offered, if nothing else, common points of departure
for grappling with constitutional questions, and the assumptions undergirding this common conceptual space often sharply diverged from the basic
assumptions undergirding modern jurisprudence. At the same time, within
this shared space, Founding-era constitutionalists often disagreed over the
nature of constitutionalism and its core concepts, disagreement that fueled
searching debate and, in turn, dynamic transformation, eventually of the
shared space itself, as it slowly began to resemble something more familiar.

When we venture back to the Founding, therefore, we find, on the one
hand, unfamiliar constitutional assumptions—distinct ways of understanding

constitutional writtenness, fixity, and law—dominating American constitutional imagination for most of the eighteenth century. Some of these assumptions were holdovers from before independence, as American constitutionalists continued to rely on those habits that had so deeply shaped them under British constitutionalism.[75] Others, meanwhile, were born of revolution, as American constitutionalists began generating new forms of constitutional understandings at a time of rupture and change.[76] Few of these eighteenth-century assumptions—those that preceded revolution and those that were a byproduct of it—fit easily with orthodox originalist thinking.

At the same time, we also begin to see more recognizable assumptions taking shape—more familiar ways of thinking about constitutional writtenness, fixity, and law—though not the inexorable result of Founding-era constitutionalists coming to terms with the Constitution's essential nature, but rather the contingent byproduct of the searching debates they had over it.[77] Here we need to appreciate not simply what was unfamiliar about early constitutionalism, but the deep constitutional contestation that was the defining feature of the period. Because the federal Constitution was constructed during a time of enormous constitutional change and experimentation unleashed by the Revolution, much about it was unprecedented, which raised doubts about the kind of thing the Constitution was and the properties that defined it.[78] The problem was not merely that the Constitution contained silences, gaps, and ambiguities that needed to be liquidated through further practice and debate.[79] Nor that the language of the Constitution was a source of instability and uncertainty.[80] More importantly still, at the most fundamental of levels, the Constitution's constitutive identity was itself open to competing, often radically distinct, readings.

As so little about the Constitution was initially clear and settled, it proved a source of persistent debate. That debate was often fueled by the fact that the Constitution functioned as an authoritative source of fundamental authority in the early United States that participants in any number of debates fervently appealed to in order to justify their claims and resolve disagreement. Yet precisely because the Constitution was an inchoate norm, the activity of appealing to it simultaneously shaped, defined, and, in certain respects, constituted it. The content and practice of using constitutional norms were thus reciprocally constitutive. Debating the application of the Constitution's principles and commands in the process helped make and remake the early Constitution.[81] Because of the unique nature of these circumstances, it did not take long for distinct *kinds* of constitutions, none easily reconciled with its competitors, to take shape in people's minds and to serve as the basis for constitutional argument.[82] Disagreement was rarely cabined to the narrow domain of meaning but, more often than not, turned on which conception of the Constitution, defined by which characteristics, was in fact legitimate. It became, at bottom, a struggle over the true referent of *"this Constitution."*

Some of our most familiar constitutional assumptions—many of which have proved so central to modern originalism—emerged from this struggle haltingly and contingently only after 1787. They did not spring inexorably from the original Constitution but were the byproduct of debates over it.[83] Nor were these assumptions, and the Constitution they made, without competitors. Throughout the 1790s and beyond, American constitutionalists remained deeply divided over how to understand the nature of the Constitution's content, its relationship to existing law, and the terms of its enforcement.[84] On into the nineteenth century, the terms of the debates remained as messy and uncertain as the positions held within them.[85] All recognized the Constitution's authority—and argued through that authority—while disagreeing over the thing they all took to be authoritative.[86]

Continuity and change; agreement and disagreement; the foreign and the familiar. If we scrutinize the Founding, what we find can seem chaotic: unfamiliar constitutional assumptions that had been around a long time, unfamiliar constitutional assumptions that were only recently the result of revolutionary debate and change, and more familiar constitutional assumptions that were haphazardly taking shape. If we stitch it all together, though— if we see both the continuity and the change—it reinforces the same basic point: orthodox originalism is not easily rooted in the Founding.

Under the guise of neutrality, originalists elevate one optional form of constitutional thinking above its competitors.[87] They ignore or distort the unfamiliar, paper over or minimize the depth of disagreement, and conflate the Constitution in their minds with the one laid down in 1787. They assume that the Constitution they so clearly recognize—the one that has become so central to modern constitutional law—must have been the one lurking beneath all that Founding-era debate, its true nature clear and settled, merely awaiting discovery. In presuming as much, originalists don't in fact take the Constitution as given but impose their own assumptions on the eighteenth-century landscape, shaping the Constitution into something it originally was not. They either substitute the familiar for the unfamiliar or treat as essential what was merely contingent and emerged only later. They pass off a constitution significantly of their own making as that of the Founders, erasing all distance in between.

4

Written Constitutionalism at the Founding

> The Constitution of a country is not the paper or parchment upon which the compact is written, it is the system of fundamental laws, by which the people have consented to be governed, which is always supposed to be impressed upon the mind of every individual, and of which the written or printed copies are nothing more than the evidence.
>
> — John Quincy Adams, 1791

TO BRING THE UNFAMILIAR WORLD of the original Constitution into focus, the place to start is with constitutional writtenness. As the putatively defining characteristic of American constitutionalism and the foundational assumption of most forms of originalism, it is the root of the problem and the source of the deepest and most consequential misunderstanding.

Originalists don't often invest much time trying to figure out what the Constitution is or might have been, for that has always seemed so apparent to them. Nothing seems quite as obvious to them as the simple fact that the federal Constitution is a written text. Surely it was evident to the Founders themselves what the Constitution was, originalists contend: not only was it the written document that lay before them, but it was alike in kind to the myriad other written constitutions they had long known—the state constitutions Americans had begun writing in 1776, the Articles of Confederation that had served as the nation's inaugural constitution, and the various charters that had governed the colonies since the first half of the seventeenth century. By 1787, there was nothing mysterious to Americans about written constitutions.

This kind of thinking badly misses the mark, however. It mistakenly assumes that just because Founding-era Americans wrote their constitutions, they understood those constitutions in ways we would expect—that certain essential constitutional features simply inhere in writtenness and, therefore, that the kind of written constitutionalism with which we are so familiar was a natural byproduct of writing constitutions. It has been too easy to assume, in other words, that wherever there were written constitutions, one readily finds written constitutionalism *as we know it*. As Quentin Skinner rightly cautioned decades ago, "the unconscious application of paradigms" on account of their "familiarity" often "disguises [their] essential inapplicability to the past."[1] Failure to heed this lesson has often left Founding-era constitutionalism buried under anachronism.

Recall how, with few exceptions, originalists think about constitutional writtenness. They jump effortlessly from the fact that the Constitution is written to a particular understanding of its character and content. *Because* the Constitution is written, it just *is* the document that we habitually call the Constitution. In practice that means that, by virtue of being written, the Constitution comes with a particular model of constitutional communication built into it. Constitutional content is created by text and communicated by the language that constitutes that text. The Constitution's content is thus the sum of propositions communicated by its words—whatever its text happens to express. Constitutional meaning is fundamentally *textual* meaning. Even if that textual meaning might be broad, either because the Constitution's language is written at a high level of generality or thanks to pragmatic enrichment that language encompasses far more than its bare semantics suggest, that textual meaning is still fundamentally rooted in text.

Revolutionary Americans assuredly embraced written constitutionalism, but their understanding of it was worlds apart from present-day understanding. They did not share modern originalists' understanding of constitutional content or modern originalists' model of constitutional communication; nor did they think that either was entailed by written constitutionalism. They did not assume that writing constitutional principles down automatically or necessarily altered the legal status of those principles, transformed constitutional content into linguistic content, or erected sharp textual boundaries between what was *in* and what was *outside* a constitution. They did not wield a clear distinction between written and unwritten constitutional meaning; nor did they draw sharp distinctions between written and unwritten sources of law. They had no trouble thinking that constitutions were at once tangible and concrete and at the same time decidedly not. To be sure, they talked about their constitutions as documents and emphasized what had been written into them. They also cared about textual meaning and constitutional language. But it does not follow that they thought that a constitution's meaning was simply the sum of propositions expressed by its words. It likewise does not follow that they thought constitutional content was solely created by and communicated through constitutional text, that the phrase "this Constitution" referred exclusively to a document, or that the nation's fundamental law was whatever had been written into the Constitution. Given how they thought about constitutions and constitutionalism, none of these propositions would have made sense.

To their minds, the content of written constitutions was not simply derived from text. And that was not simply because they believed, as modern originalists are at pains to emphasize, that constitutional text had fuller meaning when read in context, or because that text had to be given effect through legal doctrine, or because that text might prove vague or indeterminate and thus require further construction—though all those things were surely true. It was not because, as those examples stress, constitutional text could communicate beyond a literal reading of its words. That was less than half the story.[2] There were other more important ways in which, to so many at the Founding, constitutional content was not derived from enacted constitutional text. For eighteenth-century observers, it was not difficult to see how certain things were constitutional, not because of anything constitutional text expressed or implied, but because of how constitutions were *understood to work*. This was content that could not be deciphered from constitutional text no matter how carefully one interpreted it or how fully one situated it in its linguistic context. This constitutional content derived from a different source entirely: from placing the written constitution in its *constitutional* context. This unwritten constitutional content was not only compatible with Founding-era written constitutionalism but essential to it.

These facts are hardly incidental since Founding-era constitutionalists, like any group of people, wrote constitutions in light of their underlying assumptions about what kinds of things constitutions were and how constitutions worked. *Their* written constitutions were a function of how *they* understood written constitutionalism. There is no separating what their constitutions originally said from their assumptions about how those constitutions acquired and communicated content. Just as it is impossible to decode what constitutional provisions such as the Second Amendment originally meant without first understanding the particular way people at the time conceptualized constitutional rights and their relationship to state power, so too is it impossible to know what kind of content an eighteenth-century written constitution originally contained and communicated without first understanding the particular way people at the time conceptualized written constitutionalism. It's not intelligible to speak of *their* constitutions divorced from their assumptions about how constitutions worked. The federal Constitution of 1787 was originally conceived, ratified, and interpreted from an unfamiliar constitutional perspective.

To recover the Constitution that the Founders knew, we need to recreate, from the ground up, their distinctive understanding of written constitutionalism. The deeper sources of that constitutionalism were multiple. They were not unique to Revolutionary America, yet each was inflected in distinctive American ways as members of the Founding generation elaborated on them. That elaboration brought change, transforming Founding-era constitutionalism in the process.[3] Nonetheless, essential features of this thinking not only survived independence but endured well beyond the drafting of the federal Constitution, structuring how Founding-era Americans thought about written constitutions during the nation's formative period of constitution making.

Founding-era conceptions of written constitutionalism can be traced to three sources in particular: Americans' experience under British constitutionalism, their understanding of law itself, and their instinctive reliance on social contract theory. Fused together, these influences forged the logic and grammar of Founding-era constitutionalism. When we understand things from that perspective, we see why it would have been hard to imagine written constitutions as exclusive, stand-alone texts—to believe, to invoke that favored originalist conviction, that "you can carry a complete copy of the Constitution in your pocket."[4]

The Endurance of British Constitutionalism

It is all too common to treat the appearance of Americans' first constitutions, drafted in the states beginning in 1776 and shortly thereafter for the union as a whole, as a "big bang" moment—a sharp departure from what had come before.[5] In this telling, Revolutionary Americans consciously rejected the unwritten, customary, evolving British constitution they had long known in favor of something entirely different: constitutions that would be fixed through writing. This popular rendition fails to grasp, however, how Americans had understood and experienced the British constitution and, because of that, how seamlessly prior constitutional habits informed the constitutions that replaced it.[6] No doubt, American state constitutions were novel in important respects, not least because they were revolutionary manifestos announcing a break with the prior political order, a context that helped lay the groundwork for a round of searching debate throughout the states.[7] But those novelties should not distract from the basic continuities that shaped constitutional understanding before and after independence. Whatever else might have changed or was beginning to change, when it came to how American constitutionalists conceived of constitutional content, boundaries, and law, an enormous amount remained the same.

This continuity shouldn't surprise us. It's harder to see today, but if we flip things around and imagine ourselves in the eighteenth century, on the eve of American independence, we'd be struck by all that remained the same. The American Revolution, after all, was waged in the name of the British constitution, not against it. In 1776, everything white Americans knew about constitutionalism—every ingrained assumption, every belief they had about what constitutions were, how constitutions acquired and communicated content, and how constitutions regulated political and legal life, indeed the entirety of their constitutional education—was predicated on life under the unwritten, customary British constitution. They had spent decades confidently referencing a constitution consisting primarily of unwritten fundamental principles rather than a set of express textual commands.[8] Even if the British constitution often took its form in several celebrated texts such as Magna Carta, the Petition of Right of 1628, and the English Bill of Rights of 1689, it was understood to be a set of fundamental principles grounded in custom—unwritten principles that American colonists obsessively appealed to.[9] And they did not think they had been playing make-believe. "The great Principles of the Constitution, are intimately known, they are sensibly felt by [everyone]," John Adams declared shortly before independence.[10] He and his fellow colonists believed that when they referenced the British constitution they were talking about something real, something that everyone in their political world could readily pick out and interpret. They had no trouble understanding how a non-textual constitution could communicate meaning to a community of interpreters. They had no trouble understanding how constitutional principles could exist independently of textual codification. Their socialization ran deep, shaping their intuitions and habits of mind. When they thought about fundamental constitutional principles, they intuitively looked where everyone else in the British tradition looked: to custom, history, experience, written law, and deep structure. A lifetime's knowledge is not easily lost—especially when it could be so easily carried forward and applied to the situation at hand. The mere act of drawing up new constitutions to take the place of the British one they had long known hardly necessitated a dramatic shift. Rather, to a great extent it demanded more of the same.

There were so many ways in which the constitutional work of 1776 manifestly drew on prior experience. For one, when American patriots began devising regular legal governments that year, they set out less to create something radically new than to build on their existing institutions.[11] They instinctively looked to practices forged under colonial governance and, especially, the numerous quasi-legal representative institutions (committees, conventions, congresses) they had established beginning in 1765 to organize resistance to British policy, as well as the various provincial assemblies and congresses and local committees that effectively assumed power from the British beginning in 1773.[12] Institutions forged in 1776 were meant to modify earlier forms, not simply depart from them.

Even more vitally, written constitutionalism itself was nothing new at the Founding; it was a form eighteenth-century Americans had long known. That was thanks to their experience living under charters: documents that had established governance in the colonies and secured English liberties for colonial residents.[13] In addition to putting some of their own rights down on paper, American colonists also thought that their charters gave more concrete form to the British constitution they so revered.[14] The "constitution of Britain," the Suffolk Resolves stated in 1774, "was covenanted to us in the charter of the province."[15] Less than a decade earlier, Connecticut's House of Representatives had declared that "our full possession and continued enjoyment of the rights and priviledges of the British constitution" were "rendered more sacred and indefeasible by the royal grant and charter" they had received, "which we conceive to stand upon the same basis with the grand charters and fountains of English liberty," Magna Carta above all.[16] The Declaration of Independence, meanwhile, claimed that "our constitution" consisted of "our Charters," "our most valuable laws," and "the Forms of our Governments."[17]

Given that their constitutional lives had long been organized around these authoritative texts, for American Revolutionaries the act of writing new constitutions in 1776 did not mark a sharp departure from the familiar. There was no magical, instantaneous transformation from inchoate, unwritten constitutionalism to neatly focused, textual constitutionalism.[18] On the contrary, it was only natural for Revolutionary Americans to imagine their new state constitutions as logical successors to the charters they had so revered.[19] They were initially styled as charters, in fact.[20] That Connecticut and Rhode Island, the only remaining non-royal colonies, meanwhile, did not even draw up new constitutions following independence—instead merely updating their existing charters—powerfully underscores the perceived continuity.[21] "Our transition from a state of political subjection to Great-Britain, to independence, and sovereignty, was almost imperceptible," the Connecticut jurist Zephaniah Swift would later testify. "Tho we were witnesses to a most singular revolution, yet we experienced . . . no convulsion in our domestic government."[22] If the writing of constitutions beginning in 1776 marked a decisive break with the past, we should expect to find relentless testimony to this fact. Founding-era constitutionalists, after all, were not shy about drawing out the perceived significance of every aspect of their revolutionary experience, most especially their experiment in self-government. Yet we find no such testimony, and the silence is deafening.[23]

In seamlessly replacing the charters that preceded them, the first state constitutions were understood much as those charters had been: as neither an exclusive nor comprehensive repository of fundamental authority. As Mary Sarah Bilder has explained, early American "charter constitutionalism" operated under "a different assumption about the purpose of . . . written words." In charters, "words represented principles," but "principles were not defined and limited entirely by the words."[24] The charters were written, but they rested on a non-textual foundation consisting of the essential protections and fundamental law encompassing the customary British constitution.[25] The colonists' "several charters or compacts" were, as the Continental Congress suggested, tightly intertwined with, and could not be comprehended apart from, "the immutable laws of nature" and "the principles of the English constitution."[26]

The state constitutions initially worked in a similar way. Americans had declared independence in the name of the fundamental principles of the British constitution and assuredly believed that those continued to inform their new constitutional documents. Indeed, among the important things the new state constitutions were meant to do was to identify and protect the liberties that residents believed they had always enjoyed.[27] It's impossible to suppose that American constitutionalists thought they were deleting these underlying principles they claimed as their birthright and in defense of which they proved willing to die. Certainly nothing about the mere fact that they chose to write constitutions should suggest that. To them, there was nothing inconsistent about having a written constitution that was bolstered by unwritten constitutional principles. And there is no reason to believe that people who had always operated under that assumption suddenly abandoned it simply because they replaced their charters with new frameworks for government—one written instrument with another.

The persistent belief that the mere act of writing constitutions in 1776 betrayed a repudiation of British constitutionalism is ill-founded. In writing those constitutions, Revolutionary Americans relied on much the same picture of fundamental authority that had defined their colonial experience. Independence did little to disrupt the basic conceptual relationship between written constitutional standards and underlying constitutional principles. Deeply ingrained intuitions endured.

Frames and Fundamental Law

The continuities between British constitutionalism and early U.S. constitutionalism are especially evident in how Revolutionary Americans initially described constitutions. To them, constitutions were at once frames of government and, at the same time, fundamental law, or the rules that bound that government. These two descriptions were not in tension, but nor were they identical. The former described a framework—specifications that out-lined and empowered a government; the latter a legal standard—binding rules, prescriptions, and prohibitions that stood above and regulated ordi-nary lawmaking. Both senses were common, and they often were run to-gether. Sometimes when people talked about constitutions, they referred narrowly to the scheme of government. Other times, they referred broadly to the entire swath of rules, prohibitions, and principles that made up the fun-damental laws of the land. And sometimes they referred to both.

Around the time Americans declared independence, the word "constitu-tion" tended to have a narrower meaning, referring exclusively to a form of government. That emphasis was not terribly surprising given the legacy of British constitutionalism. When people referenced the British constitution, they often had in mind the structure and framework of governance within the realm.[28] The definition was descriptive in nature, and to the extent it was also prescriptive, those prescriptions were derived from the internal logic of the government's structure.[29] When it came time for Americans to devise their own constitutions, they initially followed in kind. In a characteristic move, North Carolina's 1776 document was divided into two distinct parts: the first was labeled "A Declaration of Rights," while the second was called "The Constitution, or Form of Government."[30] In a pamphlet published in 1777, Benjamin Rush sharply distinguished between a "Bill of Rights," which came first and laid out "the great principles of *natural* and *civil liberty*," and the "Constitution," which was altogether separate, describing the govern-ment that embodied and protected those "great principles."[31]

Usage of the term "constitution" gradually began to change during the de-cades that followed. Eventually, it became common to use the word more ca-paciously to refer to each of the distinct components Rush had held apart.[32] New Hampshire, for instance, titled its revised 1784 constitution "A Constitu-tion, Containing a Bill of Rights, and Form of Government."[33] The word slowly came to mean the entirety of fundamental law operative across the polity.[34]

As the word "constitution" started to take on a more expansive definition, some commentators insisted not only that a constitution was more than a form of government but also that it needed to be clearly distinct from and superior to that government. Thomas Paine stressed as early as 1776 that "[a] Constitution, and a form of government, are frequently confounded together, and spoken of as synonimous things; whereas they are not only different, but are established for different purposes."[35] While initially an outlier, this sentiment was echoed a decade later by a growing, if still relatively small, group of commentators. Thomas Tudor Tucker complained that South Carolina's 1778 constitution was "not founded on proper authority, being only an act of the legislature." Unless that was remedied, the constitution could not serve as a genuine "rule of government" that was "not alterable by it."[36] Only then, Thomas Jefferson reasoned, might a constitution stand as "an act *above the power of the ordinary legislature.*"[37]

The shift was hardly seamless, however. Even as usage of the word "constitution" changed, its original meaning endured, and for years to come, it continued to be used specifically to describe the frame of government.[38] As late as 1828, in his inaugural dictionary of the English language, Noah Webster offered a definition of "constitution" that combined the various elements that the word had come to stand for. A "constitution" was both "[t]he established form of government in a state, kingdom, or country" and "a system of fundamental rules, principles and ordinances for the government of a state or nation."[39] A "constitution" still remained "that form of being or peculiar structure and connection of parts which makes or characterizes a system or body"—such as "the *constitution* of the solar system."[40] Even as things were changing, the word retained its ancient meaning.

This linguistic indeterminacy suggests that "constitutions" described distinct things with overlapping identities: both a form of government as well as the system of fundamental law in which that frame was embedded. What we might regard as confusing and multivalent, Founding-era constitutionalists found intuitive. And why not? It was such a natural carryover from the constitutionalism they had forever known. Americans' colonial charters had primarily been constitutions of government—documents that laid out an authoritative blueprint for the governance of new settlements. In placing limitations on that government and identifying certain legal principles and protections, however, Americans had also incorporated the fundamental guarantees of the British constitution outside of those charters. Now the state constitutions functioned in a comparable way: frames of government erected on underlying fundamental principles. Constitutional text was a node in a broader constitutional and legal order.

Part of what distinguished the component meanings of "constitution," even as they were increasingly bundled together in a single definition, was the fact that frames of government and fundamental law enjoyed distinct derivations. The most vital thing a written constitution did was establish a frame of government. Not every political community needed one. Some nations, such as Britain, were governed by customary institutions that had originated centuries earlier and could carry on without anyone stipulating in writing their structure, powers, or responsibilities. But other nations, especially new nations, like the United States, enjoyed no such luxury. Although two of those states—Connecticut and Rhode Island—found their customary colonial governments sufficiently workable to maintain them, the other states experienced a sufficient power vacuum once British authority collapsed that they opted for fresh constitutions of government so that they might establish the political institutions that they lacked.[41] And there was no easy way to establish a new frame of government—practically, much less authoritatively—without codifying it in writing. In most of the independent American states, written constitutions were principally needed to constitute government.

By contrast, constitutions were not necessary to supply fundamental law. Fundamental law already existed in abundance before the formation of any polity's municipal government. American constitutionalists did not have to go looking for it in 1776. There was ample fundamental law all around from which to challenge, curb, or empower government and ground fundamental rights and protections. Reared in the British constitutional tradition, they assumed as a matter of course that all governments were automatically constrained by the fundamental principles of liberty that experience and reason had independently identified and established. To be sure, fundamental law did not have to be taken as found. There were important reasons to refine or revise it, to emphasize portions of it in more emphatic ways, or even to specify new fundamental law appropriate for the particular political communities being devised. And Revolutionary American constitutionalists assuredly did just that. But altering and adding to fundamental law was not the same thing as building it from scratch. Creating a new constitution of government did not entail nullifying or remaking existing fundamental law. Whatever a constitution of government was doing, it did not have to create fundamental law from the ground up.

Written constitutions in the early United States at once established new kinds of legal authority while leaving others as they were. Webster's definition captured this distinction as well. As the higher law—or the "fundamental rules, principles and ordinances" found in "free states"—a constitution was "paramount to the statutes or law enacted by the legislature, limiting and controlling its power." But where did this higher law come from? It was something "particular": whatever had been ordained and "made by the authority of any superior, civil or ecclesiastical." Yet at the same time it was something general: "a system of fundamental principles for the government of rational and social beings."[42] The word "constitution" described the body of rules ordained by the highest civil authority in a political community. But it also described those principles of governance that human reason and experience had invested with fundamental authority. What Webster was getting at was the idea of general fundamental law.

General Fundamental Law

The concept of preexisting fundamental law was foundational to Founding-era constitutionalism. Even more than the polysemous character of the word "constitution," this understanding of fundamental law underscored why written constitutions could never be reduced to the contents of their text. As noted, beginning in the late eighteenth century, constitutions were increasingly equated with the fundamental law of the realm. But only some of that fundamental law was created through the constitution's enactment. Other fundamental law existed before the drafting of the constitution and was simply left in place, incorporated by implication. "There are . . . certain fundamental Laws, and certain original Rights," John Adams declared, "reserved expressly or tacitly, by every People in their first Confederation in Society, and erection of Government."[43] All fundamental law was part of the "constitution," but only some of it derived from the constitution's text. Written constitutional provisions thus worked in concert with and bled seamlessly into a broader field of preexisting fundamental law.

These Founding-era attitudes toward fundamental law had broad roots. They were deeply shaped by the peculiarities of British constitutionalism and the habits it had inculcated. But these attitudes were every bit as much the result of how Founding-era constitutionalists thought about law generally. Early American constitutionalism was fundamentally built on a delicate synthesis of positive and non-positive law that permeated Founding-era legal imagination, profoundly shaping how people thought about the nature of constitutional content and writtenness.

As with Founding-era written constitutionalism, Founding-era attitudes toward fundamental law are often obscured by the modern distinctions imposed on them. Observers have had no trouble appreciating that the Founding generation tended to think about law differently than we do today. But too often observers have mistakenly assumed that those eighteenth-century views are legible on the familiar terms of modern legal theory. It's another case of square pegs being unthinkingly pounded into round holes.

Debates in modern jurisprudence have revolved around the relationship between positive law and morality—that is, law as contingently laid down by human beings in particular jurisdictions (through constitutions, statutes, executive orders, and court decisions) and moral facts that are universally valid independently of any human decision or authority.[44] Enduring debates divide theorists. Legal positivists insist that law is entirely (or mostly) a matter of social rather than moral facts.[45] Law is law, not because it is just or moral, but because it has been lawfully enacted through valid procedures. It is a social convention all the way down. Appeals to justice or moral truth merely illustrate the essential difference between what the law is and what it perhaps ought to be. Critics of legal positivism have found this account inadequate, insisting, by contrast, that law is inextricably intertwined with morality. Followers of the influential legal theorist Ronald Dworkin avow that law is best understood as a branch of political morality—not only is morality relevant to law, but law is itself a kind of morality.[46] In a related vein, meanwhile, modern defenders of the natural law tradition similarly insist that law is irreducibly embedded in morality.[47] Despite the diversity of views and the sharp disagreement dividing them, modern jurisprudence is structured by a common set of questions and categories. In broad strokes, theorists ask whether, and if so how, positive law is meaningfully shaped by non-posited morality.[48] Their answers differ, but their answers can all be plotted on the same classification scheme and readily understood on each other's terms.

When scholars have investigated the Founding generation's views on law, they have often mapped those views on this familiar modern grid. Were the Founders legal positivists? Did they think morality shaped law? Given the abundant evidence that they subscribed to natural law thinking, how did they connect those principles to the positive law of their written Constitution? These kinds of questions, intuitive as they might seem, make it hard to understand the Founders' views on law. The issue lies less with the classification than with the classification scheme itself, structured as it is by the sharp or-ganizing distinction between positive law and non-posited morality common to reigning modern debates.[49] The Founders simply didn't think this way, and if we try to map the Founders' views onto that scheme, something fun-damental will be lost. We need a new scheme.

The Founding generation had a much different view of law: an integrated view. They did not draw categorical distinctions between sources of law—natural law, customary law, enacted law. Nor did they assume that positive law could be neatly separated from non-positive law. Rather, they assumed that different sources and kinds of law naturally harmonized.[50] There are good reasons why eighteenth-century legal treatises read nothing like those written more recently—why they stitched together observations culled from what we today would call political theory, moral philosophy, sociology, psy-chology, and history without any sense that they were drawing on distinct intellectual disciplines.[51] They assumed that the study of law, in essence, was the study of human nature. The job of the jurist, or sage of law, was less to synthesize seemingly opposing elements than to understand how they har-monized of their own accord.

There was little room in this paradigm for the kinds of questions that ani-mate debates in modern legal theory or the sharply defined categories that sustain them. In the eighteenth century, there was nothing intuitive about categorically distinguishing non-positive from positive law or about asking how these distinct kinds of law interacted. It made more sense to assume that non-positive and positive law automatically bled into one another at countless points and, instead, attempt to understand how that worked. Be-cause Founding-era constitutionalists conceived of the legal whole so differ-ently, they understood the component parts differently as well. That was especially true of non-positive law. They certainly did not think of it simply as morality, as so much modern jurisprudence would have it. But neither did they equate it with something more proximate, like natural law, even if they assuredly emphasized natural law with steady regularity.[52] Calling the Found-ers natural lawyers hits closer to the mark but still cannot do justice to the complexity of their views, either how they understood the multifaceted na-ture of non-positive law—derived every bit as much from understandings of common law and customary British constitutionalism as natural law—or how they believed those legal strands fit together.[53] Non-positive law cropped up in numerous places, stretching widely across the legal domain. Its forms and locations were difficult to pinpoint, however, precisely on account of the integrated view of law through which it was understood. Because fundamental law naturally harmonized and because positive and non-positive law were not distinct and separate but compatible and intertwined, there was no simple way to delineate either.[54]

The Founders had complex synthetic views on law. We get nowhere disentangling so-called non-positive law from positive law and asking how eighteenth-century constitutionalists believed one influenced the other. We need to see how non-positive law and positive law were woven together. The best way to understand this fusion is to bring into focus the once ubiquitous legal concept with which we began: general fundamental law.

Founding-era constitutionalists often referenced various sources of law: natural law, common law, civil or municipal law, the law of nations, constitutional law, and others still. Each of these sources was, in a real sense, distinct, enjoying an independent identity and derivation, with some grounded in reason, others in custom, and still others in consent. But that seeming autonomy held up only to a point. For each source of law was shot through with a doubled-faced ambiguity that made sharp differentiation not only difficult but pointless. That ambiguity turned on the porous boundary between non-positive and positive law—law that was found and law that was made.

In eighteenth-century America, law was understood to be as much found as made.[55] Law was not treated as strictly positivist in character—simply the command of the sovereign or exclusively the enactments of lawfully authorized bodies. Law, to an important extent, rested on non-positivist foundations beyond the contingent creation of human beings. As an American writer declared in characteristic fashion in 1777, "right, and not power, is the source of law."[56] "The eternal and immutable laws of justice and morality," John Quincy Adams similarly announced a decade and a half later, "are paramount to all human legislation."[57] In vital ways, law was "out there" awaiting discovery.

These assumptions were grounded in the pervasive belief that human law was undergirded by natural law, which was preexisting, universal, unchanging, and divinely sanctioned.[58] "By the natural and moral law," explained the judge Jacob Rush in 1796, "is understood, that law which is founded upon the *eternal reason and fitness of things*, and enjoins those duties, which, as dependent creatures, we owe to our Creator, and to each other, and which necessarily result from *those* relations."[59] "The law of nature is immutable ... [and] universal," wrote James Wilson, and "having its foundation in the constitution and state of man, has an essential fitness for all mankind, and binds them without distinction."[60] Natural law was paramount and binding. Any human law contrary to it, went the familiar refrain, was null. Whatever was "contrary to natural right and justice," declared George Mason in Virginia's General Court in 1772, "are, in our laws, and must be in the nature of things, considered as void."[61] But natural law was not easy to pinpoint. It was known only through felt intuition and rational reflection.[62] "The science of law is grounded on certain first principles," explained Zephaniah Swift, "derived from the dictates of reason."[63] "We discover it," echoed Wilson, "by our conscience, by our reason, and by the Holy Scriptures."[64] Because the law of nature was abstract and deciphered principally through reason, it was often referred to as the law of "right reason."[65] Given its broad applicability, moreover, natural law was necessarily general in its pronouncements.[66] On account of these two characteristics—that it was inferred by reason and general in its tenor—natural law was shot through with indeterminacy.[67]

In a straightforward sense, civil or municipal law was distinct from natural law. Natural law had governed human beings in the state of nature—that pervasive Enlightenment thought experiment—but entry into civil society had led to the establishment of a new kind of law that was not derived from reason alone but was instead grounded in human will and consent.[68] "By a positive law," explained Jacob Rush, "is understood a law, which does not necessarily flow from the nature of things, but is founded solely on the *will* of the law-giver, and adapted to some particular *time* or *occasion*."[69] As James Wilson succinctly put it, "municipal law" was "[t]hat which a political society makes for itself."[70]

Despite these seemingly clear differences, natural and municipal law blended together in myriad ways. For one thing, it was widely assumed that civil law needed to conform to natural law. As James Wilson stressed, "municipal laws are under the control of the law of nature."[71] Natural law was thus often treated as a set of fundamental background principles for construing civil law.[72] It was presumed that legislators could never have intended to contravene, as the South Carolina Court of Common Pleas stressed in 1789, "the plain and obvious principles of common right, and common reason." "We are, therefore, bound," the court continued, "to give such a construction [to the statute] . . . as will be consistent with justice, and the dictates of natural reason."[73] Meanwhile, because natural law was often so broadly conceived and relatively undefined, it was widely assumed that municipal law fleshed out natural law in various ways, either by expounding its deeper logic, filling in its details, providing the best evidence of its content, or enforcing it by declaring what it otherwise required.[74]

There was an even more important reason yet why non-positive and positive law blended in the eighteenth-century American legal imagination: the multifaceted character of the common law. It is impossible to overstate the common law's centrality to Founding-era constitutional thought and experience. It was at the center of the constitutional and legal tradition in which Revolutionary Americans came of age and was celebrated as the great bulwark of English liberty on both sides of the Atlantic. The "common law" kept "the great ends of liberty," proclaimed James Wilson, "steadily and constantly in view."[75] The language of early American constitutionalism unsurprisingly was saturated with references to it. And the idea of constitutionalism itself, as Founding-era Americans initially understood it, was deeply inflected by the idea of the common law and all it was taken to embody. As the jurist Peter Du Ponceau would put it a generation after the Revolution: "We live in the midst of the common law, we inhale it at every breath, imbibe it at every pore." It is "interwoven with the very idiom that we speak, and we cannot learn another system of laws without learning at the same time another language."[76] Today, the common law is usually understood in avowedly positivist and realist terms, as judge-made law found in the decisions of courts. That was not how the common law was understood in the eighteenth century, however.[77] At that time, it carried a much wider set of meanings, followed a far different logic, and derived from a much different set of legal sources. It was not simply a set of discrete legal rulings, rules, and procedures, but the conception of law and method for deciphering it that lay beneath those particular legal outcomes and requirements. From this wider conceptual perspective, the common law helped harmonize the seemingly competing criteria—the immutable dictates of reason and the consent of the political community—upon which natural and civil law were based.

The common law was grounded in custom. It originated not in written enactment but long practice.[78] It consisted of "those principles and doctrines, which have become law by the usage and practice of the people," stressed Zephaniah Swift.[79] In that regard, as the Virginia jurist and law professor George Wythe declared, "the whole common law is founded on custom."[80] As the famed English jurist William Blackstone wrote in his *Commentaries on the Laws of England*, being "the *lex non scripta*, the unwritten, or common law," it was distinct from "the *lex scripta*, the written, or statute law."[81] The "original institution and authority" of these laws, Blackstone explained, "are not set down in writing, as acts of parliament are, but they receive their binding power, and the force of laws, by long and immemorial usage."[82] Those customs that had been practiced and sanctioned over considerable time were considered part of the common law. As the common refrain went, the merit of a custom depended on it "having been used time out of mind," or "time whereof the memory of man runneth not to the contrary."[83] A lot of times, judges and lawyers looked to past legal decisions as proof of a custom's authority.[84] But those decisions were merely a record or reminder of the common law, not its source. "It has its monuments in writing," asserted James Wilson. "But though, in many cases, its *evidence* rests, yet, in all cases, its *authority* rests not, on those written monuments. Its authority rests," by contrast, "on reception, approbation, custom, long and established."[85]

Despite its basis in custom, however, the common law was not thought to be at odds with democratic consent.[86] In fact, in the eyes of many Founding-era constitutionalists, custom, rightly understood, was the strongest evidence available of consent.[87] James Wilson was especially engaged on this point.[88] "[C]ustom is, of itself, intrinsick evidence of consent," he submitted.[89] It carried the mark of "internal evidence, of the strongest kind, that the law has been introduced by common *consent*."[90] As he explained: "How was a custom introduced? By voluntary adoption. How did it become general? By the instances of voluntary adoption being increased. How did it become lasting? By voluntary and satisfactory experience, which ratified and confirmed what voluntary adoption had introduced."[91] In that regard, "this consent rests upon the most solid basis—experience as well as opinion."[92] Jesse Root, a Connecticut Superior Court judge, echoed this account. Those "unwritten customs and regulations which are reasonable and beneficial, and which have the sanction of universal consent and adoption in practice, have," he wrote, "the force of laws under the authority of the people."[93] This was especially true in the American colonies, argued Zephaniah Swift, since "[o]ur ancestors . . . were under no obligation to . . . observe the laws of the country, from whence they emigrated." The "voluntary reception of the English laws, by the general consent of the people," was "the only foundation of their authority."[94] Custom was not just the evidence of consent, however; it also helped realize that consent. Privileging custom built flexibility into the law, enabling it to change to accommodate those it governed.[95] "It is the characteristick of a system of common law, that it be accommodated to the circumstances, the exigencies, and the conveniences of the people, by whom it is appointed," explained Wilson. "The same principles, which establish it, change, enlarge, improve, and repeal it."[96]

At the same time, the common law was also believed to be founded on reason.[97] It was not merely the contingent customs of the realm, instantiated in so many celebrated political episodes, judicial rulings, and legal treatises. By drawing on the wisdom of experience and the successions of the ages, the common law promised to work out the "artificial reason," or inner logic, of the law.[98] In deciphering the deeper pattern that custom made, the common law revealed what was inherently reasonable and pointed the way to the deeper principles of legal reason, thus helping the law work itself pure. "The common law," as Zephaniah Swift claimed, "is a highly improved system of reason, founded on the nature and fitness of things."[99] The "[c]ommon law is the perfection of reason, arising from the nature of God, of man, and of things," Jesse Root declared in a similar spirit. "It is universal and extends to all men . . . ; it is immutable, and cannot be changed or altered, without altering the nature and relation of things; it is superior to all other laws and regulations, by it they are corrected and controlled . . . the usages and customs of men and the decisions of the courts of justice serve to declare and illustrate the principles of this law; but the law exists the same."[100] The common law also was found, not made. That fact helped underscore a deeper commitment: that the reason of the common law helped reveal the dictates of natural law, often itself called the law of reason. Indeed, it was sometimes said that the common law provided the best evidence of the content of natural law.[101] Even more strikingly, it was also said that the common law was simply natural law applied to human society.[102] The "Maxims and Principles, which form the ground-work of the Common Law," the Pennsylvania lawyer William Barton wrote, "are Rules, deduced from Reason, Natural Law and Justice."[103] The common law, in short, harmonized with natural law.[104]

There was nothing perceived to be incompatible about these distinct common-law ingredients. Custom, consent, and reason worked together. Custom was the best marker of both consent and reason and thus the site where
they became entwined. The "common law," insisted Wilson, was "nothing
else but common reason—that refined reason, which is generally received by
the consent of all."[105] Alexander Addison, meanwhile, claimed that "[t]he
common law is founded on the law of nature and the revelation of God" in the
same breath that he claimed that it was "founded on an implied common
consent, from long acquiescence in its authority and use" and, thus, on "the
will of the community."[106] Or, as William Barton put it, "the *common* municipal law . . . is founded on ancient, immemorial usage, and common consent" and "derives its sanction from its reasonableness, the equity of its
maxims, and the justness of its fundamental principles."[107]

The common law was also seen as both contingent and timeless, changing
in light of circumstance and need while remaining constant over time.[108]
Here, too, eighteenth-century Americans perceived no contradiction. As Wilson put it, as "circumstances, and exigencies, and conveniencies insensibly
change; a proportioned change, in time and degree, must take place in the
accommodated system. But though," he went on, "the system suffer these
partial and successive alterations, yet it continues materially and substan-
tially the same."[109] Dynamic yet steady, the common law evolved without
ever fundamentally changing.

In at once embodying contingent consent and timeless reason, the common law synthesized positive and non-positive law into an integrated whole.
The common law was not judge-made law. It was found, not made. But unlike natural law, which too was found and not made, the common law was an
inseparable blend of positive and non-positive law. By looking to venerated
custom, the common law at once discovered the distinctive positive law of a
discrete political community while also uncovering the immutable principles of reason undergirding it. There was no disentangling one from the
other. The common law was neither strictly positivist nor the opposite.[110] It
was the combination of the two, the synchronizing of consent and reason
through the medium of custom. The common law improved over time
through experience—indeed, as Wilson proclaimed, "[t]he common law is
the law of experience"—adapting to social needs while disclosing the deeper
foundation of law itself, its "general principles."[111] The common law at once

revealed the law (of the community) and the law (generally), each of which inflected the other.

What helped reconcile these components was the fact that the common law was more an orientation to and vision of law than a set of substantive principles or doctrines—a method of legal thinking as much as the determinations that followed from it.[112] Deciphering the common law meant thinking like the common law, an approach that was essentially dynamic, toggling between experience and theory, findings and implications, the substance of law and the logic of law.[113] The common law was located in judicial rulings, social customs, and historical practice.[114] But it was not simply a set of positivist legal materials; it was as much the logic and principles revealed by those decisions, customs, and practices as the logic and principles derived from the study of experience and historical development. "Its foundations, laid in the most remote antiquity," asserted Wilson, had endured because it "contains the common dictates of nature, refined by wisdom and experience, as occasions offer, and cases arise." Indeed, the "common law, like natural philosophy," was "a science founded on experiment." Just as "[t]he latter is improved and established by carefully and wisely attending to the phenomena of the material world; the former," was improved and established as well "by attending, in the same manner, to those of man and society."[115] The common law was a dialectical view of law, one that embedded the substance of law in the pursuit of law. That dynamic perspective enabled it to fuse reason and will, justice and precedent, immemorial usage and adaptive change.

The onset of the Revolution fueled uncertainty about the nature and applicability of the common law, though if anything that uncertainty only reinforced the integrated conception of that law that had already come into relief. As Americans set about constructing their own legal systems, they often had to pinpoint what the common law in fact was. They were forced to reckon, in particular, with how American common law had diverged from its British counterpart, fracturing the legal field while raising important questions about which parts merited inclusion moving forward.[116] In adopting "the common law of England"—as most of the states did through either constitutional provision or reception statutes—what exactly were Americans perpetuating?[117] How much from their British past were they maintaining as part of American law? Was it the common law of England or the common law as it had developed in the colonies since the first English settlers had arrived in

North America? Had the English common law been introduced to the colonies in full or only in part?[118] Where was the substance of this incorporated common law to be found? If it was found in judicial decisions, was it found in those that had emanated from English courts, and if so, up until what date? If it was found instead in customary practice, which customs: British or American? Given the importance attached to a custom's antiquity under the common law, could customs generated in the American colonies ever be old enough to even become part of the common law?[119] Debating these intersecting questions compounded disagreement over how to define the common law, particularly following the Constitution's ratification.[120] In turn, these debates fueled opposition to the distinctively British features of the common law and led a host of early national Americans to begin calling for the abolition of English common law.[121] These debates and criticisms encouraged Founding-era legal commentators to reframe custom, even more than they already had, to align it with consent and, at the same time, underscore the general spirit of the common law at the expense of its particularity or British flavor.[122] Even before independence had been declared, Roger Sherman had insisted that the "Colonies adopt the common Law, not as the common Law, but as the highest Reason."[123] In the years following independence, support for this view only deepened. Americans had helped create a superior form of common law predicated not on British judicial rulings or customs but, as the leading jurist and legal theorist James Kent put it in the 1820s, on "the dictates of natural justice, and of cultivated reason."[124] In other words, the disunity of the common law as a *body of law*, which the revolution had so clearly exposed, encouraged even greater emphasis on the unity of the common law as an *orientation toward law*. Americans could say, and did say, that in adopting the common law they were adopting a legal foundation and accompanying jurisprudence rather than a particular body of law. The most cherished features of the common-law tradition endured in the United States, then, because they were suited to American needs, had received the people's consent, and boasted universal foundations.

This emphasis came rather easily to American constitutionalists since they had long equated the common law principally with the most ancient and essential features of their British constitutional inheritance: with what counted as the fundamental law of the realm. In celebrating the common law, they had rarely set their sights on the decisions of English common-law courts. They had instead sought to elevate certain aspects of the common law to the status of fundamental law to make it part of the British constitution from which they sought protection.[125] In so doing, they were mirroring British practice itself. England's ancient constitution emerged in the seventeenth century as various politicians and lawyers began applying common-law reasoning to fundamental law, elevating those particular principles that had supposedly been sanctioned since time out of mind to higher constitutional status.[126] As the British constitution took shape over the ensuing century, this conception remained central to it, and American constitutionalists were quick to latch onto this version of the constitution that incorporated and embodied fundamental common law.[127] On the road to independence and thereafter, when American constitutionalists invoked the "common law," they had in mind the celebrated protections found in Magna Carta and the English Bill of Rights, not the ordinary rulings of common-law jurists. That's certainly what the Continental Congress was referring to in 1774 in resolving that "the respective colonies are entitled to the common law of England."[128] Those parts of the common law that were most ancient in origin, most essential in practice, and most rational in nature were afforded fundamental status.

This brings us to general fundamental law. The legal harmony that the common law so vividly embodied was nowhere more prominent than in the domain of fundamental law. Here was where the Founding generation's integrated view of law was most pronounced. That was partly because, for those immersed in Anglo-American constitutionalism as we have just seen, the distinctive perspective of the common law had become the basis of fundamental law itself, undergirding the legal vision through which fundamental legal principles were most readily identified. Fundamental law was distinct from other kinds of law—it was the highest form of municipal law that stood above ordinary statutory law and common law and was separate from natural law—but it was also the site where the most important aspects of each of those other forms of law merged.[129] It was where seemingly distinct kinds of law (written law, positive common law, non-positive common law, and natural law), as well as seemingly distinct sources of legal authority (popular consent, ancient custom, and the dictates of reason and justice), rather than being distinguished one from another or held in tension or opposition, harmonized. Rather than distinguishing these elements, fundamental law integrated them, seamlessly fusing enacted law with preexisting legal principles derived from natural law, common law, and British constitutionalism. Justice Joseph Story, writing from the Supreme Court in 1815, succinctly captured the outlook: "[W]e think ourselves standing upon the principles of natural justice, upon the fundamental laws of every free government, upon the spirit and the letter of the Constitution of the United States."[130] These sources of law joined into a unified whole.

Fundamental law derived both its authority and content from each of these elements, picking out and fusing their most essential mandates into a set of general legal principles that necessarily undergirded any sound constitutional system. These were the "fundamental Principles of Law" that James Otis and so many other Revolutionary Americans conspicuously and confidently invoked before and after independence.[131] They were principles based on "the great Law of Reason, the Rules whereof are deducible from the Nature of Things," and known from custom, "right reason," "principles of justice," and "the dictates of common sense."[132] The sovereign people made fundamental law, and yet law was fundamental only if it aligned with immutable principles.[133]

The vision of law embodied in the concept of general fundamental law is not easily mapped onto modern categories. It emphasized consent but judged law on the basis of its merit and deeper alignment with justice; it viewed custom simultaneously in positivist and non-positivist terms; and it assumed that law was as much found as made. It valued constitutional text but saw that text in non-exclusive terms, presuming that written constitutions worked in concert with the general legal principles against which they were invariably set. It was steeped in natural law but owed as much, if not more, to British constitutional and common-law thinking. Above all, it rejected so many of the distinctions that have come to define legal debates, particularly those that sharply distinguish between positive and non-positive law, law and morality, text and principle, or distinct sources of law. It presumed that different kinds of law harmonized into a common whole by privileging the perspective on law through which that harmony was most clearly seen.

This understanding of general fundamental law ran through the Founders' written constitutions. It was not outside of or separate from, nor did it merely supplement, those constitutions. Constitutionalism, in its broadest sense, incorporated all of it. That's what it meant to have an integrated view of fundamental law. We should, thus, not ask how general fundamental law, or the numerous ingredients constituting it, shaped the Constitution; we instead need to understand how general fundamental law was part of Founding-era constitutions. In an age before constitutional law as we've come to understand it had yet emerged, constitutionalism was entangled with general fundamental law.

Given this prevailing understanding of law when Americans wrote their first constitutions after independence, and later the federal Constitution in 1787, it makes little sense to treat their written words as constitutive of their full content.

No doubt much of these constitutions' content was constituted by text. As was the case with the charters that preceded them, the state constitutions relied on textual provisions to frame the government and crucial aspects of its operations. For Revolutionary Americans who needed to reconstitute municipal government, writing out the framework and rules of governance was a practical necessity. The federal Constitution followed this example, relying on text where essential. There was no existing legal referent in customary or fundamental law that could specify the composition of the various branches of government (such as the number of executives or senators), the federal ratio of representation, or the number of legislative bodies. These kinds of rules, and many more, needed to be stipulated through text. In the context of the federal Constitution, there is one president (rather than three), two houses of Congress (rather than four), two senators per state, and a system of presidential electors allocated according to a state's congressional representation, only because the text of the Constitution happens to say so.[134]

As a technology, moreover, constitutional text offered crucial advantages that Founding-era constitutionalists came to embrace through the activity of making constitutions. What had initially been a practical tool became a beneficial tool as well. Constitutional text wasn't just useful for establishing a new government, it could also entrench particular rules of governance, affording them the status of fundamental law and thus exempting them from ordinary legislative change and the whims of future legislatures. At the Federal Convention, delegates frequently debated whether to cement certain rules through constitutional text—making them higher-order constitutional rules—by weighing the advantages and disadvantages of limiting future legislative discretion on the subject. As James Madison said at one point: "The

qualifications of electors and elected were fundamental articles in a Republican Govt. and ought to be fixed by the Constitution."[135] At another point delegates debated the virtues of establishing a permanent rule governing the
time of Congress's meeting as opposed to allowing it to be "varied by law."[136]
And at many other points, recognizing the consequence of codifying particular constitutional rules in text, and thus what Alexander Hamilton articulated the following year—that "Constitutions should consist only of general
provisions: The reason is, that they must necessarily be permanent, and that
they cannot calculate for the possible changes of things"—delegates worked
hard to adopt language that was sufficiently general and adaptable.[137] These
kinds of insights reveal how the turn toward written constitutions, initially
born of practical need and happenstance, came to represent an improvement
over what had preceded them. Under the British constitution, too many fundamental rules of governance were too easily manipulated by Parliament.[138]
By entrenching written constitutional rules beyond the control of ordinary
government, Americans could chart a surer course. They could help ensure
that their constitutions would in fact be "the first and fundamental law of the
State" (as the British constitution often could only pretend to be) by codifying rules and structures that would be "paramount to all acts of the Legislature."[139] Written constitutions provided unique and substantial benefits and
securities for which they were celebrated as a notable innovation in the history of constitutional government.[140]

    That said, just because constitutional text mattered and did essential con-
stitutional work (and in a great many instances entrenched constitutional
rules) didn't mean that non-textual constitutional content suddenly disappeared. That only would have been the case had people at the Founding re-
nounced their working understandings of fundamental law and the nature
of political society, which they demonstrably did not.

    Just because *some* constitutional rules were constituted by text did not mean
all of them were.[141] A lot of constitutional text was non-constitutive, reinforcing or calling attention to preexisting powers, principles, or rights. Nor, moreover, was the constitution fully integrated in the text—that is, not all relevant
constitutional rules and principles could be derived from it. Constitutional
text was presumed to be embedded within a broader web of fundamental law
that was not, by definition, exclusively textual in nature. In sharp contrast to a
strong positivist understanding of constitutional enactment, Revolutionary

American constitutionalists presupposed that their written constitutions effectuated, elaborated on, and harmonized with general fundamental law. American constitutions both codified new fundamental law and presupposed its independent existence without drawing sharp distinctions along the way.

Originalists, therefore, often assume a false dichotomy: that the Constitution's text is either exclusive and comprehensive, or unimportant. This binary would have baffled the Founding generation. Constitutional text assuredly mattered—much constitutional content was created by it. Yet, given the nature of fundamental law, that text was necessarily embedded in a wider field of unwritten legal authority. Fundamental law, that is, was inextricably entangled with general fundamental law. In a world so deeply shaped by the idea of preexisting legal principles, the seamless interaction of enacted text with given law made intuitive sense. As John Quincy Adams wrote in 1791, responding under the pseudonym "Publicola" to Thomas Paine's denunciation of British constitutionalism, "the Constitution of a country is not the paper or parchment upon which the compact is written." Rather, "it is the system of fundamental laws, by which the people have consented to be governed, which is always supposed to be impressed upon the mind of every individual, and of which the written or printed copies are nothing more than the evidence."[142]

Text and Rights

Founding-era constitutionalists' distinctive understanding of fundamental law saturated their understanding of rights. Today, it is usually assumed that constitutional rights are grounded in a common source: constitutional text. Americans have claim to certain fundamental privileges and immunities because these rights have been enumerated in their constitutions—be it the federal Constitution or those enacted within the states. Constitutional text *creates* the rights and establishes their legal standing. That was not the case in the eighteenth century, however. For the most part, fundamental rights existed independently of and before the writing of constitutional text. "The sacred rights of mankind are not to be rummaged for, among old parchments, or musty records," declared Alexander Hamilton. "They are written, as with a sun beam, in the whole *volume* of human nature."[143] Assuredly, many rights came to be enumerated in American constitutional text, including most famously in the federal Bill of Rights ratified in 1791. That enumeration was meaningful. But in most instances, that text was declarative, not constitutive of the rights themselves. It served as a reminder of certain rules and principles that had already been settled by nature or custom. Rights-bearing Americans would have enjoyed most of the constitutional rights found in written constitutions whether they had been enumerated or not, which is among the reasons for the inclusion in the federal Constitution of the Ninth Amendment, now largely ignored, which states that the enumeration of certain rights is not to be "construed to deny or disparage others retained by the people."[144] By and large, as Jud Campbell has emphasized, the Founding generation "did not treat rights as textual objects."[145]

This attitude toward rights and text had deep roots. Before independence, American colonists were adamant that their rights existed independently of textual codification. James Otis thought it absurd that Americans' "essential rights" might be " 'expressly granted' . . . by charter."[146] If something were "to annihilate all those charters," that could not possibly "shake one of the[ir] essential, natural, civil or religious rights."[147] The "charters were *declarations* but not *gifts* of liberties," added John Dickinson. Liberty was "not annexed to us by parchments and seals."[148] In the same vein, Silas Downer proclaimed that "[t]he great charter of liberties, commonly called *Magna Charta*, doth not *give* the privileges therein mentioned, nor," he went on, "doth our *Charters*." They "must be considered as only declaratory of our rights, and in affirmance of them."[149] Such testimony is found almost anywhere one turns.

These habits endured. The act of writing new constitutions in the states, which often involved declaring rights, did little to alter these long-standing assumptions. To see why, we need to grasp how rights were understood at the Founding. Few areas of the period's history are a more persistent source of confusion. Just as scholars have struggled to grasp the pre-liberal conception of liberty that ran through the eighteenth century (and that made it impossible to see rights as the inverse of government powers), so they have struggled to understand the relationship between different kinds of fundamental rights and why, initially, virtually none of those rights needed to be constitutionally enumerated in order to have effect.[150] Eighteenth-century Americans certainly talked about a bewildering variety of rights in ways that can appear contradictory.[151] Too often, scholars have tried to overcome this difficulty by privileging one set of rights at the expense of others, as seen in the enduring debate over whether the American Revolutionaries favored natural rights derived from universal principles or customary common-law rights derived from the British constitutional tradition—a false dichotomy we ought to move past.[152] Thanks to the work of Jud Campbell, we now have a much clearer sense of how eighteenth-century American constitutionalists conceptualized and debated fundamental rights—and how seemingly conflicting categories of rights operated within a common conceptual space.[153]

As they did before the break with Britain, Revolutionary American constitutionalists continued to reason about rights from the perspective of social contract theory—the third pillar of Founding-era constitutional thought. Social contract theory provided an indispensable framework for thinking through the origins of political society. It imagined people in a pre-political state of nature, each person in possession of equal natural rights, consisting of all forms of human liberty, and constrained only by natural law. "Men in a State of Nature," proclaimed Richard Bland of Virginia, "are absolutely free and independent of one another as to sovereign Jurisdiction."[154] It was then supposed that people left that state of nature by unanimously forming a political society, or social compact—which created a distinct polity and people. As the Connecticut minister Timothy Stone expounded in a 1792 election sermon, "all civil communities have their foundation in compacts, by which individuals immerge out of a state of nature, and become one great whole, cemented together by voluntary engagements; covenanting with each other, to observe such regulations."[155] Once the body politic was formed, its people established a constitution of government to specify the powers and rules of governance.[156] When people "enter into a Society," Bland explained, "and by their own Consent become Members of it, they must submit to the Laws of the Society according to which they agree to be governed" and subject themselves "to the Authority of that Body in whom, by common Consent, the legislative Power of the State is placed."[157] The constitution of government thus rested on a prior social compact that powerfully shaped that government's operation. "The right of society to make laws of any description," Theodore Dwight put it, "depends entirely on the original compact, which formed the society."[158]

Along the way, it was widely assumed that individuals either retained or acquired certain fundamental rights. There were three distinct kinds.[159] First came inalienable natural rights. These were facets of natural freedom that individuals could not rightfully forfeit to the body politic, such as the freedoms of conscience and thought.[160] Second, there were retained natural rights. These were most aspects of natural freedom—far greater in number than inalienable natural rights and often summarized as the rights to life, liberty, and property—which individuals retained upon entering political society.[161] Unlike their inalienable counterparts, these natural rights did not place clear limitations on governmental power.[162] Instead, they could be regulated and constrained, but only by the people's consent and only in the interest of the public good.[163] In fact, they *needed* to be regulated when the public good demanded it.[164] In *The Essex Result*, published in 1778, Theophilus Parsons neatly captured both sentiments. "Each individual," he asserted, "surrenders the power of controuling his natural alienable rights, ONLY WHEN THE GOOD OF THE WHOLE REQUIRES it."[165] Third, and last, were fundamental positive rights. These rights—often called civil, social, or political rights—were a product of political society (they did not exist in the state of nature) and, unlike natural rights, were defined in relationship to governmental power. The most important of these positive rights, such as the right to trial by jury or the right of habeas corpus, acquired fundamental status and were regarded as part of fundamental law.[166] As James Madison explained, "[t]rial by jury cannot be considered as a natural right, but a right resulting from the social compact which regulates the action of the community." Despite this difference, it "is as essential to secure the liberty of the people as any one of the pre-existent rights of nature."[167]

Before and after independence, American constitutionalists spoke freely about their fundamental rights. But precisely because of how they conceived of these rights, they placed less importance on textually enumerating them. Given the precepts of social contract theory, as Jud Campbell has explained, "Americans naturally viewed fundamental rights as being recognized *before* constitutional ratification, making it generally unnecessary to enumerate them in a bill of rights. After all, it was the social contract—not the constitution—by which individuals became citizens. And so it made perfect sense that rights of citizenship were recognized in that agreement."[168] This was certainly true of natural rights. Inalienable natural rights were preserved through the social contract, whereas retained natural rights were preserved through republicanism—the act of empowering representative institutions to regulate retained natural liberty in the interest of the public good. Enumerating natural rights had no impact on their legal status; nor

was it necessary for their enforcement.[169] Things were a bit more complicated when it came to fundamental positive rights, but by and large, enumeration was still incidental to their legal existence. That was because
such rights were believed to be grounded in custom. Their constitutional
status could be traced to certain well-known episodes in the history of Anglo-
American common law.[170] Given this basis, Founding-era constitutionalists
tended to assume that long-standing common-law rights were already inherent to the social contract. Most of these rights, then, also did not need to be
enumerated to enjoy the status of fundamental law. They were already settled rules and principles of constitutional life.

As a result, the first declarations of rights that accompanied several of the
state constitutions were understood to *declare* rather than *create* fundamental
rights.[171] That only about half of the new states even wrote declarations confirms as much. Citizens of New Jersey or New York would have been shocked
to learn that they lacked the fundamental rights that had been codified in
Virginia or Delaware.[172] Among those states that did write declarations,
meanwhile, there was considerable divergence—both in what they enumerated as well as how much.[173] The only thing that can explain this hodgepodge
is the fact that these declarations were understood to merely reaffirm widely
recognized fundamental rights. The notion that rights were constituted by
written text, Thomas Paine declared in late 1776, was "truly ridiculous." Instead, "all the great rights which man never mean, nor ever ought, to lose,
should be *guaranteed*, not *granted*, by the Constitution."[174]

Enumeration was hardly meaningless. It afforded rights a certain "degree
of explicitness and clarity" they might otherwise have lacked.[175] It also helped
constitutionalize *some* positive rights (never more than a small minority)
whose fundamental status was less clearly established by custom.[176] And in
some cases, it determined the legal content of preexisting rights, by specifying certain determinate rules regarding the scope and exercise of those
rights.[177] In these select instances, constitutional text served as the basis of
these fundamental privileges and immunities, either by constitutionalizing
rights or by altering existing law by determining the content of preexisting
rights. Even more importantly, enumeration served an important pedagogical purpose, reminding citizens, lest they forget, of their fundamental
rights.[178] Indeed, the manner in which early declarations of rights were constructed served an educative function. These declarations either came at the

beginning of the new constitutions or were issued separately from them, positioning that underscored the social-contract premises undergirding these instruments.[79] As Benjamin Rush noted, bills of rights and constitutions served distinctive purposes: "The BILL OF RIGHTS should contain the great principles of *natural* and *civil liberty*," whereas "[t]he CONSTITUTION is the executive part of the Bill of Rights."[180] The declaration of rights, in other words, operated as an avowal of the underlying social compact. Its purpose was to remind citizens of the origins of their political society and thus the reasons why their government had been constructed in the first place. The constitution that followed was meant to carry into effect the principles of the social compact that were expressed in the declaration of rights.

While enumeration served a variety of functions, each of these purposes tended to underscore the more basic point: that in most instances, constitutional rights were neither made by nor entrenched through constitutional text. In at least two vital ways, the logic that Rush unpacked explained why. First, by calling attention to the underlying social compact, these declarations served as express reminders that some fundamental law preceded the enactment of the constitution. Indeed, that constitution would need to be interpreted in light of the underlying compact and especially the rights guarantees inherent to it. And while the constitutional text might help illuminate the nature of that social compact, outlining its core features called for an inherently socio-historical form of analysis rather than a textual or legal one: the interpreter needed to understand the nature of the political community, its people, and the promises they had made to one another.

Second, in stressing that constitutions *executed* bills of rights, Rush betrayed a pervasive view of constitutional rights and their protection that placed limited weight on text. Few captured this thinking better than James Madison, who, throughout the 1780s, famously denounced written constitutional securities as mere "parchment barriers."[181] Although he would later modify his views, the phrase succinctly captured the then-widespread notion that enumerating rights or specifying precise limits on government did little to secure liberty.[182] Rights, as so many Founding-era commentators stressed, were best secured through effective representative governance, through a well-structured government that mirrored the people's will and interests.[183] Rights were enumerated toward this end—to guide the government and remind observers of the purposes for which it had been constituted.

These attitudes toward text and rights, so central to the early Revolutionary experience, were still dominant when the federal Constitution was drafted. In 1787, William Paca, a former governor of Maryland and signer of the Declaration of Independence, assumed that constitutions instantiated fundamental law as much as they delineated it. In a series of extensive newspaper essays, he asked whether Americans, when resisting British tyranny, had "rest[ed] the rights of America on the[ir] charters or compacts? Or did they deduce them from a higher source, *the laws of God and nature*? Did any *patriot* or *judge*," he went on, "broach the absurd doctrine, or make the absurd position, that the people could exercise no other rights or powers, except those mentioned and defined in their respective charters, compacts and constitutions?"[184] Whatever else had changed in American thinking in the preceding years, it continued to be assumed that protecting fundamental rights preceded the writing of constitutions.

The next spring, during the ratification debates, John Dickinson echoed Paca: essential "corner stones of liberty . . . were not obtained by *a bill of rights*, or any other records, and have not been and cannot be preserved by them." What, then, "are a bill of rights," he asked, "or any characters drawn upon paper or parchment, those frail remembrancers?" Certainly not the source of those rights.[185] Numerous Federalists reiterated this sentiment to explain why, in the face of Anti-Federalist complaints, the proposed federal constitution lacked a bill of rights. As George Nicholas asserted in the Virginia ratifying convention: "A Bill of Rights is only an acknowledgement of the pre-existing claim to rights in the people. They belong to us as much as if they had been inserted in the Constitution."[186]

And perhaps most revealing of all, the first amendments to the Constitution, now christened the Bill of Rights, were on balance declaratory in character.[187] Drafted in the First Federal Congress in 1789 and ratified in 1791, they need not have taken that form. As Jud Campbell has shown, while declaratory bills of rights were the norm at this time, some prominent figures, such as Thomas Jefferson, were eager to move from merely declaring settled rights to, in addition, specifying their legal content in more textually determinate ways.[188] For several years, Jefferson had favored this approach, and, in his extensive correspondence with his confidante James Madison on whether the recently ratified Constitution ought to be amended, he expressed the hope that these sorts of textually specified provisions would be added.[189]

Jefferson craved something more than textual placeholders—he hoped to use language to fix concrete legal content by specifying firm standards or rules not easily derived from natural law or customary practice. While Madison ended up pushing for amendments in Congress, most of which enumerated fundamental rights, importantly he did not agree with Jefferson on the character they should take. Nor, it seems, did most of his congressional colleagues. They instead opted for a standard declaratory approach.[190]

In the end, crucially, the Bill of Rights that was added far more decisively reflected Madison's rather than Jefferson's preferences. Some of that was because Madison's interest in adding a declaration of rights was political and strategic—he hoped to appease former Anti-Federalists who had complained during ratification that the Constitution failed to protect fundamental rights and thus quell whatever appetite there was for a second constitutional convention; in short, he aimed "to quiet the minds of people."[191] But some of it was because, for Madison, a properly constructed declaration of rights would only make explicit what was already constitutionally implicit. By declaring rather than creating rights and by enumerating to underscore rather than concretely determine, a federal bill of rights would more or less leave the existing Constitution as it was. Madison convinced his otherwise hesitant colleagues to pursue the project in part because he made clear that "alterations might be made, without effecting the essential principles of the Constitution, which would meet with universal approbation."[192] Upon seeing the initial proposal for amendments that Madison took the lead on drafting, Roger Sherman spoke for many in the House of Representatives when he declared, "The amendments reported are a declaration of rights, the people are secure in them whether we declare them or not."[193] Because the amendments would not be adding much in the way of new constitutional content, Sherman questioned their necessity—because they were strictly declaratory in character, they were perhaps superfluous. While Madison thought a declaratory bill of rights served useful purposes, he did not disagree with Sherman's premise, which had long been his own.[194] On the floor of Congress, he was happy "to admit the force" of the previously standard Federalist position that "a bill of rights is not necessary"; but while enumerating rights was not essential to establish or enforce their constitutional existence, and could be "rather unimportant" in the eyes of the law, doing so could still have a "salutary tendency" by impressing their importance on the public mind.[195]

With that aim in view, they should only pursue "an enumeration of simple acknowledged principles," Madison emphasized, while avoiding those "of a doubtful nature."[196] The point was to declare fundamental rights that the people already enjoyed the protection of, not to create new rights that gained their force or content through constitutional enumeration. Regardless of whether the proposal for amendments was a good idea or not, in other words, Madison agreed with Sherman that the people were secure in their rights whether they were declared or not. To be sure, the amendments did not exclusively take this declaratory form. Some of them hewed closer to Jefferson's preferred approach, such as the Seventh Amendment's amount-in-controversy requirement, which specified precise legal content through text.[197] The decisive majority of the amendments that were eventually added, however, simply declared preexisting rights, which meant that textualizing them did little to alter existing fundamental law.[198]

The choice mattered.[199] There were ways to enumerate rights that would have placed greater, even exclusive, emphasis on text—that would have made constitutional content a matter of what the text said and did. Jefferson's approach to amending was available. But members of the First Congress expressly rejected that form of rights declaration. On balance, they enumerated rights neither to establish their legality nor to fix their legal content by specifying how the rights would operate in particular instances. The text did little substantive work, neither creating constitutional rights nor determining their content. Instead, it underscored the pre-textual basis of most rights while leaving it to future decision-makers to more concretely determine their scope and effect. The text affirmed the rights but did not limn their content. For the most part, the constitutional substance of these constitutional rights was not a function of constitutional language.

Countless more examples could be deployed to illustrate the essential point, but an especially revealing episode from the Constitutional Convention drives it home. When considering whether to include a prohibition against ex post facto laws, several delegates balked. Oliver Ellsworth of Connecticut asserted that such laws were automatically "void of themselves," and that "there was no lawyer, no civilian who would not say that."[200] Even more emphatically, James Wilson complained that including such a prohibition would show Americans "ignorant of the first principles of Legislation" or that they were "constituting a Government which will be so."[201] The prohibition

was ultimately included on precautionary grounds, but no one disputed Ellsworth's or Wilson's deeper point: that ex post facto laws were *already* prohibited no matter what the text of the U.S. Constitution said, because such laws
violated general principles of law.[202] The debate, strikingly, was not about the
creation of constitutional content and, in fact, presupposed that some things
would be part of the Constitution regardless of what was enacted.[203] The
Constitution's Ex Post Facto Clause was a paradigmatic example of non-
constitutive text, no different in kind from the numerous enumerations of
rights found in so many American constitutions. It emphasized what, as a
matter of the underlying social compact, was already part of the constitutional order. Ellsworth and Wilson were among the most sophisticated legal
thinkers in the nation—each would soon be appointed to the Supreme Court.
And they assumed, as a matter of course, that the constitution they were
making would be embedded in a wider field of general fundamental law,
composed of a diverse array of materials—some expressed, some not; some
positively enacted, some already part of the social contract—none of which
could easily be separated from the rest. Indeed, that *had* to be the case for
their comments to make any sense. They were not operating under the assumption that "this Constitution" would pick out a textually circumscribed
object. Clinging to long-standing assumptions about fundamental rights,
law, and writtenness, they did not think that written constitutions drew a
sharp boundary between the text and what was outside of it.[204] That was not
how constitutionalism or fundamental law worked.

Judging Constitutionality

Early American judicial behavior displays a similar dynamic. It is almost
incomprehensible unless understood in the context of general fundamental
law, social contract theory, and the related ideas charted thus far.

We are often told that the distinctive American brand of judicial review was
a direct by-product of written constitutions: that judges claimed the authority
to nullify legislative enactments (and got away with it) only because they could
point to the novel American invention of a written constitution.[205] That was
the story, after all, that John Marshall famously told in *Marbury v. Madison* in
1803. Yet Marshall, following on the heels of other jurists, was spinning a
myth many years after the fact. Judicial review was not inherently tied to writ-

tenness, certainly not at first.[206] As a conceptual matter, all judicial review required was the idea of constitutional repugnancy: that acts in violation of the constitution were void.[207] This concept—which was hardly new—implied nothing specific, however, about the nature or content of the constitutional standard in question. During the years following independence, when Revolutionary-era judges evaluated (and sometimes nullified) state laws, they treated general legal principles—various forms of legal authority from natural law to common law to the law of nations, as well as fundamental legal standards such as equity, right reason, and natural justice—as inherent parts of the state's fundamental law.[208] And they did so without any indication that they were referring to something other than the constitution or what *it* mandated.[209] These were neither distinct nor competing sources of law.[210]

A few cases begin to tell the story. In New Jersey in 1780, in *Holmes v. Walton*, the state supreme court struck down a statute permitting a six-man jury, despite the fact that nothing written in the state constitution required otherwise, on the basis that it was "contrary to the constitution, practices and laws of the land."[211] In the 1786 Rhode Island case *Trevett v. Weeden*, Weeden's lawyers successfully challenged a statute denying him a jury trial, on the grounds that it violated "the constitution," by which they meant not simply the state's updated colonial charter but also the "fundamental laws" and rights that had been central to "the English constitution" and Rhode Island's colonial experience under it. In addition, they argued, "[t]here are certain general principles that are equally binding in all governments," principles that the statute in question infringed.[212] The judges agreed, declaring the law "repugnant and unconstitutional" for violating the "laws of the land," even though it did not clearly violate anything expressed in the state's charter.[213]

There is perhaps no more striking example of judges' willingness to base their decisions on general legal principles in the early United States, however, than the ruling in *Rutgers v. Waddington*, which illustrated how the law of nations interacted with state constitutional law. The case, which came before the Mayor's Court of New York City in 1784, emerged when Elizabeth Rutgers sued Joshua Waddington under the state's Trespass Act, a controversial statute that was enacted in 1783 and designed to punish former loyalists. During the War for Independence, Waddington had occupied the Rutgers family brewhouse, one of several pieces of abandoned property that the British army had commandeered. Waddington had subsequently turned the property back over to Rutgers, but the new law enabled Rutgers to sue for back rent while denying Waddington the right to claim a military order as a defense.[214] Alexander Hamilton, who was eager to defend former loyalists against this kind of retaliation, represented Waddington.[215]

Hamilton argued that New York's statute was unconstitutional because it violated the peace treaty between the United States and Britain, which pledged to respect loyalist property rights and, more importantly, the law of nations—the body of legal principles that governed relations between nations and permitted, via the laws of war, armies to use abandoned property during wartime.[216] The "law of nations," Hamilton explained, was "the law of nature applied to nations," which meant its principles could be discovered, as with natural law, through "Reason" and, as with the common law, by consulting "[t]he opinions of Writers" and "the practice of Nations." This law was binding and enforceable in New York, Hamilton claimed, because "it results from the relations of Universal society" and because "our constitution adopts the common law of which the *law of nations is a part*."[217] The New York Constitution incorporated the common law as it stood at the onset of hostilities with Britain, and Hamilton's interpretation was yet further reminder that the common law was, for many, not a particular body of positive law but rather a general fundamental law.[218] In arguing that the law of nations was an extension of the common law while also implying that the law of nations applied regardless, Hamilton demonstrated how fundamental law was so often perceived to interact with constitutionalism. New York's constitution necessarily incorporated general principles of fundamental law while simultaneously reinforcing them through enacted constitutional provisions. Such principles were at once simply a part of the constitution and yet, thanks to its non-positive character, independent from it, blurring to form "part of the law of the land."[219]

James Duane, who decided the case on the Mayor's Court, accepted the thrust of Hamilton's argument—offering one paean to the law of nations after another—as well as the deeper logic for which it stood.[220] Because it was assumed that authoritative sources of law ultimately harmonized (in this case the law of nations and the state's constitution), Duane interpreted the Trespass Act narrowly so as not to violate the law of nations, upholding the statute while denying the plaintiff relief. The legislature could not have intended to disregard such an important body of law, he asserted. Duane was doing far more than exploiting ambiguity or appealing to background principles of natural law to equitably interpret the positive law that he considered himself bound by.[221] Critics of his ruling reasonably claimed that his interpretation of the Trespass Act effectively rewrote the statute (inverting its meaning and clear intent).[222] Duane was not merely disambiguating positive law; he was challenging a narrow view of positive law by defending a more capacious and muscular conception of general fundamental law. His creative interpretation of the Trespass Act offered a glimpse into how Founding-era legal assumptions often worked. Because fundamental law was at once written and preexisting, its sources were neither sharply distinct nor opposed. Early defenders of judicial review instinctively made sense of written constitutions by this legal logic.

This thinking carried beyond the drafting and ratification of the federal Constitution. Hamilton and Duane were by no means alone in assuming that the law of nations was incorporated into U.S. constitutionalism. Throughout the 1790s, it was widely believed that this law was binding on the national and state governments, particularly when it came to treaty obligations.[223] Constitutional partisans who otherwise deeply disagreed (such as Hamilton, James Madison, Thomas Jefferson, and Edmund Randolph), as well as the nation's preeminent early jurists (John Jay, James Wilson, and James Iredell), repeatedly declared that the law of nations was part of the law of the land of the United States.[224] As Jay matter-of-factly put it in a grand-jury charge, "the Laws of Nations make Part of the Laws of this, and of every other civilized Nation." "They consist," he went on, giving voice to the conception of law on which so much eighteenth-century legal thinking was based, "of those Rules for regulating the Conduct of Nations towards each other, which resulting from right Reason, recieve [sic] their obligation from that Principle and from general Assent and Practice."[225]

The law of nations, moreover, was but one aspect of general fundamental law that shaped jurists' decisions in this period. Indeed, it is simply impossible to comprehend the reasoning that emanated from the early Supreme Court from the perspective of our brand of written constitutionalism.[226] In numerous cases, the justices appealed to general jurisprudence to elaborate the Constitution.[227] William Paterson, in one case, looked to "the principles of justice and the dictates of the moral sense" to determine what accorded with "right reason and natural equity."[228] In another, William Johnson deemed a state action void given "the reason and nature of things."²²⁹ In yet another, *Calder v. Bull*, Samuel Chase famously defended prohibitions on government enactments that were "contrary to the great first principles of the social compact" and that "the general principles of law and reason forbid."²³⁰ These justices did not invoke those standards because they believed that the standards were superior to the Constitution; nor did they treat those standards as encompassing—as we might assume—an unwritten constitution distinct from the written one.²³¹ Investigating these complementary sources of law provided different ways of accessing the fundamental authority that the Constitution created, recognized, and sanctioned. Because the Constitution was fundamental law, the justices assumed that it incorporated certain general principles of law. This idea was what Chase was getting at when he declared in *Ware v. Hylton* that "laws should not be repugnant to the Constitution, or fundamental law."²³² We have been socialized to dwell on Chase's use of "or" and to ponder whether these were distinct standards in people's minds. But that is the wrong question to ask. As the Constitution was fundamental law, it recognized general fundamental law. There were no sharp breaks or discontinuities to account for or think through.

The fact that critics of judicial review, meanwhile, rarely objected to jurists' appeals to general principles of law in their decisions suggests that they, too, thought that a constitution was more than just its textual provisions. While judicial review was controversial at the Founding, the spirited debate it provoked only rarely turned on the character of constitutional content. Like defenders of the practice, its detractors assumed that constitutions extended beyond their express contents. The debate centered, instead, on the proper scope of judicial authority in a republic. Defenders of judicial review had come to believe that judges, who were previously viewed with suspicion, were as capable of defending fundamental law as other officeholders.²³³ As Jack Rakove has explained, judicial review took on new meaning beginning in the 1780s, as things around it profoundly changed. No factor proved more important than the explosion of state legislation that often interfered with contract and property rights. This torrent of statutes led some observers to rethink the nature of legislative power and whether local legislatures were indeed the best guardians of republican liberty.²³⁴ Critics of judicial review, meanwhile, remained wedded to orthodox republican thinking and continued to maintain that only the people's genuine representatives, or the people themselves, could enforce the people's constitution.[235] Richard Dobbs Spaight, one of North Carolina's delegates to the Federal Convention, defended this view in 1787 upon learning that North Carolina's superior court had nullified a state law. "It can not be denied," he conceded, "that the Assembly have passed laws unjust in themselves." But "it is immaterial what law [the court] have declared void," he went on, since "it is their usurpation of the Authority to do it that I complain." Were judges to possess "any such power," then, "instead of being governed by the representatives in general Assembly," the people would be subject to judicial rule.[236] Since "the judiciary are independent of the people," Zephaniah Swift echoed, "it is a total prostration of the government, to vest them with a power of deciding that legislative acts are null."[237] Critics, in other words, did not complain that judges had misconceived the constitution either by ignoring its inherent boundaries or illegitimately appealing to general legal principles. Rather, they denied that judges had the institutional authority to decide when the legislature had violated its constitutional duty. That was somebody else's call. It was a debate over constitutional *enforcement*, not *content*.

It was in this context that Thomas Jefferson and James Madison famously pondered judicial review of constitutional rights in 1789. Given that each of these men at different points that year seemed to suggest that enumerating rights in the federal Constitution would enable judges to enforce them, observers have long assumed that these leading Founding-era constitutionalists were drawing a tight link between judicial review and enumerated constitutional rights and in so doing emphasizing the distinctive importance of written constitutionalism.[238] But in different ways, that assumption misreads both Jefferson and Madison. In a letter to Madison in which he endorsed adding a federal bill of rights, Jefferson indeed stated that one of the great "arguments in favor" was "the legal check which it puts into the hands of the judiciary."[239] In so doing, however, Jefferson wasn't necessarily promoting written over customary constitutionalism so much as he was describing what would be necessary for judges, in particular, to credibly police constitutional boundaries. Enumerating rights alone would not be sufficient. Those textual enumerations would also, as we have seen, need to determine the shape and limits of rights through specific legal rules and standards. Only then could judges ever contemplate the awesome authority to challenge an overreaching legislative body. As would be true throughout his life, Jefferson was deeply

distrustful of the willful exercise of judicial power.[240] He was staunchly opposed to judges engaging in broad construction of the Constitution, or even
really interpreting it. What they could do was enforce explicit legal determinations specified expressly in text. Jefferson, then, was tethering judicial review
not only to written text but to particularly explicit and detailed text. Over the
course of his life, he was generally more partial than others to the power of
written constitutions to determine and constrain political power of all kinds.[241]
But in writing to Madison, Jefferson was principally channeling the critics
of *Rutgers v. Waddington* or Richard Dobbs Spaight rather than disclaiming
customary constitutionalism and general fundamental law.

Madison seemingly echoed Jefferson in the First Congress, but in so doing
he was even less interested in subverting customary law in favor of exclusive
written constitutionalism. As we have seen, Madison departed sharply from
Jefferson's favored scheme for enumerating rights, primarily opting instead
to declare broad settled principles—just the kind of underdetermined constitutional rules Jefferson thought judges were ill-equipped to enforce. What
then was Madison implying when, in his congressional speech calling for
amendments, he claimed that if fundamental rights were enumerated in the
Constitution, "independent tribunals of justice will consider themselves in a
peculiar manner the guardians of those rights" and "will be naturally led to
resist every encroachment upon rights expressly stipulated for in the constitution by the declaration of rights"?[242] Madison clearly wasn't endorsing Jefferson's view that judges could enforce only those rights that had been clearly
determined in text—otherwise he would have proposed a declaration of rights
that did just that. Nor was he suggesting, as many have assumed, that judges
could enforce only those fundamental rights that happened to be enumerated
in some way. Like many of his peers—including those who had defended the
judicial review of state laws to that point—he thought judges could enforce
the customary constitution.[243] At least up to a point, anyway. (As discussed in
chapter 7, Madison was also skeptical of excessive judicial power.) Like most
American constitutionalists at this time, Madison didn't think judges should
flesh out underdetermined constitutional principles. But if the laws in question manifestly violated already settled and determined rights, he believed
judges could act. What he was suggesting in his congressional speech, then,
was that one advantage of enumerating certain customary rights was that
judges would be encouraged to defend them. Enumerating rights was neither

a necessary nor a sufficient condition for judicial enforcement of those rights.[244] Much as enumerating rights had pedagogical value in reminding the broader public of their underlying rights, so too could textualized rights shape judicial psychology by encouraging judges to perform their underlying duty.[245] Importantly, then, nothing Madison was endorsing in terms of judicial behavior or how enumerating rights might shape judicial behavior implied that constitutional content necessarily or even primarily derived from constitutional text. He was even less willing than Jefferson to do anything to disturb customary constitutional legal principles. He left general fundamental law just where he found it.

Traditional accounts have obscured a similar dynamic in Samuel Chase and James Iredell's well-known 1798 dispute on the Supreme Court in *Calder v. Bull*.[246] The case revolved around the Connecticut legislature's decision to authorize a new trial in a probate case, which was promptly challenged on the grounds that the Constitution's prohibition on ex post facto laws prohibited retroactive civil legislation of that kind.[247] It often attracts attention, though, less for what was decided (that the Constitution's Ex Post Facto Clause applies only to criminal legislation) than for the arguments over the sources of constitutional law it provoked. In most renditions, it is presented as a debate between natural and positive law—whether judges could nullify laws that violated unwritten principles of natural law, as Chase insisted, or needed to stick to the positive law of the written constitution, as Iredell maintained. "The purposes for which men enter into society will determine the nature and terms of the social compact," Chase wrote, "and as they are the foundation of the legislative power, they will decide what are the proper objects of it." Therefore, "[a]n act of the legislature (for I cannot call it a law) contrary to the great first principles of the social compact," he concluded, "cannot be considered a rightful exercise of legislative authority."[248] Iredell was unimpressed. He conceded that "some speculative jurists have held that a legislative act against natural justice must in itself be void" but was adamant that the "the court cannot pronounce [a law] to be void" by this standard alone.[249] At first blush, the standard story seems correct and thus might be noteworthy for illustrating, if nothing else, that at least some Supreme Court justices presupposed that natural law supplemented the written Constitution, even if other justices denied the proposition.

The better reading of the case, however, is that Chase and Iredell both accepted customary constitutionalism but were instead debating whether it was appropriate for judges to enforce it. Iredell was not playing the hard positivist to Chase's natural lawyer. Each believed that the written Constitution was entangled in a thick framework of preexisting law. Chase clearly thought that the U.S. Constitution incorporated general fundamental law, but Iredell seemingly did too, noting in his opinion that the Connecticut legislature's action was "sanctioned by a long and uniform practice."[250] Beyond the fact that both justices accepted aspects of customary constitutionalism, they also both agreed that it was someone else's job to determine those fundamental legal principles in the American polity. Whereas Iredell was skeptical that judges could ever do so, Chase (perhaps like Madison nearly a decade earlier on the floor of Congress) was claiming that when preexisting rights were clearly settled and determined, judges could enforce customary constitutional commitments. He might have also been pushing further in his opinion and claiming that judges could also "recognize the invalidity of *clearly unreasonable* legislative determinations" of underdetermined natural rights that were unquestionably part of the social compact upon which the Constitution sat.[251] Whatever the precise scope of Chase's argument, his debate with Iredell focused far more on the judicial role than on the written character of U.S. constitutionalism. Chase thought judges could at least enforce settled features of the social compact. Iredell, by contrast, contended that judges were best positioned to enforce clearly determined limits on legislative power—those "marked and settled boundaries" expressed in written constitutional text.[252] The same was not true of the inherently uncertain boundaries found in natural or customary law. The "ideas of natural justice are regulated by no fixed standard," he emphasized, which was why "the ablest and purest men have differed upon the subject." For that reason, courts should not question the attempts of a legislature—"possessed of an equal right of opinion"—to determine those crucial features of the social compact.[253] Just because judges were ill-positioned to make those determinations didn't mean the legislature could not. He reiterated what he had stressed throughout his many defenses of judicial review to that point: judges ought to defer to legislative judgment, exercising that "delicate and awful" authority to declare such judgments void only "in a clear and urgent case."[254] Once again, a debate over judicial review hinged on institutional enforcement rather than constitutional content—*who* could enforce general fundamental law, not whether it was part of the United States' fundamental law.

WRITTEN CONSTITUTIONALISM

Too often, we read eighteenth-century American judicial opinions, espe-cially those emanating from the early Supreme Court, in light of our own familiar conceptions of constitutionalism and law, our own legal questions, and our own long-standing disputes over interpretation. When we do so, however, we obscure the early justices' own understanding of constitutional-ism and, from there, misconstrue what the justices were trying to say. To be sure, decades later, things would change, and justices would begin sounding more like they do now. But that marked a dramatic shift. And we still have a hard time seeing what preceded that revolution.

Seeing Their Constitutions

The Founding generation embraced written constitutionalism. Indeed, it would be a mistake to claim that they subscribed to what we might call un-written constitutionalism. But their written constitutionalism was not ours. If our aim is to see *their* constitutions, we need to see those constitutions as they did—from the perspective of their constitutionalism.

Their vision clouded by anachronistic assumptions and distinctions, orig-inalists struggle to adopt this Founding-era perspective. Originalists typically assume that because early U.S. constitutions were written, these instru-ments, by their own terms, announced themselves as the comprehensive, stand-alone texts that originalists routinely take them to be. Originalists of-ten believe, moreover, that eighteenth-century observers saw their constitu-tions in this way, since those observers unsurprisingly can be found referring to their constitutions as documents or emphasizing their tangible, textual forms. These convictions obscure far more than they reveal. Seeing why al-lows us to pull together the various strands of Founding-era constitutional-ism we have traced to this point.

One of the standard ways originalists insist upon the exclusively textual nature of the U.S. Constitution is by fixating on the so-called communicative content of its written text. They quietly define this concept in a thoroughly linguistic fashion: as the set of propositions that the Constitution's text com-municated in context to readers at the time.[255] In so doing, they struggle to see how an eighteenth-century constitution might have communicated in non-linguistic ways or, in fact, how that might have been the dominant form of constitutional communication at the Founding. It might be hard for us to understand how people could so readily and instinctively decipher unwritten commands—yet for most Founding-era constitutionalists, that was all they had ever known.

Put yourself back in 1775, on the eve of American independence. White American colonists had no trouble thinking constitutionally at this time—identifying constitutional principles and imperatives and appealing to them for authoritative guidance. They had been doing so for as long as they had been alive, even though the British constitution to which they appealed was mostly unwritten. For them, unwritten constitutional communication had long been the default. It was what they knew best and took most readily for granted. Leading modern originalists seem to assume that only a written constitution can have communicative content—that it's the only sort of constitution that can *mean* something. But that claim would have baffled eighteenth-century American constitutionalists, who were confident that the largely unwritten British constitution communicated precise content that carried the authority of fundamental law. If originalists are going to assume that a constitution's communicative content is tethered to its words, then they need to explain whether and how the British constitution communicated content at the time of the Revolution. Unless they are going to argue, surely implausibly, that the British constitution didn't communicate any content to eighteenth-century interpreters who routinely said otherwise, then it won't do to assume that a certain model of constitutional communication necessarily attaches to a written constitution, when the people who wrote those constitutions had themselves only ever known a radically different model of constitutional communication. Perhaps Americans' first written constitutions obliterated the forms of constitutional communication that had long been second nature to them—maybe they jettisoned everything they had ever known in favor of something radically new without so much as noting it, let alone justifying or debating it. Or perhaps the change in consciousness only came later through reflection, concern, and debate, crystallizing by 1787. But one would have to show how that happened, rather than merely assuming that codifying a written constitution necessitates an attendant brand of constitutional communication. That would be a heavy lift, for as we have seen, there was no sudden change in constitutional thinking, no testimony insisting that constitutions had been one sort of thing in 1775 but by 1776 were now something wholly different. And even if one pursued the more moderate claim that constitutional thinking only later changed under the pressure of events and debates—an argument that would itself concede that written constitutions themselves need not entail a text-bound theory of constitutional meaning—one would have to explain why familiar habits of appealing to unwritten fundamental law and constitutional principles persisted in such powerful ways through 1787 and beyond.

Related difficulties undermine more concrete originalist attempts to establish that early U.S. constitutions presented themselves as spatially bounded texts. Most recently, the originalists Evan Bernick and Christopher Green have latched onto one example in particular to establish this point: the fact that the texts of both the 1780 Massachusetts Constitution and the 1784 New Hampshire Constitution state that they "shall be enrolled on parchment, and deposited in the Secretary's office."[256] Bernick and Green would have us believe that this single provision confirms that these constitutions were circumscribed texts. But the people who made and validated these constitutions did not share this understanding. To sharpen the differences between their constitutionalism and that of originalists, it pays to explore why.

As we have seen, early state constitutions were understood against the backdrop of social compact theory and thus consisted of at least three distinct components: a social compact (which defined the nature of the political community), a declaration of rights (which explained some of the basic terms of that compact), and a form of government (which laid out the government that would preside over that community).[257] As we have also seen, given entrenched understandings of general fundamental law, written constitutions enacted new fundamental law while leaving other fundamental law in place. Constitutions were at once codified (the kind of thing you could cite chapter and verse) and yet also consisted of far more than that, which either could not or did not need to be codified.

Consider what those eighteenth-century Massachusetts and New Hampshire constitutions in fact say in full: "This form of government shall be enrolled on parchment, and deposited in the Secretary's office, and be a part of the laws of the land."[258] The terminology tells the story. The *form of government* was to be enrolled on parchment and deposited in the Secretary's office, at which point it would become *part of the laws of the land*. The "constitution" was to be enrolled on parchment insofar as this word described the form of government that was to be erected. The other parts of the constitution—the social compact and declaration of rights, both of which were necessarily pre-textual—were undisturbed by this instruction. The enrolled parchment, moreover, would not become *the* law of the land, but *part* of the *laws* of the land. Could it be clearer? These states were codifying fundamental law that would join preexisting fundamental law to form the laws of the land that would govern their political communities.

Nothing about this formulation should surprise us. At the Founding, as we have seen, constituting a new government required outlining the frame of government in writing. But that did not mean that the constitution was fully constituted by what was written down on that parchment, for significant portions of that constitution were created before the enactment of any constitutional text. To assume otherwise, we would have to believe that constitution writers in Massachusetts or New Hampshire, simply by stating that the forms of government they had codified would be stored for official reference, inadvertently abolished their own constitutional assumptions. Through this single provision, they apparently nullified the constitutional significance of their underlying social compact, their preexisting fundamental rights, and preexisting fundamental law—and entirely by accident. Surely we should not blithely assume that these constitutions' purported self-definition somehow erased their authors' own conception of constitutionalism.

Nor should we, in turn, misread the numerous and unsurprising ways Founding-era constitutionalists referred to their constitutions as documents. Once Americans began codifying new frames of government in 1776, printed versions of their work soon circulated through special issues of newspapers and almanacs—a natural result of an expanding world of political print and a valuable means for enabling the people at large to scrutinize and legitimate new revolutionary forms of governance.[259] Thomas Paine would later claim that the Pennsylvania Constitution of 1776 was "the political bible of the state" and "[s]carcely a family was without it," even going so far as to say that "[e]very member of the government had a copy" and "nothing was more common, when any debate arose on the principle of a bill, or on the extent of any species of authority, than for the members to take the printed constitution out of their pocket, and read the chapter with which such matter in debate was connected."[260] Paine, as he often did, was exaggerating. While there seem to have been more printed state constitutions in Pennsylvania than anywhere else, they were nowhere near as plentiful as he claimed. Indeed, some state constitutions, it seems, weren't even printed as stand-alone docu-ments at this time.[261] The smallest surviving version of the Pennsylvania Constitution, moreover, was only a duodecimo pamphlet, while most others were octavo sized.[262] Nonetheless, printed constitutions circulated, and their printed nature mattered—for publicity, popular legitimacy, and much else—so it's not hard to find examples of American commentators referring to these printed documents as "constitutions."

The same was true when copies of new constitutions circulated privately. Individuals often sent copies of new forms of government to correspon-dents, reporting when doing so that they were enclosing a "copy of the Con-stitution" for consideration. Official bodies occasionally did the same, relaying the work of a convention to another body for assessment—as hap-pened, most famously, when the Federal Convention sent the constitution it had drafted to the Confederation Congress with a cover letter that referred to "the preceeding Constitution."[263]

Capturing many originalists' unexamined assumptions about the Consti-tution's distinctively textual character, Bernick and Green have collected various references of this kind, convinced that they straightforwardly dem-onstrate that "[o]ur constitutions are textual" and that "[t]hat's what the founders thought the Constitution *was.*"[264] But their examples demonstrate no such thing. One could emphasize the textual features of written constitu-tions without seeing those instruments as bounded texts. Founding-era con-stitutionalists were untroubled by such false dichotomies. They could debate among themselves the precise meaning and significance of constitutional documents without losing sight of core constitutional assumptions. What we have trouble seeing was obvious to them.

In analyzing their selected examples, Bernick and Green fail to appreciate the multiple senses that the word "constitution" enjoyed in the eighteenth century. As we've seen, at this time it was commonplace to use the word "constitution" to refer specifically to a frame of government. In the vast ma-jority of instances in which writers mentioned enclosing a "copy of the con-stitution," they were using the word in that conventional way. Often it was explicit, such as when Charles Thomson, in 1779, requested that Thomas Jefferson "transmit . . . a copy of the constitution or form of government adopted by your State."[265] The document Thomson hoped to receive would embody only a portion of the constitution. As we've also seen, however, the meaning of "constitution" was beginning to change. Even if the word still referred often to a "frame of government," it now also referred to the entirety of the fundamental law of a particular sovereign jurisdiction. Nonetheless, even among the minority of writers who, in relaying a copy of a constitution, had a more capacious meaning of "constitution" in mind, nothing about that usage required the assumption that the constitution they were relaying was itself textually bounded. The sender would have assumed that the enclosed constitution would be read *as a* constitution in light of what constitutions were understood to be and how they were perceived to function.

Any eighteenth-century reader, for instance, would have known that any constitutional document presupposed a social compact—itself as much a part of the "constitution" as the form of government outlined in text—and that deciphering that compact demanded sociological and historical analysis that had less to do with parsing constitutional text than with understanding the history and makeup of a polity and its people. Sometimes portions of the written constitution—often the declaration of rights that preceded the form of government—offered important clues into the nature of the social compact. But even those clues merely led the interpreter beyond and below the text, serving more than anything as a reminder of the unavoidable need to do so. You could figure out the social compact only by looking elsewhere—that was a given—and you couldn't understand the "constitution" without understanding the social compact, and everyone knew that.

The same was true when the public was called upon, in the few instances when they were, to breathe life into a proposed constitution by ratifying it— when they were asked to approve or reject a proposed constitutional document, as most famously in the case of the federal Constitution of 1787. Originalists often assume that Founding-era Americans ratified *documents*. But they in fact ratified *constitutions*. *What* exactly they ratified was a function of what they understood themselves to be ratifying given what they understood constitutions to be and how they understood constitutionalism to work. If they took themselves to be ratifying a bounded constitutional text, that would be one thing. If they took themselves to be ratifying something else, however, perhaps a constitution that presupposed social compact theory and general fundamental law, then that would be another thing entirely. There was no fact of the matter independent of the thick cultural context in which people at the time conceived of the precise activity in which they were engaged.

So we're back to square one. People in the eighteenth century would have read a constitution in light of their understanding of constitutions and how they worked. And given how Founding-era Americans understood constitutions, it would have been nearly impossible for them to see those instruments exclusively as texts. Otherwise, we're left with an apparent contradiction: mountains of evidence showing that Founding-generation constitutionalists assumed that written constitutions contained far more than what had been written into them, alongside other sorts of evidence emphasizing the textual nature of what the Founding generation created. If we actually listen to this evidence, and try to see how a "constitution" could be at once written, tangible, and concrete and at the same time decidedly, *necessarily*, not, that contradiction suddenly vanishes. Perhaps we should understand why Founding-era constitutionalists spoke so regularly about social compacts, fundamental rights, and bodies of fundamental law existing before constitutional enactment. Perhaps we should grasp why, even as constitutions were written, printed, distributed, and circulated, it would have been strange to most people at the time to suggest that you could somehow "carry a complete copy" of a constitution "in your pocket."[266] Perhaps, in short, we should stop trying to see their constitutions through our eyes, and instead see their constitutions through their eyes.

Doing so would certainly better equip us to understand what the framers of the federal Constitution imagined themselves to be doing in the summer of 1787. The delegates assumed they were there to frame a new federal government and recalibrate the federal system and, in the process, add to, delete, shape, enhance, modify, declare, or leave in place existing fundamental law. The act of codifying constitutional text was a vital part of their work. But they would constitutionalize new rules of federal governance against a background of preexisting fundamental law and an existing social compact. If we are asked to suppose otherwise—that through certain stray textual references, including the repeated use of the phrase "this Constitution," the Constitution somehow self-defined as a bounded text—then let us make no mistake about what we are being asked to believe: that Founding-era Americans made a constitution that directly contradicted—indeed erased—their own stated understanding of constitutionalism.

How the Founding generation understood written constitutionalism was often sharply at odds with the kind of hyper-textualist brand of written constitutionalism on which orthodox originalism so commonly depends. The blithe assumptions about writtenness that have long undergirded conventional originalist argument, from Justice Antonin Scalia to Justice Neil Gorsuch, obscure crucial differences between past and present. Originalists assume too much when they find themselves and their ideas so readily at the Founding. The Founders' constitutionalism was not ours. It would take many subsequent changes—some of which came relatively quickly, while others took much longer—before the former gave way to the latter. Even then, little about our constitutionalism was foreordained. Our written Constitution could have remained tethered to a once predominant and now largely invisible form of written constitutionalism.

5

Federal Constitutionalism and the Nature of the United States

Adverting to the act by which the United States became a free and independent nation ... from that declaration, solemnly recognized at home and abroad, they derive all the powers appertaining to a nation thus circumstanced ...

— John Vining, House of Representatives, 1791

NOTHING ABOUT WRITING constitutions down ever required treating constitutional content as exclusively written. Given that for so much of the eighteenth century, and especially the period leading up to the drafting of the Constitution in 1787, few assumed otherwise, the interesting question to ask is not, How could anyone have ever seen written constitutionalism in such non-exclusive, non-positivist terms? But rather, How did it ever become intuitive to see written constitutionalism otherwise? It is *our* strange conception of written constitutionalism that needs to be explained, not assumed. We err in assuming that our familiar, habituated way of thinking about constitutionalism logically flowed from, let alone was required by, the original Constitution. It took *work* to see the Constitution as we tend to today—to see its content and boundaries in such sharply textual terms and to see it as an independent source of law so plainly distinct from other authoritative sources. None of that immediately followed from the mere activity of drawing up and enacting forms of constitutional government. Our familiar habits of mind had to be learned, and in the process much else had to be unlearned.

To be sure, at the Founding, American constitutionalism was as much defined by change as continuity. The federal Constitution was not simply predicated on long-standing assumptions. It was also, to a great extent, the result of new ways of thinking about constitutionalism that had developed only in the years immediately prior.[1] While many unfamiliar assumptions endured for decades to come, they were gradually joined by new, more recognizable habits of thought, propelled forward by the transformative energy of revolution. Around the time the Constitution first appeared, some commentators *did* begin anticipating a more familiar form of constitutionalism by emphasizing the exclusivity of constitutional writtenness and the positivist nature of fundamental law.

But even as things were changing, in essential ways early U.S. constitutionalism remained a world apart from our own.

New Attitudes Toward Constitutional Text

One major reason why constitutional assumptions were changing was the dramatic transformation, so famously explicated by Gordon Wood, in how Revolutionary Americans understood the legal foundations of constitutions.[2] In most cases, the first state constitutions had been written and enacted by the same legislative bodies whose authority derived from those constitutions.[3] As time passed, some observers began worrying that these constitutions were, on account of their origins, legally deficient. Unless elevated beyond the control of ordinary lawmaking bodies, these constitutions would be equivalent in kind to the ordinary law they were intended to regulate. They would not obviously enjoy the status of fundamental law. To remedy this defect, these commentators emphasized the importance of constitutional conventions, special bodies that, in gathering independently of sitting governments, could embody the sovereign people's will and thus create constitutions that expressly spoke for that people.[4] This new emphasis on conventions, in turn, supplied fresh importance to the idea of formal legal enactment in the domain of fundamental law, which, in turn, focused attention on a single, discrete moment of constitutional creation and the single, discrete product of that convention. This shift would ultimately have important consequences for American constitutionalism. It enabled Americans to begin thinking in fresh ways about how consent was sought and obtained.[5] What had been a mostly open-ended, ongoing process could begin to be seen instead as a closed, bounded action. Just as importantly, the new focus on conventions made it easier to associate constitutions with their written form—the thing those conventions made. Older ways of thinking—about the importance of customary consent and the diffuse sources of fundamental law—endured, but core concepts were beginning to change.

Related to this transformation, before the fall of 1787, when the Constitution went public, there had been occasional remarks—scattered amid the cacophony of commentary—that hinted at a new understanding of written constitutionalism. In 1787, writing in defense of the exercise of judicial review in *Bayard v. Singleton* (the North Carolina Superior Court ruling that Richard Dobbs Spaight found so alarming), the jurist James Iredell claimed that "[t]he Constitution" of the state "limiting the powers of the Legislature" was not only "*a fundamental Law*" but also "*a law in writing*," defining the former in terms of the latter in a way few had. Consequently, "the Constitution" was not "a mere imaginary thing, about which ten thousand different opinions may be formed, but," he asserted, "a written document to which all may have recourse."[6] In a similar vein, the unbending radical Thomas Paine, drawing on thoughts he had first expressed in Pennsylvania in 1776,[7] declared in 1791 that "[a] constitution is not a thing in name only, but in fact. It has not an ideal, but a real existence; and wherever it cannot be produced in a visible form, there is none." It was, he insisted, "the body of elements, to which you can refer, and quote article by article."[8]

Only after the Constitution was circulated, however, did this sporadic commentary acquire coherence and weight. During the ratification debates, Anti-Federalists pulled together previously inchoate ideas to advance a novel argument about the relationship between writtenness and constitutional content.[9] In the Virginia ratifying convention, for instance, Patrick Henry refused to accept that principles of state sovereign immunity might persist as a matter of general law, instead demanding express support in "the paper" that would affirm as much.[10] Several other opponents of the Constitution, meanwhile, demanded the textual enumeration of cherished common-law rights, refusing to accept Federalist reassurances—no matter how conventional those assurances were and how much experience they rested on—that the federal Constitution would leave those protections in place.[11] "[I]t is doubtful, at least," warned the Anti-Federalist Federal Farmer, "whether [fundamental common-law rights] can be claimed under immemorial usage in this country," since "we generally claim them under compacts, as charters and constitutions."[12] From our perspective, these Anti-Federalist complaints are sound and prescient, so much so that we often fail to appreciate how innovative (even desperate) they were and how understandably perplexed Federalists were by them.[13]

Slowly, these Anti-Federalist impulses took on greater force. In the First Congress, during the fateful debate over the removal of executive officers, a few congressmen channeled them to insist—ultimately to no avail—that the Constitution's content was largely coextensive with the meaning of its words.[14] Two years later, congressional opponents of Alexander Hamilton's proposed national bank provided these earlier musings a clarity and vigor they had previously lacked, issuing an even stronger account of the written Constitution's exclusivity.[15] These kinds of arguments thereafter became a doctrinaire feature of Jeffersonian Republican ideology, perhaps captured nowhere more emphatically than St. George Tucker's defense of "the visible constitution" of the United States.[16] By 1825, a Pennsylvania jurist could matter-of-factly remark, "The principles of a written constitution are more fixed and certain, and more apparent to the apprehension of the people than principles which depend on tradition and the vague comprehension of the individuals who compose the nation, and who cannot all be expected to receive the same impressions or entertain the same notions on any given subject."[17] In discussing the Constitution in 1821, James Madison succinctly captured this emerging attitude: "[T]he legitimate meaning of the Instrument must be derived from the text itself."[18]

Federalist judges, meanwhile, in sharp contrast to jurists' earlier rhetorical practices, began justifying the exercise of judicial power and review on the basis of the writtenness of the Constitution. In a circuit court case in 1795, Justice William Paterson drew a sharp contrast between American constitutions and what they had replaced. Unlike "in England," where "there is no written constitution, no fundamental law, nothing visible, nothing real, nothing certain," he argued, in the United States, constitutions were "reduced to written exactitude and precision," providing something concrete "by which a statute can be tested."[19] Later, in *Marbury v. Madison* in 1803,

Chief Justice John Marshall even more emphatically tethered judicial review to written constitutionalism. The "very essence of judicial duty," Marshall famously explained, was to "void" legislative acts that were "repugnant to the Constitution." Nothing about this declaration was novel. The innovation lay in claiming that this familiar principle was in fact "essential" to, and thus predicated on, that "greatest improvement on political institutions—a written Constitution." That explained, he declared, why "in America" written constitutions were "viewed with so much reverence."[20]

If a more modern way of describing, defending, and understanding written constitutionalism began to emerge in these years, however, the chronology, prevalence, and explosiveness of such claims reveal that there's still far more to this story.

First, the evidence is plain that these habits of mind took shape almost entirely *after* 1787—that is, they were a product of the development of a written constitution, rather than the mentality in which one had been forged. They emerged contingently from debate *over* the Constitution and its core character.[21] Only as they emerged did others begin to ascribe novel significance to the Constitution's purported form, subtly transforming how the Constitution came to be perceived.[22]

Second, the older habits that had informed written constitutionalism throughout the century still endured and proved vital. Even as commentators like Thomas Paine began insisting that constitutions needed to take "visible form," others forcefully defended the long-standing conventional wisdom. John Quincy Adams, for one, countered Paine extensively in print, offering, in his words, "an examination of certain principles and arguments contained in a late pamphlet of Mr. Paine's, which are supposed to be directly opposite to principles acknowledged by the constitutions of *our* country."[23] The constitutional principles, in other words, that Paine disparaged and claimed to be absent from American constitutionalism in fact remained a key feature of it. Others agreed. In defense of Connecticut's mostly unwritten constitution, which could be traced back to the seventeenth century and remained largely customary in character, the leading legal theorist Zephaniah Swift proclaimed that, while "[s]ome visionary theorists, have pretended that we have no constitution, because it has not been reduced to writing," the state's constitution enjoyed an "existence" that was "well known and precisely bounded."[24]

Even those Federalist jurists, such as Marshall and Paterson, who seemed from their pronouncements to have lined up squarely behind modern written constitutionalism held more complex views. Their oft-quoted declarations—which helped mythologize a distorted tale of American constitutional exceptionalism based on an invidious, and as we have seen deliberately overstated, distinction between American and British constitutionalism—are routinely misread as descriptive common sense when they were, in fact, polemical moves made as part of a concerted effort to defend what remained controversial at the time: the exercise of judicial power in a republican system of government.[25] Proof of this fact is nowhere more evident than in the judges' own behavior. While they emphasized constitutional writtenness with greater frequency, they didn't abandon their basic jurisprudential view that preexisting general law infused the Constitution. They continued seamlessly connecting the formally codified elements with general legal principles. The reasoning foregrounded in *Marbury* did not upend these long-standing assumptions; far from it. They endured well into the next century.[26] It would take decades before eighteenth-century orthodoxy was fully supplanted by a new conception of constitutional law. An important part of this transformation took place in the decade following ratification.[27] But the complete transformation would take many more years still, and was not even close to finished until the early twentieth century.[28] In the decades after *Marbury*, constitutionalists continued to believe in and readily appeal to general fundamental law, blend natural law with common law, and conceive of common law as a dynamic combination of non-positive and positive law that could never be reduced to the particular rulings of courts.[29] The "brooding omnipresence in the sky" that Justice Oliver Wendell Holmes, Jr., so famously disparaged a century ago continued to brood on in the early United States.[30] And constitutionalism—however textualist and archival it was becoming—continued to presuppose a perspective strongly at odds with modernist legal sensibilities.

Finally, and most importantly, combining the two prior points underscores that the collision of older and new ways of thinking about constitutional writtenness produced conflict, debate, and doubt, particularly over the Constitution's nature and the character of its content. Exacerbating this problem was the novelty of the federal constitutional project itself—that in addition to the complex questions about its written character lay the intricacies of the polity it was established to govern. The Constitution reflected and created a federal system that neither clearly consolidated power in a national government nor unambiguously recognized a confederacy of sovereign states but instead established something in between, the likes of which was unprecedented and thus not easily understood.[31] It erected a government that was seemingly, as James Madison famously argued, neither wholly national nor federal, that represented a polity and a people, each of which might be imagined in a host of competing ways.[32] All questions of written constitutionalism aside, then, it was decidedly unclear what kind of community the Constitution governed, and when it came time to sort out the Constitution's content, the two questions were inextricably intertwined.[33] It was impossible to know what the Constitution said—and thus licensed or prohibited—without first understanding the nature of the federal union for which it spoke.[34] And, as Alison LaCroix has shown, the dispute over federalism that was set in motion at the Founding and that soon saturated constitutional debate across the first half of the nineteenth century produced a dizzying array of competing *federalisms*.[35] As the Constitution was increasingly called upon to resolve thorny jurisdictional issues triggered by the movement of commercial goods, people (both enslaved and free), and much else, the distinct ways in which disputants described the union quickly multiplied.[36] And efforts to clarify the Constitution's operative provisions often descended into a deeper set of debates over the federal union itself.

Although it became easier to see the written Constitution in textual terms, therefore, it simultaneously became even clearer that the written Constitution itself, no matter how it was understood, could not resolve its own meaning. Most interpretive claims presupposed a robust theory of constitutionalism that could not itself be derived from the text. No one could fully understand the Constitution's commands merely by scrutinizing its words. Drawing complete and coherent meaning from those words would invariably require a sociological and historical investigation into the kind of union the Constitution could be said to govern. For decades to come, the shape of U.S. constitutionalism remained the same: understanding what the Constitution meant required understanding what sort of thing it was, which usually required understanding what kind of polity it represented. Interpreting constitutional text necessarily carried the interpreter far beyond it.

Which means that, even as more familiar attitudes toward constitutional writtenness eventually began to take shape, and even as members of the

Founding generation seemingly began to talk more like us, these new attitudes still failed to neatly correspond to those presupposed by most modern originalists. Despite any new emphasis on the textual nature of the Constitution, it was still widely assumed that "this Constitution," in the fullest sense, could not be reduced to its written text, for its content was determined as much by the underlying nature of its union as by what its words proscribed.

Just as the content of constitutional rights could not be reduced to the content of written constitutions (the principal subject of the prior chapter), then, the same was true of the content of constitutional powers. One might be tempted to distinguish between rights and state power and claim that precisely because the former was understood in non-textual terms, the latter never could have been. Because rights were grounded in nature or long-standing custom and thus preceded the formation of government, the argument might proceed, the point of government was to secure those preexisting rights. To achieve this end, constitutions needed to precisely enumerate those few powers that the government required. A broad commitment to rights, therefore, might have placed more emphasis on the express written-ness of constitutions, not less. Those originalists who have stressed the legitimacy of unenumerated rights seem to embrace such an argument, explaining how they manage to marry a non-textual vision of constitutional rights to a hyper-textual vision of constitutional powers (and most other features of the Constitution's content as well).[37] From the perspective of the Founding, however, this disjuncture between rights and powers wouldn't have made sense. Even as various constitutional assumptions were beginning to be remade, and even as some constitutionalists began emphasizing constitutional writtenness in new ways following 1787, powers, no less than rights, remained linked to pre-textual foundations. Probing Founding-era debates over the delegation of national power and the composition of the federal union shows how.

The Nature of the Federal Union

It is well known that members of the Founding generation disagreed about the nature of the federal union—and that these divisions coursed through antebellum America before eventually precipitating a bloody civil war.[38] What is far less appreciated is how deeply entangled this debate was with the Constitution's own content: that it proved impossible to identify the scope of that content without clarifying the union itself. The nature of the polity and the meaning of the Constitution were inextricably intertwined. This is among the reasons it is so misleading to think of the Constitution's earliest years as a series of interpretive disputes over a common object—to assume that Hamilton, Madison, Jefferson, and company agreed on the thing they were interpreting, just not what it said.[39] The early republic witnessed not merely competing *interpretations* of the Constitution but, more fundamentally, competing *conceptions* of the Constitution.[40] Partisans came to hold in their minds distinct images of the Constitution based on divergent theories of the federal union.[41]

The best way to bring these original fault lines into focus, and to expose the tight (and seldom-appreciated) connections between the nature of the federal union and the Constitution's content, is to briefly focus on an especially important and enduring issue: the relationship between constitutional text and the delegation of national authority. How much power did the Constitution delegate to the national government that it set up? Could the Constitution's text, on its own, answer this question? It is often assumed that the written Constitution *does* neatly address this matter. As orthodoxy has it, the Constitution does not grant the federal government plenary power. Instead, national authority, as the familiar incantation goes, is "limited and enumerated."[42] Congress's powers, most notably, are those expressly listed in Article I, section 8. There has always been debate over how narrowly or broadly to interpret each of those enumerated powers, as well as what counts as a "necessary and proper" means for carrying each into effect, but this debate, we are told, runs squarely through the written Constitution, turning, fundamentally, on how to interpret its express text. The sum of all delegated national authority is, one way or another, conveyed and constrained by the Constitution's language.[43]

When the Constitution was originally constructed, most American political and legal elites imagined a very different relationship between textual enumeration and the delegation of power.[44] Back then, it was widely assumed that the scope of the national government's power was not determined simply by the language of the Constitution but instead by the nature of its underlying polity. Depending on the character of the union, the exact same constitutional words might yield a different ambit of constitutional power. Nationalists—

those who most vigorously championed national power, such as James Wilson, Gouverneur Morris, Alexander Hamilton, Rufus King, and Fisher Ames—were adamant that the character and scope of governmental power could not be understood apart from the nature of the federal union. They contended that, because the United States was a genuine nation—a national community of individuals that transcended the borders of the separate states—the government that represented it was entitled to significant authority. What proves striking is not just how powerful this kind of nationalist thinking was at the Founding, but how broadly its underlying premise was shared.[45] Nationalists' opponents surely contended that the Constitution established a federal government of limited powers—but only because nationalists' account of the federal union was wrong. In other words, the federal government's power was limited to textual enumeration *because* a certain kind of political community had authorized it. The two sides bitterly disagreed over how much power the Constitution delegated to the national government. But both sides agreed that this was not a question the Constitution's text could answer on its own. The answer necessarily turned on a set of facts beyond the text—facts concerning what sort of polity the United States truly was.

Nationalist Constitutionalism

Nationalists assumed that the full scope of national power under the Constitution turned on the matter of sovereignty and union: *Who* had authorized the Constitution, and *what kind* of polity did that agent speak for? Not only did nationalists assume that these were the operative questions, but they also assumed—with considerable justification—that on this point almost everyone agreed.

These questions would have been familiar to most Founding-era constitutional disputants since they were guided by the familiar premises of social contract theory, which (as discussed in the prior chapter) was utterly ubiquitous at the time. To refresh: Social contract theory imagined a two-step process in which individuals formed, first, a social compact (a body politic) and then, second, a system of government (a constitution).[46] "The first 'collection' of authority," John Adams explained, was an "agreement" among individuals "to form themselves into a *nation, people, community, or body politic*."[47] Then, "[t]he society being formed," James Wilson elaborated, next came "the formation of a government."[48] The powers and obligations of the government were directly informed by the constitution of the polity because the body politic both established the government to act in its name and retained sovereignty following that delegation. "When the society was formed," Wilson continued, "it possessed jointly all the previously separate and independent powers and rights of the individuals who formed it," but also "all the other powers and rights, which result from the social union." The "aggregate of . . . powers" that "compose[d] the sovereignty of the society or nation" was thus determined, in part, by the *kind* of union that had been formed.[49] Different social compacts produced different accumulations of power, which were delegated, in turn, to the governments presiding over those compacts. A government's power thus reflected the nature of the sovereign entity that had given life to that government.[50]

In the context of the United States, sorting out the character of the polity and its attendant sovereignty was complicated by the federal nature of the union. There was wide agreement that the people were, in some way, sovereign. During the revolutionary struggle against Britain, Americans had rallied around the concept of popular sovereignty; and then during their initial efforts to construct an independent constitutional order, they had refined their understanding of it.[51] But even if it was clear that *the people* wielded sovereign authority, in the context of authorizing a national government to preside over the entire American union, it was much less clear *which* people had delegated the relevant authority: the people of the United States or the peoples of the separate states. The choice would determine whether the body politic was a union of sovereign states or a nation. These were the foundational questions necessary to comprehend the full scope of the federal government's power: Which kind of sovereign people had constituted the government, and which kind of polity did the Constitution speak for?

Nationalists defended an expansive vision of national power on the basis of their belief that the Constitution had been established by a national people speaking for a national polity.[52] James Wilson, the prominent Pennsylvania framer and jurist, had laid out the essence of the theory even before the Constitution was drafted, in defense of the national government's authority under the Articles of Confederation (the United States' first, short-lived constitution) to establish the nation's first national bank: the Bank of North America.[53] The Articles had both failed to enumerate the relevant power and made clear that the state governments retained all powers "not . . . expressly delegated."[54] But, Wilson explained, the inquiry into whether the national government could nevertheless create a bank should not begin with the Articles but instead with the Declaration of Independence, which had established not thirteen autonomous states but a single nation and, with it, a national people.[55] Consequently, the government presiding over that nation was the creation not of the people of the separate states but of the sovereign people of the United States. This meant that the national government derived its powers from two separate sources. Some powers were expressly delegated by the states through the Articles, but others "*result[ed] from the union of the whole.*" For many purposes, "the United States are to be considered as one *undivided, independent* nation; and as possessed of *all the rights,* and *powers,* and *properties . . . incident* to such."[56] Any power that was "*general*" in character, that the separate states could not competently exercise on their own, was delegated independently of the states.[57] Upon breaking from Great Britain, those powers were assigned to the union as a whole. And the subsequent "confederation" did not "weaken or abridge the *powers* and *rights,* to which the United States were *previously* entitled."[58] These broad powers did not amount to national plenary power—many significant powers were reserved to the states. But there was enormous space between a national government vested with plenary authority and one whose powers were limited to those expressly delegated. It was easy to reject the latter without embracing the former. Wilson, drawing on social-contract premises, concluded that any credible account of national power lay somewhere between those poles.[59] For Wilson, the logic was clear: the Declaration of Independence had created a specific initial body politic (a national people) that was separate from the subsequent bodies politic created by the state constitutions (the peoples of the separate states). Because the national government was constructed for a national people, it automatically assumed all general powers of union.

Wilsonian thinking subsequently shaped the drafting of the United States Constitution in profound ways.[60] In an early debate, Wilson brandished the Declaration and quoted from it at length, confident that it confirmed that "the *United Colonies*" were originally "independent, not *Individually* but *Unitedly.*"[61] This understanding of the polity shaded the way many delegates understood the enumeration of legislative powers eventually written into Article I. The mere fact of an enumeration of national legislative powers did not mean that national legislative power was limited to that enumeration. This theory of delegated national authority surely shaped one of the most famous provisions in the Constitution. As John Mikhail has shown, Wilson dramatically revised what became the Necessary and Proper Clause while serving on the Committee of Detail (the committee charged with compiling a working draft of the Constitution roughly halfway through the Convention).[62] When his work was complete, the Constitution declared that the national legislature would enjoy the power to make all laws necessary and proper to carry out not only its "foregoing powers" (those enumerated in what would become Article I, section 8), but also "all other Powers" that had been vested "in the Government of the United States" by "this Constitution." Here, in the plain text of the Constitution, was an explicit reference to "other Powers" independent of anything that had been enumerated in Article I, section 8—powers, one could claim, that had been delegated to the national government as a result of the nature of the preexisting union.[63] These revisions provided a textual reminder of what, from a Wilsonian nationalist perspective, was already necessarily the case: that certain national powers resulted from the formation of the American union itself. These powers were not "vested" via text but instead were conferred through an entirely different mechanism. And thus, the phrase "this Constitution," found in the Necessary and Proper Clause and elsewhere throughout the document, described not merely the textual content being written in Philadelphia but also, necessarily, the underlying composition of the polity upon which that text would be fundamentally based. Those powers "vested" by "this Constitution" could not be identified solely on the basis of text or enumeration, because the content of "this Constitution" was not only the discrete textual provisions written into it but a reflection of the kind of sovereign people who had established it.

Wilson's Committee of Detail work was soon fortified by his ally, Gouverneur Morris, on the Committee of Style—which was assigned the task of producing a final draft of the Constitution. Morris, quite possibly with Wilson's assistance, dramatically reworked the Constitution's Preamble (which Wilson had initially drafted on the Committee of Detail).[64] Although earlier drafts had listed each of the peoples of the individual states as the constitutive entity, the final version recognized just one national people in this role. It unambiguously established "We the People of the United States" as the Constitution's founding agent.[65] When combined with rules for ratification—

which leapfrogged state legislatures and instead empowered the people themselves, acting through special ratifying conventions rather than the state legislatures, to consider the new Constitution—these opening words made plain that the new government would not be a compact of the states, as most thought the Articles had been, but something else entirely. From Wilson and Morris's view, it had already been the case under the Articles that the states could delegate or retain only those powers that they could competently exercise; but by so dramatically undermining the states' initial claim to sovereign authority, the Constitution further underscored the primacy of the union. In addition, and as importantly, the final Preamble specified six specific purposes for which the new national government would be established, which could be read as the referent of the "all other powers" so conspicuously referenced in the revised Necessary and Proper Clause: a set of national ends that a national people licensed its national government to pursue.[66] The Preamble served as the clearest evidence imaginable of a Wilsonian reading of the final Constitution. Like the "all other powers" clause, it did not vest any power in the government but rather reinforced what was already vested, serving as both proof of a particular understanding of the federal union and a reminder of what necessarily followed from that fact. As under the Articles, the proposed national government would lack plenary authority, but thanks to the polity and people who were set to establish that national government, it would enjoy the authority to legislate on all inherently national ends and thus command vastly more authority than the sum of textually enumerated powers written into the Constitution.

Of course, many Founding-era Americans sharply disagreed with the nationalists' aims and underlying assumptions about the union, but to a remarkable degree, disputes over the Constitution were defined on their terms.[67] Indeed, it was precisely because Wilson and his allies were right—not about how much national power was preferable, but about the relationship between the constitution of the polity and the constitution of its government—that during the ratification debates opponents found the proposed Constitution so threatening. "I confess, as I enter the Building I stumble at the Threshold," Samuel Adams uneasily reported. "I meet with a National Government, instead of a federal Union of Sovereign States."[68] The opening words of the Preamble, Robert Whitehill claimed in the Pennsylvania ratifying convention, showed "the principle of confederation excluded, and a new unwieldy system of consolidated empire . . . set up upon [it]."[69] The proposed Constitution—as revealed in the Preamble—presupposed a certain kind of federal polity, one that, Anti-Federalists assumed, entitled the national government to more power than was enumerated. "The inference is natural," Brutus complained, given "[t]he design of the constitution" as "expressed in the preamble," it followed that "the [national] legislature will have an authority to make all laws which they shall judge necessary for the common safety, and to promote the general welfare."[70] These implications were only reinforced, An Old Whig believed, by the inclusion of a clause "for carrying into execution ALL OTHER POWERS," which signaled that "other powers may be assumed hereafter as contained by implication in this constitution."[71]

Those Federalists who were less committed to expansive national power, such as James Madison, worked to reassure Anti-Federalists that the proposed Constitution delegated powers that were, in fact, "few and defined."[72] Even Wilson, cognizant of the rhetorical and political needs of the moment, offered some reassurances. Yet he left ample room for his own genuine understandings. For instance, "where the powers are particularly enumerated," he assured the Pennsylvania ratifying convention, "the implied result is, that nothing more is intended to be given, than what is so enumerated." "[U]nless," he added, "it results from the nature of the government itself."[73] The federal government would be able to exercise only those powers delegated, but that, of course, begged the question of how power was delegated under a constitution like the one proposed. And here Wilson reminded listeners: "I consider the people of the United States, as forming one great community," while "the people of the different states" formed communities "on a lesser scale." And, he explained, "[f]rom this great division of the people into distinct communities," different allotments of power were "given to the governments, according to the nature, number, and magnitude of their objects."[74] As John Jay emphatically declared later in ratification, "[t]he Convention," recognizing what was "indispensably necessary," had created "a national government competent to every national object."[75] The national government established by the Constitution would enjoy the power to pursue every object of this kind on account of the polity that had constituted it. It was a function of the compact, not the constitutional text. The sum of delegated authority was limited to those powers enumerated if—and only if—the underlying polity was a collection of sovereign states rather than a national sovereign people. If it was the latter—as nationalists insisted—the sum of delegated power was necessarily greater, extending to, as Jay put it, all national objects.

We might mistakenly assume that Federalists hid the ball from the ratifying public, but that is only because we fail to see the original Constitution as members of the Founding generation did: embedded in the framework of social contract theory. From that shared vantage, it was obvious that the Constitution's delegation of power was, at least in part, a function of the polity that constitution represented. That was precisely why so many Anti-Federalists objected to the Preamble and complained that the Constitution, in the words of one Massachusetts writer, "proposes the beginning of one new society."[76] The Constitution's critics understood what they were looking at. For decades, they and their brethren had been engaged in a long-running conversation about the basis of representative government, much of which had swirled around practical efforts to construct new governments in the states. So no matter how many Federalists hinted otherwise to help ensure ratification, few skeptics were pacified by such assurances. The inescapable relationship between the constitutional text and the underlying polity resonated.

What the Text Could Not Resolve: Debating
the Nature of the Polity

After ratification, these fault lines continued to shape constitutional debate in profound ways. To an extent rarely appreciated, defenders of national power instinctively appealed to Wilsonian arguments in a range of important debates, nowhere as prominently as during the congressional debate over Alexander Hamilton's proposed national bank.[77] Nationalists emphasized that the character of the union determined the scope of national power. "Adverting to the act by which the United States became a free and independent nation," John Vining of Delaware declared that the United States "derive[d] all the powers appertaining to a nation."[78] "[B]y the very nature of government," contended Fisher Ames, the sardonic representative from Massachusetts, "the legislature had an implied power of using every mean not positively prohibited by the constitution, to execute the ends for which that government was instituted." The Preamble, he continued, "vested Congress with the authority over all objects of national concern or of a general nature."[79]

Whether the national government could charter a national bank came down to, as Vining, Ames, and so many others believed, the question Wilson would pose as a justice on the Supreme Court in 1793 in *Chisholm v. Georgia*: "[D]o the people of the United States form a Nation?" Wilson's answer, which Chief Justice John Jay echoed in his own separate opinion, captured nationalists' thinking perfectly.[80] Properly read, the Constitution disclosed that "the people of the United States intended to form themselves into a nation for national purposes," because "they established the present Constitution" in their "collective and national capacity."[81] Because a constitution had to be read in conjunction with the terms of the social contract, interpreting the federal Constitution turned on the nature of that prior compact. Because the people of the United States had formed a nation and set up the federal Constitution to act in their name, therefore, that constitution delegated all distinctively national powers to the government it established.[82]

Nationalists' ideological opponents—those who rallied around the opposition Republican Party being formed by Thomas Jefferson and James Madison—vigorously challenged nationalists' conclusions, insisting, in sharp contrast, that federal power was strictly enumerated. Initially, they tried to combat nationalist arguments by pressing the Constitution's writtenness into service. They insisted that, as Madison argued in the congressional debate over chartering a national bank, the Constitution's "essential characteristic" was that it established a government "of limited and enumerated powers."[83] William Giles of Virginia took this argument a step further, asserting that "the peculiar nature of this government" was that it was "composed of mere chartered authorities," meaning that any "authority not contained within that charter" was off limits. The soon-to-be Tenth Amendment, which declared that all powers not delegated were retained, Giles argued, underscored this essential point.[84] Throughout the 1790s, as the nation divided into discernible political coalitions, these became common refrains among Republicans.[85]

Ultimately, however, Republicans rested their case against broad federal power on a rival account of union. Though they reached a radically different conclusion, Republicans shared a guiding premise, concurring with nationalists that the question could be settled only by appealing to the true nature of the underlying compact.[86] Republicans, in short, recognized that truly limiting the scope of the federal government's power required establishing that nationalists were mistaken about the nature of the federal union.

Pointing to the enumeration of federal powers or clamoring about the Tenth Amendment only reinforced that the debate turned not on the Constitution's written content but on the operative meaning of "delegated." Claiming that something about the Constitution's writtenness settled the matter presupposed a robust understanding of how federal power was delegated and, thus, what kind of polity had constituted the government in the first place. That Republicans did not rest their case—indeed *could* not rest their case—on the inherent limitations of textually expressed powers but rather based their case on their own rival conception of the federal union served as striking acknowledgment that, to virtually everyone at the time, the core social-contract premises on which nationalists relied were irresistible.

In broad terms, Republicans defended two distinct positions. The first, most readily associated with Jefferson, simply denied that there was a national polity or national social contract, either before or after the Constitution was ratified. Consequently, the federal Constitution was not, in fact, a constitution at all, but rather a compact among sovereign states. As Jefferson asserted in 1798, in protest of the Alien and Sedition Acts, the Constitution was a "compact under the style and title of a Constitution for the United States." The Constitution's own style and title were misleading. Its Preamble, which seemed to establish a national polity, was not to be taken at face value. Instead, the "several states composing the United States of America," Jefferson argued, "[had] constituted a General Government for special purposes, delegat[ing] to that Government certain definite powers" while "reserving . . . the residuary mass" to themselves.[87] Compact theory (as this position came to be called) was, in effect, the nationalist position inverted. The federal government's authority was limited to those powers strictly enumerated *because* the Constitution had been agreed to by the peoples of the separate states rather than the people of the United States. Power was limited to the text *not* because of the text or something inherent to written constitutionalism but because of what preceded the text. As Jefferson himself conceded, if the Constitution's own style and title were in fact accurate, then the national government would have claim to more authority than if they were not. Whether the United States was a nation of individuals or a compact among states, the Constitution's text would be identical, yet the extent of power delegated by that constitution to the federal government would not be. The exact same text could delegate radically different sums of authority depending on the nature of the political community for whom that text spoke. On at least this much, Jefferson assumed that nationalists were right.

Compact theory took on greater weight over time. A few years after Jefferson elaborated it, in 1803, the leading legal theorist of the Republican movement, St. George Tucker, systematically defended compact theory in an extensive essay that was appended to his annotated, and Americanized, edition of Blackstone's *Commentaries*.[88] The federal government's powers were confined to those written, Tucker argued, because the Constitution was a compact among sovereign states. There was no national polity, just a national government brought into being by separate peoples in separate political communities in separate states.[89]

The second Republican position, articulated most forcefully by Madison, fell between the strong nationalist and Jeffersonian views, by conceding that there was a quasi-national social contract, but rejecting that it was either truly national in character or that it preceded the Constitution. Defenders of this intermediate position recognized federal sovereignty, accepted that the Constitution was, in fact, a constitution (not merely a compact styled as one), and therefore acknowledged that there was at least a federal body politic that transcended the states. In all these respects, they broke with hardline Jeffersonians. But even if, like nationalists, defenders of this intermediate position recognized a social contract beyond the states, they accounted for its origins much differently. The distinctively federal polity they imagined was not a compact between individuals that had been created through the act of independence, but rather a compact formed from the states' individual decisions to divest their authority through the act of ratifying the Constitution. This federal polity, in other words, did not predate the Constitution—as Wilson, Jay, Vining, and so many others had claimed—but came into being alongside the new federal charter. Ratification was not, therefore, an exercise of a preexisting national people's sovereignty but in fact the act that had brought something like a nation into legal existence.

Madison had hinted at these arguments during ratification,[90] but he made the case most fully in the *Report of 1800*, written in defense of the Virginia and Kentucky Resolutions (the latter in which Jefferson had laid out his own argument).[91] The Virginia Resolutions had asserted that "the powers of the Federal Government" were "no farther valid than they are authorised by the grants enumerated in that compact."[92] This was the case because those powers "result[ed] from the compact to which the states are parties."[93] Here, however, Madison was clear to differentiate his argument from compact theory. He recognized that the term "states" had several distinct meanings. When invoking it, he referred not to the thirteen separate political units but to the peoples within them: "the people composing those political societies, in their highest sovereign capacity," who had received and ratified the Constitution.[94] The states did not maintain sovereignty after ratification, but because the state polities had been the original font of national sovereignty, the federal government's authority was confined to "a particular enumeration of powers."[95]

The Constitution's earliest years were marked by conflict and contestation, not just over its meaning but the basis of that meaning. What the Constitution said, permitted, and required turned on the nature of the federal union, which itself was subject to sharply competing interpretations.[96] Throughout this period, nationalists captured something significant. The point of emphasizing them—and the nationalist theory they defended—is to show that debates over constitutional interpretation typically presupposed the fundamental importance of the questions nationalists repeatedly asked. Virtually everyone believed that there was a tight relationship between the Constitution's meaning and the sovereign people for whom it spoke. Beneath the bitter disagreement, disputants readily conceded that constitutional meaning was entangled with the nature of the underlying polity. On this point nationalists and their opponents were in consistent agreement. This was just how constitutionalism worked.

All at the time recognized that "this Constitution" did not—and could not—simply describe the express constitutional text written down in 1787 (or added via amendment in 1791). Set in the foundational context of social contract theory, "this Constitution" described the entwined relationship between the formation of a political community and the constitution of government that followed. The latter could not be read independently of the terms of the social contract. What the Constitution *said* was a function of the kind of people and union for which it spoke. And the constitutional text could not resolve these foundational issues; it could not, on its own, specify what kind of federal union stood beneath it. The document's meaning was shaped by the nature of the polity, and the nature of the polity could not be derived from the document—no matter how hard some today might be inclined to try. The

Founding generation knew well how futile this move was, and thus never assumed they could interpret the Constitution without probing its deeper foundation. To know what the Constitution communicated necessarily required a theory of constitutional union and sovereignty derived from history, sociology, and political theory, not law or text. Whatever else changed after 1787, through at least Reconstruction, this conceptual framework dominated American constitutional interpretation and debate.[97]

This recognition exposes, more broadly, that just-so appeals to constitutional writtenness (then and now) presuppose *some* theory of constitutionalism that shapes *how* that writtenness ought to be understood. Even as the written Constitution took on new significance in the years after 1787, it still was not possible to resolve the Constitution's full meaning by pointing to what had been written into that Constitution. Sorting out what the Constitution meant required resolving its contested nature and ultimately deciphering the nature of the political community for which it spoke. These were things the text simply could not resolve.

To put the point about constitutional writtenness most broadly: The original U.S. Constitution was written. It took "visible form," and significance was attached to that fact, increasingly over time. But what that writtenness amounted to was a function of the particular languages in which the Constitution was initially written, above all the languages of social contract theory and general fundamental law. And those languages compelled interpreters to see the Constitution as far more than a text. For eighteenth-century constitutionalists who spoke these languages fluently, this was easy to grasp. For us today, for whom these languages are not second nature, what was once obvious is now mostly invisible. If we don't reacquaint ourselves with these languages, we will misunderstand *their* written constitutionalism and, in turn, risk erasing the very eighteenth-century Constitution we seek to recover.

6

Fixing Fixity

> All new laws, though penned with the greatest technical skill, and
> passed on the fullest and most mature deliberation, are considered as
> more or less obscure and equivocal, until their meaning be liqui-
> dated and ascertained by a series of particular discussions and adju-
> dications.
>
> — James Madison, *The Federalist* 37, 1788

ORIGINALISTS CONTEND THAT, BY committing their constitution to writing,
Founding-era Americans not only ensured an exclusively textual understanding of its contents, but also fixed its meaning. In their minds, in fact,
fixity is inescapably tethered to writtenness—fixity is simultaneously a function and a requirement of writtenness. They believe, that is, that the act of
writing something down inherently fixes its meaning and that the only way
to fix something's meaning is to write it down. By opting for a written constitution, therefore, the Founding generation opted for a fixed constitution.

By this logic, not only are writtenness and fixity tightly linked, but writtenness is a prerequisite of fixity. The only way a constitution *could* be fixed is if
it's written. The only kind of constitutional meaning that *could* be fixed is
textual meaning. To ask whether a constitution's meaning is fixed is to ask
whether the meanings of its *words* are fixed. As a category, fixed meaning can
only ever refer to textual meaning.

But just as constitutional writtenness was conceptualized quite differently at the Founding than it is today, so too was constitutional fixity. At the Founding there was a distinct, long-standing way of understanding constitutional fixity, an understanding that was detached from writtenness and not automatically disturbed by the fact that Americans committed constitutional principles to writing. This unfamiliar form of fixity worked in harmony with the unfamiliar understanding of law and constitutional writtenness that, as we have seen, also once predominated. In the late eighteenth century, it was assumed constitutions were and ought to be fixed, but *how* those constitutions were understood to be fixed and *what* exactly was constitutionally fixed followed a different logic. Just as the Founding generation held an alternative conception of written constitutionalism, so too did it embrace an alternative understanding of fixed constitutionalism.

Like our own modern understanding of writtenness, our own modern conception of fixity did not spring inexorably from the original Constitution. It resulted, instead, from a particular way in which people came to imagine fixity in the decades after the Constitution was first drafted. Indeed, the way we understand fixity today owes far more to the vagaries of constitutional practice and disputation than it does to anything essentially laid down in 1787. Our familiar understanding of fixed constitutionalism did not come fixed.

A Different Kind of Fixity

Originalist dogma makes it impossible to grasp what was a settled eighteenth-century truth: that the unwritten, largely customary British constitution, like all constitutions, was fixed.[1] Writing from London in 1773, Henry St. John, Viscount Bolingbroke explained that "[b]y constitution we mean . . . that assemblage of laws, institutions, and customs, derived from certain fixed principles of reason." All "riches" and "strength" was owed to "the British constitution," for in "preserving this constitution inviolate, or by drawing it back to the principles on which it was originally founded . . . we may secure to ourselves, and to our latest posterity, the possession of that liberty which we have long enjoyed."[2] James Otis reiterated this point in Boston in 1764. There are "bounds, which by God and nature are fixed," that formed "the great barriers of a free state, and of the British constitution."[3] The "fundamental Laws and Rules of the Constitution," wrote Joseph Galloway in

1760, existed "to fix the Bounds of Power and Liberty."⁴ This was precisely why, as one Maryland essayist announced in 1748, "*Parliament cannot alter the Constitution*" and why colonial Americans (like many Britons) always insisted that Parliament was checked by a higher authority.⁵ Such sentiments reached a crescendo in the midst of the colonial crisis. "The Parliament has a right to make all laws," the Massachusetts House of Representatives declared in opposition to the Stamp Act, but only "within the limits of *their own constitution*."⁶ In the face of American complaints about Parliament's omnipotence, even defenders of Parliament's authority throughout the empire conceded that the body's activities were answerable to the fixed constitution.⁷ Perhaps nowhere was this thinking more clearly expressed than in the Massachusetts Circular Letter of 1768, which pronounced that "in all free states the constitution is fixed," speaking not aspirationally but in reference to "the fundamental rules of the British constitution."⁸

If we're to understand what these various Anglo-Americans meant, we need to come to terms with the different concept of constitutional fixity they had in mind. Long before anyone claimed that constitutions had to be written, it was widely assumed that constitutions were, and ought to be, fixed. Fixity had little to do with word meanings; it relied to a far greater extent on unchanging underlying principles. As we've seen, this was how American colonists understood the fixed content of their written charters.⁹ And following independence, they had no difficulty seeing their state constitutions in proximate terms. Given how they thought about central aspects of constitutionalism, such as fundamental rights, they had no choice but to think this way. Because most fundamental rights (be they retained natural rights or fundamental customary rights) were constitutionally entrenched through the formation of the social compact, and thus preceded the written codification of the constitution of government, it would have been impossible to imagine that the words of textually enumerated rights declarations (either in those state constitutions that happened to have them or in the federal Constitution's celebrated first amendments) were what had been fixed. Indeed, most textually enumerated rights provisions in the early constitutions, as we have seen, were declaratory in character—announcing rights that had already been constitutionally entrenched.¹⁰ Therefore, in a great many instances, the words were largely beside the point.¹¹ The content of the right, which preceded textual enactment, was what had been fixed, not the linguistic meanings of the words that happened to find their way into the provision recognizing its underlying existence. The substance of the rights declared through the First, Second, or Fourth Amendments might have been fixed, in other words, but that didn't mean that the meanings of those amendments' words were also fixed. *What* was constitutionally fixed, not *whether* it was fixed, marked the distinctive difference. Founding-era constitutionalists at first assumed no necessary connection between fixity and writtenness. Constitutions could be fixed without being written, and nothing about having a written constitution automatically changed the basic ways in which constitutions were understood to be fixed.

In part because it was understood apart from writtenness, constitutional fixity was readily compatible with the notion of evolutionary constitutional change.[12] It followed a logic almost incomprehensible to us now. We assume that if a constitution's content is fixed, it cannot evolve; that would amount to a contradiction in terms. Yet, throughout the eighteenth century, fixity and evolutionary change worked in tandem. As the famed common-law jurist Matthew Hale explained in 1713, "Use and Custom . . . might introduce some *New* Laws, and alter some *Old*. . . . But tho' those particular Variations and Accessions have happened in the Laws," he explained, "we may with just Reason say, They are the same English Laws now, that they were 600 Years since in the general." He then turned to metaphor to underscore the point: "the Argonauts Ship was the same when it returned home, as it was when it went out, tho' in that long Voyage it had successive Amendments, and scarce came back with any of its former Materials."[13] As with this example from Greek mythology (Hale surely meant the "Ship of Theseus"), the British constitution had been transformed over time and yet remained the same. Changes in its content had only clarified the constitution that had always been. As the constitution evolved through usage, debate, and controversy, it converged on its ancient fixed principles.[14] This was how "enquiry into the nature of our ancient constitution," as one British writer put it in 1767, "discovers what improvements have been made, and learns us to value and esteem them."[15] Across the Atlantic, a Massachusetts author writing under the pseudonym Aequus said much the same thing in 1766. "Time and a change of circumstances," as well as "successive usage," if "ratified by repeated authoritative acquiescence," the essayist claimed, could turn an "indulgence into a right."[16] Constitutional meaning evolved within a fixed constitution.

Because reducing constitutions to writing did not complicate this under-standing of fixity, the real questions are when and why Americans' sense of this concept ever changed—when and why, that is, Americans came to un-derstand fixity and change as antithetical. There is virtually no evidence of a shift in such thinking as Americans drafted their first written constitutions. Indeed, the fact that two states—Connecticut and Rhode Island—decided not to write constitutions at all, and instead carried on under their old colo-nial charters, is a clear indication that constitutions could still be understood as fixing fundamental principles and, at the same time, evolving to meet new circumstances.

Perhaps, though, change came not in the 1770s but in the decade that fol-lowed, thanks to significant transformations in constitutional thinking.[17] As we have seen, in the wake of the initial wave of state constitution making, certain Americans began rethinking the relationship of fundamental law to ordinary lawmaking, underscoring the importance of special constitution-making practices. These commentators argued that to obtain the status of fundamental law, constitutions needed to be drafted by special conventions and ratified by the people at large.[18] These observers were anxious that so many of the state constitutions had been written and enacted by the very legislative bodies that now governed under those constitutions. If these con-stitutions were seemingly no different from ordinary legislative enactments, and thus could be changed by any subsequent legislative enactments, then these constitutions were themselves nothing more than conventional ordi-nances, and thus not properly constitutions at all. As Thomas Jefferson noted, a "constitution" must mean "an act above the power of the ordinary legislature."[19] The way to remedy this deficiency and ensure that American constitutions would be "unalterable by ordinary acts of assembly," was to "delegate persons with special powers" to sit in "special conventions." Only such a "convention," Jefferson insisted, could "fix the constitution."[20] Once drafted by a special convention, the constitution could be still further fixed through the people's express ratification of it. Only then would constitutions embody the people's sovereign will.

As Americans were rethinking the mechanisms by which constitutions might be fixed, they were also seemingly rethinking the modes by which fixed constitutions might be changed. Most of the early state constitutions had failed to include formal amendment provisions. Some protected certain

features from legislative change, others installed supermajority requirements, and still others mandated special councils to perform constitutional
review. But from these early experimentations emerged the procedures for
formal amendment that were written into, first, the Articles of Confederation, and then later, more famously, the federal Constitution.[21]

One might conclude that the new emphasis placed on these lawmaking
practices generated a new understanding of constitutional fixity. Perhaps in
adopting these novel procedures for fixing a constitution (through conventions and popular ratification) and subsequently changing a fixed constitution (through formal amendment), Revolutionary Americans had made it
hard, if not impossible, to continue to think, as they long had, of constitutions as at once fixed and evolving. Constitutions were now express enactments, not fluid registers of the people's will. Constitutions could no longer
evolve through practice and experience; they could change only through formal amendment. Constitutions were now deliberately fixed in such a way as
to ensure that they *couldn't* informally evolve.

Yet these innovations, significant as they might have been, did not upend
the form of fixity that had long pervaded the English-speaking world. Old
habits and old ways of thinking persisted. A closer look at the emerging practice of ratification, which we've long misunderstood, demonstrates as much.

The familiar story suggests that Massachusetts pioneered the technology
of popular ratification by sending its draft constitutions to the towns for consideration and approval.[22] The first version, submitted in 1778, was rejected.
Only once the requisite number of towns had approved the second version
in 1780 did it become the state's fundamental law. New Hampshire, which
had initially drawn up an emergency temporary constitution months before
independence was even declared, followed suit when it revised its constitution a few years after Massachusetts by submitting its constitution to the
state's towns for approval. The delegates in Philadelphia in 1787 then appro-
priated this idea, the story goes, convinced that ratification was the
essential procedure by which constitutions were made supreme law in the
name of the sovereign people.[23] The only problem with this account is that
it's wrong. As Anne Twitty has observed, far from having been cemented as
one of the signature features of American constitutionalism, ratification was
almost immediately abandoned and forgotten at the state level thereafter,
and it would be decades until ratification was again used as the standard

procedure for approving American constitutions.[24] The decision to have the U.S. Constitution put up for popular ratification reflected the pressing need, unique to a particular set of circumstances, to circumvent the state legislatures and place the new federal Constitution on legal footing superior to that of the states more than it signaled a sea change in how Founding-era Americans understood popular sovereignty and constitutionalism. Some people might have believed that such a transformation had occurred, but it seems evident that most did not. If they had, then eighteenth-century Americans would have broadly demanded that all subsequent constitutions made in their name be adopted by popular ratification, as that was now the single way that the sovereign people could express themselves constitutionally. But that plainly did not happen, as ratification was overlooked or rejected in the decades to follow.

The supposed ascendancy of the practice after it was adopted at the federal level, meanwhile, did not appear to raise any concerns about the legitimacy of existing state constitutions, hardly any of which had been ratified, and none of which were subsequently reapproved by new methods to conform to the supposed emerging legal orthodoxy. At the Constitutional Convention, several delegates openly cast doubt on the need to do so. While Oliver Ellsworth acknowledged that "a new sett of ideas seemed to have crept in," which appeared to vest "[c]onventions of the people . . . with power derived expressly from the people," with unique authority, he nonetheless stressed the limits of this thinking.[25] That was because such arguments, if extended to their logical conclusion, Elbridge Gerry explained, were liable to "prove an unconstitutionality in . . . some of the State Govts."[26] If only popularly ratified constitutions merited the label "constitution," Gerry noted, then virtually none of the existing American constitutions met the legal standard. "Inferences drawn from such a source," therefore, he concluded, "must be inadmissible."[27]

Even as new ideas and practices emerged, then, older ways of eliciting the people's consent endured. As Twitty shows, even after 1788, few Americans seemed to believe that constitutions, in order to be fixed, needed to be ratified.[28] Zephaniah Swift certainly did not think that ratification was necessary, writing about Connecticut's constitution (at the strikingly late date of 1795): "Some visionary theorists, have pretended that we have no constitution, because it has not been . . . ratified by the people," but the state's constitution "has been accepted and approved of by the people" by "tacit

agreement," and thereafter "ratified, confirmed, and approved by all suc-
ceeding ages."[29] Some may have embraced new forms of constitution making, but the transformation was neither uniform nor complete.

Meanwhile, it was one thing to accept or celebrate the importance of popular ratification and formal constitutional amendment as means of empowering the sovereign people to fix and alter constitutional norms, but quite
another to believe that these processes exhausted the means by which the
people could express their sovereign will. The new emphasis on conventions
seemed to sharply disaggregate sovereignty from government—the sovereign people now expressed themselves not in ordinary lawmaking but
through the constitution that they had expressly ratified.[30] But for years to
come, broad segments of the American population continued to assert that
the people's sovereignty was dynamic and mobile and could instantiate itself
in any number of settings—within and beyond the government.[31] Certainly,
some claimed that the "people" could exercise their sovereignty only through
proscribed constitutional mechanisms. But many others denied this proposition. The original impetus, after all, for devising novel mechanisms for the
adoption of constitutions and amendments had not been to circumscribe the
people themselves but rather to curtail the capacities of ordinary lawmaking.
To claim that Americans had arrived at a clear consensus by 1787 about the
nature of popular sovereignty—how it expressed itself constitutionally, and
when and how it could speak—is to brush away a huge swath of post-ratification history. Many Americans continued to assume that the sovereign
people could adjust or enforce *their* Constitution depending on circumstance
and need.[32]

That more capacious conception of popular sovereignty had undergirded
American rights declarations from the beginning. Most of those declarations
were, as we've seen, declaratory in character—using constitutional text to
identify preexisting rights, rather than using that text to determine the content of those rights. The substance of the underlying right, not the precise
textual formulation used to declare it, was, alone, what was fixed. Rights
declarations of this sort left the legal contours of those fundamental rights
underdetermined, precisely so that the people themselves could provide the
legal determinations that such a declaratory approach to constitutional rights
failed to specify. Most of the time, the people exercised their reserved authority to determine the content of their fundamental rights by acting through

their representative institutions, most especially legislatures and juries. But they also determined their rights through common law, which the people supposedly shaped and approved over time, and which judges could enforce on the perceived basis that they were finding, not making, law. What that meant was that fundamental rights were fixed, but determinations of those rights could evolve over time as the people wished.[33] In those instances in which a fundamental right was underdetermined and nothing in the consti-tutional enumeration of that particular right more concretely determined it—which was most of the time at the Founding—the determination of the right was not itself fixed, and certainly not fixed in the text declaring the right.[34] Neither the right nor the determinations of its exercise were often fixed in text. Because the former, while fixed, preceded textual enumeration, determinations of it could more easily change over time.[35] To ensure the sovereign people's self-governance, fixed constitutionalism would work in tandem with evolving constitutionalism.

All of which meant that, even after ratification of the U.S. Constitution, it was still easy for Americans to think of constitutional fixity much as they had before. Constitutions were and ought to be fixed; they embodied the people's sovereign authority and could be changed only with their sovereign approval; and certain special lawmaking practices seemed well suited to speak for the people themselves. Yet these ideas could easily be squared with a dynamic conception of fixity, especially if the conditions under which the people could exert their sovereignty remained a source of uncertainty. It would take more than an emerging commitment to popular ratification or conventions to re-make fixity itself.

A New Brand of Fixity

Only after the federal Constitution was written do we begin to see changes to the concept of fixity. Constitutional debates following ratification began to remake the idea of constitutional fixity. As the Constitution was increasingly tethered to distinctive notions of textual and archival constitutionalism, fixity and change were slowly, if not fully, disaggregated from one another. The Constitution's meaning was perceived to be fixed, as it always had been, but now in a potentially new kind of way. As American constitutional imagina-tion gradually fixated on the Constitution's physical locus (the language of its text) as well as its temporal one (a particular moment of founding), it became easier to see changes from that original fixed meaning as departures from, rather than elaborations of, that original meaning.[36] Things did not change all at once—it would take a long time and additional conceptual modifications to dislodge such firm habits. But the ground was beginning to shift. Whereas it had been second nature to think of constitutions as simultaneously fixed and evolving throughout most of the eighteenth century, it was becoming harder to see the American Constitution in that once conventional way. In fact, thanks to this transformation, some of those living on the other side of it had a hard time even recognizing what had once been. Commentators in the 1790s began claiming with mounting ferocity that the British constitution, because it was unwritten and customary, had never in fact been fixed and that American constitutions were, in sharp contrast, "certain and fixed," all because they had been "reduced to written exactitude and precision."[37] The significance of the conceptual transformation can be measured by what it was able to erase.

Once jettisoned, moreover, this older conception of fixity has never returned. Modern observers have followed the lead of some post-ratification Americans in assuming that the Constitution is *either* fixed or living, but never both, because the only way the Constitution could be fixed is if its word meanings are unchanged by practice and usage. In the 1790s, then, it was not that, as some might have it, an unfixed Constitution was fixed, or that everyone suddenly came to believe that the Constitution was fixed in this new way. Rather, under the pressure of transformative debate, the concept of fixity began to shift, altering the argumentative landscape and available possibilities. That originalists today assume there is one single way for the Constitution to be fixed is testament to what the 1790s helped bring about. The same goes for non-originalists, who rather than revive a long-forgotten brand of fixity typically reject the idea of a fixed constitution (at least in any determinative sense). In other words, positions that would have been unimaginable when the Constitution was first conceived came to define the terms of debate and shape how people imagined the Constitution.

Exploring how Americans' conception of fixity changed shows that nothing about the original Constitution mandated these positions. One can maintain fidelity to the original Constitution without asking whether its meaning is fixed or evolving. Assuming the logic of that choice presupposes a way of thinking about the Constitution that is separable from its original requirements. The easiest way to remind ourselves of this fact is to respond to originalist incantations that "the Constitution's meaning is fixed" with the simple query, "Fixed how?" With too little appreciation for the constitutional world from which the Constitution emerged, originalists write as if this were a redundant question, as if the Constitution could be fixed only in one way. In 1787, however, it was possible to think the Constitution was fixed in a radically different kind of way.

Liquidation

Recently, some originalists have latched onto the concept of constitutional liquidation to carve out space for a form of post-ratification constitutional change outside the amendment procedures specified in Article V that is nonetheless consistent with originalists' overarching commitment to constitutional fixity.[38] Inspired by its various invocations at the Founding, particularly by both James Madison and Alexander Hamilton in *The Federalist*, these originalists have contended that some indeterminate constitutional meanings were settled, or liquidated, over the course of the early republic, often outside of the courts.[39] Madison's well-known comment in *Federalist* 37 has been the touchstone: "All new laws, though articulated with the greatest technical skill, and passed on the fullest and most mature deliberation, are considered as more or less obscure and equivocal, until their meaning be liquidated and ascertained by a series of particular discussions and adjudications."[40] This idea, which Madison first penned in 1788, continued to preoccupy him throughout his life. Later, in 1819, he reiterated much the same point. It "was foreseen at the birth of the Constitution," he asserted, "that difficulties and differences of opinion might occasionally arise, in expounding terms & phrases necessarily used in such a Charter . . . and that it might require a regular course of practice to liquidate and settle the meaning of some of them."[41] Liquidation is not simply a curiosity, originalists maintain, but an important feature of the Founders' law: a legitimate way in which the Constitution could be fleshed out through post-enactment historical practice by non-judicial actors in the earliest years of the republic.

The Supreme Court's recently adopted "history and tradition" standard has been compared to liquidation. Rather than looking to the meaning or

understanding of a constitutional provision at the time of its enactment, this
standard considers whether a particular rights claim or form of legal regulation is "deeply rooted in the Nation's history and traditions"[42] by looking
broadly beyond judicial precedents and doctrines to general social practices
and pervasive social norms as instantiated in legal enactments, customs,
mores, or simply vibes that endured across the early decades of American
history.[43] Unlike vague appeals to enduring practice or tradition, however,
liquidation presumes settlement at some moment in time.

Although Caleb Nelson was the first to draw attention to liquidation in
originalist circles,[44] William Baude has offered the fullest account of the concept and its value to originalist theory through an analysis of Madison's extended commentary on it.[45] According to Baude, Madison thought that three
conditions needed to be met to liquidate the Constitution's meaning. First,
there needed to be textual indeterminacy—only genuinely ambiguous or
vague provisions were candidates for liquidation. Second, there needed to be
a course of deliberate practice—the indeterminacy had to be the source of
serious and sustained debate. Finally, third, there needed to be settlement—
where a particular candidate for interpretation was accepted by defenders
of competing interpretations and sanctioned by the public.[46] For Baude,
this process explains how President Madison could unhypocritically authorize a bill chartering a national bank in 1816, even though, in 1791, he had
proclaimed that bank's predecessor unconstitutional. In the intervening
years, Baude asserts, a once uncertain constitutional question had under-
gone a course of deliberate practice before being settled in the eyes of the
public. Madison thus acquiesced and accepted that a new constitutional
meaning had been liquidated.[47]

Liquidation thus provides an alternative originalist path to fixed linguistic
meaning, one seemingly endorsed at the Founding itself. Perhaps the Constitution was not born wholly fixed but became so shortly thereafter.[48] Perhaps early uncertainty, indeterminacy, and disputation are not at odds with
originalism but easily handled by it. Perhaps fixed meaning and deliberate
practice don't follow different paths but work in tandem. Liquidation offers
an intriguing wrinkle to originalists' long-standing notion of fixed constitutional meaning—one that seems eager to reconcile constitutional fixation
with (some) constitutional contestation, constitutional text with (some) constitutional practice, original meaning with (some) updating.

There is much to be said about this latest originalist innovation, perhaps most obviously that, by acknowledging a legitimate process through which the meaning of constitutional text might evolve, it constitutes a major concession, maybe even complete surrender, to the living constitutionalism that originalism was designed to combat. This is especially the case because, on originalists' own terms, liquidation remains remarkably ambiguous. What are the circumstances in which the Constitution is truly indeterminate? What counts as a genuinely deliberative practice that might properly liquidate meaning or as evidence of the public's clear approbation of a newly liquidated meaning? When has a dispute been clearly settled? These are but some of the questions that remain unanswered.[49] Pretty soon, liquidation simply becomes shorthand for the unruly history of American constitutional practice. Constitutional debate has almost always centered on indeterminacies of one kind or another. Most of these conflicts have been settled over time through a fluid constitutional politics and have remained only as settled as public opinion and the willingness of constitutional disputants have allowed. If most of this thick practice is consistent with originalism, then it becomes much harder to tell the difference between the theory and its competitors. If, moreover, liquidated meanings can be re-liquidated following the same procedures used in the first instance, as at least Baude and some originalists concede, then it becomes harder still.[50] It would seem yet another example of originalism slowly morphing into what it originally set out to defeat. Whither originalism?

But it is also unclear what this new originalist account of liquidation amounts to. Was the doctrine, as originalists have developed it, broadly endorsed at the time of the Founding, enough that it should be considered a constitutive feature of the Founders' law?[51] Or was the doctrine primarily of interest to Madison (and perhaps a smattering of like-minded elites)? Surely a Madisonian principle, however interesting, is nothing more than any other feature of Madison's constitutional thinking: one leading theorist's particular views. Baude is upfront about the fact that he has focused in depth only on Madison and that a more systematic review awaits completion, but he suggests that others at the Founding were drawn to the idea.[52] And other originalists seem convinced, having argued that liquidation was part of "[t]he framers' law."[53] Liquidation was surely a recurring motif and reference point in the early United States, but it hardly seems to have acquired the theoretical clarity or coherence that Madison attempted to give it. To the extent that liquidation was broadly accepted, it was likely little different from tradition- ally non-originalist ideas such as precedent or historical gloss.[54] Whatever liquidation may have meant at the time, however, it also certainly had its share of detractors, including especially the so-called Old Republicans who encompassed a crucial faction of Madison's own political party, and who criticized the core principles inherent to liquidation.[55]

The Madisonian imprimatur, of course, still matters. There's a good reason liquidation's champions have branded it in this way: linking this constitutional doctrine to the heroic aura of one of the foremost framers might impart just the Founding-era pedigree that it needs.[56] It likewise matters, then, whether Madison in fact ever settled on a clear theory of liquidation. It's doubtful that he did.[57] Throughout his life, Madison assuredly wrestled with the vital prob- lem the concept was devised to solve, but by his death he had yet to arrive at a decisive remedy.[58] He had much better luck posing the problem, and debunk- ing tidy solutions to it, than he did solving it.[59] He had a conception of liquida- tion, not a doctrine, as Baude and other originalists imply. And given Madison's own understanding of constitutionalism, it's doubtful he thought he needed the latter. For what's most clear, and most important, is that Madison never conceived of liquidation in the narrow fashion originalists allow. By their tell- ing, when Madison thought about constitutional liquidation, he adopted a quasi-judicial focus that was centered solely on the ambiguity of precise con- stitutional text. But this sketch fails to grasp that Madison had in mind a deeper sense of constitutional indeterminacy and, accordingly, a more capa- cious and robust brand of constitutional politics.[60] He was less preoccupied with fixing text and legal rules than he was with identifying a framework for political practice capable of stabilizing and, when needed, revising the regu- larities of a working constitutional system. He assumed, as a matter of course, that genuine forms of constitutional doubt would need to be resolved by the sovereign people through their elected representatives.[61] Like most constitu- tionalists at the time, he never thought judges could adequately settle these questions, above all because they lacked the institutional credibility to do so.[62] From this view, Madison recognized how deeply constitutionalism, of any kind, rested on practice and thus understood liquidation less as a recipe for narrowing the text's meaning and more as an account of how practice might narrow the terms of constitutional debate at the center of that practice.[63]

At the Founding, then, liquidation meant many things to many people, arguably never amounting to much more in theory or practice than the recognition that a dynamic brand of constitutional politics would be necessary for a working constitutional system; if it was Madisonian, it was not evidently more than that; and even then, its Madisonian imprimatur seems misplaced. Above all, liquidation was, at its core, largely inconsistent with the idea of judicial supremacy. Members of the Founding generation grabbed hold of it because they lived in a world of constitutional enforcement so radically different from our own, one in which few believed that Supreme Court justices would settle major constitutional controversies—like those that emerged over the boundaries between two rival branches of the federal government or the limits of federal power.[64] Taking liquidation seriously requires imagining a constitutional world in which judicial supremacy as we have come to understand it was largely unthinkable. To be sure, not all originalists endorse judicial supremacy. Baude, for instance, does not. But most originalists, including many who embrace liquidation, tend to presuppose a judge-centered view of constitutional interpretation and settlement. After all, their overarching goal has been to provide a method for interpreting the Constitution today, which principally has meant equipping federal judges with the interpretive tools they require. Originalists have thus attempted to marry Founding-era liquidation to a modern understanding of judicial enforcement, even though the former, purely understood, is incompatible with the latter. As with so much else, in uncritically assuming continuity between the constitutional past and present, originalists have inflected a Founding-era concept with the discordant trappings of current legal thinking, unaware they are deforming the very idea they've championed.

Be all that as it may, all this renewed interest in liquidation reveals, at base, that far more than the Constitution's bare meaning needed to be fixed in the decades following 1787. Originalists are surely eager to defend a relatively narrow brand of liquidation—deployed only when textual meaning is clearly indeterminate and acknowledged as binding only when that meaning is clearly settled. But that kind of narrow liquidation was rare in the decades following ratification. At that time, constitutional indeterminacy ran much deeper than the meaning of the Constitution's text. There were of course plenty of ambiguous constitutional clauses to debate and settle. But those living in ratification's immediate shadow craved something much broader: a more determinate sense of what the Constitution was and the characteristics that defined it. Efforts to liquidate the Constitution, not simply its meaning, could never be anything but large-scale struggles to settle a working vision of what the Constitution was, what kind of content the Constitution had, and thus what it even meant to claim that the Constitution had been fixed. What sort of thing, after all, were they trying to fix: the Constitution's linguistic meaning, its underlying principles, general fundamental law, something else? Fixity itself needed fixing.

Perhaps all these things were liquidated in the early republic. One could imagine originalists responding in that way. Over the course of the 1790s, it became easier to see the Constitution in textualist and archival terms, and from there to understand constitutional fixation in terms of time-locked language.[65] Even if nothing about the original Constitution necessitated these developments, perhaps those distinctive ways of understanding the U.S. Constitution were eventually settled through a course of practice. Maybe the entire Constitution, then, not simply its meaning, was liquidated in the first decades of its existence? If so, no originalist has yet made this argument, or worked out the implications of such an ambitious claim. It is one thing (though not a small thing) to square originalism with the liquidation of bits of constitutional meaning here and there, quite another to accept that the original Constitution *itself* was unsettled, even if it was subsequently liquidated. More than this, the argument would face a steep climb because, in the 1790s, American political leaders fixed neither the Constitution nor its meaning; what they fixed, at most, was a novel understanding of constitutional fixity itself. This transformation altered, and in some ways narrowed, the parameters and possibilities of constitutional argument, but it merely recast and restructured disagreement over fixity rather than eliminated it. Perhaps through this process, and the debates that shaped it, liquidation itself took on new meaning. As constitutional fixity and change became antagonists, perhaps liquidation came to focus primarily on textual meaning. But even if liquidation was liquidated as fixity was fixed—massive *ifs*—the essential point remains: the original Constitution did not necessitate any of these developments. It was done to the Constitution.

Taking liquidation seriously, in other words, underscores how unfixed the original Constitution initially was—not simply its meaning, but its essential nature. That there was robust discussion of liquidation throughout the early

republic underscores the depth of that contestation. Taking liquidation seriously also emphasizes how unfixed fixity initially was.

Contrary to what originalists often assume, constitutional fixity was not always as we recognize it. It had long been assumed that a fixed constitution
could also be an evolving constitution. Even as people gravitated toward new
ways of conceiving of fixed constitutions, older habits of thought lived on.
Even as some celebrated fixed constitution-making procedures, others continued to defend a dynamic vision of the people's sovereignty. Even as greater
emphasis was placed on constitutional text and the distinctive mechanism
for fashioning it, major questions continued to be resolved through a fluid
constitutional politics. At the Founding, the very concept of fixity was up for
grabs.

7

Before the Legalized Constitution

> A constitution ought to be understood by everyone. The most hum-
> bling and trifling characters in the country have a right to know what
> foundation they stand upon.
>
> — William Lenoir, North Carolina Convention, 1788

THE ORIGINAL CONSTITUTION WAS neither written nor fixed in the ways we might assume, but perhaps nowhere is the difference between past and present quite as clear as the Constitution's early relationship to law. Here, the anachronisms run especially deep.

Originalists, by and large, tend to assume that the Constitution is distinctively lawlike. It is a lawyer's and judge's instrument, to be interpreted by known rules of legal interpretation, and to be understood within the framework of constitutional law.[1] Some originalists have even made these pervasive assumptions the basis for a distinct version of the theory: original methods originalism. John McGinnis and Michael Rappaport are its most devoted defenders.[2] Their core claim is that meaning follows method: to recover the Constitution's original meaning, originalists should employ the interpretive methods that would have been used at the Founding to construe an instrument such as the Constitution.[3] This charge rests on two basic premises. First, it assumes that the Constitution is, in essence, a conventional legal text, written in the technical language of the law.[4] Second, it asserts that, because the Constitution is a legal text, the original methods for constitutional interpretation are simply the conventional rules of legal interpretation that were familiar and widely agreed upon at the Founding.[5] When the Constitution was enacted, there was broad agreement over what kind of rules ought to guide its interpretation because the Constitution was a familiar form of law. McGinnis and Rappaport have even asserted, more specifically, that the Constitution was essentially like a statute, and thus the original rules for interpreting it were simply the known rules of statutory construction.[6] Other originalists, meanwhile, have claimed that the Constitution was originally akin to a power of attorney.[7] Still others have asserted that the law of nations supplied background rules of interpretation for understanding the Constitution's key enactments.[8] While not all originalists would agree with these particular conclusions, most of the theory's champions assume the validity of what precedes these specific claims: that the Constitution is comparable to other kinds of law and thus is subject to familiar forms of legal reasoning.[9]

At the Founding, however, whether the Constitution was a distinctively legal instrument was a subject of bitter and ongoing debate. The Constitution was obviously law of a kind—the fundamental law of the United States—that both created a host of legal powers and privileges and imposed various legal duties and obligations. But that didn't mean the Constitution was alike in kind to other more familiar forms of law. And even among those who were willing to concede that the Constitution was akin to conventional law, it was decidedly unclear what, if any, rules existed to guide the Constitution's interpretation. Ratification did not quickly give way to the legalized Constitution that originalists so often take for granted. Only over an extended period of time, and as a result of considerable constructive work, was the Constitution *turned into* a common legal artifact. Only at this later moment did something like the genre of constitutional law become imaginable. And even at that point, different ways of thinking about the Constitution still endured. The Constitution wasn't *just* law when it was written and ratified, nor, indeed, for a long time thereafter. Consequently, the foundations of original methods originalism, as well as the broader set of originalist attitudes that breathe life into them, are deeply mistaken.

Debating Legalism

One of *the* defining debates of the early republic, as Gerald Leonard and Saul Cornell have explained, was over "legalism," the notion that the Constitution was a form of conventional law to be interpreted by legal techniques and enforced in courts of law.[10] During this period, anti-legalists vigorously maintained that the Constitution was distinct from conventional law and meant to be enforced by institutions other than courts. This was a debate the legalists ultimately won. But their victory was hardly foreordained. Indeed, from the perspective of the Founding, it is remarkable that a legalized understanding of constitutionalism ever came to predominate in the United States.

Anti-legalism had deep roots in eighteenth-century America. It was widely assumed, both before and after the Revolution, that fundamental and ordinary law were distinct in kind, and thus constitutions (be they British or American) were categorically different from other legal standards.[11] Following independence, American constitutionalists emphasized that their constitutions were a unique brand of popular law derived from and answerable to the people's authority.[12] These general attitudes at once grew out of and helped fuel a powerful brand of popular constitutionalism that was especially hostile to elite legal authority.[13] Popular constitutionalists believed that the people themselves, not legal elites, should control the interpretation and enforcement of a constitution. That meant empowering those institutions (legislatures, juries, militias, and even crowds) that most closely embodied the people to enforce constitutional authority and resolve fundamental disputes arising under it.[14] Popular constitutionalists were often deeply distrustful of lawyers and judges, convinced that they often circumvented the people's authority through artful legal reasoning and manipulation.[15] Naturally, popular constitutionalists were skeptical of judicial review of duly enacted laws.

Thanks to how pervasive these attitudes were, efforts to defend legalist principles, however tame, never went unchallenged and, given the prevailing belief that fundamental law was distinct in kind from other forms of law, often faced major blowback. During the ratification debates, many observers recoiled at the idea that the proposed federal Constitution might be a legal instrument. To preserve the promise of the Revolution, the Constitution needed to be treated as a "people's" document.[16] "A Constitution," insisted Patrick Henry, "ought to be like a beacon, held up to the public eye so as to be understood by every man."[17] Several Anti-Federalists who shared Henry's sympathies complained that the Constitution was likely to be colonized by lawyers. It seemed to have been constructed so that "the Scribes & Pharisees only will be able to interpret, & give it a Meaning."[18] Federalists recognized the force of this charge and were quick to dispel the myth behind it. "It is an excellency of this Constitution," declared the future Supreme Court justice Oliver Ellsworth, "that it is expressed with brevity, and in the plain common language of mankind. Had it swelled into the magnitude of a volume, there would have been more room to entrap the unwary, and the people who are to be its judges, would have had neither patience nor opportunity to understand it." Indeed, he went on, "[h]ad it been expressed in the scientific language of law," it might have been clear to lawyers, "but to the great body of the people altogether obscure, and to accept it they must leap in the dark." Adopting a technical dialect would have been a profound mistake. "The people to whom . . . the great appeal is made, best understand those compositions which are concise and in their own language."[19] The Constitution was emphatically not written in the "scientific language of law"; it was written for and in the vernacular of the people. Anyone who claimed otherwise misunderstood both the Constitution and the very purpose of constitutionalism.

At the time it was ratified, the U.S. Constitution was not conventional law in any plain sense. Those who championed popular constitutionalism wholly rejected any insinuation that it might be. Even those who did not share popular constitutionalists' hostility toward judges and legal reasoning, moreover, assumed that fundamental constitutional disputes could be resolved only through "an appeal to the people themselves."[20] As James Madison wrote in 1788 while commenting on his ally Thomas Jefferson's draft constitution for Virginia: "In the State Constitutions & indeed the Fedl. one also, no provision is made for the case of a disagreement in expounding them; and as the Courts are generally the last in making their decision, it results to them." Troublingly, "[t]his makes the Judiciary Dept paramount in fact to the Legislature, which was never intended, and can never be proper."[21] Jefferson emphatically agreed, carrying the point even further. Even if he had exercised caution during his presidency as the more radical elements in his party waged war on the judiciary, he never backed down from his belief that final interpretation of the Constitution belonged to the people, not judges.[22] The idea of "judges as the ultimate arbiters of all constitutional questions" was, in Jefferson's estimation "a very dangerous doctrine indee[d] and one which would place us under the despotism of an Oligarchy." The "constitution has erected no such single tribunal" to decide contested constitutional questions. "I know no safe depository of the ultimate powers of society," he concluded, "but the people themselves."[23] The Constitution was not only superior to ordinary law but distinct in kind from it.[24]

It would be years before the Constitution resembled conventional law. This transformation was not inevitable, easy, or complete. It was born of political conflict over the Constitution's relationship to the people's sovereignty, between popular constitutionalists, who continued to insist that the people themselves should wield constitutional authority, and elites, especially jurists, who, in the face of popular constitutionalists' challenges, began, with mounting conviction, to defend legalist principles.

The dynamics of the debate mirrored its substance. The struggle over who controlled the Constitution and its interpretation was litigated across political society. Not easily confined to courthouses or legislatures, it spilled out into the public sphere, onto the pages of newspapers and pamphlets, into the raucous proceedings of public meetings, and through the boisterous clamors of the streets.[25] The popular and public nature of constitutional debate was nothing new. From the imperial-crisis debates that had precipitated American independence to the far-reaching ratification debates that had ripped across the union, American constitutional debate had long been a broad, relatively open conversation among thousands, shaped by ordinary citizens and popular agitators as much as political elites.[26] Such disputes only turned more democratic and raucous in the 1790s, as the dramatic expansion of print further extended the constitutional conversation and the people "out-of-doors," who had long been a formidable presence in American political and legal life, asserted their power more than ever before.[27] Along with their allies in political office, they rallied around popular constitutionalism, insisting that the true meaning of the Revolution and the Constitution's opening words could be realized only if the people writ large energetically exercised their supreme sovereignty. The mere fact that debate over popular constitutionalism was so avowedly popular in character underscored what an uphill climb defenders of legalism faced in these early years.

By the end of the 1790s, clear fault lines had emerged from the debate over legalism. At least three distinct groups defended three distinct conceptions of the Constitution's relationship to law.[28] Federalists defended a legalist Constitution that embraced core common-law principles and protections, especially for property and contract, and afforded judges considerable control over the Constitution's meaning. Radical, more democratically minded Republicans thoroughly rejected Federalist legalism, championing a populist, anti-legalist Constitution in its place. They criticized judge-controlled common law and proclaimed that the sovereign people alone had final say over the Constitution's meaning. The Georgia legislature's decision in 1796 to rescind the notorious Yazoo lands sale—on the grounds that the legislature was popularly authorized to perform such an extraordinary form of constitutional review—personified this vibrant brand of popular constitutionalism and its anti-legalist ideology.[29] And it was but one of many examples. Moderate Republicans, meanwhile, fell in between these two camps.[30] They shared many of the radicals' misgivings but valued an independent judiciary and charted a middle course, as illustrated in their opposition to the Alien and Sedition Acts.[31]

These were not mere interpretive divisions but disagreements over the essential nature of the Constitution, and the debate only intensified following Jefferson's election as president. The "Revolution of 1800" carried not only Jefferson but Republican majorities in both the House and the Senate to power. But Federalists retained control of the judiciary, and their cause was soon bolstered by the appointment of John Marshall as chief justice on the Supreme Court.[32] From this remaining "strong hold," as Jefferson famously put it, Federalists' legalism continued to calcify, until pretty soon most of them were treating the Constitution as conventional law that only they could rightfully interpret.[33]

It is crucial to understand how and why the thinking of elite jurists changed over the quarter century that followed ratification. During this period, they firmly defended the value of legal reasoning and the role of judges in republican society, but the character of this defense, and what it implied about the Constitution, transformed in subtle yet significant ways. In defending legal reasoning and judicial authority in the early 1790s, Federalists were not pointing the way toward something recognizably modern. On the contrary, they were clinging to the standard features of classical jurisprudence, especially the assumption that common-law thinking helped discover the laws of consent, reason, and nature in which the Constitution as fundamental law was essentially embedded. In their minds, there was no tension between popular sovereignty and the common law.[34] As Jesse Root asserted in 1798, "unwritten customs and regulations," much like statutes enacted by popularly elected legislatures, "have the force of laws under the authority of the people," and therefore it was assumed that "the courts of justice recognize and declare them to be such."[35]

This posture changed as popular constitutionalists and their allies began denouncing this brand of common-law jurisprudence.[36] Among a bevy of charges, they complained that the common law was not suitable for republican America. "There have been strong prejudices against what is called the Common Law," an observer noted in 1801, "from an idea, that it is a system imposed upon us, by a power now foreign to our national existence."[37] Even more stridently, popular constitutionalists stressed how dangerous it was to leave the law in the hands of lawyers and judges who were prone to exploit formal and technical readings to obfuscate understanding and impose their own will. "[T]he decision of the judges," declared Philadelphia radicals in 1807, "is the most artful and terrible engine, in a country, which believes itself free." Through legal cunning, "the judges very often discover that the law, *as written*, may be made to *mean some thing which the legislature never thought of.* The greatest part of their decisions are in fact, and in effect, making *new laws.*"[38]

From these complaints sprang support for legal codification: the desire to replace obstruse, ad hoc, undemocratic judge-made law throughout the states with simpler, formal, democratic legislative law.[39] It is "of great importance, that those legal principles, which have been thus established by the people themselves, should be reduced . . . to a system," declared James Sullivan, the Republican attorney general of Massachusetts, in 1801, "so we may know by what laws we are governed. We have no method to come at this knowledge, in our present situation," he complained, "but by turning over a multitude of books, and by spending a great length of time in our courts of justice."[40] As a corollary of this struggle, populist critics of judicial machinations also targeted the idea of a federal common law—the idea that federal courts enjoyed a general common-law jurisdiction similar to state courts—that a range of Federalists had supported since ratification.[41]

According to Republicans, and a growing swath of the American people, judges now stood squarely in the way of the Revolution's democratic energy.

In leveling these charges with such ferocity, Republicans were driving a wedge between the common law and the people's consent. Although Federalist jurists remained committed to legalism, the ground beneath their feet had shifted. A crisis of legitimacy was imminent.

Such attacks forced Federalist jurists to redefine themselves—to take refuge in a new professional practice and identity. Henceforth, they would no longer brand themselves as classical constitutionalists engaged in a harmonious synthesis of human nature and society but instead as modern legalists who practiced a technical science of legal analysis.[42] As such, they called for legal reform. They insisted that law was a science demanding specialized training, that lay lawyers and judges ought to be replaced by qualified professionals. And to ensure that these legal professionals would have adequate resources, they called for the systematic compilation and dissemination of legal decisions and opinions.[43] Eventually, by the middle decades of the nineteenth century, lawyers of most every political stripe presented law as scientific, methodical, and apolitical.[44] Throughout, Federalist jurists maintained their allegiance to common-law reasoning even though through these shifts it had lost so much of its earlier valiance.

Legalizing the Constitution

Against this backdrop, the Marshall Court legalized the Constitution.[45] That is, Marshall and his colleagues began treating the Constitution as akin to ordinary law—interpreting it as though it were a statute. In subjecting the Constitution to the tools and methods of statutory interpretation, they made it easier to see the Constitution as a kind of super-statute—superior in nature but alike in kind.[46] They made the Constitution seem as though it was just another kind of law, to be adjudicated by legal professionals who now increasingly saw themselves as practitioners of a technical science that was removed from partisan politics.[47] These habits of constitutional interpretation, which spread rapidly across the legal landscape, had the effect of domesticating the Constitution in courts of law—making conventional legal interpretation and adjudication of the Constitution ubiquitous and ordinary.[48] In turn, these developments helped lay the groundwork for the modern genre of constitutional law, defined as it has been ever since by a narrow brand of legal analysis and exposition, a tidy conception of doctrine built around case law, and an increasingly legalistic conception of constitutional substance.[49] Marshall and his colleagues, working in tandem with other lawyers and judges, helped turn a robust, popular, quasi-political process into a mandarin-controlled, technical exercise. Even more, with the concerted assistance of an army of supporting jurists, they helped erase the transformation they had helped bring about. In the swelling volumes of professional legal literature, they presented this new legalized Constitution as "neutral, objective, scientific."[50] At the center of this literature were treatises, none of which more clearly embodied the twin processes of legalization and erasure than Joseph Story's *Commentaries on the Constitution* published in 1833.

Perhaps nothing better captures this transformation than the fate of the Constitution's Preamble. Originally, when the Constitution was treated as "an ordinance and establishment of the people," the Preamble had been its cornerstone.[51] In the eyes of many, from Supreme Court justices like James Wilson to ordinary Americans who fervently believed that the promise of the Revolution was tethered to the promise of popular sovereignty, the Preamble had been proof positive of the Constitution's exceptional character.[52] The "single sentence in the Preamble is tantamount to a volume," Wilson had once declared, "and contains the essence of all the bills of rights that have been or can be devised."[53] As legalists treated the Constitution more and more like a statute, however, the Preamble became like any other statutory preamble—a bit of pretty poetry that merely prefaced the main event. Four decades later, its import had eroded to the point that Story would identify it only as a resource for resolving ambiguity in the rest of the instrument.[54]

But however ascendant, the legalized Constitution was not without competitors. Even after it had triumphed within the federal judiciary, popular constitutionalism endured.[55] In 1825, the chief justice of the Supreme Court of Pennsylvania, John Bannister Gibson, wrote in dissent, "I am of [the] opinion that it rests with the people, in whom full and absolute sovereign power resides to correct abuses in legislation, by instructing their representatives to repeal the obnoxious act." And for that reason, the "judiciary . . . cannot take cognizance of a collision between a law and the constitution."[56] While the Marshall Court defended one particular normative legal order, moreover, other nineteenth-century Americans—from free Black, enslaved, and Native peoples to white women, and scores of middling white men— successfully defended competing legal orders of their own.[57] Even after the

Constitution became law to some, it remained something else to many others.[58] As a result, when originalists emphasize the Constitution's conventional lawlike character, they privilege one normative order that happened to take shape above others that were no less legitimate.

But surely much of the reason originalists privilege the legalized Constitution is that it remains hard to see how the Constitution might ever have been different. Early nineteenth-century jurisprudes proved quite successful in convincing, first, lawyers and then, later, a broader segment of American society that the law-centric Constitution was not only logical but inevitable. Yet, if our goal is to see the original Constitution as it once was, we have to look beyond this erasure: we have to see the Constitution before it was legalized and before the genre of constitutional law existed or made much sense.

In the beginning, constitutional expectations were vastly different. Nothing more clearly illustrates just how distinctive they were than the remarkable fact that, throughout the 1790s, none of the major constitutional questions that Americans debated ended up in court.[59] Virtually no one thought that core constitutional controversies—not ordinary legal disputes arising under federal law, but debates that touched on the inherent structure of the constitutional system or raised fundamental doubts about its central principles or operations—ought to be adjudicated in court. Those questions needed to be resolved by the people themselves through their elected representatives in the political branches. The most important constitutional debate of the era—over chartering a national bank—ended just that way. The question was fiercely debated in Congress and then sent to President George Washington for consideration. He solicited an opinion from his secretary of state, Thomas Jefferson, who wrote, "The negative of the President is the shield provided by the Constitution to protect against the invasions of the legislature."[60] Jefferson's meaning was clear: Washington needed to take his veto decision seriously because it would be *the* decision. In sharp contrast to today, no one contemplated the possibility that one could or should challenge the legislation in federal court. Once the political branches had decided the fundamental limits of federal power, that was the end of the debate—and indeed it was. Only decades later would anyone think differently.

From our perspective, this is all unfamiliar. It can't be emphasized enough. The idea that the Constitution would ever be controlled or shaped primarily by legal processes organized around the Supreme Court is thoroughly un-originalist. Perhaps nothing better captures how far we've traveled, and how profoundly we've departed from the original Constitution, than the extent to which we've accepted judicial control of our constitutional order. In the Constitution's earliest years, no one anticipated that peculiar development.

In part through the work of the Marshall Court, the unthinkable eventually became commonplace. But we should not anachronistically impose later developments back onto the original Constitution. We must see the legalized Constitution for what it was: a later invention—an unexpected, contingent development born of years of debate, maneuvering, intellectual innovation, and change. Joseph Story was not referring to the original Constitution in his *Commentaries* so much as establishing a Constitution that he, and those who shared his predilections, had helped invent. It would be a significant mistake to confuse the two.

Fighting over the Rules of Interpretation

Because the Constitution's relationship to law was initially so contested, so too was the method of its interpretation. When the Constitution first appeared, there were simply no agreed-upon rules for interpreting it.[61]

There were, to be sure, various kinds of legal interpretive rules available. But these varied depending on the legal instrument in question— statutes, contracts, and treaties were each governed by distinct interpretive protocols—and the kind of law it embodied.[62] And, as the protracted debate over legalism reveals, it was an open and contested question whether any such rules even applied to the federal Constitution in the first place. Some analogies were seldom used—the Constitution, for instance, was hardly ever compared to a power of attorney.[63] But others proved more common as interpreters sought to establish a foothold.[64] It is understandable why, in hopes of finding interpretive traction, various American political and legal elites drew on different methods proscribed by William Blackstone, Emmerich de Vattel, Thomas Rutherforth, and other widely cited legal theorists. But it is every bit as understandable why such efforts invited resistance and critique. To those desperate to defend popular constitutionalism, these appeals to legal authorities fundamentally misjudged the task at hand.[65] But even those who were willing to accept that the Constitution resembled conventional law were often struck by the instrument's sheer novelty, at least enough to conclude that no existent set of interpretive rules automatically applied.[66] Doubt thus ran along several dimensions.[67]

The issue of fit was clearest when it came to common-law rules for statutory construction (laid out most famously in Blackstone's *Commentaries*).[68] Founding-era Americans who were friendlier to legal reasoning sometimes instinctively drew on those common-law rules, but whenever they did others were quick to raise powerful objections. Their detractors noted that the content of such rules was contested.[69] Or they stressed that such rules, being meant for statutes, were inapplicable to a constitution. "A Constitution differs from a law," declared Edmund Randolph, the nation's first attorney general, in Virginia's ratifying convention in 1788. "For a law only embraces one thing," he explained, whereas "a Constitution embraces a number of things," and on account of those differences, "is to have a more liberal construction."[70] Elite jurists, meanwhile, as we have seen, initially clung to a conception of fundamental law that set constitutions apart from statutes.[71] Interpreting the Constitution, they argued, often meant applying general legal principles to the case at hand, not analyzing words or grammar in light of familiar interpretive techniques.[72] Anti-legalists, meanwhile, went so far as to claim that interpretive rules like Blackstone's, embedded as they were in British legal culture, were inapplicable in a republic. "[W]hy should these States be governed by British laws?" Benjamin Austin asked skeptically. "Can the monarchical and aristocratical institutions of England, be consistent with the republican principles of our constitution?"[73]

If familiar legal rules presented intractable issues of fit, perhaps there were rules specifically suited for constitutions? After all, the U.S. Constitution of 1787 was not the first constitution Americans had known. But here the federal Constitution's uncertain and contested character posed particular difficulties. Not only was it unclear whether the Constitution could be usefully analogized to other legal instruments, so too was it unclear whether it could be analogized to other constitutions. In broad strokes, the federal Constitution shared much in common with the British constitution, Americans' colonial charters, their state constitutions, and the Articles of Confederation. But it was not exactly like any of them. The British constitution was largely customary in character and shaped by the needs and practices of a distinct society and legal order. The state constitutions departed in obvious ways from those meant to govern a federal system rather than a single state and, with the advantage of time, struck many American observers as tentative and flawed attempts to constitute republican government and fundamental law rather than mature models to emulate. The Articles of Confederation were the immediate successor to the federal Constitution, so offered the most promise. But they rested on a distinct foundation and, by 1787, had been the source of little interpretive scrutiny that was liable to provide useful guidance.[74] More importantly still, the Revolutionary American experience of debating the British constitution and then drawing up new state constitutions had raised so many fundamental questions and transformed so many crucial constitutional assumptions that, by 1787, little about constitutionalism itself was clear and settled.[75] Americans were still trying to sort out what a constitution precisely was, including what of their inheritance should be incorporated or rejected and how, if at all, a national constitution designed for a federal system deviated from other examples.

Such uncertainty hindered any effort to draw on available interpretive protocols for construing transfers of sovereignty in public law, especially those found in writings on the law of nations. Originalist scholars Anthony Bellia, Jr., and Bradford Clark have provocatively claimed that because the Constitution was an instrument designed to transfer sovereignty, it incorporated these interpretive rules when it was enacted.[76] Unlike rules of statutory construction, these interpretive guidelines derived from the law of nations seemed more applicable to instruments like constitutions that were authoritative expressions of sovereign authority, especially those like the U.S. Constitution that reconstituted a federal union of states. In addition, as we have seen, Founding-era legal elites regularly drew on the law of nations for guidance in understanding their legal and constitutional order.[77] That said, while the law of nations could delineate the various rights and obligations of states and confederacies, it couldn't explain, as an initial matter, what *kind* of state or confederacy the United States of America happened to be. Thus, while authoritative commentaries on the law of nations helped explain how to interpret transfers of sovereignty, for those rules to guide U.S. constitutional interpretation, one first needed to understand who or what was sovereign in the United States and how the Constitution had altered or reinforced that arrangement—matters that were deeply uncertain and contested from the beginning.[78]

Discerning how or even whether certain interpretive principles drawn from the law of nations applied to the U.S. Constitution required first clarifying the nature of the American federal union: the locus and distribution of sovereignty within it, the legal status of the individual states, and the nature of the American people (or peoples) whose authority was said to be fundamental. As we saw in chapter 5, there was nothing straightforward about this task. From the start, Americans debated whether the union or the states had come first.[79] Related, there was broad uncertainty over the legal status of the states—whether they had ever been sovereign or remained so after the Constitution replaced the Articles of Confederation.[80] Complicating matters further still, in the years leading up to the Federal Convention, Americans had begun remaking the concept of sovereignty, locating it outside of government in the people themselves—a move that called into question the notion that any government could claim traditional rights of sovereignty.[81] These thorny matters weren't easily ignored either, for the nature of both the union and the constitutional instrument that structured it hinged on what sorts of parties had putatively formed each. The issues were tightly entwined. Maybe the United States was a confederacy of sovereign states bound together by a federal treaty; or perhaps it was a national union held together by a constitution. To many observers, the move to replace the Articles of Confederation with a genuine constitution of government signaled a dramatic transformation.[82] In the Federal Convention, James Madison sharply distinguished between "*a league* or *treaty*," which the Articles of Confederation had been, and "a *Constitution*," which they now sought to erect.[83] For many, this one fact— that the U.S. Constitution was a genuine constitution—immediately nullified all comparisons to treaties and, with that, arguably many of the interpretive rules supplied by law of nations theorists, which were best suited for construing agreements made between sovereign powers. Later, however, some interpreters would come to claim controversially that the federal Constitution was nothing more than a treaty between sovereign states, to justify the separate states' retained authority to nullify federal law and secede from the union.[84] But in so doing, these so-called compact theorists revealed how contested the nature of the union remained well into the nineteenth century. For every step of the way, others emphatically rejected their understanding of the United States and its attendant claims about the Constitution and sovereignty within the federal system.[85]

By focusing attention on how sovereignty had been transferred under the U.S. Constitution, then, law of nations principles helped frame the debate.

But those principles couldn't explain who or what had been sovereign in the American union before 1787 or how the Constitution had altered that uncertain arrangement. To figure that out, interpreters had to turn elsewhere. For that reason alone, interpretive principles drawn from the law of nations simply could not supply ready-made rules for U.S. constitutional interpretation.

When it came to rules of interpretation, there was simply no escaping a basic fact: the Constitution of 1787 was simply an unprecedented kind of thing.[86] Its deeper nature, and thus the kind of interpretive rules necessary to explicate it, could only be worked out over time. In this early unsettled context, any claim about which interpretive rules applied to the Constitution necessarily amounted to a provocative argument about what the Constitution was and required.[87] Therein lies the true history of rules for U.S. constitutional interpretation. From ratification on, countless constitutional disputants claimed that certain rules suited the situation at hand, but always in hopes of making a controversial proposition a reality. Their success would hinge not on the true nature of the Constitution or the right understanding of law but instead on how well they could convince others to follow their lead.

Interpretive rules were forged in the cauldron of constitutional debate. Founding-era constitutionalists knew better than to presume that the Constitution came with a clear set of interpretive rules; they debated what those rules ought to be in hopes of establishing the rules. They fought over whether existent rules or techniques were applicable or whether new rules were needed for a new kind of constitution and, if so, where those might come from. When someone claimed that certain rules applied, that often became a source of debate. There were thus no clear original interpretive methods or, as some have claimed, obvious default rules for construing an object like the Constitution.[88] Nor was this uncertainty easily worked out.[89] Whether the Constitution was going to be treated as closer in kind to a statute, treaty, or corporate charter, or recognized as wholly distinct in kind from any of these analogues, was going to be determined through debate. As we have seen, it was only after judges successfully legalized the Constitution that it become common to interpret it like a statute. Yet, as early disagreement over interpretive methods reveals, this later development hardly amounted to legal professionals figuring out what the Constitution required from the beginning. Instead, it marked an effort to turn the Constitution into something that few would have originally accepted it to be. This later judicial commitment to legalized interpretation can only be

understood as a product of original interpretive disagreement, not used to explain it away.[90]

If we look closely at the Constitution's earliest years, it's impossible to see
anything but a series of debates *over* methods of interpretation.[91] To consider
just one prominent example: the famous debate over chartering a national
bank in 1791 was nothing if not a debate over interpretive rules.[92] The participants in Congress and beyond explicitly debated which rules were needed
to decipher whether the Constitution allowed the national government to
exercise the contested power. This was not a narrow debate over the gram-
matical meaning of particular words, such as "necessary and proper," or the
application of familiar canons of construction. Disputes over those things
unfolded amid a much wider debate over whether the Constitution erected a
government of, as James Madison put it, "limited and enumerated powers"
or a national government equipped with certain inherent powers.[93] The parsing of "necessary" and the (occasional) invocations of Blackstone's rules
were part of a broader struggle over how the Constitution ought to be read.
The rules for interpretation that Madison outlined in his opening speech
challenging the bank amounted to a larger rule: interpret the Constitution as
though it vested no powers save those expressly specified and any necessary
incidents that followed.[94] Fisher Ames, Madison's most able challenger on
the House floor, countered by advancing a radically different rule: interpret
the Constitution as though it vested all powers "necessary to the end for
which the constitution was adopted."[95] Madison's rule discounted the Preamble, under the assumption that it offered no evidence of additional government power.[96] Ames's rule, in contrast, underscored the fundamental
significance of the Preamble, treating it as sure evidence of additional national power.[97] Beneath their competing rules were competing views of federal union: Ames thought the United States was a full-fledged nation,
whereas Madison did not. Their exchange was hardly a debate over the application of agreed-upon rules, but a debate over the rules themselves.

The urge to locate underlying interpretive agreement in debates like these
has ever diminishing returns. Without needing to unpack the other constitutional arguments made for and against the bank, we can simply consider what
archnemeses Thomas Jefferson and Alexander Hamilton had to say once the
congressional debate had concluded: Jefferson defended strict construction of
the Constitution, whereas Hamilton advocated broad construction. In short,

they offered radically different methods of constitutional interpretation.[98] If such sharply opposed interpretive approaches, which yielded such profoundly conflicting results, can somehow be lumped together as variations of a common commitment to shared interpretive methods, then the category of interpretive rules ceases to have meaning. Once we find ourselves at such an elevated level of generality, it is easy to identify consensus—everyone in the debate tacitly agreed on the interpretive rule that they should be interpreting the Constitution and not something else. But if that counts as agreement on interpretive rules, then we've lost the thread.

Most importantly of all, a fruitless search for common ground precludes us from seeing what matters: Founding-era Americans had to work out methods for constitutional interpretation, not simply appeal to neatly packaged preexisting recipes and formulas. And that search for the rules of American constitutional interpretation proved a generative source of debate and creativity that has never ceased.

8

Were the Founders Originalists?

[I]t is ... dangerous ... for the historian of ideas to approach his
material with preconceived paradigms.
— Quentin Skinner, 1969

GIVEN HOW DEEPLY CONTESTED the constitution—both its nature and the
appropriate method for interpreting it—initially was, perhaps we can finally
put to rest an age-old question that has proved remarkably resilient: Were the
Founders originalists?

The question itself has enjoyed a tumultuous career. Early forerunners to
originalism called for the Constitution to be interpreted by recourse to the original intent of its framers, often assuming that the Founders themselves endorsed
this method of interpretation.[1] After H. Jefferson Powell famously argued that
the Founders did not in fact endorse this method of interpretation, originalists
retreated from the claim.[2] One of the reasons so many originalists gravitated to
public meaning originalism was because that version of the theory supposedly
neutralized the critique that the Founders were not themselves originalists by
disaggregating the Constitution's meaning from the early history of its interpretation. Yet originalists never quite abandoned the argument, and of late, it has
enjoyed a powerful resurgence, proliferating across the originalist landscape
once again.[3] Perhaps few contemporary originalists would unflinchingly assent
to Ilan Wurman's extravagant claim: "[M]ake no mistake about it: The Founders

were originalists."[4] But the sentiment nevertheless enjoys broad support among the theory's champions.[5] Even as originalism has reinvented itself many times over, the idea that the Founders were themselves originalists has endured.

In many respects, originalists' continued commitment to the idea that the Founders saw the Constitution in the same way they do is not surprising. Originalism fundamentally relies on the cultural authority of the Founders. Academic originalists like to claim that they are immune from the broader political and rhetorical dimensions of the debate, but it is obvious that the theory's resilience is entangled with the broader authority the American Founding has always enjoyed in American civic life.[6] Naturally, then, even if originalists claim not to care about subjective attitudes at the Founding, it bolsters their case to be able to claim that the Founders were like them—that originalism was sanctioned from the start. As several scholars have noted, argument from honored historical authority has long been a dominant feature of American constitutional culture.[7] While most originalists claim to be focused on the Constitution, not the Founders, they are still eager to enlist the Founders' support.

It's not all cultural politics either. No matter the stated commitments of originalist theorists, no matter how aggressively they separate meaning from early practice and expectations, it is hard to make a convincing case for originalism— for a return to the nation's *origins*—if the Founders did not endorse it too. If an account of the Constitution, its meaning, and its interpretation is at odds with the generation who brought that Constitution into being and set it in motion, it is more easily dismissed. Originalists seem to appreciate as much, which is part of the reason they have always been unwilling to move on from the Founders' own interpretive lessons, no matter what else they might maintain.

Whatever might be driving them, it's clear that the question—Were the Founders originalists?—can be revived, time and again, in part because it seems like such an obvious place to start. But it turns out that it's simply the wrong question to ask, one that exposes yet more ways in which originalists bury the past beneath anachronism.

Myth and Anachronism

It is not hard to canvass constitutional rhetoric across the long Founding—the half century or so that followed 1787—and find statements that seem to resemble originalism. Throughout this period, Americans of all

political stripes were fond of evoking the Constitution's framers and pledging loyalty to the true meaning that they had laid down.[8]

Keen to place the Founders firmly in their camp, originalists have routinely drawn our attention to a handful of well-worn quotations. For obvious
reasons, the purported "father of the Constitution," James Madison, has
been a particular focus. A few passages from the course of his long career in
American political life play an outsized role in originalist work. Their favor-
ite is an excerpt from a letter Madison wrote in 1824, in which he declared:

> I entirely concur in the propriety of resorting to the sense in which the Con-
> stitution was accepted and ratified by the nation. In that sense alone it is the
> legitimate Constitution. And if that be not the guide in expounding it, there
> can be no security for a consistent and stable, more than for a faithful exer-
> cise of its powers. If the meaning of the text be sought in the changeable
> meaning of the words composing it, it is evident that the shape and attributes
> of the Government must partake of the changes to which the words and
> phrases of all living languages are constantly subject. What a metamorphosis
> would be produced in the code of law if all its ancient phraseology were to be
> taken in its modern sense.[9]

In addition to this passage, originalists also routinely make recourse to two far
pithier quotations. First, they cite Madison's 1791 declaration—during the debate over the national bank—on the floor of the House of Representatives that
"[i]n controverted cases, the meaning of the parties to the instrument, if to be
collected by reasonable evidence, is a proper guide. Contemporary and concur-
rent expositions are a reasonable evidence of the meaning of the parties."[10]
And then, they reference another Madison speech, this time from 1796: "If we
were to look, therefore, for the meaning of the instrument beyond the face of
the instrument, we must look for it, not in the General Convention, which
proposed, but in the State Conventions, which accepted and ratified the Constitution."[11] Madison's words, however, are not the only ones originalists like to
brandish. A portion of Chief Justice John Marshall's decision in the landmark
Supreme Court case *Gibbons v. Ogden* in 1824 is similarly beloved:

> As men, whose intentions require no concealment, generally employ the
> words which most directly and aptly express the ideas they intend to convey,
> the enlightened patriots who framed our constitution, and the people who
> adopted it, must be understood to have employed words in their natural
> sense, and to have intended what they have said.[12]

To be sure, at casual glance, these statements, among several others found in the earliest decades of the republic, sound in originalism. But it would be a grave mistake to classify them as such. Reading these quotations as though they demonstrate the Founders' commitment to originalism constitutes a textbook example of the various interpretive mythologies once classified by the famed political theorist and intellectual historian Quentin Skinner.[13] Justly influential, these mythologies merit repeating here. While Skinner formulated them with the study of iconic political texts in mind, they could not be more pertinent to the issue at hand.

First, by insisting that such quotations prove the originalist affinities of the Founders, originalists commit the mythology of origins. A corollary of Skinner's mythology of prolepsis, this mythology assumes that earlier statements anticipate what developed only much later.[14] Once ideas have taken shape, there is a natural tendency to find and identify antecedents in earlier times—to find the logic of present intellectual forms prefigured and lurking in the past. It can be valuable to chart an idea's endurance and development over time. But we must be sure we have the right idea in mind and are not confusing a superficial resemblance for the thing itself. Consider the above Madison and Marshall testimony, which illustrates common arguments from the nation's first decades. There is nothing surprising about the fact that eighteenth- and nineteenth-century Americans inquired about original constitutional intent. For as long as people have interpreted legal or constitutional texts—indeed, seemingly for as long as human beings have engaged in hermeneutics of any kind—interpreters have cared, at least some of the time, about what authors intended or what the accepted meaning of a text at the time of its composition was. But that is no proof of originalism. Originalism has always amounted to a far stronger claim: that original intent, meaning, or understanding is dispositive in constitutional interpretation—that it is the *only* thing an interpreter should look for or the single factor that surmounts all others. These stronger commitments are absent from the Founders' testimony. Equating their earlier interest in the framers' intent with originalism assumes that prior use of an idea signals or anticipates something more robust that came only later. In fact, the causal arrows run in the opposite direction. The passages from Madison and Marshall are not early examples of originalism that helped lead the way to the modern theory; they only look that way when filtered through the modern legal debates in which originalism has become salient. The modern disputes do the work of transforming arguments that originally served a different purpose and had a different meaning into precursors of what we now know and treat as so natural.[15]

By reading Madison's and Marshall's words as a benediction of their own practices, originalists also fall victim to Skinner's mythologies of doctrines and parochialism. The mythology of doctrines assumes that past authors, in speaking about a particular subject matter, must have been speaking to the doctrines that are taken to define it.[16] Relatedly, the mythology of parochialism occurs when observers, failing to construe what they are interpreting on its own original terms, instead impose on it "familiar criteria of classification and discrimination," which allows them to mistakenly " 'see' something apparently (rather than really) familiar" and afford it "a misleadingly familiar-looking description."[17] Originalists often classify Founding-era interpretation according to familiar criteria and discriminations, perceiving in every appeal to framers' or ratifiers' intent a recognizable move in modern constitutional argument. The organizing framework shapes and distorts the empirical evidence, privileging what we naturally see over what the Founders themselves would have seen.[18]

This is a recurring problem in the history of ideas. Calling the Founders originalists is akin to claiming that early defenders of natural rights were anticipating modern human rights, believing that theorists of mixed constitutionalism were somehow saying something about the modern doctrine of separation of powers, or pondering what the Founders thought about strict scrutiny. Each of these mistakes features the imposition of anachronistic concepts, born of much different contexts, onto historical actors who knew nothing of them. It is historical malpractice to collapse earlier arguments and ideas onto the terms of something that developed only later—to render those prior concepts mere forerunners and precursors to something yet unseen. It is to engage in mythmaking, not genuine historical recovery. It is to see the past through the prism of the present instead of taking it on its own terms.

Arguing from Absence

Even if one was willing to entertain the idea that Madison and Marshall somehow anticipated originalism, however, they were hardly the only Founders who offered prescriptions on how to properly interpret the Constitution. The crippling fact is that the Founding generation, as we have already seen, didn't agree about what the Constitution even was, let alone how to interpret it. How then, we might ask, could people who disagreed over interpretive method, at times so deeply and bitterly, have commonly subscribed to one particular interpretive methodology that can be fairly labeled originalism? The only way to conclude that the Founding generation shared an interpretive method would be to attach such broad and inclusive meanings to "interpretive method" and "shared" as to strip them of all practical significance. If we applied those same broad, inclusive standards to our own contemporary practices, we would have to similarly conclude that almost everyone today is committed to a common set of interpretive conventions and priorities—that beneath our own sharp disagreements we in fact share a set of methods for interpreting the Constitution. That marks no small irony given that the entire reason for arguing that there was such a thing as shared original methods at the Founding is to make a move in a present-day debate in which it is assumed that we today unambiguously and meaningfully disagree over how to interpret the Constitution. The guiding premise is that we today don't share a method for interpreting our Constitution. So what is necessary to identify shared interpretive conventions at the Founding (elevating to a sufficiently high level of generality to locate broad consensus) eliminates the basis of our own current debate. If the Founders somehow broadly agreed on interpretive method, then, at the same broad level, surely so do we. For "shared interpretive methods at the Founding" to mean anything of significance, then, the methods that are said to be shared must be sufficiently specific that they can be distinguished from potential competitors. And once we require such particulars, the statement once again becomes implausible. There were no original methods for interpreting the Constitution, just fundamental disagreement over how to interpret the Constitution—over what those methods *ought to have been*.

If we look closer, however, we can see what is going on. Identifying originalist-sounding arguments among the Founders is only half the story. What has originalists convinced that the Founders are on their side is not just what those sages said but also what they didn't say. It is an argument derived from absence. What makes it *seem* plausible that the Founders agreed where we disagree is belief that none of the Founders overtly endorsed living constitutionalism. If one studies Founding-era interpretation, we are told, "all . . . roads likely lead to Rome . . . to some form of originalism" because, no matter the disagreement back then, "the key point is that there is little or no evidence supporting dynamic interpretation or living constitutionalism."[19] For originalists, what really stands out is not that members of the Founding generation spoke often about recovering the original intent of the Constitution's authors or ratifiers but that they rarely claimed that the Constitution's meaning needed to evolve, or had evolved, to keep up with social and cultural change. The Founders' failure to invoke living constitutionalism, in the end, does the heavy lifting. Because the Founders plainly *weren't* living constitutionalists, the argument goes, they must have been originalists.

There are three equally important problems with this argument. First, it ascribes mistaken significance to the absence of living constitutionalism. Second, by obsessing over that particular absence, it papers over earlier interpretive divisions, lumping together opposed eighteenth- and nineteenth-century views on constitutional interpretation instead of appreciating how they clashed. Third, it fails to identify the real importance of the absence of living constitutionalism: without it, appeals to original intent amounted to a different kind of commitment than they do today. Combined, these points show that the issue lies not with the empirics but the criteria of classification itself.

Originalists make much of the fact that the Founders were not outspoken living constitutionalists—at least not of the kind we find familiar. But here originalists should reckon with another kind of silence. It should not be surprising that living constitutionalism, *as we understand it*, did not quickly emerge following the Constitution's creation.[20] Its emergence required, at minimum, significant time to have passed during which social, economic, and cultural change proved sufficiently transformative that some naturally began to wonder whether a constitution created so long ago still served the changed society in which they found themselves. In addition, it surely required the development of new ways of conceiving of human beings in society, ushered in by, among other things, Darwinism, modernism, pragmatism, and legal realism.[21] None of these conditions were met in 1795, 1810, or 1825, so it should come as no surprise that, when looking at any of these historical moments, we fail to find people asserting that the Constitution had evolved to keep up with social change.[22] In the debate over chartering a national bank in 1791, for instance, are we to be struck by the fact that none of the participants claimed that the Constitution had once (way back in 1787 or 1788) meant something different but that the changed circumstances wrought by the intervening years had given the document a new meaning? Surely not. There is nothing meaningful about the absence of such claims.

Obsessing over living constitutionalism's absence allows originalists to feel more comfortable in claiming that a remarkable diversity of constitutional interpretation during the long Founding, itself born of divisive debate, somehow converged toward the same broad commitment to their own interpretive method. Never mind the ample endorsements of flexible interpretation, constructive interpretation, common-law interpretation, or broad construction of the Constitution. Never mind that jurists such as John Marshall construed the Constitution so flexibly and favored such a judge-controlled form of common-law development that they faced criticism for handling the Constitution, in the words of Jefferson, like a "mere thing of wax . . . which they may twist and shape into any form they please."[23] Never mind that modern originalists, if pressed, would reject so many of the interpretations defended during the Constitution's first half century as contrary to original meaning, precisely because they were so broadly derived. Never mind that James Wilson, John Jay, Alexander Hamilton, and other leading nationalists assumed that the Constitution, properly interpreted, gave the national government extraordinary power. Never mind that they assumed that the Constitution, as a matter of law, incorporated the law of nations and wide swaths of unwritten general law. Never mind that they recognized no obvious distinction between right reason and textual content. Never mind that they, like their leading opponents, assumed that the nature of the polity determined the scope of the Constitution's content. By virtue of an unremarkable absence, it seems, all of these disparate interpretations are to be classified as originalism.

Defined strictly as the absence of living constitutionalism, originalism becomes so attenuated that it can describe almost everything anyone has ever argued about the Constitution. It does not matter how frequently interpreters appealed to general fundamental law, how broadly they construed the Constitution, how readily they interpreted it in the flexible spirit of the common law, or how quick they were to insist that the Constitution was written to adapt to unforeseen circumstances—as so many eighteenth- and nineteenth-century politicians, jurists, and reformers assuredly did. As long as they claimed to be recovering the Constitution's original intent or applying its settled meaning, they were apparently originalists.

Indeed, according to this thinking, it would seem the only reason living constitutionalists today are in fact living constitutionalists is that they claim to be. If they simply dropped the label and the posture and instead claimed that their interpretations fulfilled the original meaning of the Constitution, then they too could be originalists—ones who interpreted the Constitution as broadly and flexibly as did James Wilson, Alexander Hamilton, or John Marshall, but originalists all the same. Of course, there would continue to be substantive interpretive disagreements *beneath* this new consensus. But those would be no different in kind from the precise sorts of disagreements we find coursing through late eighteenth- and early nineteenth-century America. If the endurance of those sorts of disagreements is enough to disprove that "we are all originalists now," then the same holds true for the long Founding. If we are inclined to lump almost all interpreters into a common category, no matter the depth of disagreement otherwise separating them, then that suggests our classification scheme is unsuitable for the task.

Finally, while the absence of living constitutionalism in Founding-era disputes is not meaningful in any of the ways originalists believe, it is significant in one vital respect: without living constitutionalism serving as a conscious foil, calls to recover and enforce original intent during the Constitution's first decades did not imply the same commitment that such calls do today. After all, a modern originalist defends that idea *in contrast to* living constitutionalism—the idea is constituted as much by what it opposes, and thus what it is *not*, as by what it defends. Earlier appeals to the framers' intent were not informed by that same opposition, so we should doubt that the argument captured the same idea. One of the essential principles of sound intellectual history is to appreciate how ideas acquire their substance from the distinctions drawn proximately to them. If a past idea looks familiar but a distinction that is so central to that idea's substance did not yet exist, we ought to wonder whether the idea was indeed so similar. If, today, we recognize ideas A and B in opposition to one another, then key to the substance of both A and B is the distinction *between* A and B. If we look to the past and find something that looks like A or B but no evidence of a recognized distinction between A and B, we should not assume that we have actually found anything quite like A or B. This is especially true if we not only fail to find the distinction but also fail to find either of the halves. If we find something like A but not something like B, we would also be mistaken

to assume we have found anything quite like A. Thus, while it might be problematic, for instance, to think of John Marshall as an early living constitutionalist (since the intellectual conditions and ingredients upon which the
emergence of living constitutionalism have depended had not yet taken
form), it is every bit as problematic to think of him as an originalist.[24]

All of which brings us to the most fundamental point: neither originalism
nor living constitutionalism *as we know them* existed at the Founding or for
years to follow. As Jack Balkin has stressed, they were born simultaneously,
as conjoined twins, in response to a fundamental problem of modernity:
What should be done with an old constitution in a society that has dramatically changed?[25] At bottom, originalism and living constitutionalism were,
and always have been, competing answers to this modernist dilemma. The
living-constitutionalist answer has been: that was then, this is now. By contrast, the originalist answer has been: we have drifted from our foundations
and must find our way back.[26] The theory of originalism, no matter what its
champions claim, cannot be disentangled from either this question—a question that no member of the Founding generation ever confronted—or the
legal consciousness that follows from asking it. That conscious reckoning,
which lies at the heart of originalism (and its debate with living constitutionalism), was entirely absent during the earliest decades of the nation. It does
not matter, therefore, that early Americans might sometimes have made interpretive moves that are facially similar to what originalists defend today.
That does not make those earlier moves originalist or those who made them
originalists. The people who made those arguments did so in a different
context, absent the essential ingredients and consciousness that have defined our modern constitutional debate.

Asking the Wrong Question

As should now be clear, the issue is less that originalists have reached the
wrong answer than that they have asked a thoroughly ahistorical question.
They have taken a modern binary (A or B) as natural and fixed and asked
whether the Founders were one or the other, settling on A given the absence
of B. Here we find an even stronger version of Skinner's mythology of doctrines at work. Originalists simply assume that the categories with which
they are familiar fit an earlier period. The criteria of classification and

discrimination come pre-packaged in a neat either/or: the modern divide between originalism and living constitutionalism shapes what is seen, how it is classified, and how it is grouped. Rival eighteenth-century positions find themselves sorted under the same classification scheme primarily on the basis of what they are not. And positions that *look like* A are classified *as* A even if they did not stand in opposition to anything quite like B.

All of this does violence to the past. Given that those who lived during the long Founding were manifestly not engulfed in our "originalism versus living constitutionalism" debate, we err in enlisting them in it. It is a recipe for distortion and misunderstanding. It imposes a modern consciousness on historical actors who necessarily lacked it, painting them as versions of ourselves and ventriloquizing through them, rather than taking seriously how they interpreted the Constitution on their own terms according to the conceptual categories available to them in their own time. It's playing tricks on the dead.

The question, moreover, is as unilluminating as it is ahistorical. Probing it tells us precious little about how the Constitution was in fact interpreted or debated in its earliest years. Across the long Founding, Americans argued deeply about the Constitution and its interpretation.[27] In fact, one would be hard pressed to find more fundamental interpretive disagreements across U.S. constitutional history. And it is impossible to understand those divisions on the terms of our modern debate. Thomas Jefferson versus Alexander Hamilton, Samuel Chase versus James Iredell, Spencer Roane versus John Marshall, Robert Y. Hayne versus Daniel Webster, John C. Calhoun versus Joseph Story, William Lloyd Garrison versus Frederick Douglass— none of these struggles pitted originalists against living constitutionalists; and they surely weren't recurring episodes of methodological *agreement*. Suggesting that each of these antagonists agreed on interpretive method while only disagreeing over its application strains credulity.

Rather than cavalierly plucking quotations from the period, we might consider them in conversation with one another. We've already gotten a taste of some of the things John Marshall said that originalists have seized on to claim him as one of their own. Many more could be added. In *Ogden v. Saunders* in 1827, for instance, Marshall wrote: "To say that the intention of the instrument must prevail; that this intention must be collected from its words; that its words are to be understood in that sense in which they are generally used by those for whom the instrument was intended; that its provisions are neither to be restricted into insignificance, nor extended to objects not comprehended in them, nor contemplated by its framers;—is to repeat what has been already said more at large, and is all that can be necessary."[28] Here he was echoing an argument he had made nearly a decade prior in *McCulloch v. Maryland*, when he rested the Court's decision not on what happened to be practical but on "the intention of the Convention, as manifested in the whole clause."[29]

Now consider what Thomas Jefferson, writing in retirement to Justice William Johnson in 1823, instructed on the matter of constitutional interpretation. Jefferson claimed that "there are two Canons which will guide us safely in most of the cases." One of which was "on every question of construction, carry ourselves back to the time when the Constitution was adopted, recollect the spirit manifested in the debates, and instead of trying what meaning may be squeezed out of the text, or invented against it, conform to the probable one in which it was past."[30] Here Jefferson, like Marshall, seemed to be advancing an originalist method.

By roving haphazardly from quotation to quotation, as is commonplace in debates over whether the Founders were originalists, we are sure to hear that both Marshall and Jefferson fell squarely within the originalist camp. But we might stop and reflect on the fact that Jefferson's interpretive advice was issued *as a direct criticism* of what Marshall was doing. Jefferson's own suggestion for interpreting the Constitution was entirely premised on the fact that Marshall had *not* followed it and was instead engaged in a different style of interpretation. Jefferson pulled no punches either. In not just his letter to Johnson but also letters to dozens of other confidantes, he excoriated Marshall's interpretive approach—not simply his application of a method but his method itself. In "construing our constitution" in the manner they had, Jefferson charged, the "Judiciary of the US. is the subtle corps of sappers & miners constantly working under ground to undermine the foundations of our confederated fabric."[31] Whatever else might be said, Jefferson was disagreeing—and disagreeing sharply—with Marshall *over interpretive method*. It would be defective intellectual history to conclude that Jefferson and Marshall were in broad agreement on how to interpret the Constitution when they themselves were under the impression that they so violently disagreed.

Concluding that Marshall and Jefferson were somehow fellow travelers with respect to constitutional interpretation leaves us blind to what divided the two antagonists—and thus actually defined and differentiated their own views, rightfully understood. There is more than a little irony in defending constitutional originalism by ignoring the original meaning of Marshall's and Jefferson's testimony. What infects one pursuit perhaps tells us something about the character of the other pursuit.

The only way to get to the bottom of interpretive disagreements like these—and so many others that coursed through the early United States—is to abandon the "originalism versus living constitutionalism" framework and replace it with something rooted in that earlier time. It's doing us no favors, and pressing it into service not only distorts the past but betrays a lack of interest in how the first several generations of Americans navigated constitutional interpretation. It makes it impossible to draw useful conclusions about actual interpretive activity, let alone explain how we got from then to now. Anyone still invested in establishing that the Founders were originalists, it seems, is ultimately more interested in scoring points in modern political disputes than recovering the past on its own terms.

What Constitutional Interpretation Once Was

If we are interested in understanding how early Americans thought about constitutional interpretation, we need to grasp what their interpretive moves meant in the context in which they spoke and wrote. The task is not to enlist them in our debates, which they were unaware of and which their statements did not speak to, but to figure out how to accurately catalogue, understand, and explain their own disagreements and divisions. That is how we ought to make sense of overworked statements by James Madison, John Marshall, or Thomas Jefferson that pertain to constitutional interpretation—and it is likewise how we should approach lesser-known comments on the subject by James Wilson, John Randolph, Spencer Roane, William Wirt, Joseph Story, Frederick Douglass, or anyone else before the Civil War.

All of these Founding-era interpreters, like most of their peers, appealed with regularity to the constitutional past to understand the Constitution's imperatives. We should not be surprised. It was the water in which they swam. For as long as anyone in the English-speaking world could remember, constitutional argument had been dominated by appeals to history. It was yet another way in which habits inculcated under British constitutionalism endured on the other side of the Atlantic. British North Americans came of age learning how to appeal to custom, precedent, authoritative practice, and the spirit of prior times to ground constitutional and legal claims. After devising their own constitutional system, they adapted these long-standing habits to their own revolutionary context, increasingly calling back to—and in the process creating—their putative founding moment.

On into the nineteenth century, political and legal elites as well as ordinary citizens alike pledged fidelity to the original intent and goals of the Constitution's framers and the original spirit that had imbued the constitutional system they set in motion. Over time, as the Founding generation passed and a rising generation of antebellum Americans took custody of the Founders' work, this commitment only deepened. Debates over constitutional interpretation were increasingly backward-looking, fixated on the animating spirit of the Founders who had come before them, and often became obsessed with the notion of restoring what once was.[32]

Appealing to the past was ubiquitous. But when early interpreters did so, they were making arguments in their debates not ours. Most often, they invoked history within the framework, once again, of social contract theory. Virtually all of them were trying to make sense of the Constitution in light of the social contract that undergirded it. Appeals to history were devoted primarily to deciphering and establishing the relationship between the two, and with it the true foundation of the federal constitutional system.

Those who believed that the United States constituted a national polity, no different in kind from the various state polities, assumed that the federal Constitution was just like any ordinary constitution and thus ought to be interpreted in light of the basic purpose of constitutions under social contract theory: to promote the public good. Alexander Hamilton's opinion defending the constitutionality of the national bank in 1791 rested in part on this precise point: the federal Constitution, like any other constitution of government, "ought to be construed liberally, in advancement of the public good."[33] The historical account of the federal union that James Wilson provided in *Chisholm v. Georgia* in 1793 was designed to establish a similar point. As we have seen, Wilson appealed to the history of the union and what the Declaration of Independence had purportedly wrought to prove that the powers delegated in the national Constitution should be construed in light of the broad national purposes laid out in the Preamble.[34]

Throughout the early republic, those who were skeptical of this nationalist vision of power took aim at its historical account of the underlying social contract to explain why federal power ought to be construed strictly rather than broadly. For Thomas Jefferson and other staunch Republicans, the federal Constitution was not really a constitution at all, but in effect a treaty—a compact agreed to by sovereign states—and it therefore needed to be interpreted strictly "according to the plain intent and meaning in which it was understood and acceded to by the several parties" that had originally agreed to it.[35] Given the Constitution's origins, and the fact that there was no discernable national social contract, there was simply no general welfare, common across the states, to guide constitutional interpretation at the federal level.

James Madison, as we have seen, was not willing to venture this far. He recognized that the federal government was more national than confederal, but he refused to accept that a national polity of individuals had established the Constitution. The Constitution had distinctive origins. The consent of the states qua states had been necessary to establish the national union. The federal Constitution, in contrast to its counterparts in the states, was not a direct manifestation of the people's will, but instead a mediated one. Consequently, the federal Constitution was not to be interpreted as liberally as the state constitutions were. He sketched out this middle position in 1819 in a letter to Spencer Roane, a Virginia judge and fierce Jeffersonian. Roane was exercised about the Supreme Court's recent ruling in *McCulloch v. Maryland*, which had interpreted the Constitution broadly to uphold the constitutionality of the Bank of the United States. Madison was sympathetic to the thrust of Roane's criticism if not its particulars, and he set to work specifying "the rule of interpreting the Constitution" in a dispatch to his friend. "Much of the error in expounding the Constitution," Madison wrote, "has its origin in the use made of the species of sovereignty implied in the nature of government." Some, like Roane and Jefferson, had mistakenly denied that there was a federal body politic, but others had also erred in treating the federal Constitution as an ordinary constitution, to be interpreted in light of conventional social-contract principles. "There is certainly a reasonable medium," Madison stressed, "between expounding the Constitution with the strictness of a penal or other ordinary Statute" in the way Roane insisted one should "and expounding it with a laxity, which may vary its essential character, and encroach on the local sovereignties with which it was meant to be reconcilable," as the

Supreme Court had just done in *McCulloch*. The "very existence of these local sovereignties" served as a reminder that the federal government was inherently limited, that it was different in kind from the sort of ordinary government that was, by the nature of constitutional government, vested with "any particular power necessary or useful in itself." "In the Government of the U. States," Madison explained, "the case is obviously different." Because the United States was not a single national polity—"a single State," as he put it—the federal government was not presumed to be given those powers "required for the welfare of the Community." An appropriate understanding of the federal union was a "controul on pleas for a constructive amplification of the powers of the general Government."[36]

Madison was expounding upon precisely these points in the subsequent 1824 letter to Henry Lee that originalists so frequently cite in an effort to demonstrate Madison's originalist affinities. In the oft-quoted portion of this missive, Madison encouraged "resorting to the sense in which the Constitution was accepted and ratified by the nation." As Madison explained, "if that be not the guide in expounding it, there can be no security for a consistent and stable, more than for a faithful exercise of its powers." If national officeholders could construe federal powers in light of the public good, then the terms of the Constitution, into which the peoples of the separate states had entered as parties, could not remain "consistent and stable." It would be a recipe for "a destruction of the states, by transfusing their powers into the government of the Union."[37] Unless interpreters remained wedded to the terms of the original social contract, Madison warned, there would be no maintaining the distinctively federal nature of the union. His interpretive argument hinged on social contract theory rather than originalism.

It was in opposition to these various Republican approaches to constitutional interpretation, moreover, that John Marshall issued his own historical claims. Marshall did not agree with James Wilson and his allies that the national body politic could be traced back to independence. He largely accepted Madison's claim that the national social contract originated with the ratification of the federal Constitution.[38] But because the Constitution's original authority rested on a national body politic, he thought it reasonable to treat that polity as equivalent in kind to those already existent in the states and thus to interpret the Constitution like any other constitution. This was among the leading reasons the chief justice famously declared in *McCulloch v. Maryland* (the case that had ignited Roane's and Madison's ire), "[W]e must never forget, that it is *a constitution* we are expounding."[39] He did not mean simply to distinguish the Constitution from an ordinary "legal code," the "prolixity" of which would prevent it from being "adapted to the various *crises* of human affairs," important though that surely was.[40] He also intended to emphasize that the U.S. Constitution was no different in kind from other constitutions, especially those found in the American states. There was, thus, no justification to "deny to the government those powers . . . which are consistent with the general views and objects of the instrument."[41] There was no grounds for treating it as something other than a conventional constitution.

To justify his account of the federal polity, Marshall claimed that the Constitution had originated from a single national intent. In several Supreme Court opinions, he emphasized that a singular public had originally agreed to the federal Constitution—"the people of America adopted their government," as he put it in *Gibbons v. Ogden*.[42] In stressing the unitary character of the public, he was refuting Jefferson's and Madison's divergent ways of emphasizing an original plural public and suggesting that the Constitution had been approved by a single author: a solitary national polity. Joseph Story, Marshall's fellow justice on the Supreme Court, would make much the same point in his 1833 *Commentaries* by asserting that "[t]he sense of a part of the people has no title to be deemed the sense of the whole."[43] Because the Constitution was the work of the whole people, it was to be interpreted broadly in light of the first principles of social contract theory: advancing the common interest. "Was it not framed for the good of the people, and by the people?" asked Story.[44] "The Government of the Union" was "emphatically, and truly, a government of the people." Hence, it was "an effective Government" and to be interpreted accordingly.[45] Marshall, in other words, did not appeal to original constitutional intent to translate interpretive questions into historical ones. Rather, he developed a historical account to explain why the Constitution could be construed liberally, to promote the public good, in the present.

These were among the most important interpretive debates in which early constitutional partisans participated. This is how they typically used and appealed to history and the origins of the Constitution in interpreting the nation's fundamental law. None of their positions, or the interpretive fault lines they created, make much sense from the standpoint of the modern originalism debate. Some original interpreters such as Madison, given his commitment to conceiving of constitutional authority in more historical and fixed terms, were closer to something we might associate with that label. But the distance was still significant. Madison still continued to believe that constitutional politics, not judicially controlled textualism, would serve as the final arbiter of the Constitution's meaning. As we have seen, moreover, Madison's several antagonists—be they Wilson and Jay or the comparatively more moderate Marshall—countered not by denouncing Madison's search for an original intent but instead by locating it in a different place. The debate was not between those who favored historical foundations and those who favored interpretive dynamism, but between those who thought the Constitution was straightforwardly a constitution and those who did not. Additionally, Madison, and many who agreed with him, hoped to limit the interpretive authority of national politicians and jurists in order, ultimately, to empower the people themselves as the ultimate arbiters of disputed constitutional questions. The point of reining in interpretation had less to do with privileging historical meaning than facilitating the supreme authority of the sovereign people, in the present, to determine the Constitution's true meaning. In short, understanding these earlier appeals to original intent and the Constitution's origins demands a different context altogether.

From Past to Present

Appealing to the past has always been profoundly important to American constitutional interpretation, and it was especially so in the half century following the Constitution's inception. But we shouldn't misunderstand what all that talk of history supposedly signaled. Despite its dominance, it didn't offer any consensus on how to interpret the Constitution but rather channeled disagreement no less fierce that what we now know. We shouldn't lose sight of the extent of those earlier disagreements.

As we've seen, both Jefferson and Marshall appealed to the history of the founding moment. Yet they violently disagreed over how to approach that history and what one could claim to find there. And that was in large measure because they simply disagreed about the character of constitutional interpretation itself—a disagreement that was far simpler than anything that hinged on the use history. Jefferson championed strict construction and Marshall broad construction. Long before the originalism debate swallowed everything up, that's actually what Americans fought over. And as obvious as it may seem to remind all of us of that earlier fault line, it's one that is surprisingly hard to place in our modern debates.

The "were the Founders originalists?" obsession has proved so hard to suppress, in large measure because it's not clear how the "strict construction versus broad construction" debate maps onto the "originalism versus living constitutionalism" one. Because originalists have needed to solve so many interpretive dilemmas and have been happy to take the theory in so many different directions, originalism can now seemingly permit the strictest of strict construction or the broadest of broad construction. The imperative is to recover original meaning, however strictly or broadly that recovery entails. Consequently, the theory now happily accommodates a host of interpretive moves and impulses that, in Jefferson and Marshall's time, were sharply and irreconcilably opposed. This state of things has bred considerable confusion. Do a strict-construction originalist and a broad-construction originalist agree on interpretive method? Few would have thought so in the nineteenth century. Do a broad-construction originalist and a living constitutionalist disagree on interpretive method? It often is hard to see exactly how, much as originalists insist otherwise.

We can begin to make sense of this muddle by coming to terms with how we got here—by appreciating the sheer contingency of the originalism–living constitutionalism divide. If certain early twentieth-century Americans faced with the modernist predicament hadn't chosen to defend the idea that the Constitution's meaning had evolved, we likely never would have lost touch with the "strict versus broad construction" debate. If we still found ourselves in something like that world, it likely wouldn't matter who claimed fidelity to the original Constitution (be it the Constitution's intent, text, spirit, or purpose), but whether they were committed to the Jeffersonian or the Marshallian side of the earlier debate. The Jeffersonian likely would recoil no less at the modern originalist defense of *Brown v. Board of Education* than at President Franklin Delano Roosevelt's defenses of the New Deal as consistent with the guiding principles of the Founders' Constitution, detecting in each the kind of malleable and unrestricted approach to interpretation that was so threatening.[46] But we shouldn't be surprised. After all, we have been told that Jefferson and Marshall agreed on a method of constitutional interpretation when they spent the entirety of their mature years claiming the opposite. Something curious has happened to bring us to a place where that's possible.

The challenge is not figuring out whether eighteenth- and nineteenth-century Americans favored one side of our debate. The challenge is understanding how and why we got from then to now—how one kind of dispute over constitutional interpretation morphed into another—and perhaps whether the fact that we so instinctively lump early constitutional antagonists into a common interpretive pot suggests that there is something peculiar, if not impoverished, about our own way of thinking.

We still need to plot the course from past to present. Even if it is misguided to ask whether the Founders were originalists, it is understandable to wonder how originalism's intellectual ingredients came into existence—to understand the deeper roots of our modern obsession and the preconditions of its later development.[47]

Important aspects of its development can surely be traced to the 1790s. Over the course of that decade, there was a transformation in constitutional imagination that made it possible to see the Constitution as fixed in a new kind of way. Essential to this process was the fusion of a textualized and an archival understanding of the Constitution that enabled Americans to start thinking about their Constitution in time-locked ways and at the same time made it harder to reconcile fixity and evolutionary change as they long had.[48] Originalists might interpret these developments as evidence of how quickly originalism emerged and permeated American constitutionalism. But the point is not that the Founders became originalists in the years following ratification but rather that they created a new way of *arguing over* the Constitution. They continued to disagree over the nature of interpretation, but now that disagreement was channeled in new ways. This new form of constitutional thinking was reinforced when jurists began treating the Constitution like a statute, willfully enacted at a discrete moment by known framers. The Constitution might be stipulated, written, fixed law or it might be customary, unwritten, evolving law, but the older notion of fundamental law as simultaneously fixed and evolving had begun to dissipate. Founding-era Americans gained one deep, organizing concept at the expense of another. But that did not mean they suddenly agreed on whether the Constitution was fixed or how to interpret it. To conclude either of those things is to misunderstand what happened in the early republic and why it proved consequential. Americans

had created a new lingua franca of constitutionalism, predicated on new understandings of textual meaning, historical meaning, positive enactment,
original intent, and the Constitution's relationship to historical time. By the
early nineteenth century, much of the disagreement now ran along those
channels—just as fundamentally and divisively as before, but now increasingly adjudicated in light of novel understandings of what the Constitution
was and required.

If we dwell on this early transformation, we learn a lot about why American constitutional debate took the form it did, why so many in antebellum
America and beyond fought over the framers' intent and expectations, and
why, so much later, modern originalists and living constitutionalists could
adopt their competing positions confident that the terms of their debate naturally followed what came before. Unpacking that constitutional history,
however, wouldn't tell us whether the Founders were either originalists or
living constitutionalists. Far from it. It would encourage us, instead, to see
how their disagreements evolved, how, over time, those disagreements
turned into our modern constitutional debates, and how, in the process, the
original Constitution was steadily obscured. The new ideas that emerged
across the decades following the Constitution's ratification—novel understandings of constitutional writtenness, fixity, and history—eventually
helped lay the groundwork for the modern originalism debate. But they were
a break with the past, not a restoration of it. They created a new understanding of the Constitution that, ironically, helped erase crucial features of the
original Constitution as it had been originally conceived.[49]

PART THREE

ORIGINALISM AND HISTORY

9

Making, Not Finding, the Constitution

What we are destroying is nothing but houses of cards and we are
clearing up the ground of language on which they stand.
— Ludwig Wittgenstein, 1953

WHEN WE HISTORICIZE THE CONSTITUTION, and not simply its meaning, we see
how different the originalists' Constitution is from the one that Founding-era
Americans conjured in their own minds. And we can return to where we began.

As we saw at the beginning of our exploration, the standard originalist
formulation—if not uniformly held then nonetheless pervasive among
champions of the theory—goes something like this:

> The Constitution's meaning is what its text communicated to the public at the
> time of its enactment. Because fixation is a function of writtenness, the Con-
> stitution's meaning remains the same until its words are formally changed.
> This meaning, until changed, is therefore the law. Because the Constitution is
> the fixed meanings of its words, the task of interpretation is to recover those
> meanings, which is accomplished by focusing on the words themselves and,
> when necessary, by utilizing conventional methods of legal interpretation.

This conception of constitutional meaning presupposes that the Constitution is its words (that its language delimits its content and boundaries), that
its word meanings are what are fixed (because fixation is an empirical fact

that follows from writtenness), and that those word meanings are the law because the law of the Constitution is, by character, formally enacted. It presumes, in essence, that the Constitution is akin to a statute: a written text enacted by authorized decision-makers to be deciphered by familiar canons of legal construction. And it thus presumes that authoritative text makes authoritative law.

As we can now see, however, the original Constitution did not initially rest on any of these premises, at least not necessarily so. Nothing about the Constitution simply being written down meant that its content was coextensive with the contextually enriched meaning of its words. The idea of constitutional fixation need not have been correlated with language in the slightest. And because law was still understood as a delicate synthesis of positivist and non-positivist elements, there were no sharp boundaries to be drawn between the Constitution as a textual instrument and the Constitution as preexisting fundamental law. Interpretation was not simply focused on word meanings or textual provisions; nor was it structured by non-existent default methods of constitutional interpretation. The image of the Constitution upon which orthodox originalism depends, and upon which each of these premises relies, was a creation of later times. That image effaces the original Constitution.

What happens when we press these differences—when we force originalists to think about the numerous ways in which Founding-era constitutionalism diverges from their foundational assumptions? What happens when we see how different the Founders' Constitution was from the originalist Constitution?

If we recall, orthodox originalists assume, often without much justification, that the Constitution is just as they describe it—that the way they conceive of the Constitution is given and essential. It is not the product of choice, constructive work, or optional presuppositions. In the face of the significant historical evidence we have just presented, however, orthodox originalists need to explain why, in fact, the Constitution is just as they readily assume. The historical evidence shows clearly that the originalist Constitution that courses through modern jurisprudential debates is predicated on an optional set of historically contingent assumptions about writtenness, fixed meaning, and law. One *could* think of the Constitution in any of the ways originalists usually do, but one certainly does not have to. Those conceptions don't inevitably follow from the Constitution's essential character.

Earlier, we also observed that originalists have never seemed to consider what would follow if their arguments from logic pointed in a different direction from history—if it turned out that the Founding generation's understanding of the Constitution's essential characteristics contradicted originalist orthodoxy. We now know this to be the case—logic and history are at odds, in some instances starkly so. When forced to choose, what will originalists do? Will they, at last, historicize the Constitution and take seriously the different ways in which eighteenth-century American constitutionalists understood constitutional writtenness, fixity, and law—overhauling their theory and method in the process? Or will they try ever harder to disaggregate the Constitution's original essence from the constitutional assumptions, commentary, and beliefs that originally surrounded it?

If pushed, most originalists are sure to opt for the latter. They've been engaged in that kind of evasion for some time now. In fact, one can already hear their likely rejoinder—a version of which is now so familiar that it has become a cliché. Some originalists might be persuaded that recovering the *original* Constitution requires more history rather than less, but if past is prologue, the more likely response would be to dismiss most of the historical evidence we have considered here as largely irrelevant to the originalist project. While the historical evidence presented in the prior chapters is potentially helpful in sorting out important issues of interpretation or construction, none of it tells us that much about the Constitution itself or what originalists claim to be bound by. Perhaps some or even most of the framers might have failed to appreciate the Constitution's true nature, but nonetheless, in spite of themselves, they constructed a written, fixed Constitution, because it is just in the nature of things that writing down constitutional principles eventually results in a distinctively fixed and textual Constitution of the kind originalists describe. Originalists would surely reiterate, as they so often have, that the strictly empirical matter of recovering the Constitution's original meaning is categorically distinct from the separate normative matter of defending that meaning's contemporary legitimacy.[1] And that their commitment to the original Constitution is derived from separate normative commitments—to popular sovereignty, justice, supermajoritarian rule, the rule of law, judicial constraint, and so on—rather than the Founders' own intentions about what they might have been doing.[2] Originalists are fond of insisting that they don't require "originalism all the way down," for they have no intention of bootstrapping their theory to the Founders' authority.[3] It makes little difference, they are sure to claim, what the Founding generation thought about constitutions or what made constitutions authoritative.

If, moreover, these skeptics happened to subscribe to public meaning originalism in particular (as the majority of practicing originalists and most originalist jurists do today), they would surely remind us that originalists are not ultimately bound by the original intentions, expectations, assumptions, interpretive methods, or constitutional practices of the Founding generation, only the original public meaning of the text itself.[4] "Textual originalists are not committed to everything the Founders believed," Evan Bernick and Christopher Green stress, only "to the *meaning* that the Founders expressed by means of the Constitution's text in context."[5] That was what the Founding generation ratified—that alone was what they made fundamental law. And the Constitution's original meaning, as originalists repeatedly stress, is purely a matter of objective, empirical fact.[6] As Randy Barnett, a leading originalist, has stressed, "We are searching for an empirical fact," one recovered through a straightforward question: "What information would these words on the page have conveyed to a reasonable speaker of English in the relevant audience at the time of enactment?"[7] It is not that hard, originalists claim, to cleanly separate that original meaning—the content the Constitution communicated when written—from the subjective attitudes that its authors or original readers brought to bear on it.[8] Whatever the Founding generation thought about writtenness or law is thus, for originalists, inessential to the recovery of original public meaning. That kind of historical evidence might raise issues for some originalists—such as those who champion original methods or cling to original intent—but for the vast majority of the theory's defenders, it poses few, if any, difficulties.

Originalists, as they are quick to remind us, are invested not in adjudicating the Founders' intramural squabbles, but rather in deciphering the Founders' objective creation. Scientists determine the makeup of water by identifying the hydrogen and oxygen molecules that constitute it; originalists purport to do much the same thing with the Constitution. *What* the Founding generation created—not *how* they conceived of it—is all that ultimately matters. The original Constitution is separable from the substantive Founding-era attitudes that initially surrounded it. The object can be neatly disaggregated from the assumptions. The Constitution can stand on its own.

This counterargument fails. And it fails precisely *because* of the historical evidence we have thus far canvassed. That evidence, properly understood, illustrates why doctrinaire originalists cannot bracket Founding-era assumptions about writtenness, fixity, and fundamental law as they presume—why they *cannot* disaggregate the original Constitution from the conceptual world from which it issued—not, that is, without abandoning the original Constitution and with that originalism's most important commitment: that it finds rather than makes a constitution.

Our remaining task is to see why this is the case. Given that originalists' favored tactic is to deflect and dismiss the relevance of the sort of historical evidence we have been at pains to present, it is essential to explain why they can't do that without fatally undermining their theory on its own stated terms. If the goal is to recover the *original* Constitution, we can't ignore how Founding-era Americans understood constitutionalism. We can't separate "the Constitution" from the constitutive assumptions that originally undergirded it, at least not without losing the original Constitution in the process.

Defining the Historical Evidence

Orthodox originalists will dismiss the historical evidence presented in part II only if they misunderstand what it is evidence *of.* They are sure to catalogue it with so much other historical evidence they've invested so much effort discounting. What the Founding generation intended or expected is often relevant to originalist interpretation, but it isn't binding. All we are bound by today, they'll say, is the Constitution's original public meaning— just the rules that the framers laid down. We're not bound by what the framers subjectively thought about those rules or assumed would follow from their enactment, or by what went into interpreting them. Just the rules; just the meaning of the words; just what the Constitution says—that's all that matters: what the Founding generation actually ratified.

The evidence presented in part II is sure to be classified similarly. The Founding generation's views on natural and common law, the federal union, or rules of constitutional interpretation as well as early commentators claiming the Constitution's meaning could not be reduced to its text, early jurists presupposing that the Constitution incorporated wide swaths of general fundamental law, and nationalists and their opponents assuming that the

Constitution's content turned on the nature of the underlying polity: it's all just so much evidence of original intentions, original expected applications, or original interpretive methods.

Whatever else this evidence might tell us, and however interesting it might be in its own right, originalists are sure to insist, it is simply not evidence of the Constitution's original public meaning. It is evidence of what people subjectively thought about the Constitution, not what it objectively communicated. And since none of those things count as original public meaning, none of them are essential to figuring out what the original Constitution requires of us today. That broader historical evidence, they'll say, might be relevant in other ways—in establishing context and clarifying ambiguity or in helping to choose among competing constructions—but that evidence is often not central to deciphering the Constitution's communicative content. We can figure out what the Constitution originally meant without knowing a whole lot about the wider field of constitutional beliefs and understandings that originally surrounded it.

Here we have a category error. The evidence presented in part II is primarily evidence not of original intentions, practices, or interpretations but of something more fundamental: eighteenth-century understandings of what constitutionalism was and how it worked. Maybe originalists can bracket what they call original intentions or original expected applications. But they cannot bracket what the Founding generation assumed about constitutionalism. And we will see why.

Constitutions Embedded in Constitutionalism

By failing to understand what Founding-era views on constitutionalism are evidence *of*, originalists fail to understand why those views matter *to* *originalism*—they fail to see that, because the *original* Constitution was embedded in those assumptions and understandings, it cannot be separated from them. The things that defined the original Constitution and determined its meaning—the nature of its content, its boundaries, its character, its relationship to fundamental law—were the product of how constitutionalism was understood to work. The Constitution *was made* of those assumptions. It was impossible to read the Constitution when it first appeared without knowing what you were reading, and you could understand what you were reading only if you understood how constitutions worked—how they acquired and communicated content, how they interfaced with fundamental law, how they presupposed (or didn't) the formation of a certain kind of constitutional polity. You could make sense of the Constitution circa 1787 only if you understood, in a word, constitutionalism. And the historical evidence we marshaled in part II is evidence of just that: eighteenth-century American constitutionalists' foundational assumptions about how constitutionalism worked. It is evidence of what made the Constitution what it originally *was* and thus what determined what it originally *meant*.

The original Constitution (like all constitutions) was embedded in history, in culture, in politics, but especially in a thick constitutionalism: in assumptions about constitutional substance and communication, in understandings of fundamental law and rights, in beliefs about the federal union. To rip the Constitution from the constitutionalism in which it was initially embedded is to change it, to turn it into something different than it once was.

Constitutional Communication

This point is perhaps most clearly illustrated by considering the standard originalist view of constitutional communication that has come to predominate.[9] Most originalists believe what they do about original meaning—and especially their conviction that it is separable from other kinds of original constitutional beliefs—because of how they assume the Constitution inherently communicates. They assume that the Constitution, by virtue of being written down, implies a comprehensive model of constitutional content and communication. Their sequence of logic goes something like this: the Constitution is a written document—the thing behind glass at the National Archives; therefore, the Constitution is constituted by its words; therefore, it communicates through the medium of language; therefore, what the Constitution communicates is a function of how language communicates, and to understand constitutional communication, you need to understand linguistic communication; therefore, what the Constitution originally communicated is whatever its language empirically communicated at the time of original enactment according to the linguistic conventions and usages of the day combined with what is true of how language generally works. Plug the right linguistic empirical inputs into the model and you get the Constitution's original communicative content:

the set of propositions that the written words of the constitutional text objectively communicated circa 1787 to a hypothetical original reader.[10]

Because the Constitution comes hardwired with this communication model, originalists argue, their standard interpretive techniques logically follow. The Constitution is a piece of linguistic communication that conveys its contents through formally enacted legal words. That is why originalists so readily liken originalism to textualism, and why they so comfortably analogize the Constitution to a statute, contract, or other written legal instruments.[11] Reading the Constitution like a textualist is just the same thing as reading it. Because the Constitution communicates through its language, meanwhile, it makes all the sense in the world to draw on general principles of linguistic communication to understand what the Constitution communicates. Understanding what the Constitution is saying requires understanding how language itself works. If that's the essential medium by which the Constitution relays its content, constitutional interpretation is seamlessly transformed into textual interpretation.

A growing stable of originalists are especially convinced that making sense of the Constitution is just a matter of figuring out language.[12] For them, originalism often has much more to do with understanding the philosophy of language and linguistics or the relationship between things like semantics and pragmatics, sense and reference, communicative meaning and communicative intent, and explicature and implicature than it does with eighteenth-century constitutional history.[13] They seem confident they can circumvent most of what happened or was said at the Founding through linguistic theory. Knowing how language communicates meaning, they assert, can tell you what an eighteenth-century written constitution *actually* communicated at the time of its ratification by virtue of the fact that it enacted one set of words rather than another. By contrast, for these originalists, canvassing eighteenth-century testimony on that constitution will likely tell you only what some fallible, potentially misguided, and likely partisan commentators subjectively believed *may have been* communicated by the enacted constitution. Fact trumps opinion, especially when informed by cutting-edge linguistic knowledge. The Founding generation knew so much less about how language works, so we are in a better position today, armed with advanced techniques and refined views, to comprehend what they in fact enacted and what the content in fact communicated. Philosophy of language better illuminates the Constitution's original communicative content than any-thing eighteenth-century legal commentators had to say about fundamental law, anything Federalists and Anti-Federalists had to say about the underly-ing social compact, or anything James Wilson and Thomas Jefferson had to say about the nature of the federal union. If *what* the Constitution said turns on *how* it communicated, then knowledge of language, not Founding-era constitutional commentary, holds the key.

While other originalists might not go so far, most of them nonetheless share a view of the Constitution that has given rise to this overly refined brand of linguistic theorizing. They accept that the Constitution is princi-pally a text that communicates its content through its textual commands. That certainly embodies, for instance, the textualist brand of originalism that Justice Antonin Scalia made so famous and controversial and that continues to influence the majority of originalists in the federal judiciary and the legal academy. By virtue of reducing U.S. fundamental law to written text, they reason, Americans created a constitution that communicated in a distinc-tively textualist kind of way. And that fact, above all, explains why originalists can separate the Constitution's original meaning (what the text says) from the commentaries that originally surrounded it (what Founding-era Ameri-cans thought about what it said).

What originalists enamored with this picture of public meaning fail to realize, however, is that their favored model of constitutional communica-tion is not necessitated by the Constitution, and indeed radically departs from the one Founding-era constitutionalists initially employed. These orig-inalists assume, rather than justify, that the Constitution communicates as they stipulate—that their communication model simply inheres in the origi-nal Constitution itself. They jump breathlessly from the fact that the Consti-tution is written to a particular understanding of textual communication without recognizing that the latter need not follow from the former. As we have seen, at the Founding there were much different ways of understand-ing how a written constitution acquired and communicated its content—based on deep-seated assumptions about social compacts, general fundamental law, and the nature of law itself. These alternative understand-ings demonstrate, if nothing else, that written constitutionalism did not au-tomatically dictate the model of constitutional communication upon which orthodox originalism depends. Indeed, not only were there alternatives, but hardly anyone at the Founding believed that constitutions communicated in the distinctive linguistic and textualist way that most modern originalists assume must be inherent to our Constitution.

Originalists, in other words, move too quickly in their analysis. They begin by asking the wrong question, namely, What did the Constitution originally say? They should, instead, start by asking, How did the Constitution originally speak? The questions are entwined: the *what* turns on the *how*. You cannot understand *what* an eighteenth-century constitution originally communicated (its original communicative content) without understanding *how* it originally communicated. Too few originalists have given much thought to *how* the Constitution—as a historical matter—might have communicated when it first appeared. They breeze past that consideration confident that they already have a handle on it: the Constitution is a text, and texts communicate like texts. Yet that assumes too much and, worse, imposes a model of constitutional communication on the Founding that is not only optional but anachronistic. It forces the Constitution to speak in a particular privileged way rather than taking seriously how the Constitution might in fact have spoken at the time of its inception.

Rather than assuming that the Constitution is a text that communicated like a text, the starting point ought to be that it was a *constitution* that communicated *like* a constitution, and to figure out what *that* originally entailed. However eighteenth-century constitutions happened to communicate is a function of how they were originally understood to communicate. There is no disentangling these things. How one could possibly have known what an eighteenth-century constitution was saying when it first appeared without understanding what *kind* of thing one was reading and what followed from the fact that one was reading that kind of thing and not some other kind of thing is difficult to fathom. No one could *just* look at a constitution's text or words and make sense of what one was reading independently of the essential fact that one was reading a constitution and all that implied. Only by understanding what one was reading and why it mattered that one was reading that sort of thing could someone decipher what it was saying. People at the Founding wrote and ratified the Constitution in light of their understanding of how a constitution, by virtue of being a constitution, acquired and communicated constitutional content. That invariably shaped what they thought they were making and what they thought they were enacting. If we wish to know what the Constitution originally said, we need to know how it originally acquired and communicated its content, and if we wish to understand how it originally acquired and communicated its content, we need to understand how constitutionalism itself was understood to work. And there is simply no understanding any of *that* without understanding the precise sort of historical evidence we explored in part II. Any well-rounded account of original constitutional communication would have to begin with the Founding generation's own understanding of constitutionalism.

Even if originalists' goal is relatively narrow and all they aim to do is decipher what the original Constitution communicated, they still can't bracket the kind of historical evidence canvassed in part II. The testimony presented there is evidence of how constitutions were understood at the Founding to acquire and communicate their content by virtue of the fact they were constitutions. It is evidence of how the Founding generation understood constitutions to operate as complex legal instruments that established both an authoritative framework of governance as well as the polity's fundamental law by simultaneously entrenching existing fundamental law and creating new fundamental law. It is evidence of how *constitutional communication* worked.

Founding-era Americans, as we've seen, wrote constitutions in light of what they presupposed about general fundamental law, social contract theory, and the essential harmony between non-positive and positive law. Given those essential assumptions about how constitutionalism worked, the Founding generation assumed that constitutions communicated much of their content through their text. But Founding-era Americans also assumed that constitutions communicated a lot of their content by virtue of the fact that they were *constitutions*. Because they were constitutions, they incorporated wide swaths of general fundamental law. Because they were constitutions, their commands turned in part on the underlying social compact that preceded enactment of constitution of government. Because they were constitutions, their rights provisions often merely declared—rather than created—the fundamental rights that already enjoyed constitutional protection. In the case of the federal Constitution, its content was inseparable from the nature of the union it represented. And so on. In important instances like these, the U.S. Constitution did not speak through its text—not primarily anyway. None of these different kinds of constitutional content were, strictly speaking, products of writing or enacting constitutional text. None of them were decipherable through or communicated *by* the language found in constitutional text. You could only know that these things were part of the constitution and identify the content that they added to it if you understood how that constitution—because it was a *constitution*—acquired and communicated its content.

If originalists' stated goal is to understand *what* the Constitution originally communicated, we first have to understand *how* it originally communicated. That demands knowing far more about eighteenth-century constitutionalism than most originalists tend to believe. Because what the Constitution *originally* expressed was a function of the constitutional language in which it was *originally* written—above all, as we've seen, the languages of general fundamental law and social contract theory. The specific historical evidence canvassed in part II, which is evidence of these original constitutional frameworks, is thus inextricably intertwined with any plausible account of the Constitution's original meaning—of what the Constitution in fact originally communicated to readers at the time of its enactment.

Because what the Constitution said was a function of how it communicated, originalists cannot escape history through language. There is a particular sense in which Chief Justice John Marshall's famous declaration in *McCulloch v. Maryland* that "[w]e must never forget, that it is *a constitution* we are expounding" is especially apt for the originalism debate.[14] In assuming too much about the nature of constitutional communication, too many originalists have mistakenly transformed a problem of constitutionalism into a problem of language. Suppose everything these leading originalists have said about language and meaning were correct. Putting aside the fact that much of it is controversial and debatable,[15] suppose that every bit of it were true—that they have settled these enormous questions that have vexed luminaries for centuries and gotten the nature of linguistic meaning exactly right. Why would these insights necessarily be relevant to interpreting the original U.S. Constitution? If we want to figure out what that Constitution said back when it was conceived, our task is not to understand how language generally communicates, but how constitutions specifically communicate. The two become one and the same only if American constitutions, simply by virtue of being written, communicate exclusively through language, communicate *as* language—if, that is, constitutional communication is no different in character from linguistic communication. That could be true. But we know that it wasn't true at the time of the Founding when the Constitution's original meaning was laid down. In eighteenth-century America, constitutions did not communicate as language; they communicated instead in ways particular to the nature of constitutionalism. Much of their content stood independent of constitutional text and could be deciphered only with knowledge of how fundamental law, social compacts, rights, the law of nations, or popular sovereignty worked. Originalists are fond of stating over and again that the Founding generation "adopt[ed] a text."[16] But the Founders did not; they adopted a constitution. And there's a difference.

Originalists often remind us that we need to be clear about what we mean by original meaning—that we need to make sure we understand the meaning of meaning as it were.[17] It's a valuable point, if not for the reasons they tend to emphasize. As interpreters, we target *constitutional* meaning, not *linguistic* meaning or *legal* meaning. Those other kinds of meanings are obviously relevant to constitutional meaning, and, in practice, there is liable to be considerable overlap between these categories. But the latter two, which dominate interpretive debates and do significant work in originalist theory, are poor substitutes for the thing we're actually looking for in the past: the specific kind of meaning that things called constitutions communicated in thick context. In many instances, likening linguistic to constitutional meaning leads us astray. In the eighteenth century, understanding what a written constitution communicated required understanding far more than the mysteries of language: it required understanding how fundamental law and social contract theory worked, the difference between constitutive and non-constitutive constitutional text, and the relationship between the common law and popular sovereignty. Knowing how language happened to communicate in other contexts—in day-to-day conversations, instruction manuals, letters of recommendation, novels, or campaign literature—was of limited help on this distinctively constitutional front. One had to understand constitutional content and what determined it, how constitutional text interacted with unwritten constitutional principles, and how any of that was communicated to savvy interpreters.

Then as now, a theory of language is no substitute for a theory of constitutionalism.[18] The content of the Constitution is determined not by the nature of language but by the nature of the Constitution. Only *if* the nature of the Constitution was essentially linguistic would it be possible to limn the Constitution's boundaries according to the inherent properties of language. And this initial, foundational point is not something that knowledge of language can establish. Only knowledge of constitutionalism could do that. Constitutional communication, in short, cannot be outsourced to linguistic study.[19] Understanding how the original U.S. Constitution communicated content to interpreters requires understanding how constitutional communication was originally understood to work. And that in and of itself demands deep historical excavation of how eighteenth-century constitutional minds worked.

If public meaning originalists are still inclined to resist and cling to their favored understanding of the Constitution's original communicative content—if they want to claim, in essence, that it doesn't matter how Founding-era Americans understood constitutional communication because those earlier Americans were ignorant of linguistic theory—then let's be crystal clear about what they're in fact arguing, which is that the original communicative content of the Constitution is *different from* the actual content that the original Constitution actually communicated at the time of its actual inception. There's the content the Constitution communicated according to eighteenth-century understandings of constitutional communication, and there's the content the Constitution is said to have communicated according to originalists' set understanding of constitutional communication. If originalists are adamant that the Constitution simply must speak in the way they have stipulated, given what supposedly inheres in the nature of a written constitution, then they are accepting that the original Constitution's original communicative content was, at least partially, invisible to those who actually lived at the Founding. What the Constitution in fact communicated, in this scenario, would be different from what real people believed it communicated according to their own distinctive understanding of how constitutions worked. Originalists' argument would need to take that form. It would seem, then, that either mainstream originalists adjust the concept of communicative content to account for how eighteenth-century constitutions in fact communicated to actual people at the time, or they jettison that concept altogether. If, by definition, it simply must refer to "the set of propositions communicated by the constitutional text," then it's of much less help in illuminating the original meaning of the original Constitution.[20] By presupposing a brand of written constitutionalism and an attendant model of constitutional communication at odds with those that predominated at the Founding, this formulation obscures the very thing it purports to illuminate.

Maybe originalists, or at least *some* originalists, can bracket certain kinds of original constitutional understandings, like what the framers intended constitutional provisions to mean or the changes the framers and ratifiers expected to follow from enacting those provisions, while maintaining a coherent interpretive theory. Maybe public meaning originalists, unlike original methods originalists, can sever the Constitution's original meaning from the original interpretive rules that supposedly would have been used to divine that meaning. But no originalist can bracket eighteenth-century constitutionalism itself. Because *any* meaning the Constitution had circa 1787 (original public meaning or otherwise) was a function of how constitutions were understood to acquire and communicate their meaning—that is, how they were understood to work. *What* the Constitution originally said was inextricably entangled with *how* it spoke. And the latter was as much the product of history as the former. There is no escaping that essential fact.

The Nature of Law

Just as originalists frequently claim that original public meaning is separable from Founding-era constitutional assumptions, they also frequently claim that original meaning is wholly separable from Founding-era views on the nature of law. We are not bound by the Founders' theory of law, originalists maintain, just the meaning of the actual law the Founders made by virtue of enacting the Constitution. Whatever eighteenth-century constitutionalists happened to think about natural law, common law, the law of nations, or the relationship between non-positive and positive law, it's separable from the search for original constitutional meaning. As the originalist Lawrence Solum, capturing a widely shared originalist belief, has emphatically put it, "it is simply a fallacy to equate [the Founding generation's] beliefs about the nature of law with the actual nature of law in 1787."[21]

This view is mistaken. As with their claims about constitutional communication, this popular originalist argument fails to understand how original constitutional meaning was essentially embedded in original conceptions of law. To see why, we first need to draw some distinctions that Solum's statement— which encapsulates what many originalists think—papers over. Whether the Founders' beliefs about law circa 1787 are the same thing as the actual nature of law circa 1787 is a separate matter from whether the Founders' beliefs about law circa 1787 are inextricably entangled with the Constitution's *original* meaning circa 1787. The Founders might well have been mistaken about law—and nothing argued to this point turns on it. But the Constitution's original meaning is surely inseparable from the Founders' understanding of law —unless "original meaning" describes something radically different from what originalists have long defended and thus fails to uphold many of the cardinal virtues that originalists have long emphasized. Let's consider how.

Eighteenth-century constitutions did not simply communicate meaning; they said things about law. The reason is obvious: they established systems of fundamental law, creating, in the process, a legal world in concrete and decisive ways. They did so by laying out how lawful governance would operate, how powers of governance would be regulated, and how essential features of liberty would be protected. In so doing, they determined where fundamental law came from and how it would work in a particular polity. They necessarily assumed things about the nature of law—its sources, its hierarchies, its logic, its basis.

Just as it was (and is) impossible to construct a constitution without some thick conception of constitutionalism, it was (and is) impossible to construct a system of fundamental law without some thick conception of fundamental law. What people thought about fundamental law at the Founding invariably shaped the nature of the Constitution they made and, by extension, the precise content it expressed.[22] Whether those who designed and adopted eighteenth-century constitutions accurately understood law or not, what they created and what it initially established and communicated was inseparable from their legal thinking. Whatever eighteenth-century American constitutions said about fundamental law was a function of how fundamental law was understood to work.

How could it be otherwise? As we have seen, what eighteenth-century U.S. constitutions communicated about fundamental rights was inseparable from the assumptions of social contract theory, especially the conviction that most fundamental rights were *already* afforded constitutional status before the writing of the constitution. It is impossible to understand *what* these constitutions were saying about rights without understanding what they *assumed* about law. In 1787, only about half of state constitutions enumerated most fundamental rights, and the U.S. Constitution, as initially ratified, enumerated hardly any. That was because those constitutions, according to the theory of law upon which they were predicated, already protected rights that might otherwise have been enumerated in text. Bracketing the theory of law fundamentally alters the content of the constitution those eighteenth-century people made and adopted. As we have also seen, eighteenth-century constitution making was tightly entwined with the concept of general fundamental law—not just the distinct body of legal principles assumed to be contained within it but the mode of legal thinking that animated it. If people believed that fundamental law was where positive and non-positive law fused into an integrated whole, that necessarily shaped what they thought their constitutions were saying about fundamental law through their particular enactments. James Wilson's and Oliver Ellsworth's insistence that the federal Constitution need not expressly prohibit ex post facto laws since they would already be "void of themselves" illustrates how tethered the Constitution's content initially was to assumptions about law itself.[23] The original Constitution presupposed particular understandings of fundamental law. To make fundamental law of any kind, it needed to.

Maybe Wilson and Ellsworth, as well as Samuel Chase, Alexander Hamilton, John Jay, Zephaniah Swift, Nathaniel Chipman, St. George Tucker, William Cushing, and their many peers, were all mistaken about law. Maybe they were wrongheaded to treat law as found more than made, to reason from social compacts, or to assume that written constitutions worked in concert with general fundamental law. Given Founding-era figures' careful and often penetrating reflections on law, I'm not sure why modern originalists automatically have claim to a deeper understanding of law than them. But even if we today can more accurately grasp the "true nature of law in 1787," it's still hard to see why that would change anything about the nature of "original constitutional meaning," given how inextricably entangled that original meaning was with eighteenth-century legal thinking. It is impossible to untangle one from the other without fundamentally changing what the original Constitution said.

Originalists could, of course, read the original Constitution in light of what they deem to be superior modern jurisprudence—but at considerable cost. It would seem more than a little odd to defend a theory that purports to recover the law of the original Constitution—the law that the Founding generation laid down, agreed to, and put in motion—by recovering some other law that they didn't think they were laying down, agreeing to, or putting in motion.

Originalists inclined to tread this path would likely intone that *what* the Founding generation adopted was the written Constitution we still call supreme law, and nothing else. Maybe those who made and adopted the Constitution didn't fully understand what they had legally created, because they didn't understand the nature of law the way we do today. But despite their ignorance, they made it all the same. The implication that naturally follows is that the law they made was, to a substantial degree, invisible to them—and perhaps remained murky to interpreters for decades to come. They thought they had one kind of fundamental law, but they in fact made another, one they couldn't easily see from their benighted legal perspective.

However plausible this idea might be, it directly undercuts two leading defenses of originalism: that it respects popular sovereignty by hewing to the Constitution that "We the People" originally enacted and that it upholds the rule of law by preserving cardinal virtues essential to that principle such as transparency, reliance, and notice.[24] If we discount the Founding generation's attitudes toward fundamental law and assume that they made a Constitution different from the one they tried to make and thought they had made, it's hard to see how we're fulfilling either of those stated aims. We're instead assuming that the sovereign people were originally blind and that few, if any, who followed them knew what the law even was for generations to come. Such an approach presumes that the nation's fundamental law only came into view slowly over time, as constitutional interpreters abandoned their flawed jurisprudential assumptions for more enlightened alternatives. This approach imagines that if the Constitution's original architects and ratifiers had only had the benefit of that learning, they would have been able to appreciate what they had in fact created—by accident.

The Intersubjective Constitution

The point runs deeper still. The ultimate reason why originalists cannot tidily separate the Constitution's original meaning from the constitutionalism in which it was embedded is that the Constitution, at base, is an intersubjective object. Originalists often fail to appreciate this fact. Most originalists like to believe that they can separate the object called "the Constitution" from so many of the things thought and said about that Constitution in the eighteenth century—that they can extract the Constitution from the intellectual, legal, and constitutional world in which it was originally rooted. The Constitution is whatever it is, they suggest, which is simply distinct from anything the Founders said about it. The object, they insist, should not be confused with the commentary that has surrounded it. The two can be neatly separated. What might work for other interpretive objects, however, doesn't work for constitutions.

When originalists attempt to separate the Constitution from the Founders' views on it, they typically draw on examples from natural science. The physics of buildings or bombs or the right understanding of chemistry, they indicate, follows a particular logic no matter what anyone in the past happened to think about them.[25] We don't need the Founders' testimony to accurately describe the properties of a building that the Founders occupied or a body of water they drank from. With the help of our superior science, we can sort out the essential properties of these kinds of objects independently of their (potentially) mistaken conceptions of these objects. The same is perhaps also true of bare facts.[26] If we are talking about the population of a state in 1790 and the Founders erred in calculating it, what matters legally is the actual fact of the matter—that is, what is required by the rule they laid down, even if they mistakenly thought something else would follow from implementing that rule. The truth of the matter is easy to separate from potentially faulty opinions about it. Accordingly, as originalists have claimed time and again, they are bound only by what the Founders laid down (the objective Constitution), and surely not the Founders' jurisprudential views, legal assumptions, or interpretive attitudes. Those things, originalists insist, are no different in kind from faulty views people held in the past about physics or chemistry—easily separable from the historical objects they seek to interpret.[27]

But these examples (factual, natural, or physical) don't get us very far with the U.S. Constitution. Perhaps it is possible to talk about the essential physical attributes of a building or the essential natural attributes of a body of water, regardless of what anyone has ever thought about them.[28] But the Constitution is neither a physical nor a natural object. It is, by contrast, a distinctively intersubjective one. It was made by human beings for human needs, and it was—and always has been—inextricably intertwined with a whole network of supporting concepts and assumptions. It is impossible to disentangle the Constitution from various contingent understandings of government, liberty, rights, and public power or various contingent assumptions about the nature of fundamental law and the inherent ways in which liberty and governance intersect. We can imagine how a building might be the same at T1 and T2 and, thus, how better science at T2 would equip us to better understand that building at T1 than the people who constructed it. But this analogy does not hold for an intersubjective object like a constitution. If we take our "better" constitutionalism from T2 (based on whatever theory we have dreamed up or imported from philosophy or jurisprudence) back to the Constitution at T1, we don't make better sense of the Constitution at T1, we just end up distorting it to look more like something we would recognize at T2. Because a constitution is necessarily predicated on a host of supporting concepts and assumptions, we need the "worse" constitutionalism at T1 to make out the Constitution at T1—if that is indeed our aim, as originalists claim it must be. The original Constitution cannot be separated from the original constitutionalism on which it was based and in which it was embedded. And there is no making sense of that constitutionalism without reckoning with Founding-era understandings of constitutional writtenness, fixity, and law. Originalists cannot bracket these kinds of Founding-era attitudes and beliefs, for they determined what the *original* Constitution actually said and did.

It is therefore mistaken to insist that originalists can somehow be bound by original meaning but *not* the Founding generation's views on constitutionalism, law, and rights. *If* we are bound by the Constitution's original meaning, then we are bound by whatever defined and determined that meaning. It's a package deal. You cannot simply attend to *what* the Founding generation laid down or *what* they ratified or what the Constitution *communicated* while ignoring how eighteenth-century people understood constitutionalism and fundamental law to work. *What* they laid down and what the Constitution *communicated* was a function of how constitutionalism and fundamental law were assumed to work. The two were inseparable. A constitution is not a bridge or an atom. It doesn't work that way. What the Constitution originally was and what it originally said were distinctly shaped by what actual people originally thought about it. Whatever the U.S. Constitution or any of the state constitutions that preceded it happened to say or do was deeply entangled with the many things Founding-era constitutionalists believed about the nature of law, the various things they assumed about the nature of liberty, the working assumptions almost all of them held about social compacts and their relationships to constitutional governance, and the basic ways people defined and debated the idea of a constitution itself—all things, we have seen, that were undergoing important change as the activity of constitution making placed fresh stress on them and ignited waves of uncertainty and disagreement. These are the things that made the original Constitution *original*. Any attempt to sever that Constitution or its original meaning from that thick constitutional context merely wrenches it out of the eighteenth century, quite possibly effacing the meaning that Constitution originally possessed.

Those who made, ratified, and first used the U.S. Constitution actively invested it with an identity and distinctive characteristics. There was no Constitution to speak of without those things. Otherwise, we must entertain the possibility, again, that the Founding generation created a constitution that was invisible to them—that the *original* Constitution existed in a form that no one at that time easily recognized. The better approach is instead to accept that the Constitution cannot be separated from the intersubjective processes that fundamentally shaped it. It is difficult to escape the conclusion, in fact, that the former fundamentally derived from the latter. The question is not whether the Constitution is a thing or a set of practices, but whether our capacity to see and speak intelligently about the Constitution *as a thing* is dependent on our intersubjective practices. There is every reason to believe that is the case.[29] If we fail to appreciate the intersubjective nature of the Constitution, we'll fail to grasp what constituted the original Constitution and its meaning.

Liberty and Commerce

Two concrete debates that have roiled modern American jurisprudence—over fundamental rights and the scope of federal regulatory power—help illustrate why originalists can't separate *original* meaning from *original* constitutionalism.

When it comes to deciphering the original meaning of particular fundamental rights, originalists fixate on constitutional text and the meaning of individual words and phrases. But in so doing, they quietly presuppose a broader understanding of the nature of constitutional rights themselves— "where rights come from, what purpose they serve in the constitutional order, and who has authority to define their meaning."[30] In searching for original meaning, as Jud Campbell has explained, interpreters often make three assumptions: "constitutional rights come from being enacted in the Constitution's text, they serve as counter-majoritarian limits on governmental power, and their content is defined by judges." For most originalists, "[t]his is just what constitutional rights are."[31] Thus, in the recent landmark Second Amendment case *New York State Rifle & Pistol Association v. Bruen*, which ruled that New York's concealed-carry law violated the right to keep and bear arms, Justice Clarence Thomas's originalist analysis first identified the scope of the right to keep and bear arms through the text of the Second Amendment (because, he assumes, the right is created by text) before asking whether certain regulations of that right were deeply rooted in the nation's history and traditions (because, he imagines, fundamental rights are meant to be protected from burdensome governmental interference).[32] This search for original meaning, in other words, already presupposed a thick conception of constitutional rights and, in turn, constitutionalism itself—a conception that determined the very meaning that the Court claimed it was merely recovering in its unvarnished historical form.

But as we have seen, the Founding generation did not share any of the thinking on which *Bruen* rests.[33] Eighteenth-century constitutionalism was predicated on a different understanding of, as Campbell has put it, "where fundamental rights come from, what purpose they serve, and who gets to define them."[34] Fundamental rights were not, in most instances, created by text but preceded textual enactment; these rights were not meant to limit governmental activity but to ensure legitimate and robust self-governance; and these rights were to be defined, not principally by judges, but by the "people themselves" acting through the institutions that most readily spoke for them.[35] In presupposing that constitutional rights gain their force through textual enumeration and, once enumerated, are fully determinate and non-regulable, *Bruen* is thus squarely at odds with the essential premises and logic of the original Constitution. As we know, like most of the original amendments, the Second Amendment was declaratory in character—its text neither created nor precisely determined the constitutional right it announced. At the time it was written, sorting out what the amendment said was not a matter of linguistic interpretation—of closely parsing the semantics and pragmatics of its text—but a matter of conceptual analysis based on the particular right it identified. By the terms of originalism, beginning with the text is a mistake, as is closely analyzing the precise formula of the text as if that determined the right or communicated its precise content. As Campbell has instructively put it, "[i]nstead of starting with a search for the original meaning of certain words and phrases," originalists ought to "begin by recovering, at a more conceptual level, how the Founders thought about rights."[36] As we have also seen, like most fundamental rights at the time, the right announced by the Second Amendment would be regulated by the people's representatives in the interest of the public good. Nothing about constitutionally enumerating a particular right stripped the people of their power to engage in the precise kind of means-ends analysis *Bruen* seeks to curb. Finally, like all underdetermined constitutional rights at the time, the right announced by the Second Amendment would be more precisely determined only over time, usually through the people's representative institution. A fixed right did not mean fixed determinations of that of right, and it certainly did not mean that it had been fixed by declaratory text.

Bruen's defenders can't ignore any of this by claiming that the Court is simply after the original legal meaning of the Constitution, not the premises upon which that legal meaning might have been constructed. For the very legal meaning the Court seeks to recover was inextricably tied to a broader vision of constitutional rights. These premises about rights, enumeration, and regulation were woven into the very fabric of that original meaning. *How the Founding generation understood the nature of constitutional rights determined* what the original amendments communicated. By fixating on textual meaning, insisting that rights are inherently threatened by legislative regulation, and assuming that judges are meant to protect those rights, *Bruen* distorts the very understanding of constitutional rights that the Second Amendment, like so many of the original amendments, was constructed to serve—and, in the process, forces the amendment to say something it didn't say in 1791. By assuming that constitutional text speaks on its own apart from these deeper eighteenth-century assumptions, *Bruen* makes it impossible to see the very different way that constitutional text once spoke *on account of* those assumptions. It is a perfect illustration of how originalists, through their tacit presuppositions, so often quietly rewrite the original Constitution into a modern one they prefer. Contrary to what *Bruen*'s originalist defenders might claim, the justices who decided it neither privileged original public meaning over irrelevant historical context nor favored legal over historical reasoning. They instead warped the Constitution's original legal meaning by deleting the understandings of rights, law, and constitutionalism that originally determined it.

The same can be said of *Bruen*'s proposed method for using post-ratification history to judge the legitimacy of contemporary regulations of Second Amendment rights, a method that supposedly showed New York's concealed-carry law to be unconstitutional. In place of a balancing test, the Court laid down an alternative test that looked to "history and tradition." Instead of asking whether modern regulations on the right to keep and bear arms served a compelling governmental interest, the Court declared that these regulations needed to be consistent with the nation's history and traditions. Those defending today's regulations, the Court declared, would need to demonstrate that they are analogous to regulations from the nation's earliest years. What exactly constitutes a historical tradition remained uncertain, especially given that the Court selectively—many would say arbitrarily—counted or dismissed evidence of public-carry regulations from the decades following the Founding.[37] But even more problematic than the Court's arbitrary application of its own arbitrary method was the ahistorical way the majority sought to execute its own approach. To identify past regulations, the Court looked primarily to eighteenth- and nineteenth-century state statutes.[38] Assuming that law must have worked then as it does now, they looked in the places familiar to them. But, as Laura Edward and Mandy Cooper have shown, local law—where most regulations took place—worked quite differently back then. Local law was a robust system of customary practices and norms not easily seen from an anachronistic modern legal perspective that privileges statutes. It becomes visible only by attending to a broader constellation of legal practice and a broader set of legal archives.[39] This system of customary legal practice also constituted something much closer to a deeply rooted tradition than anything the Court claimed to find through its selective statutory analysis. The Court looked in the wrong place, and not for sound modern legal reasons—as defenders are sure to claim—but out of historical ignorance. By failing to understand how early U.S. law worked, by assuming that law must have worked as law works now, the Court obscured the very historical traditions it sought to recover. The Court invented traditions rather than finding them in history, much as the Court had rewritten the Second Amendment rather than locating its original historical meaning in its original constitutional context.

Here, then, we have a concrete example illustrating why originalists can't recover the Constitution's original meaning without first understanding how the Founding generation thought about constitutionalism itself. When originalists try to recover the Constitution's original meaning, too often they "begin with deeply engrained premises about the nature of what [they] are looking for."[40] By defining original meaning in terms of text, Justice Thomas's opinion in *Bruen* quietly molded the past to conform with the assumptions of the present.

The same lessons apply when we turn from fundamental rights to federal regulatory power. Once again, the conventional search for original public meaning presupposes a vision of constitutionalism that is anything but neutral and indeed at odds with the key assumptions upon which Founding-era constitutionalism was predicated.

In modern constitutional doctrine, the limits of federal power usually turn on the interpretation of the Commerce Clause. That is unsurprising since the power to regulate interstate commerce has long been used, especially since the New Deal era, to defend a more expansive regulatory state. Modern originalists, wary of ever-expanding federal power, have trained their sights on the originalist foundations of this particular doctrine by investigating the original meaning of this clause and, in particular, the meaning of the word "commerce" in order to evaluate the constitutional legitimacy of the modern U.S. state.[41] Looking at usage of the term at the time of the Founding, they contend that, when the Constitution was written and ratified, "commerce" did not enjoy a broad meaning—denoting any "gainful activity"—but was instead employed only in reference to "trade and exchange."[42] Such work of originalist scholars built on and then helped propel the Supreme Court's reading of the Commerce Clause in important cases like *United States v. Lopez* and *National Federation of Independent Business v. Sebelius* (better known as the Obamacare case), in which the Court, for the first time since the New Deal, placed limits on the commerce power.[43] Often drawing on originalist scholars, originalists on the Court insisted that the expansive readings that had been given to the Commerce Clause by past justices were unsupported by historical evidence.

Fixating on the original meaning of "commerce," however, turns out to be an anachronistic exercise. Originalists are obsessed with the Commerce Clause because modern constitutional law has long shared the same preoccupation. It's become the standard vessel through which the Supreme Court limns the boundaries of federal power. But as we have seen, that was not how the Founding generation thought about the scope and outer limits of national power.[44] And that wasn't because they ignored the Constitution's so-called public meaning but because they presupposed a different understanding of constitutionalism altogether, one that focused their attention on alternative interpretive questions.

At the Founding, the action lay elsewhere. The Commerce Clause was an important part of Article I, section 8—especially to ensure that states would not restrict trade across state lines as they had under the Articles of Confederation—and it would take on outsized importance in the first third of the nineteenth century as the movement of goods and people created controversies over interstate commerce that federal courts needed to adjudicate.[45] But back when the Constitution was first drafted, the field of debate was markedly different. As we have seen, initially debates over national power often turned on competing theories of union—disagreements about whether the federal government established by the U.S. Constitution represented a genuine nation, a confederacy of sovereign states, or something in between. The meaning communicated by the enumerated powers of Article I, section 8, the Necessary and Proper Clause that punctuated it, or the Preamble that came well before it was a matter of what kind of union the United States was and, because of that, what kind of government had been created to represent it. Unsurprisingly, then, early debates over national power—between Wilsonians, Hamiltonians, Madisonians, Jeffersonians—rarely turned on competing interpretations of the Commerce Clause. They were organized instead around a different set of constitutional questions and touchstones, and a different underlying debate over federal constitutionalism itself.[46]

The great irony is that originalist investigations into the original meaning of "commerce" are, in crucial respects, living constitutionalist in character—they are predicated on how constitutional doctrine, assumptions, and debate have evolved since the Founding rather than how people reasoned about federal power at the time the Constitution was drafted. These investigations are based on a question that matters now but would have been beside the point when the Constitution was first debated.

The crucial point, as with fundamental rights, is that decoding the Constitution's original meaning requires coming to terms with the constitutionalism in which that meaning was embedded. Asking what the word "commerce" originally meant doesn't cut to original meaning by helpfully bypassing the Founders' intentions or expectations; it obscures the original meaning that the Founders created by obscuring the underlying understanding of delegated authority in a federal constitutional republic on which that meaning was premised. By zeroing in on "commerce" and ignoring the social-contract premises that initially breathed life into that clause, originalists quietly supply their own robust understanding of how the Constitution delegates authority: through the textual enumeration of powers. Text makes and circumscribes constitutional powers much like it makes and circumscribes constitutional rights. But the Founding generation thought that federal power was delegated not simply through enacted text but also as a result of the kind of polity and people who had delegated that power. The original scope of national power was not determined by the linguistic meaning of "commerce"— or the Article I Vesting Clause or the Tenth Amendment. It was determined by the nature of the United States.

Whether it's decoding fundamental rights or limning the boundaries of national power, the search for original meaning cannot be separated from the history described in part II.

Rewriting the Constitution

Originalists cannot continue to ignore what the Founding generation thought about constitutionalism—not without abandoning the core tenets of originalism in the process. This is no small matter or simple fix—it cuts to the heart of the theory.

Originalists tend to presume that their conception of the Constitution is given. That is why they feel justified in bracketing the kind of Founding-era evidence we've emphasized to this point. That is why so many of them are confident that the Constitution communicates in a distinctively textual way. That is why so many of them claim that original meaning is a matter of linguistic fact. That is why so many of them assume that fixed constitutional meaning implies fixed textual meaning. That is why so many of them presume that the Constitution is a conventional legal instrument. Those things are just so. But there is nothing given about any of this, much less the robust conception of the Constitution made of these various assumptions. That givenness is a myth.[47]

In taking their own understanding of the Constitution for granted, doctrinaire originalists erase the Constitution's historical identity. They impose their own assumptions onto it, assumptions that take the place of the Founding-era assumptions they've quietly discarded. They don't take the Constitution as they find it; they twist it into novel form. In defining how the Constitution speaks, they change what it says. In ripping the Constitution from the original context in which it was embedded, they transform its core features. In disaggregating the Constitution from its original constitutional world, they rewrite it. Under the auspices of passively reading the Constitution, they invest it with an identity and substance it did not initially possess. They define its content, redraw its boundaries, alter its character. They, in effect, turn it into something new, something of their own making. Originalists don't simply find a Constitution in the past, as they so emphatically claim. They *make* one in the present.

In so doing, they undermine what has long been the defining narrative of the originalist project. For beneath the various normative theories that are often layered on top of it, originalism has long depended on one consistent defense: that, as an interpretive approach, it does not *make* a constitution; it merely *finds* and *interprets* one. Whereas other theories get caught up in what the Constitution *ought* to be, originalism alone supposedly respects the Constitution for what it *is*. Originalism's most important defense has always been that it purports to be a neutral method of interpretation, the lone approach that merely unearths what the Constitution objectively means. "The deeper reason that Originalism will not die," Tara Smith has insightfully noted, "is that it has staked out the moral high ground, championing the *objectivity* of interpretation that is essential to the ideal of the rule of law."[48] Justice Antonin Scalia, meanwhile, put it his own way. "The conclusive argument in favor of originalism is a simple one: It is the only objective standard of interpretation even competing for acceptance."[49] Such a description equates originalism with pure constitutional recovery. As one leading originalist has asserted, originalism alone restores "the essential forms of the Constitution."[50] A real originalist Constitution is juxtaposed against an invented non-originalist one, and non-originalists are assumed to be altering and revising the Constitution to suit their desires and needs. By virtue of its method, by virtue of recovering the Constitution as it *is*, originalism alone is faithful to the Constitution. That has always been originalism's central narrative: constitutional fidelity by way of constitutional recovery and restoration.

But in defining the Constitution's content according to the terms of modern law and jurisprudence, orthodox originalists don't merely describe the Constitution but in fact *give* the Constitution an identity and core characteristics that, at its inception, it did not obviously possess. Consider our historical evidence. In taking their conception of the Constitution as given, doctrinaire originalists foreclose the possibility of ever seeing the Constitution as so many Founding-era constitutionalists instinctively did, of ever allowing it to communicate the content that those framers, ratifiers, and interpreters assumed it necessarily conveyed. Those ways of thinking about the Constitution and what it communicated are automatically excluded from consideration under the guise of an allegedly neutral definition of what the Constitution is. By its own logic, orthodox originalists' method assumes that the Constitution does not and cannot communicate what so many early constitutional thinkers assumed it necessarily did. Which means that originalists' method is not adjudicating the matter but determining it beforehand; not deciphering public meaning but in fact constituting it. In describing and analyzing the Constitution in the contingent way that they do, originalists erase the possibility of vast swaths of original constitutional content. In so doing, they don't merely follow the Constitution "as it is" and as they claim, but rather make it into what they think it must have been. Before interpreting anything, in other words, much of originalists' argumentative work is complete. How, then, are originalists not imposing something—and something fundamental—on the precise thing they claim merely to be recovering? How are they not guilty of doing what they so often accuse living constitutionalists of doing and what originalism was purportedly designed to prevent: of *making* rather than *finding* a constitution?

Consider how the leading originalists Randy Barnett and Lawrence Solum have described the originalist task: "Historical evidence is the lifeblood of originalism. Historical linguistics is the key to the original meaning of the words and phrases that make up the constitutional text. Historical context disambiguates and enriches semantic meaning. Historical practice and historical doctrine frequently provide evidence of original meaning."[51] Historical evidence is the lifeblood of originalism, they say, yet the manner in which they describe that evidence anachronistically presupposes lots about the Constitution, its content, and the ways it communicates. Original constitutional meaning is simply original *linguistic* meaning; historical context and practice help clarify the meaning of *words*. If historical evidence was truly the lifeblood of originalism, then originalists would take the evidence on its own terms and follow where it leads. They wouldn't assume *anything* about the nature of original constitutional meaning or communication but would instead allow the historical evidence and context to tell them how constitutional meaning and communication worked in the eighteenth century. Rather than narrowly contextualizing constitutional words, they would broadly contextualize the Constitution. Rather than studying historical practice to clarify particular constitutional phrases, they would look to historical practice to understand how people conceptualized constitutional meaning. Rather than stipulating a robust conception of constitutionalism, constitutional meaning, and constitutional communication, and *only then* turning to the historical evidence, they would try to recapture the Founding generation's own conceptions of those things. Originalists would do as they say and consider what eighteenth-century Americans laid down, rather than assuming that constitutionalism as they understand it must have been there from the beginning. They wouldn't bracket all the historical evidence presented here—they would realize that *that* evidence is the lifeblood of any historically grounded form of originalism.

As these reflections suggest, originalists' point of entry usually assumes too much. Originalists typically start with the text and ask what the words of that text meant in their original context. Originalists should start instead with the Constitution itself and ask how it acquired and communicated meaning in its original constitutional context. They should ask how the original Constitution spoke, instead of assuming that it's obvious how it did. Starting in the right place is vital. As we have seen, if one starts with the words of the Constitution's enumerated rights provisions without first understanding the particular way eighteenth-century Americans conceptualized liberty and fundamental rights, or if one starts with the Constitution's enumerated powers without first understanding how the powers of union turned on the underlying nature of that union, or if one starts with the Constitution's status as law without first understanding how eighteenth-century fundamental law worked or what might have differentiated a constitution from other forms of law, one runs the risk of obscuring the very eighteenth-century Constitution one aims to recover, all while pretending that a faulty image is in fact the real thing.

The eighteenth-century Constitution was enmeshed in eighteenth-century constitutionalism. In trying to recover the former while ignoring the latter, all originalists have done is fashion a Constitution of their own making. That isn't ultimately surprising, for as long as originalism has been defended and practiced, it's been largely detached from the eighteenth-century Constitution it purports to respect. Originalism is a position staked out in modern jurisprudential debates and based on the logic of modern constitutional law, which makes it, like its various competitors, a version of living constitutionalism. And the latest brand of originalism to burst on the scene—one we have yet to consider in depth—helps us see why.

10

Imposing the Modern on the Past

> [W]e have . . . the natural desire to talk to people some of whose ideas
> are quite like our own. . . . Such enterprises in commensuration are,
> of course, anachronistic. But if they are conducted in full knowledge
> of their anachronism, they are unobjectionable. The only problems
> they raise are . . . whether [they] are to be viewed as "making clear
> what the dead really said," and . . . whether [they] are "really" doing
> *history*.
>
> — Richard Rorty, 1984

THE STANDARD ORIGINALIST CONCEPTION of the constitution is unfounded
and ahistorical. It quietly effaces eighteenth-century constitutionalism by
imposing modern understandings of fundamental law, legal interpretation,
and rights culture onto an unsuspecting past. In so doing, it substitutes a
modern Constitution in place of the original one.

There is, however, one kind of originalism, treading an unbeaten path,
that describes the Constitution in fundamentally different terms: original
law originalism. Tantalizingly, its acolytes seem interested in historicizing
the Constitution in ways that other originalists have proved unwilling to pursue. Through its heterodox assumptions, this new version of the theory exposes just how optional orthodox originalism's conception of the Constitution
has long been. Yet, at the same time, original law originalism reveals something fundamental to all forms of originalism, something that helps clarify

what originalism is and has always been. Originalism is not, ultimately, as its champions maintain, a form of historical recovery, a concerted effort to remain faithful to what original lawmakers laid down. Instead, originalism is a form of modern legal rhetoric that, by presupposing the genre of modern constitutional law and the contingent jurisprudential logic that structures it, is focused on the present far more than the past. In that regard, this new brand of originalism reveals perhaps the deepest truth about originalism: in its many diverse forms, it is living constitutionalist to its core.

Original Law Originalism

The architects of original law originalism, William Baude and Stephen Sachs, have broken from the conventional originalist approach to the Constitution, transforming originalism from a prescriptive theory of interpretation into a theory of law. Baude and Sachs have done so by adopting H. L. A. Hart's influential theory of legal positivism and applying it to the originalism debate.[1] Following Hart, they see law as a matter not of stipulation but acceptance. Instead of looking to expressly posited law (the written Constitution) as most originalists do, they focus on positive social practice.[2] Specifically, Baude and Sachs consider what legal officials take the law to be given their own legal system's rule of recognition—that is, the rule that sets out the criteria of legal validity itself. Baude and Sachs thus start with a positivist account of our present law. They contemplate what our law actually is today—as revealed by legal practice and social fact—and, on the basis of that alone, have contended that our legal system is originalist in character and orientation because it recognizes the Founders' law (with whatever changes have been made along the way in accordance with the Founders' rules for valid change) as our law today.[3] "If originalism is legally required," they suggest, that is "a question solely of *modern* law."[4] It is because of *our* law today that we must look to the past.[5] Our rule of recognition sends us in search of the original rule of recognition that accompanied the Constitution and forces us to follow the chain of legal development from then to now. By tying law to social acceptance, rather than formal enactment, this positive turn directs our focus away from the text of the original Constitution and toward the system of law existent at the Founding (its sources of legitimacy, its content, its rules, and its rules for lawful change), which the Constitution was a part of and which our current practices still purportedly authorize.[6] This picture is nothing if not striking.

At present, it is unclear what this novel form of originalism will amount to. Many observers are deeply suspicious that originalism is in fact our law. They cast doubt on Baude and Sachs's account of our legal system and the rule of recognition that purportedly structures it.[7] It is doubtful, moreover, that in adopting such a capacious (and, it seems, dynamic) understanding of Founding-era law and its avenues for change, and in turn legitimizing such a wide range of interpretive possibilities, original law originalism will preserve any of the features, aims, or ambitions that have traditionally defined originalism or distinguished it from leading competitors.[8]

These two critiques converge on a common skepticism: it is not clear that much ultimately hinges on declaring originalism to be our law. The statement is either trivially true or self-evidently false depending upon how we define the operative term. One is reminded of W. V. O. Quine's observation about the possible existence of magical creatures: we can always twist our concepts into whatever shape necessary to fit empirical reality, he explained, in order to make certain statements true, though doing so is not likely to shed any light on what originally motivated the inquiry.[9] Originalism can easily be made to describe our law and our settled social practices, depending on our (re-)definition of originalism itself. If making the statement true necessitates a dramatic redefinition of originalism, however, it's unclear what doing so ultimately accomplishes. Defined at a certain level of generality, originalism can be made consistent with almost everything anyone has ever argued about our Constitution. So the interesting questions become: Do Baude and Sachs define originalism in such a way that they can retain some of originalism's core features and goals while delivering on their positive account? Or must one come at the cost of the other? Whatever the case, the statement "originalism is our law" does minimal initial work. The point of making such a statement is, presumably, to learn more about both originalism and our constitutional practice, but it still remains to be seen whether the positive turn will clarify either or whether instead, to make it all work, this new form of originalism must ultimately muddy the waters, redirecting rather than resolving the debate.[10]

Original law originalism might, at first glance, appear to suffer from the same issues that plague original methods originalism. Indeed, it not only bears a resemblance to the latter, but the comparison is one that Baude and Sachs have themselves occasionally drawn.[11] Like John McGinnis and Michael Rappaport, they conceive of the Constitution principally as law and emphasize the centrality and determinacy of Founding-era legal rules.[12] They are legalists through and through. But it would be a mistake to simply lump Baude and Sachs in with other originalists. For upon closer investigation, original law originalism is actually quite different from original methods originalism—and indeed every other kind of originalism.

In fact, the most striking thing about original law originalism is how sharply it departs from orthodox originalism. As we have seen, orthodox originalists conceive of the Constitution as a formally written and expressly enacted text—something that is strictly posited. They reduce originalism—and the law that the Constitution produced—to original meaning precisely because, to their minds, the Constitution is just the set of linguistic meanings expressed by its text. Those original meanings *are* the original law of the Constitution. Regardless of their other disagreements, public meaning originalists, original intent originalists, and original methods originalists all begin with the Constitution's text and its textual meaning. Their disagreements turn on the correct way to read that text. Some favor its ordinary meaning, others its legal meaning; some see it as a typical species of linguistic communication, others see it as technical law; some read the words like other English sentences, others read them through the lens of familiar rules of legal construction; some read those words for what they communicate linguistically, others read them more historically as expressing the particular subjective understandings of those who wrote and ratified those words. But in all cases, the Constitution *is* the text, and its original meaning is, accordingly, textual in nature. This, at bottom, is the originalism long advocated by most leading originalist academics and championed from the bench by originalist jurists such as Justices Antonin Scalia, Neil Gorsuch, and Amy Coney Barrett.

Original law originalism rejects the basic outlines of this originalist orthodoxy. Baude and Sachs favor original *law* over original *meaning*.[13] They refuse to see the Constitution as a circumscribed text whose content is derived from the deliberate act of bringing it into being.[14] Nowhere is this more apparent than in Sachs's avowed (and dramatic) efforts to rescue originalism from its obsession with constitutional writtenness.[15] Instead, Baude and Sachs see the Constitution as a considerably larger—and in certain respects amorphous and shifting—body of law that is fundamentally intertwined with the techniques and practices that determine its content.[16] In their work, the Constitution is treated more like a set of intersubjective practices than a discrete object.

The distinctive way in which Baude and Sachs understand the determinants of original law makes it especially plain that they see the Constitution differently than their originalist counterparts do. Contrary to most originalists, they privilege legal *acceptance* over legal *enactment*. According to Baude and Sachs, original law is not simply what an enacting authority posited at a particular moment in time. Following Hart, they believe original law is, instead, a function of social practice, a reflection of what the Founding generation took the law and the Constitution to be—as a positive matter—and the practices in which those entities were embedded.[17] Law is not something that is laid down; it's something that is recognized.[18]

Accordingly, Baude and Sachs offer a dramatically different account of how the original Constitution made law. Some original law, they acknowledge, was a direct product of the enactment of the Constitution's text. But the act of creating the Constitution also left lots of existing law in place and brought vast swaths of general law on board.[19] The Constitution also, they claim, authorized unwritten rules of change that allowed this large body of amorphous law to shape-shift over time.[20] As Baude and Sachs imply, the Constitution's drafters did not create constitutional law from scratch; they were not painting on a blank canvas. Instead, they altered a preexisting picture, deciding what to leave in place, what to modify, and what to scrap. According to Baude and Sachs, the framers understood that the whole body of law would operate in concert with techniques of legal reasoning and accepted understandings of how law worked.[21]

The Constitution, according to them, is therefore far more than the law made by its words. It was as much the law it left in place—the preexisting law derived from the common law, the law of nations, and general legal principles. Other originalists no doubt would hastily point out that they too believe that the Constitution incorporates various elements of customary law.[22] But only to the extent that these forms of law are recognized by the Constitution's text, which is no modest difference. Thinking that the Constitution incorporates those kinds of law because its text says so, as most originalists believe, and thinking that the Constitution incorporates those kinds of law because that is how law works, as Baude and Sachs believe, embody two fundamentally distinct accounts of how the Constitution acquires content. From the standpoint of original law originalism, moreover, one does not use original legal methods to interpret the Constitution's text. Instead, one uses original legal methods to understand which parts of which sorts of existing law were incorporated—and in what ways—through the legal act of creating the Constitution.[23] There is no way to successfully read the Constitution, according to Baude and Sachs, without understanding the unwritten law of interpretation, which is found in few of the obvious places that originalists usually look for constitutional content and whose legitimacy hardly relies on the conscious, authoritative choice of constitutional enactors.[24] Where most originalists have been allergic to the idea that the Constitution could recognize, let alone rely on, general law and jurisprudence—for them the Constitution *is* the text written, enacted, and amended, after all—original law originalism not only accepts the presence and authority of general law but fundamentally depends on it.[25] Orthodox originalists have long disparaged the "brooding omnipresence in the sky"; original law originalism extols its indispensable virtues.[26]

These are not small differences. In conceiving of the Constitution in such a radically different way, Baude and Sachs take a wrecking ball to core originalist thinking. Given how sharply original law originalism breaks from orthodox originalism, attempts thus far to synthesize the former with mainstream originalist theory unsurprisingly have proved awkward. Taking original law originalism fully on board would force orthodox originalists to fundamentally rethink how they have long envisioned the Constitution—which is perhaps why they have been unable, or perhaps unwilling, to acknowledge the extent of Baude and Sachs's break from the standard originalist portrait.[27] Original law originalism is simply talking about a different kind of constitution than most other originalists are, including those originalists who privilege legal meanings and interpretive methods. It's a version of originalism that completely breaks the mold.

All of this marks a significant step forward. In approaching the Constitution and its history so differently, Baude and Sachs help expose how impoverished most prior originalist treatments of the early Constitution have been. In breaking with originalist orthodoxy, original law originalism helps reveal how nonessential the standard originalist conception of the original Consti-tution really is. More positively, by favoring original law over original mean-ing and law as social practice over law as posited text, Baude and Sachs encourage a superior approach to Founding-era constitutionalism, one that at least has a fighting chance of avoiding the sort of sweeping anachronism that plagues most other forms of originalism. As we have seen, we can bring the original Constitution into focus only if we first embed it in eighteenth-century constitutionalism and the myriad interconnected assumptions that were central to that constitutionalism. Original law originalism at least car-ries the potential to do that.

With all of that said, however, fundamental issues remain. By conceiving of the Constitution distinctively as law and in emphasizing the determinacy of Founding-era legal rules, original law originalism minimizes the depth of early constitutional contestation (interpretive and otherwise) and presup-poses the kind of legalized Constitution that was so fiercely challenged at the Founding.[28] Additionally, Baude and Sachs tend to derive the law of the Founding from the commentary of a small cadre of legal elites, even though early constitutionalism was the product of a far greater number of voices drawn from a far greater diversity of society.[29] They also minimize disagree-ment among legal elites, which at the Founding was often every bit as fierce as it is today. One need only consider the debates prompted by *Chisholm v. Georgia* over the interpretive approach taken by Justices James Wilson and John Jay, which ran about as deep as anything could.[30] In addition, Baude and Sachs take for granted the kind of Constitution that early nineteenth-century jurists only later polemically and politically constructed as though it was an inexorable byproduct of ratification and conventional legal thinking. On account of their legalism, moreover, Baude and Sachs's conception of the past is also stubbornly narrow.[31] Because they are interested only in whatever part of history modern law deems relevant, they claim that they can look at an exceedingly slender slice of the past to decipher original law.[32] Concretely, they draw a sharp distinction between what was *internal* to the law of the Founding and what was *external* to it—bracketing most political struggles over the Constitution that engulfed the young republic on the grounds that they fall into the latter category. Originalists need concern themselves, Baude and Sachs argue, only with those facts and developments that happened to be internal to the law. Everything else can be brushed to the side. What they

fail to recognize, however, is that so many of the early constitutional struggles they are quick to bracket or minimize—particularly the ones we probed
in detail earlier—*were* internal to Founding-era law. Those struggles were
not disputes over how to apply or interpret the law, or whether that law was
good or bad, or where it might lead; they were disputes over the essential
nature of the Constitution—over the very determinants *of* law. The struggle
between Wilsonians, Jeffersonians, and Madisonians over the nature of
the federal union was as internal to the law of the Founding as anything
could have been. Debates between legalists and their opponents were no different. In both cases, and in many others, the contest was over what the law
of the United States even was—over what the Constitution as a legal matter
established.

   Baude and Sachs also need to contend with the fact that, on a variety of
fundamental issues that cut right to the Constitution's core, there were not
any descriptively "right" or settled answers. Was the federal union a national
social compact or a collection of states that had compacted together? Was the
president the first magistrate of a commonwealth or the chief executive of-
ficer of a European-style state? Were individual states in the union sovereign? Was the Constitution a legal instrument to be enforced by the judiciary
or a people's document to be enforced by the terms of popular constitutionalism? These questions were internal to Founding-era law, and that law could
not settle them. Any attempt to appeal to a preexisting law of interpretation
necessitated passing judgment on the precise issues in need of clarification.
Legal elites thus used the common law to defend their belief that the Constitution was a common legal instrument, much as nationalists and compact
theorists each claimed that the Constitution's text affirmed their understanding of the federal union. But in none of these cases was anyone using law
to settle a charged legal question; they were attempting to stake out what
the law even was and what, as an internal matter, determined its use and
operation. They were not playing by established rules but attempting to establish which set of rules—which internal vision of law—would take priority.
That is why Baude and Sachs's attempts to neatly separate legal and political
questions at the Founding doesn't work.[33] Surely, then as today, there was a
recognized distinction between what we might call policy and legal questions. In early constitutional debates, such as the one over chartering a national bank, disputants sometimes debated whether the bank was good

policy, while at other times they debated whether it was legal, all while appreciating the difference. It's not that they lacked the distinction; it's that the boundary between politics and law was unclear and a source of debate—that the boundaries of what constituted constitutional "law" was necessarily bound up in constitutional politics. There wasn't a body of law that could explain where a constitutional claim ended and a policy claim began—the distinction that made the difference had to be negotiated through the precise kind of constitutional politics that Baude and Sachs try to shield original law from. Baude and Sachs thus fail to grasp the depth of Founding-era constitutional struggle—over both the nature of law and the rules for interpreting and enforcing it. They are eager to bracket so much of the period's history in order to redeem their positivist account of what, as a descriptive matter, the creation of the Constitution legally established. But that leads them to furnish an implausible account of Founding-era law and legal rules, one that looks past the defining features of the period and the defining struggles that constituted our fundamental law.

It also leads them to misconstrue the primary ways in which constitutional law has changed over the course of our nation's history. Not only was our constitutionalism initially constituted through the kinds of debates already mentioned, but it was changed through these debates as well. Baude and Sachs are comfortable with a much broader swath of constitutional change than most originalists. For them, any rule of change that was part of the Founders' law—not just the formal amendment procedure found in Article V of the Constitution but also the informal processes of liquidating meaning through practice and debate or establishing precedent through judicial rulings—can lawfully change the Constitution, provided that it's consistent with original law.[34] Most constitutional change, however, has arguably not followed these rules for change. The Constitution's character and meaning changed as Americans debated the fundamental underlying issues raised in the decades following ratification—debates over, among other things, the nature of the union and the Constitution's relationship to legalism. In this charged context, the Constitution's meaning was not liquidated through an established legal formula. The change, rather, was essentially political and cultural in nature.

Perhaps even more significantly, Baude and Sachs's approach fails to account for the fact that constitutional law has often changed as a result of conceptual rupture—as modes of thinking about law have subtly transformed. The Marshall Court's steady rejection of early jurists' synthesized view of law, a move that made it easier to see the Constitution like a self-contained statute, was one such change. The gradual shift toward legal positivism and the dramatic ways in which that altered the nature of common law and legal science itself was certainly another.[35] The invention of the genre of constitutional law, of making constitutionalism essentially lawlike, was yet another. These changes were immense. As after a Kuhnian paradigm shift, on the other side of such conceptual transformations it was impossible not to read the Constitution and its provisions differently.[36] As Lawrence Lessig has astutely noted, "law is a culture, not a logic board."[37] Whether people took for granted the existence of general fundamental law, treated common law as simply the rulings of courts, or believed that constitutional law was positivist in nature invariably shaped what they even thought they were doing in deciphering the Constitution's legal commands.[38] And none of those changes followed the rules of change that had been established as part of the Founders' law. How could they? Are we to believe that the Founding generation established rules of change for when future people stopped thinking about constitutionalism and law in the various ways they treated as natural and essential? The Founders did not anticipate or speak to these kinds of ruptures, let alone somehow implicitly ratify them and their often unexpected consequences. It was not part of the Founders' rule of recognition in any sense we can fairly describe. Because law, as Baude and Sachs rightly stress, emphasizes continuity, jurists and legal practitioners over the years have certainly proved able, however unconsciously, of erasing these kinds of ruptures by stressing the broader tradition that has persisted uninterrupted. But that kind of rhetorical continuity, which portrays change on the terms of prior legal rules, should not obscure the conceptual rupture it surely works to mask.[39] A great deal of constitutional change, in other words, has resulted not from the application of the Founders' own rules of change but as our legal consciousness increasingly departed from that of the Founders—as we left the Founders' legal imagination behind.

Original law originalism, by its own terms, is a manifestation of that change. Even if it takes seriously the kind of general law that modernism washed away, in deeper ways the theory's approach to law evinces the socialization of a modern lawyer—the subjects, problems, and techniques common to it, as well as the approach to law implicit in it.[40] In that regard, the theory's view of law and its theoretical makeup bears limited resemblance to the one assumed by the Founding generation. Original law originalism might embrace the category of general law, if not the full legal worldview that once breathed life into it. Original law originalism thus quietly testifies to the various conceptual ruptures that carried us away from the Founders' law. It itself bears the mark of earlier paradigm shifts in legal consciousness that, being fundamental and conceptual in nature, neither could have been fueled by prior rules of change nor could have been anticipated by them.

That said, even if original law originalism suffers from these defects, its social-practice account of our constitutional system nonetheless does seem to reimagine the Constitution in a way that is far more consonant with the Constitution's history and development. Among originalists, only Jack Balkin has been similarly willing to embrace such a fractured and histori- cized version of the Founding (and, when it comes to originalism, he has long been the exception that proves the rule).[41] By looking to original law, Baude and Sachs take a wider vision and treat the Constitution as a capa- cious body of law. But they seem to do far more than even this. In situating the Constitution in the context of an original legal system, predicated on the social practices that informed and authorized it, they don't merely set an authoritative text against certain legal backdrops or rules of legal interpreta- tion.[42] Rather, they flirt with erasing the firm distinction between text and law by depicting legal content and the practices through which it is accessed and generated as mutually constitutive, and thus mutually irreducible. While they problematically stress the Constitution's legal character, they are more inclined to emphasize a vast, interlocking system of doctrines, rules, as- sumptions, and norms than a stand-alone text interfacing with stand-alone interpretive legal rules. Original law originalism thus seems far more capa- ble of handling an inchoate Constitution embedded in a complex array of recognized authorities (from the common law to the law of nations to prec- edent) in which intense and fundamental disagreement at the Founding nonetheless betrayed commitment to certain shared rules and norms and, even more importantly, the process of working certain contingent rules and norms out.[43] Original law originalism seems capable, at least in principle, of historicizing the Constitution on its own terms. The previously identified issues that stand in the way of this goal are important and perhaps fatal. Yet, if only by hinting at how it might reckon with the Founding in a new way, original law originalism perhaps points a new way forward.

This might be wishful thinking, however. It could betray an eagerness to see in Baude and Sachs's conceptual revisions a move toward a more authentic and richly textured constitutional historicism when, in reality, their brand of originalism might be fueled by a competing impulse: not to historicize the Constitution but in fact to clarify (in no less thoughtful a manner) why—in the domain of legal interpretation—such an exercise is largely beside the point. Here, original law originalism reveals something about originalist orthodoxy, not by breaking from it, but instead by concurring with it. Even if original law originalism is willing (at least partially) to depart from orthodox originalism's conception of the Constitution, it nonetheless seems wedded to something that has long pervaded all forms of originalism: a strong, almost stubborn, sense of continuity between present and past. Despite adopting a more capacious and historicist form of Founding-era constitutionalism, Baude and Sachs are ultimately less interested in recovering the Founders' Constitution as it actually was than they are in forcing the Founding to speak to the needs of our constitutional present. Indeed, they are invested in returning to the Founding primarily in order to clarify our law today. They are compelled to do so for the same reasons they think the Founders' law matters to begin with: because they believe, as a matter of positive fact, that we operate in legal continuity with the Founding—that we today are interpreting, elaborating on, clarifying, or adding to the constitutional system that eighteenth-century Americans enacted.[44] The way we reason about constitutionalism today, by identifying "modern law by way of . . . past law," is alone what gives "the law of the past" force and thus what makes originalism the " 'deep structure' of our constitutional law."[45]

By taking this positive turn, and construing originalism as a modern legal practice, Baude and Sachs help us see what distinguishes originalists' original Constitution from the one the Founders themselves knew. Whether Baude and Sachs are correct about our law today, they do seem right that modern constitutional practice—especially among originalists—typically engages with the Founding in just the way they describe. Rather than deciphering Founding law on its own, we consult it in order to clarify modern law. Rather than understanding the Founders' constitutionalism as the Founders themselves understood it, we contrive a narrative that seamlessly connects their constitutionalism to ours. Rather than understanding the Founding generation on their own terms, we force them into conversation with us, on our terms. We investigate what they thought and did in light of what we care about, demand that they speak to our problems and answer our questions, and repackage their observations as a direct commentary on a Constitution they would scarcely have recognized.[46] We see their Constitution through the lens of *ours*. We make them speak to us in *our* constitutional tongue. We make them a part of *our* story. Maybe this is all done for compelling legal reasons, in light of the demands of the present and how we reason about law. But the whole thing is designedly anachronistic. It is the past shaped by and reduced to the terms of the present.[47]

Modern Fiction

What this suggests, and what Baude and Sachs themselves hint at, is that originalism, as practiced, is in fact primarily a contrived modern legal fiction—a way of construing the past in light of our present commitment to a single continuous legal and constitutional tradition that enables us to neatly apply law to unanticipated developments across time.[48] Originalism is a way of constructing and filtering the Founding so that it may speak to us in our language, on our terms, for our purposes.[49] As a description of our actual practices, that seems broadly accurate. As a way of harmonizing our constitutional tradition and forging a civic identity, it is understandable, maybe even essential. As a mode of interpreting relics of the past, it is common and even intuitive. As a way of doing modern constitutional law, it might be broadly legitimate (such fictions are often foundational to societies and their legal orders and ought not to be discredited simply because they are contrived). But as a way of recovering the *actual* Constitution brought into being in the *actual* eighteenth century, it is surely inadequate. The unbroken continuity that we often assume with the Founding reveals a great deal about our modern cultural and legal practices and the "structure of legal justification" that seems to underlie them.[50] But that assumed continuity ultimately tells us far less about the actual Founding and the Constitution it produced.[51]

Recovering that historical Constitution requires an altogether different approach. It requires appreciating the sharp discontinuities (in conceptual thinking and thus legal imagination) that separate past and present, the Founders' constitutionalism and our own. And, in light of that recognition, it requires reconstructing the Founding generation's own constitutionalism from the ground up, without the warping influence of our modern assumptions and legal disputes. It requires joining the Founders' own constitutional conversations rather than dragging them into our own. It requires learning how to navigate their constitutional world rather than imposing what we take to be perennial concerns onto their unique challenges. It requires starting with their terms rather than our own.[52] Recovering the original Constitution requires, in short, historicizing it—grasping it on its original eighteenth-century terms.

The illuminating distinction that Richard Rorty once drew between what he called rational and historical reconstructions of philosophy helps clarify the sharp differences between these rival ways of engaging with the Constitution of the past. Rational reconstructions of the past, Rorty explained, consist of anachronistically imposing our own vocabulary and problems on historical figures to enlist them as our conversation partners—forcing their ideas to speak to us on our own terms. Historical reconstructions, in contrast, require rendering historical figures on their own terms by reference to the concepts and problems that those figures would have recognized.[53] A rational reconstruction and a historical reconstruction of the original Constitution are inherently different. The former, predicated on a stipulated sense of continuity, constructs a historical Constitution on the terms of the present. The latter, working to comprehend discontinuity, recovers an actual historical object that once existed in the past.

When it comes to law generally, there is nothing inherently defective about rational reconstructions of the past. They pervade legal practice. Law is different from history. It asks different questions, solves different problems, and accordingly, relies on different techniques. Unsurprisingly, its use of the past is often quite different.[54] The purpose of ordinary legal work is to adjudicate modern legal disputes. Lawyers and judges draw on historical evidence principally to serve this aim—to explain why a case should be resolved one way and not another. In the common-law tradition especially, turning to the past to resolve contemporary legal conflicts is expected. In doing so, the past is made to speak to the legal categories, questions, and controversies of the present. The goal is not to render the past accurately on its own terms, but to wrench historical evidence into the present to serve modern-day conceptual

needs. By its inherent structure, then, legal interpretation promotes historical anachronism. Ordinary lawyers' work purposefully distorts the past
according to the imperatives and logic of law. The standard interpretive techniques common to it—the use of analogies, the mining of precedent, the
tracing of doctrine—amount to a stylized form of rhetoric quite distinct from
genuine historical recovery. It answers not to the past but to the criteria of
law's various language games. The modern lawyer does as the common-law
judge always has: grabs hold of the past to make it speak the language of the
legal present. Like literary or political theorists who read historical texts with
an eye toward what they tell us across time and place rather than what they
might have originally meant in their own times and places, or like most philosophers who purposefully turn past philosophical thinkers into modern
conversation partners in order to illuminate philosophical issues at the expense of historical ones, modern legal practitioners can happily accept that
there is a sharp difference between their use of the constitutional past and
that past as it actually was.[55]

Assuredly, then, modern constitutionalists—not just originalists—have
helped create and reproduce the social practices and supporting culture that
have made the constructed original Constitution. Modern lawyers of all
stripes often cannot help but see the Founding through the perspective of
modern constitutional law.[56] The questions they pose, the things they look
for and *see* when they confront the past, are profoundly shaped, distorted,
framed, and illuminated by the terms of modern legal argument and the
distinctive mindset those terms have quietly inculcated. The socialization
runs so deep and structures so many essential intuitions that this lawyerly
approach to the Founding has become a kind of second nature. One of Baude
and Sachs's important points is that originalists and non-originalists alike
sanction many of the practices that structure appeals to and uses of the
Founding.[57] "[C]onstitutional law," as the legal scholar H. Jefferson Powell
once suggested, presupposes a "coherent tradition of argument."[58]

But the disjuncture between the contrived original Constitution and the
historical one poses few of the same difficulties for non-originalists. Not only
do non-originalists almost uniformly accept that the Constitution is essentially shaped by evolving practice, they also have refused to tether their understanding of the Constitution to its actual historical recovery. They treat
history as a resource, not a command—one source of constitutional legiti-

macy among many of equal weight. Nothing about doing constitutional law, appealing to its historical development, or looking to the constitutional past for legal guidance commits them to the historical project of recovering the actual eighteenth-century Constitution.

Originalists, by contrast, have committed themselves to the project of excavating and restoring the Founders' Constitution. It is the crux of their theory. For them, history is no mere resource, but indeed a command. While other lawyers might be able to justify anachronistic engagement with the legal past, originalists can't. That hasn't stopped them from trying. To deflect historians' critiques, they call attention to fundamental differences between law and history, often of the precise variety just outlined.[59] Baude and Sachs have been especially eager to press these differences, but they are not alone within the originalist ranks.[60] Where originalists err is not in thinking that such differences are real (they are), but in believing that those differences absolve originalists of their historical sins. For originalists have committed themselves, by the terms of their own theory, to a fundamentally different kind of relationship to the past. The anachronisms baked into legal practice undermine their own stated commitment to recovering the original Constitution as laid down and understood by eighteenth-century actors. To interpret the Constitution today along the lines of what Baude and Sachs call ordinary lawyers' work is, as a matter of course, to anachronistically drag it into the present. That's what ordinary lawyers' work tends to do. It's un-originalist by orientation; and, as a result, it is in tension with originalism. Originalists, then, cannot claim that they are merely doing ordinary lawyers' work, which depends on an artificial construction of the past, while also insisting that they are recovering the Constitution *as it was*. They try to have it both ways. They distort the historical past in light of the logic, fictions, and needs of modern jurisprudence while also vowing to have recovered something authentic from that same past. The sleight of hand is often unintentional. As Jud Campbell has aptly put it, "one worries that originalists often do not appreciate how much th[eir] approach *creates* a new past."[61] Whether they mean to do so or not, however, originalists unwittingly conflate the two distinct kinds of original Constitutions—the one constructed by our modern legal practices and the one actually found in history—as if they are one and the same.

Originalists need to make a fundamental choice. Either originalists can recognize how our modern constitutional practices and habits of mind distort the original Constitution and embrace them for the modern fiction that they are (thus acknowledging that originalists' narratives of historical recovery are merely a form of rhetoric derived from legal language games); or originalists can recover the original Constitution that the Founders actually knew. But originalists cannot do both. Original law originalism, whatever its shortcomings, helps reveal—and perhaps even explain—originalists' unfounded original Constitution.

Living Constitutionalism by Another Name

By seeing the distinction between constructed and historical reconstructions of the past, we can appreciate what originalism is and what it is not. In particular, it helps us understand why originalists have been so hesitant to historicize the Constitution, why they have been so quick to treat the Constitution in a certain defined way, and what the consequences of those decisions have been for their theory.

Originalism, we can now see, is a position taken up in the context of *modern jurisprudence*. It is not really about the past, but the present.[62] It is thoroughly shaped by a set of modern constitutional practices that inexorably collapse the Founding and the present into a common constitutional conversation structured by common constitutional terms, assumptions, practices, and doctrines. The whole endeavor is organized around modern legal questions, the genre of modern constitutional law, and the organizing logic of legalistic jurisprudence. Originalism takes for granted the Constitution—an underlying theory and conception of the Constitution—at the heart of modern constitutional practice, the one that lawyers and jurists have shaped into its recognizable form, and the one that modern constitutional doctrine identifies and makes sense of. Originalism situates constitutional interpretation in a decidedly legal context, in light of a host of assumptions about how law works and how courts enforce it, and makes sense of that interpretive enterprise by reference to a long-running tradition of legal doctrine and analysis that fundamentally frames the argumentative field and the kind of moves that can be made within that field. Originalism is a position taken in *this* tradition—a rhetorical move within a modern legal language game.

That means that originalism is predicated on a conception of the Constitution that is neither original nor essential but has instead evolved over time through social practice. It is a constitution whose basic conceptualization (as manifested in its outlines, content, character) has developed according to how people (legal professionals most of all) have grown accustomed to identifying, analyzing, interpreting, and debating it. The Constitution that originalists (and other moderns) bandy about was forged through and by history. It is a product of habituated practice. It is a conventional constitution, not an essentialist one. Originalism's Constitution, in other words, is a living constitution.

Originalists wage merciless war against the idea of a living Constitution while nevertheless embracing one. They question how any document, not just the Constitution, could be interpreted in a manner contrary to its original meaning and wonder how the basic values of constitutionalism could possibly be upheld if the Constitution's meaning has evolved with the times. That makes it especially ironic that nothing more clearly illustrates that our Constitution is living than originalist interpretations of it. By unwittingly imposing the modern on the past, by assuming that their constitutionalism was the Founders' constitutionalism, originalists pull the Constitution into the present and turn it into something it was not. With rare exceptions, originalist readings of the Constitution are about something other than the eighteenth century. They show us just what happens when our conceptual scheme changes, when our views on constitutionalism and law undergo subtle but profound changes over the course of decades, when our conceptions of constitutional content, communication, and interpretation morph in unexpected ways. Those standing on the other side of these changes, content to take them as given, will bear the imprint of the present. Their interpretations of the Constitution will presuppose everything that has fundamentally changed the Constitution. The strongest proof that we have a living Constitution is how originalists matter-of-factly talk about it.

It is understandable why originalists gravitate toward the Constitution as we know it today. It's the one that legal professionals, through years of disciplinary and intellectual acculturation, have been conditioned to see. It's the one debated in modern federal courts and essential to understanding their rulings. How could a participant situated in that world see the Constitution differently? It probably makes good sense, moreover, that this kind of constitution is at the heart of modern discussion and debate. For better or worse, it is the one that speaks to the kinds of constitutional questions that our society generates. Certainly, no modern lawyer should feel any need to step outside of these social practices. Yet it is surely ironic, in light of their stated commitments, to find originalists uncritically immersed in them.

It points to a paradox in originalism. The Constitution itself has changed, but apparently its meaning cannot. We must not interpret a Constitution that is itself the product of evolving conventions and commitments, according to those evolving conventions and commitments. We must recover the original eighteenth-century meaning of a non-original Constitution that is itself a modern invention of originalists and their legal foes. We must locate the original meaning of, not the original Constitution, but a living Constitution—one that the Founders themselves would have struggled to recognize. If this seems more than a little peculiar, that's because it is.

It also points to a problem in originalism. By failing to historicize the Constitution, by conceiving of it in such avowedly modernist terms, originalists wrench the Constitution into the present. Originalism stands as just another version of the present imposed on the past. One solution might be to simply accept that originalism is a modern legal fiction, to concede that it is a way of appealing to a contrived past from within the genre of modern constitutional law and jurisprudence. This approach would take the modern conception of the Constitution that has developed in legal study and Supreme Court discourse as given—*on the basis of the settled practices of modern law*. Within the conceptual scheme created by that settlement, it would then defend versions of textualism and historical recovery that make sense within that contrived rhetorical space. It would also differentiate those who insist on following that Constitution's text from those who insist on supplementing it with other sources of consideration. Finally, as part of the process of taking the text seriously, this approach would look to historical evidence of how different bits of language were used and understood. All these moves would be predicated on the shared anachronism baked into modern law, but since the intent would be to clarify modern legal questions, it could be defensible on its own terms—at least as long as originalists were to relinquish all claims to *genuine* historical recovery.

Among self-identified originalists, only Jack Balkin seems prepared to fully and explicitly concede the historicist character of the Constitution and the contingent, constructed nature of the category of original meaning itself. But he is the exception that proves the rule. Alone among originalists, he has attempted to fuse originalism with living constitutionalism.[63] Where other originalists have maintained that those are irreconcilable approaches, he has defended their inherent compatibility. In the process, he has conceded the historicist character of the Constitution and its meaning while also conceding that originalists *construct* historical meaning on the basis of modern legal thinking. Indeed, as he has put it, originalism engages in a "theoretical reconstruction" of the past according to the imperatives of modern legal theory. Those theories "filter, shape and configure the history" into something that can address the needs and terms of present law.[64] Originalism is compatible with living constitutionalism, then, in part because originalism inherently transforms the past into something distinctively modern and legal. It does not recover the past or the Constitution as they were; it shapes them into something usable and new, on the terms of our legal present.

Less obviously, the same might be said of Lawrence Lessig's constitutional translation, which he defends as a kind of originalism (calling it "two-step originalism"), though it's far more akin to Balkin's "living originalism" than the dominant versions defended by other originalists. "Translation itself is a two-step process," Lessig explains. "In the first step, the translator understands the text in its original context. In the second step, the translator then carries that first-step meaning into the present or target context."[65] It is a search for "an equivalence between two contexts."[66] This activity is inherent to U.S. constitutional interpretation, Lessig argues, because the Constitution is very old, so there's often a significant gap between the context in which it was written and the context modern interpreters find themselves in. That means, importantly, that in translating original meaning into a modern context, interpreters will often have to seemingly change original meaning (at least as it appears in its original context). A meaning in one context might not be the same in another context. To preserve the original Constitution, the interpreter needs to identify what an equivalent interpretation in the changed context would look like. Like Balkin, Lessig embraces a historicist account of constitutional development and, on account of that, he advances an unconventional brand of originalism. It's a brand of originalism that presupposes important discontinuities over time—that assumes that modern constitutionalism presents problems and contexts that do not neatly interface with those found two centuries ago. "Time bends everything," Lessig tells us.[67] As a result, he continues, originalists cannot stop once they have arrived at the Constitution's original meaning in its original context. They will need to wrest that meaning into the present and fit it into a new context. They will have to take something written in one register and alter it so that it might speak in a different register. Lessig's brand of originalism fully acknowledges the modernist impulse that must propel originalist interpretation—it fully acknowledges that preserving original meaning across time has often meant defeating that original meaning as understood in its original context. Lessig is explicit: doing originalism properly means making an old Constitution speak a modern tongue.[68]

The fundamental problem, however, is that other originalists cannot accept these sorts of concessions without sacrificing the essence of the originalist project. Originalists could mount a hitherto untested defense of their tacit assumptions, but only at the cost of admitting that originalism is not actually what it has always claimed to be and that it can no longer deliver on its core promises.[69]

If originalists admitted that theirs is a modern theory designed to interpret a modern constitution embedded in modern jurisprudence, doctrine, and law, they would have to abandon the idea that they are merely recovering what the Founding generation (and subsequent amenders) understood themselves to be doing. They would have to acknowledge that originalism interprets a Constitution that was either unknown to that Founding generation or deeply contested within it. There are important reasons why they haven't done so and would be loath to do so. Were originalists to concede, first, that the Constitution they take for granted is very different from the Constitution that prevailed at the Founding and, second, that the "original legal meaning" they speak of is not to be confused with the Constitution's actual eighteenth-century meaning, it would be hard to justify originalism to a public that has long been told that originalism is genuinely grounded in the eighteenth-century past. The appeal of originalism has always been that it urges us to look to something objective and real outside our own subjective interpretive preferences. In looking to the Constitution's past, we can ensure that there's a " 'there' there" governing constitutional interpretation.[70] But it's a lot harder to make that case if it turns out that the "there" there is something that originalists themselves have *put* there—if the past they're appealing to is simultaneously one they've created.

There's a reason why the Supreme Court, when it has relied on originalist arguments, has acted as though it's recovering the actual past. The justices certainly haven't implied that their use of historical evidence is purposefully anachronistic or premised on distinctively legal fictions. In the landmark Second Amendment case *District of Columbia v. Heller*, which is widely considered the modern Supreme Court's most originalist ruling, Justice Antonin Scalia's majority opinion never suggested that the Court was interpreting the amendment from a modern legal perspective.[71] Indeed, he never so much as hinted that the Court's analysis of what the amendment meant in 1791 was somehow different from what the amendment actually meant to actual people who were actually alive in 1791. Nor did the Court claim that it was engaged in a distinctively legal practice of anachronistically reading the past on the terms of the present by pretending that eighteenth-century Americans approached constitutionalism and law the way modern lawyers do today. As it has in so many other cases, the Court instead suggested that it had straightforwardly recovered what the amendment meant when it first appeared, without any caveats. There's good reason why. It is powerful to stake one's interpretive activities to the actual past, especially in our constitutional culture. To say:

> We are recovering what the framers and ratifiers actually laid down as they understood it; we are interpreting the same Constitution that they did—the one that James Madison and John Marshall held in their minds—in light of all the premises about constitutionalism and law that informed it.

By contrast, it is a much weaker argument to say:

> We are recovering a constructed and, from the standpoint of historical study, fictive account of the legal past. Our goal is not to understand this matter as people in the eighteenth century understood it—on their terms. Our goal, instead, is to understand what those people laid down *if we pretend that they thought about law and constitutionalism as we do today*. We know that's sure to be anachronistic. We know we won't be talking about the same Constitution that James Madison or John Marshall held in their minds. We're not historians; we're lawyers in a common-law system doing lawyer's history, which is a practical tool designed to aid legal decision-making. When we declare the original meaning of the Second Amendment, we therefore do so from this modern legal perspective. That shouldn't be confused with what the Second Amendment may have meant to real eighteenth-century people at the time of its enactment—with *that* kind of original meaning rooted in the actual past.

For good reason, originalist jurists never say anything like this. They never imply a gap between original meaning according to *law* or *originalism* and original meaning according to *history*. Acknowledging any discontinuity would vitiate the very cultural and political authority on which originalism both rhetorically and substantively depends.

And that's not just because the Founders enjoy a special authority in our culture, as vital as that may be, but also because a concession like that would mean abandoning (as discussed in the prior chapter) what has long been the defining originalist commitment: that originalism restores the Constitution *just as it is* and, thus, offers the neutral and objective theory of interpretation its competitors can't. Every just-so and just-is claim would have to be relinquished alongside the immense argumentative authority that originalism has long derived from those claims. Originalists would have to abandon their meta-narrative about fidelity and restoration and defend the theory in entirely new and different ways. To concede that their conception of the Constitution might be optional would be to abandon their foundational, authoritative argument: that originalism is required by the Constitution and is, alone among interpretive theories, faithful to it. Originalists have long emphasized other contingent goods that their theory purportedly delivers: it respects popular sovereignty, promotes the rule of law, protects reliance interests, gives "We the People" legal notice, promotes stability, protects individual rights, and so on. But the value of each of these goods presupposes that originalists recover an authentic historical Constitution. Their theory is ultimately defended on the basis of its supposed constitutional fidelity. Originalism, at bottom, has always claimed to recover the Constitution *as it was and is* because fidelity to the Constitution requires fidelity to the Constitution *as it was and is*. Originalists have never so much as hinted that their descriptions of the Constitution are a matter of choice—mere food for thought. The properties they identify in the Constitution are neither accidental nor merely possible; they are essential.

For conceptual and theoretical reasons as much as rhetorical and political ones, then, originalists need to claim that their theory is continuous with the work of the Founding generation. Originalism has long been founded on the belief that it is staked to and continuous with a deeper history. The very idea that originalism entails a neutral recovery of the law as originally laid down necessitates that orientation to the eighteenth-century past.

Herein lies the fundamental importance of the historical critique of origi-nalism we have developed here. Our historical investigation has confirmed, if nothing else, that there is nothing essential nor especially originalist about originalists' just-so conception of the Constitution. The Founding genera-tion thought differently about constitutionalism, and thus the federal Consti-tution of 1787, than most originalists do today. The conception of the Constitution that most originalists take for granted is optional. It is anything but a fixed feature of our constitutional order; it is anything but an essential byproduct of the ratification of the Constitution as fundamental law. The his-tory we have documented, therefore, strips originalism of its dominant de-fenses. The contingency of originalist thinking does not automatically diminish it—most ideas that human beings celebrate and are willing to die for are similarly optional, having emerged only through complex contingent cultural processes. But whether it is good or bad, defensible or illegitimate, in keeping with long-standing practice or novel, the originalist conception of the Constitution is emphatically not given, necessary, or required. *Nothing* about fidelity to *this* Constitution, *on its own*, demands that originalist con-ception. *Nothing* about what the Founding generation laid down necessitates it. We can clearly conceive of the Constitution in a host of different ways while remaining faithful to it. We could, as just one concrete example, merely adopt what many of the Founders took the Constitution to be. We could see its writtenness in non-exclusive terms, its fixed meaning as perfectly com-patible with informal evolutionary change, its underlying sovereignty as mo-bile and dynamic, and its status as law entirely apart from any kind of legalism. If we elected to embrace any of those things, not one of them would be incompatible with the original Constitution. Originalists can cling to their favored conception of the Constitution, but they can no longer claim that that conception is necessitated by the Constitution itself. If they wish to treat the Constitution as exclusively written, incompatible with evolutionary change, and distinctively legal in character, then they will have to explain why anyone else is beholden to their thinking. They can no longer insist—as their theory has long assumed—that the Constitution simply demands that we see it in these ways.

Once we appreciate this fundamental point, we can dislodge originalists from their authoritative perch and force them to defend their theory on equal footing. Originalists have long assumed, explicitly or surreptitiously, that their understanding of the Constitution—as a fixed legal text—is inherent to the Constitution itself, as confirmed by the fact that their understanding happened to be the understanding that prevailed at the Founding. Moving forward, originalists must either rebut the history of the Founders' Constitution or, alternately, concede that their conception of constitutional adjudication and jurisprudence is, as a matter of historical fact, an anachronism—and defend their theory as the fully modernist endeavor it is. That can be done, but not without conceding the bulk of originalism's rhetorical force, argumentative appeal, and most important of all, its own account of its legitimacy.

Stripped of the authoritative grounding of history, originalism will need to stand on its own. Originalism might be able to survive that transformation, but only by reinventing itself and abandoning what it has long claimed to be.

Conclusion: Our Historical Constitution

> I have always called our Constitution a Game at Leap frog.
> — John Adams to Benjamin Rush, Sept. 8, 1808

ORIGINALISM IS STAKED TO HISTORY—but that history proves its undoing. At bottom, it is a theory founded on the authority of the past—premised on recovering what was laid down centuries ago—and yet, to its core, it is predicated on the assumptions and sensibilities of modern constitutional law. Originalism's avowed modernism is sharply at odds with the theory's stated fidelity to recovering the past on its own terms. By its posture and presuppositions, the theory quietly wrenches the Constitution into the present, while claiming to recover the Constitution in its pure original form. Originalism takes for granted—indeed depends upon—a Constitution and brand of constitutionalism largely unknown at the time of the Founding.

By and large, originalists have always assumed that the Constitution and constitutionalism so familiar to them and modern legal debate has been around since the beginning. The object of interpretation, the methods for interpreting that object, the character of fundamental law, the essential ways that constitutions acquire and communicate content—originalists believe that all of it has more or less held steady since 1787.

But eighteenth-century constitutionalism was markedly different from the brand of constitutionalism familiar to us today. The Founding generation understood constitutions differently than we do because they understood law (natural law, common law, and fundamental law), liberty (representation, rights, and governance), and above all constitutionalism (the content, character, interpretation, and enforcement of constitutions) much differently than we do. Only once we've done the painstaking work of inhabiting a different constitutional worldview can we begin deciphering the complex things the Constitution expressed at the time it first appeared.

This disjuncture between constitutional past and present matters. It shows that originalists' dominant conception of the Constitution is not grounded in history as they assume it must be. It shows that originalists' Constitution is anything but given. Originalists can no longer take the Constitution for granted.

Originalists can't have their cake and eat it too. They cannot claim the mantle of neutrality and objectivity while substituting a modern Constitution for a genuinely historical one. Originalism will require a deeper historical defense than its champions have thus far offered—one that presses beneath their familiar claims about original meaning, fixation, or constraint and reckons with the original Constitution itself. But if originalism is, instead, a modern jurisprudential fiction, it must be defended as one. Originalists must concede that their constructed Constitution is different from the one known to the Founding generation. They must explain why their constructed Constitution preserves any of originalism's long-standing aims. And they must show why their constructed Constitution deserves our fidelity.

However originalists choose to handle the challenge of history, we should all reckon with the fact that our constitutional past was so very different from our present. Sometimes, when told that the past is a foreign country, people recoil. What value is there in learning that our constitutional history is so remote from our present needs and concerns? If true, wouldn't that only prove its irrelevance? If its significance is merely antiquarian, why bother? What purpose could there be in studying something that is said to be so removed from our own challenges? Worse, wouldn't that undermine our own commitment to the Constitution and the legal system it governs to admit that it was created with a different worldview in mind? How can we carry on if it turns out that Founding-era constitutionalism is so different from its modern counterpart—if the continuity that is so often assumed between our

Founding and our present masks sharp discontinuities between the Founders' conceptual world and our own?

This reaction is doubly misguided. It is misguided, first, because the past is whatever it is. We can't pretend it was otherwise simply because we'd like to believe that it was so. If particular legal theories, such as originalism, depend on strong continuity with the past, then that's their problem to work through, not the past's problem to accommodate. We can't lie about history just to ensure its immediate relevance to modern law. If it turns out that discontinuities between past and present create insurmountable challenges for judges and lawyers, then perhaps cases shouldn't be decided by turning to an authoritative past. That may seem like a provocative suggestion, but it needn't provoke a crisis. For well over two centuries, we've had a (more or less) functioning constitutional system whose workability has seemingly been predicated on something other than strong continuities with past imperatives. Our constitutional assumptions have been transformed many times over, and yet we're still here. And if it's true that our contemporary constitutional practices hinge on the appearance of continuity, then that tells us something about ourselves and the kinds of fictions we, like all peoples, rely on.

Denying the foreignness of the past out of fear that historicizing it diminishes its relevance, meanwhile, gets things exactly backward. Appreciating the discontinuities between our past and our present offers us something of profound value: self-understanding.[1] It puts us in a position to better understand our own constitutional practices and the historical contingencies that have produced them. It forces us to justify our approach on new grounds—as something other than what necessarily follows from honoring our Constitution. It allows us to glimpse concrete alternatives—entirely different ways of reckoning with our constitutional order—and consider anew whether any are superior to those we have embraced. In short, it lets us see what we've really been doing all along.

In reconstructing the Founding as it was and bringing the differences between constitutionalism past and present into sharper relief, what we ultimately gain is a deeper understanding of the U.S. Constitution itself. We glimpse the true nature of our Constitution and with that the essence of our constitutional project.

In the face of criticism, originalists often counter with a familiar question: If not originalism then *what*? It takes a theory to beat a theory, they insist.

Maybe originalism has defects, but to paraphrase Winston Churchill's defense of democracy, originalism still might be better than all other options. Here, as ever, originalists are skilled at building the presumption in their favor. Before anyone answers their question, originalists first should answer a different one: Why should we adopt originalism rather than merely continue to employ long-standing American constitutional practice?

The Constitution, as Jack Balkin observes, offers a framework of governance consisting of specific rules on top of which are layered broad standards and principles.[2] It offers little concrete guidance on how to construe the rules or the principles or relate the principles to the rules. It doesn't tell us what should happen when two or more principles come into competition. It can't determine whether the rules plus the principles are exhaustive or which theory of law, conception of liberty, or understanding of state power they presuppose. And it provides no clarity about which institutions (if any) should resolve this maze of uncertainties. It sets something dynamic in motion, requiring its subsequent users, through an essentially iterative process, to both work it out and work out *how* to work it out. Such might be true of all constitutions, but it is assuredly true of ours. This description best captures what has actually happened over the two-plus centuries since the framers gathered in Philadelphia in the summer of 1787. Scores upon scores of people, operating across different venues and institutional settings, from the courts to the streets, have taken the Constitution as they found it and shaped it in the ways they could, pushing out and reimagining, laying down certain interpretations, entrenching certain habits and regularities, such that anything anyone has done with the Constitution at any given moment has owed considerably more to the collective socialization of prior constitutional debate—and the accumulated precedent, doctrine, norms, and habits that have fallen out of it—than anything else. What has always mattered is not what the Constitution in some brute sense requires but the set of things that any generation of interpreters take for granted about it in light of what they've inherited: the assumed starting point for conversation, the framework of debate, and the implicit logic governing the available moves. The Constitution must be seen from somewhere. What people have seen and imagined they can do from there—what they believe constitutionalism at bottom is—has been a product of that prior debate.

No doubt a vital feature of this practice has been presumed continuity over time and a desire to remain faithful to that continuous tradition. But even if the sense of continuity has been steady, maintaining that perceived continuity has undoubtedly wrought significant change as inherited principles and imperatives have been asked to speak across time. Applying the past to the present has involved significant translation, which in and of itself has usually triggered underlying change.[3] That translation can be faithful, but surely not in claiming to honor the past on its own terms while otherwise pulling it toward the present. The history of U.S. constitutionalism has been a history of this kind of translation across time and through controversies and debates. It is the kind of activity that by its nature produces change. To translate a past that speaks one language into a present that speaks another is to creatively modify and elaborate. That's what there is. The practice of maintaining the tradition and performing fidelity to it, therefore, has unsurprisingly altered the constitutional space in unexpected and transformative ways, not least because what counts as constitutional continuity and fidelity has had to be worked out by the very practices meant to reinforce each. That historically embedded practice has been the essence of our constitutionalism.

Given that originalists propose overhauling this long-running practice of dynamic constitutional translation—which better describes our own practices—they need to explain why. The burden does not fall on non-originalists.

Too often we are unwilling to embrace our constitutional practices for what they have been. In our search for certainty and final authority, we try to turn the Constitution into the end of argument. We struggle with the idea that the Constitution itself might be enmeshed in the precise argumentative practices it is meant to regulate and control. Yet the Constitution's own history shows how entangled the two have always been.

The Constitution's early history reveals the historicist foundations upon which the Constitution has always been built. At the Founding, creating and conceiving of the Constitution were inextricably intertwined.[4] If we reckon with the contested nature of the original Constitution's character and attend to the dynamic process through which constitutional debate constituted that Constitution, we'll see how inseparable the object we call "the Constitution" has always been from the practices that have tacitly shaped and defined it. We can see how efforts to conceive of the Constitution have been continuously interwoven with the object itself—how our own ingrained assumptions about how to describe, delineate, and debate the Constitution have themselves been the product of the very historical processes they have been deployed to regulate. The Constitution cannot be separated from its history, because, in a meaningful sense, the Constitution *is* that history.

We ought to welcome this realization. The Constitution was a political creation intended to structure political argument in a political society. It was born of political debate and political compromise and broke new ground in the history of self-government. It should come as no surprise how uncertain and contested the Constitution proved to be. It needed to be worked, and so it was. Asking the Constitution to be more than it is misconceives its purpose and asks us to be something other than a democratic people. Democracy should invite and embrace historicism.[5] It should make us comfortable with the reality that our world is structured by a form of fundamental political and legal authority that is shaped by the practices we use to appeal to that authority. Our claims about the Constitution will always presuppose a set of contingent assumptions about the activity in which we are engaged.

We have tried for too long to escape the historical dimensions of our Constitution, to see it as apart from history, as though it were a set of fixed axioms awaiting discovery. The originalism debate is predicated on this unfortunate impulse, one we should overcome. At long last, we ought to appreciate what the Constitution's own history reveals: our historical Constitution.

NOTES

Introduction

Epigraph: James Madison to William Eustis, July 6, 1819, in *The Papers of James Madison, Retirement Series*, ed. David B. Mattern, J. C. A. Stagg, Mary Parke Johnson, and Anne Mandeville Colony, 4 vols. to date (Charlottesville: University of Virginia Press, 2009–), 1:479.

1. On originalism's connection to history, see Jonathan Gienapp, "Constitutional Originalism and History," *Process: A Blog for American History*, Mar. 20, 2017, www.processhistory.org/originalism-history/.

2. History has long been one of the modalities (or forms of argument) of U.S. constitutional interpretation. See Philip Bobbitt, *Constitutional Fate: Theory of the Constitution* (New York: Oxford University Press, 1982); Philip Bobbitt, *Constitutional Interpretation* (Cambridge, Mass.: Blackwell, 1991). On how history has always mattered to U.S. constitutional interpretation and all its modalities, see Jack M. Balkin, *Memory and Authority: The Uses of History in Constitutional Interpretation* (New Haven, Conn.: Yale University Press, 2024). Originalism is distinctive not in turning to history but in elevating history above all other considerations. See Mitchell N. Berman, "Originalism Is Bunk," *New York University Law Review* 84 (Apr. 2009): 1–96.

3. See *Dobbs v. Jackson Women's Health Organization*, 142 S. Ct. 2228 (2022); *New York State Rifle & Pistol Association v. Bruen*, 142 S. Ct. 2111 (2022); *Kennedy v. Bremerton School District*, 142 S. Ct. 2407 (2022). Some have wondered whether the Court's use of this "history and tradition" standard is consistent with the originalism it professes to endorse. Leading originalists have claimed that it can be. See Randy E. Barnett and Lawrence B. Solum, "Originalism After *Dobbs, Bruen*, and *Kennedy*: The Role of History and Tradition," *Northwestern University Law Review* 118 (2023): 433–94. Others, labeling it "living traditionalism," have questioned this approach's compatibility with originalism. See Sherif Girgis, "Living Traditionalism," *New York University Law Review* 98 (Nov. 2023): 1477–1555. On how originalism has always been a form of traditionalism, see Balkin, *Memory and Authority*, 67–70, 90–91, 152–68, 197–209.

4. On originalist methodology, see Lawrence B. Solum, "Originalist Methodology," *University of Chicago Law Review* 84 (Jan. 2017): 269–96. For historical critiques of originalist methods, see Jonathan Gienapp, "Historicism and Holism: Failures of Originalist Translation," *Fordham Law Review* 84 (Dec. 2015): 935–56; Jack N. Rakove, "Tone Deaf to the Past: More Qualms About Public Meaning Originalism," *Fordham Law Review* 84 (Dec. 2015): 969–76; Saul Cornell, "Reading the Constitution, 1787–91: History, Originalism, and Constitutional Meaning," *Law and History Review* 37 (Aug. 2019): 821–45.

5. Sanford Levinson, *Constitutional Faith*, 2nd ed. (1988; Princeton, N.J.: Princeton University Press, 2011), 191–94; Jack M. Balkin, *Constitutional Redemption: Political Faith in an Unjust World* (Cambridge, Mass.: Harvard University Press, 2011), 177–86; H. Jefferson Powell, *A Community Built on Words: The Constitution in History and Politics* (Chicago: University of Chicago Press, 2002).

6. Johnathan O'Neill, *Originalism in American Law and Politics: A Constitutional History* (Baltimore: Johns Hopkins University Press, 2005); Calvin TerBeek, " 'Clocks Must Always Be Turned Back': *Brown v. Board of Education* and the Racial Origins of Constitutional Originalism," *American Political Science Review* 115 (Aug. 2021): 821–34; Balkin, *Memory and Authority*, 9–10, 86–93.

7. The term *originalism* first appeared in Paul Brest, "The Misconceived Quest for the Original Understanding," *Boston University Law Review* 60 (Mar. 1980): 204–05. For Meese's speech, see Edwin Meese III, Speech Before the American Bar Association, July 9, 1985, in *Originalism: A Quarter-Century of Debate*, ed. Steven G. Calabresi (Washington, D.C.: Regnery, 2007), 47–54.

8. Ken I. Kersch, *Conservatives and the Constitution: Imagining Constitutional Restoration in the Heyday of American Liberalism* (New York: Cambridge University Press, 2019), 81–100; O'Neill, *Originalism in American Law and Politics*, 67–132; TerBeek, " 'Clocks Must Always Be Turned Back.' " Although originalism came to dominate legal conservatism, importantly, it took shape only at a later hour within a much wider field of conservative constitutional argument. Kersh, *Conservatives and the Constitution*, 27–34, 101–02, 361–63.

9. On the origins of living constitutionalism, see Michael G. Kammen, *A Machine That Would Go of Itself: The Constitution in American Culture*, 2nd ed. (1986; New Brunswick, N.J.: Transactions, 2006); Howard Gillman, "The Collapse of Constitutional Originalism and the Rise of the Notion of the 'Living Constitution' in the Course of American State-Building," *Studies in American Political Development* 11 (Fall 1997): 213–40. For an influential denunciation of it, see William H. Rehnquist, "The Notion of a Living Constitution," *Texas Law Review* 54 (May 1976): 693–706.

10. On how veneration of America's Founders has been important to originalism's popular appeal, see Jamal Greene, "On the Origins of Originalism," *Texas Law Review* 88 (Nov. 2009): 1–90, esp. 8–18, 62–64; Jamal Greene, "Selling Originalism," *Georgetown Law Journal* 97 (Mar. 2009): 657–722; Jamal Greene, Nathaniel Persily, and Stephen Ansolabehere, "Profiling Originalism," *Columbia Law Review* 111 (Mar. 2011): 356–418; Jill Lepore, *The Whites of Their Eyes: The Tea Party's Revolution and the Battle over American History* (Princeton, N.J.: Princeton University Press, 2011); Robert W. Gordon, *Taming the Past: Essays on Law in History and His-*

tory in Law (New York: Cambridge University Press, 2017), 362–65, 377; Balkin, *Memory and Authority*, 77–85. Across constitutional conservatism more broadly, the virtues of the Founders and the Founding were routinely extolled. See Kersch, *Conservatives and the Constitution*, 27–102. The definitive early originalist defense of interpretive neutrality was Robert H. Bork, "Neutral Principles and Some First Amendment Problems," *Indiana Law Journal* 47 (Fall 1971): 1–35. On the darker origins of Bork's arguments, see TerBeek, " 'Clocks Must Always Be Turned Back,' " 831–32.

11. On the political dimensions of originalism, see Robert Post and Reva Siegel, "Originalism as a Political Practice: The Right's Living Constitution," *Fordham Law Review* 75 (Nov. 2006): 545–74; Logan E. Sawyer III, "Principle and Politics in the New History of Originalism," *American Journal of Legal History* 57 (June 2017): 198–222; Paul Baumgardner, "Originalism and the Academy in Exile," *Law and History Review* 37 (Aug. 2019): 787–807; TerBeek, " 'Clocks Must Always Be Turned Back' "; Reva B. Siegel, "Memory Games: *Dobbs*'s Originalism as Anti-Democratic Living Constitutionalism—and Some Pathways for Resistance," *Texas Law Review* 101 (Apr. 2023): 1127–1204. On originalism's place in the conservative legal movement, see Steven M. Teles, *The Rise of the Conservative Legal Movement: The Battle for Control of the Law* (Princeton, N.J.: Princeton University Press, 2008); Amanda Hollis-Brusky, *Ideas with Consequences: The Federalist Society and the Conservative Counterrevolution* (New York: Oxford University Press, 2015).

12. On originalists' desire to turn the Constitution into rules, see Gordon, *Taming the Past*, 366; Antonin Scalia, "The Rule of Law as a Law of Rules," *University of Chicago Law Review* 56 (Fall 1989): 1175–88. On emphasizing the Constitution's "majestic generalities," see William J. Brennan, Jr., Speech to the Text and Teaching Symposium, Georgetown University, Oct. 12, 1985, in Calabresi, *Originalism*, 56.

13. On legal realism, see Morton J. Horwitz, *The Transformation of American Law, 1870–1960* (New York: Oxford University Press, 1992); Laura Kalman, *Legal Realism at Yale, 1927–1960* (Chapel Hill: University of North Carolina Press, 1986).

14. On these broad trends, see Daniel T. Rodgers, *Age of Fracture* (Cambridge, Mass.: Harvard University Press, 2011); Gabrielle Spiegel, "The Task of the Historian," *American Historical Review* 114 (Feb. 2009): 1–15; William H. Sewell, Jr., "The Concept(s) of Culture," in *Logics of History: Social Theory and Social Transformation* (Chicago: University of Chicago Press, 2005); James T. Kloppenberg, *Reading Obama: Dreams, Hope, and the American Political Tradition* (Princeton, N.J.: Princeton University Press, 2011), 85–149; Sarah Maza, *Thinking About History* (Chicago: University of Chicago Press, 2017), 199–234; Jennifer Ratner-Rosenhagen, *The Ideas That Made America: A Brief History* (New York: Oxford University Press, 2019), 152–72.

15. This was especially true given the emergence of critical legal studies in law schools. See Mark Tushnet, "Critical Legal Studies: A Political History," *Yale Law Journal* 100 (Mar. 1991): 1515–44; Robert W. Gordon, "Critical Legal Histories," *Stanford Law Review* 36 (Jan. 1984): 57–126.

16. On the long-standing importance of text to American constitutionalism, see Levinson, *Constitutional Faith*, 27–37.

17. On the shift to public meaning originalism, see Gienapp, "Constitutional Original-ism and History"; Lawrence B. Solum, "What Is Originalism? The Evolution of Contemporary Originalist Theory," in *The Challenge of Originalism: Theories of Con-stitutional Interpretation*, ed. Grant Huscroft and Bradley W. Miller (New York: Cambridge University Press, 2011), 16–24; Thomas B. Colby, "The Sacrifice of the New Originalism," *Georgetown Law Journal* 99 (Mar. 2011): 714–36; Keith E. Whit-tington, "Originalism: A Critical Introduction," *Fordham Law Review* 82 (Nov. 2013): 378–87; Eric J. Segall, *Originalism as Faith* (New York: Cambridge University Press, 2018), 36–121. For influential early statements, see Antonin Scalia, "Address Before the Attorney General's Conference on Economic Liberties in Washington, D.C.," June 14, 1986, in *Original Meaning Jurisprudence: A Sourcebook*, by Office of Legal Policy (Washington, D.C.: U.S. Department of Justice, 1987), 101–06; Randy E. Barnett, "An Originalism for Nonoriginalists," *Loyola Law Review* 45 (Winter 1999): 620–29; Keith E. Whittington, "The New Originalism," *Georgetown Journal of Law & Public Policy* 2 (2004): 599–614.

18. See Jack N. Rakove, *Original Meanings: Politics and Ideas in the Making of the Consti-tution* (New York: Knopf, 1996); Jack N. Rakove, "Joe the Ploughman Reads the Constitution, or, The Poverty of Public Meaning Originalism," *San Diego Law Re-view* 48 (May 2011): 575–600; John M. Murrin, "Fundamental Values, the Found-ing Fathers, and the Constitution," reprinted in *Rethinking America: From Empire to Republic* (New York: Oxford University Press, 2018), 208–12; Brest, "The Miscon-ceived Quest for the Original Understanding," 204–24; Richard H. Fallon, Jr., "The Chimerical Concept of Original Public Meaning," *Virginia Law Review* 107 (Nov. 2021): 1421–98; Erwin Chemerinsky, *Worse Than Nothing: The Dangerous Fal-lacy of Originalism* (New Haven, Conn.: Yale University Press, 2022): 144–63.

19. On issues with the historical record, see James H. Hutson, "The Creation of the Constitution: The Integrity of the Documentary Record," *Texas Law Review* 65 (Nov. 1986): 1–40; Leonard W. Levy, *Original Intent and the Framers' Constitution* (New York: MacMillan, 1988), 284–95; Mary Sarah Bilder, *Madison's Hand: Revising the Constitutional Convention* (Cambridge, Mass.: Harvard University Press, 2015).

20. On constitutional interpretation as translation across time, see Lawrence Lessig, *Fidelity and Constraint: How the Supreme Court Has Read the Constitution* (New York: Oxford University Press, 2019). On the difficulties of translating between past and present, see Gienapp, "Historicism and Holism"; Rakove, "Tone Deaf to the Past." On originalism's "modernity problem," see Chemerinsky, *Worse Than Nothing*, 115–38; David A. Strauss, *The Living Constitution* (New York: Oxford Uni-versity Press, 2010), 21–23.

21. On the problems for originalism posed by the Constitution's generalities, see Colby, "The Sacrifice of the New Originalism," 724–36, 744–76; Strauss, *Living Constitution*, 26–29; Segall, *Originalism as Faith*, 89–102; Adrian Vermeule, *Com-mon Good Constitutionalism* (Cambridge: Polity, 2022), 96–108, 115–16.

22. On originalists' historical distortions, see Saul Cornell, "Meaning and Understand-ing in the History of Constitutional Ideas: The Intellectual History Alternative to Originalism," *Fordham Law Review* 82 (Oct. 2013): 721–56; Martin S. Flaherty, "History 'Lite' in Modern American Constitutionalism," *Columbia Law Review* 95

(Apr. 1995), 523–90; Larry D. Kramer, "When Lawyers Do History," *George Washington Law Review* 72 (Dec. 2003): 387–426; Julian Davis Mortenson, "Executive Power and the Discipline of History," *University of Chicago Law Review* 78 (Winter 2011): 377–444. On how originalism can be ideologically manipulated to reach politically conservative results, see Richard H. Fallon, Jr., "Are Originalist Constitutional Theories Principled, or Are They Rationalizations for Conservatism?," *Harvard Journal of Law & Public Policy* 34 (Winter 2011): 5–28; Frank Cross, *The Failed Promise of Originalism* (Stanford, Calif.: Stanford University Press, 2013).

23. See, e.g., Julian Davis Mortenson, "Article II Vests the Executive Power, Not the Royal Prerogative," *Columbia Law Review* 119 (June 2019): 1169–1272; Julian Davis Mortenson, "The Executive Power Clause," *University of Pennsylvania Law Review* 168 (Apr. 2020): 1269–1368; Jed Handelsman Shugerman, "The Indecisions of 1789: Inconstant Originalism," *University of Pennsylvania Law Review* 171 (Mar. 2023): 753–868; John Mikhail, "The Necessary and Proper Clauses," *Georgetown Law Journal* 102 (Apr. 2014): 1045–1132; Jud Campbell, "Natural Rights and the First Amendment," *Yale Law Journal* 127 (Nov. 2017): 246–321; Saul Cornell, "Originalism on Trial: The Use and Abuse of History in *District of Columbia v. Heller*," *Ohio State Law Journal* 69 (2008): 625–40; Richard Primus, "The Limits of Enumeration," *Yale Law Journal* 124 (Dec. 2014): 576–643; Jonathan Gienapp, "The Myth of the Constitutional Given: Enumeration and National Power at the Founding," *American University Law Review Forum* 69 (2020): 183–211; James E. Pfander, "History and State Suability: An Explanatory Account of the Eleventh Amendment," *Cornell Law Review* 83 (July 1998): 1269–1382; Julian Davis Mortenson and Nicholas Bagley, "Delegation at the Founding," *Columbia Law Review* 121 (Mar. 2021): 277–368.

24. On the "dead hand" problem, see Jack M. Balkin, *Living Originalism* (Cambridge, Mass.: Harvard University Press, 2011), 41–49; Ethan J. Leib, "The Perpetual Anxiety of Living Constitutionalism," *Constitutional Commentary* 24 (Summer 2007): 353–70; Adam M. Samaha, "Dead Hand Arguments and Constitutional Interpretation," *Columbia Law Review* 108 (Apr. 2008): 606–80; Jamal Greene, "Originalism's Race Problem," *Denver University Law Review* 88 (2011): 517–22.

25. Thurgood Marshall, "Reflections on the Bicentennial of the United States Constitution," *Harvard Law Review* 101 (Nov. 1987): 1–5; Greene, "Originalism's Race Problem," 520–22; Jerome McCristal Culp, Jr., "Toward a Black Legal Scholarship: Race and Original Understandings," *Duke Law Journal* 1991 (Feb. 1991): 74–76; Mary Anne Case, "The Ladies? Forget About Them—A Feminist Perspective on the Limits of Originalism," *Constitutional Commentary* 29 (Summer 2014): 431–56.

26. Strauss, *Living Constitution*, 12–18; Balkin, *Living Originalism*, 8–12, 109–25; Chemerinsky, *Worse Than Nothing*, 92–114.

27. Non-originalists have defended several alternative approaches to constitutional interpretation. For a defense of popular constitutionalism, see Bruce Ackerman, *We the People*, 3 vols. (Cambridge, Mass.: Harvard University Press, 1991–2014); Barry Friedman, *The Will of the People: How Public Opinion Has Influenced the Supreme Court and Shaped the Meaning of the Constitution* (New York: Farrar, Straus and Giroux, 2009). For a defense of moral readings, see Ronald Dworkin, *Freedom's*

Law: The Moral Reading of the American Constitution (Cambridge, Mass.: Harvard University Press, 1996); James E. Fleming, *Fidelity to Our Imperfect Constitution: For Moral Readings and Against Originalisms* (New York: Oxford University Press, 2015). For a defense of common-law constitutionalism, see Strauss, *Living Constitution*. For a defense of interpretive pluralism, see Bobbitt, *Constitutional Fate*; Bobbitt, *Constitutional Interpretation*; Richard H. Fallon, Jr., "A Constructivist Coherence Theory of Constitutional Interpretation," *Harvard Law Review* 100 (Apr. 1987): 1189–1286; Richard H. Fallon, Jr., "The Many and Varied Roles of History in Constitutional Adjudication," *Notre Dame Law Review* 90 (May 2015): 1753–1834; Richard H. Fallon, Jr., *Law and Legitimacy in the Supreme Court* (Cambridge, Mass.: Harvard University Press, 2018); Stephen M. Griffin, "Pluralism in Constitutional Interpretation," *Texas Law Review* 72 (June 1994): 1753–70; Mitchell N. Berman, "Our Principled Constitution," *University of Pennsylvania Law Review* 166 (May 2018): 1325–1414.

28. On originalists' internal disagreements (with varying conclusions about how sharp they are), see Whittington, "Originalism," 394–404; Lawrence B. Solum, "Originalism Versus Living Constitutionalism: The Conceptual Structure of the Great Debate," *Northwestern University Law Review* 113 (2019): 1250–55, 1262–71; Thomas B. Colby and Peter J. Smith, "Living Originalism," *Duke Law Journal* 59 (Nov. 2009): 239–308.

29. See generally Robert H. Bork, *The Tempting of America: The Political Seduction of the Law* (New York: Free Press, 1990); Antonin Scalia, *A Matter of Interpretation: Federal Courts and the Law* (Princeton, N.J.: Princeton University Press, 1997), 37–47; Randy E. Barnett, *Restoring the Lost Constitution: The Presumption of Liberty*, rev. ed. (2004; Princeton, N.J.: Princeton University Press, 2014).

30. Bork, "Neutral Principles and Some First Amendment Problems."

31. Scalia, *A Matter of Interpretation*, 38–47; Rehnquist, "The Notion of a Living Constitution."

32. Keith E. Whittington, *Constitutional Interpretation: Textual Meaning, Original Intent, and Judicial Review* (Lawrence: University Press of Kansas, 1999), 15; Gary Lawson, "On Reading Recipes . . . and Constitutions," *Georgetown Law Journal* 85 (June 1997): 1823–36; Christopher R. Green, "Constitutional Truthmakers," *Notre Dame Journal of Law, Ethics & Public Policy* 32 (2018): 497.

33. Vasan Kesavan and Michael Stokes Paulsen, "The Interpretive Force of the Constitution's Secret Drafting History," *Georgetown Law Journal* 91 (Aug. 2003): 1129.

34. This kind of equation is ubiquitous. See, e.g., Antonin Scalia, "Originalism: The Lesser Evil," *University of Cincinnati Law Review* 57 (1989): 852; Scalia, *A Matter of Interpretation*, 38–39, 46–47. Originalism is often axiomatically equated with constitutional fidelity, see Fleming, *Fidelity to Our Imperfect Constitution*, 7–8.

35. On the shift, see Gienapp, "Constitutional Originalism and History." Public meaning originalism, though dominant, is not the only brand of the theory currently defended. Several originalists continue to defend original intentions. See Richard S. Kay, "Adherence to the Original Intentions in Constitutional Adjudication: Three Objections and Responses," *Northwestern University Law Review* 82 (Winter 1988): 226–92; Larry Alexander and Saikrishna Prakash, " 'Is That English You're

Speaking?': Why Intention Free Interpretation Is an Impossibility," *San Diego Law Review* 41 (Aug.–Sept. 2004): 967–96; Richard S. Kay, "Original Intention and Public Meaning in Constitutional Interpretation," *Northwestern University Law Review* 103 (Spring 2009): 703–26; Larry Alexander, "Simple-Minded Originalism," in Huscroft and Miller, *The Challenge of Originalism*, 87–98; Donald L. Drakeman, *The Hollow Core of Constitutional Theory: Why We Need the Framers* (New York: Cambridge University Press, 2020). As will be explained in chapter 1, though, most originalists still tend to share an underlying conception of what kind of thing the Constitution is.

36. Brest, "The Misconceived Quest for the Original Understanding," 212–22.

37. See Gary Lawson, "Proving the Law," *Northwestern University Law Review* 86 (1992): 875; Scalia, *A Matter of Interpretation*, 17, 38; Kesavan and Paulsen, "The Interpretive Force of the Constitution's Secret Drafting History," 1134–48; Barnett, *Restoring the Lost Constitution*, 94–95, 389–93.

38. Randy E. Barnett, "The Misconceived Assumption About Constitutional Assumptions," *Northwestern University Law Review* 103 (Spring 2009): 659.

39. Steven G. Calabresi and Julia T. Rickert, "Originalism and Sex Discrimination," *Texas Law Review* 90 (Nov. 2011): 9.

40. Public meaning originalists repeatedly stress that the Constitution's original meaning is a matter of objective fact. See Solum, "Originalist Methodology," 278; Barnett, *Restoring the Lost Constitution*, 389–95; Michael Stokes Paulsen, "Does the Constitution Prescribe Rules for Its Own Interpretation?," *Northwestern University Law Review* 103 (Spring 2009): 873–75; Gary Lawson, "Reflections of an Empirical Reader (Or: Could Fleming Be Right This Time?)," *Boston University Law Review* 96 (July 2016): 1457–80. For a critical perspective on originalists' hypothetical-reader construct, see Rakove, "Joe the Ploughman Reads the Constitution," 582–88; Cornell, "Reading the Constitution," 832–40.

41. A note on terminology is in order. To draw vital contrasts between modern originalist constitutional thinking and its Founding-era counterpart, I have had to settle on shorthand descriptions for the generation of Americans that participated in the founding of the constitutional order. Illuminating important eighteenth-century trends and recognizing conflicting views within that constitutional world—all while acknowledging that the eighteenth-century constitutional public, however large and diverse, nonetheless excluded broad segments of the population—presents terminological challenges. Most often, I have opted to use some variant of "Founding-era constitutionalists" to capture the large and diverse body of people—mostly, but not exclusively, white men—who participated in the period's constitutional debate. Though encompassing an impressive swath of the population, this group hardly could be said to stand in for Founding-era Americans as a whole, since significant portions of the population were excluded from these ranks—enslaved people of African ancestry, Indigenous peoples, most women, and less elite white men. These exclusions were never as sharp as they appeared, however, as members of these various groups not only managed to participate in constitutional debate but, at times, forced those in power to reckon with them. Sometimes, my focus is less on a broader constitutional public and instead on a narrower

group of constitutional elites who wielded outsized power and influence at the time or whose surviving testimony has most deeply shaped our knowledge of period attitudes—and where possible, I try to make that clear.

42. I have explored how foundational constitutional assumptions emerged only contingently after the Constitution's nominal creation. See Jonathan Gienapp, *The Second Creation: Fixing the American Constitution in the Founding Era* (Cambridge, Mass.: Harvard University Press, 2018).

43. There is a large and growing literature. See Michael W. McConnell, "Originalism and the Desegregation Decisions," *Virginia Law Review* 81 (May 1995): 947–1140; Akhil Reed Amar, *The Bill of Rights: Creation and Reconstruction* (New Haven, Conn.: Yale University Press, 1998); Kurt T. Lash, *The Fourteenth Amendment and the Privileges and Immunities of American Citizenship* (New York: Cambridge University Press, 2014); Christopher R. Green, *Equal Citizenship, Civil Rights, and the Constitution: The Original Sense of the Privileges or Immunities Clause* (New York: Routledge, 2015); Ilan Wurman, *The Second Founding: An Introduction to the Fourteenth Amendment* (New York: Cambridge University Press, 2020); Randy E. Barnett and Evan D. Bernick, *The Original Meaning of the Fourteenth Amendment: Its Letter and Spirit* (Cambridge, Mass.: Harvard University Press, 2021).

44. On how originalist judges tend to overlook the amendments and harken back to the Founding era, see Greene, "On the Origins of Originalism," 63–64.

45. Though, according to Mark Graber, originalists have overlooked the original purpose of the Reconstruction amendments by fetishizing section 1 of the Fourteenth Amendment and interpreting it in the textualist and legalist way to which judges have grown accustomed. Originalists have missed that few people at the time ascribed significance to section 1 because their aim was not to judicialize rights but rather to give Congress the tools necessary to reconstruct the union and destroy the vestiges of slavery. While, in other words, the amendment's framers cared deeply about the principles and rights now ascribed to section 1, in instinctively approaching constitutional reform as constitutional politicians of their day rather than constitutional lawyers of a more recent vintage, they assumed that those principles and rights would be protected through the other parts of the amendment. See Mark A. Graber, *Punish Treason, Reward Loyalty: The Forgotten Goals of Constitutional Reform After the Civil War* (Lawrence: University Press of Kansas, 2023). Meanwhile, Kate Masur has demonstrated that the history behind section 1 of the Fourteenth Amendment runs much deeper than many have realized. See Kate Masur, *Until Justice Be Done: America's First Civil Rights Movement, from the Revolution to Reconstruction* (New York: W. W. Norton, 2021).

46. See especially John Harrison, "The Lawfulness of the Reconstruction Amendments," *University of Chicago Law Review* 68 (Spring 2001): 375–462. On this originalist tendency, see Thomas B. Colby, "Originalism and Ratification of the Fourteenth Amendment," *Northwestern University Law Review* 106 (2013): 1628–31. On the Reconstruction amendments as a "second founding," see Eric Foner, *The Second Founding: How the Civil War and Reconstruction Remade the Constitution* (New York: W. W. Norton, 2019).

47. Originalists have been unwilling to accept Bruce Ackerman's argument that the Reconstruction amendments were added illegally and that, on account of those revolutionary means, they worked a broader transformation in the constitutional order. Bruce Ackerman, *We the People: Transformations* (Cambridge, Mass.: Harvard University Press, 1998), 99–100, 115–16.
48. Marshall, "Reflections on the Bicentennial of the United States Constitution," 4.

Chapter 1. Originalist Assumptions

Epigraph: Ludwig Wittgenstein, *Philosophical Investigations*, trans. G. E. M. Anscombe (New York: Macmillan, 1953), sec. 129.

1. Some originalists have concentrated on the nature of the Constitution itself. See Evan D. Bernick and Christopher R. Green, "There Is Something That Our Constitution Just Is," *Texas Review of Law & Politics* 27 (Fall 2022): 266–77, 303–04, 306–07, which builds from Christopher R. Green, " 'This Constitution': Constitutional Indexicals as a Basis for Textualist Semi-Originalism," *Notre Dame Law Review* 84 (Apr. 2009): 1607–74; Green, "Constitutional Truthmakers." Even this work, though, is noteworthy for what it assumes and its unwillingness to approach the Constitution on an unfamiliar set of terms. In more ways than not, then, it supports the trend emphasized here. A recent article by Stephen Sachs gestures in this direction as well, by distinguishing originalism as a theory of what makes certain claims about the Constitution correct (a standard) and originalism as a method for obtaining those correct answers (a procedure). See Stephen E. Sachs, "Originalism: Standard and Procedure," *Harvard Law Review* 135 (Jan. 2022): 777–830. It too sidesteps essential issues, however. For more, see chapter 7, note 87.
2. Solum, "What Is Originalism?," 32–38.
3. Lawrence B. Solum, "The Fixation Thesis: The Role of Historical Fact in Original Meaning," *Notre Dame Law Review* 91 (Nov. 2015): 1–78.
4. Lawrence B. Solum, "The Constraint Principle: Original Meaning and Constitutional Practice," 2–3n1 (unpublished manuscript, last revised Apr. 6, 2019), https://papers.ssrn.com/sol3/papers.cfm?abstract_id=2940215.
5. In addition to the former justice Antonin Scalia, current Supreme Court justices Neil Gorsuch and Amy Coney Barrett are vigorous champions of this brand of originalism, as are most self-proclaimed originalist judges on the lower federal courts. In the academy, meanwhile, public meaning originalism predominates among originalist legal scholars. "Public Meaning Originalism [is] the most prominent member of the originalist family of constitutional theories." Barnett and Solum, "Originalism After *Dobbs, Bruen*, and *Kennedy*," 436. "[T]he mainstream of contemporary originalism today seeks the original public meaning of the text, not the original intent of the framers." Kurt T. Lash, " 'Resolution VI': The Virginia Plan and the Authority to Resolve Collective Action Problems Under Article I, Section 8," *Notre Dame Law Review* 87 (June 2012): 2146. See generally Solum, "What Is Originalism?," 22–23.
6. For their writings, see the introduction, note 35.

7. Among those who seem to fit this description is Kurt Lash, who tends to look to concrete original understandings of key constitutional provisions, especially among those who ratified them, to decode their public meaning. See, e.g., Lash, " 'Resolution VI,' " 2132–33, 2146, 2152–63; Kurt T. Lash, "The Sum of All Delegated Power: A Response to Richard Primus, 'The Limits of Enumeration,' " *Yale Law Journal Forum* 180 (Dec. 2014): 189–95. More theoretically inclined public meaning originalists tend to distinguish between original subjective understanding (or the original intent of the ratifiers) and objective public meaning of the Constitution's words, which can be deciphered only through analysis of contemporary linguistic usage.

8. John McGinnis and Michael Rappaport are the leading champions of this approach. On their theory, see chapter 7.

9. In the discussion to follow, I allude to most of them, including original law originalism, which is associated with William Baude and Stephen Sachs and, in crucial respects, approaches the Constitution much differently than other forms of originalism. On their theory, see chapter 10.

10. Originalist inquiry, like most constitutional interpretation, is focused on the Constitution's more open-ended provisions ("executive power," "necessary and proper," "freedom of speech," "due process of law") that carry such enormous weight in defining the government's powers, federal-state relations, or individual liberties— or what Sanford Levinson has called the "Constitution of Conversation"—as opposed to those hardwired features of constitutional structure and design (such as the requirement that each state gets two senators or the president of the United States must be at least thirty-five years of age) that are never the source of interpretive controversy, which Levinson has called the "Constitution of Settlement." See Levinson, *Constitutional Faith*, 246–54. The only way to determine the original meaning of the first kind of provision is to look beyond the Constitution's text to contemporary usage of the key phrases found in the provision. That means in effect consulting the same body of concrete historical evidence as other originalists, looking to concrete examples of framers' intent, ratifiers' understanding, or early debate and practice, not because original intent, expected application, or post-ratification practice either determines or trumps original meaning, but because they are our best, and often only, evidence of that meaning. So most of the time, an original intent originalist can be found consulting original intent because that holds the key to original meaning, while an original understanding originalist can be found consulting original understanding because that holds the key to original meaning. And a public meaning originalist, despite resolutely distinguishing original public meaning from either framers' intent or ratifiers' understanding, can be found consulting much the same evidence as these other originalists because it is said to be good evidence, not of subjective intent or understanding, but of public meaning itself. As Michael McConnell has stated, "a practitioner of original public meaning will necessarily rely on much the same sources and methods as a practitioner of original intent." Michael W. McConnell, *The President Who Would Not Be King: Executive Power Under the Constitution* (Princeton, N.J.: Princeton University Press, 2020), 13. No matter then the clear theoretical distinctions that have been

mapped separating them, public meaning originalism and other kinds of originalism tend to look quite similar in practice.

11. On originalism's diversity, compare Solum, "Originalism Versus Living Constitutionalism," 1250–55, 1262–71 (arguing that, despite its diversity, originalism is coherent and unified), with Colby and Smith, "Living Originalism" (arguing that originalism's ever-increasing diversity suggests that it is anything but coherent and unified).

12. On how this tendency is endemic of all prescriptive legal theories, see Jeremy K. Kessler and David E. Pozen, "Working Themselves Impure: A Life Cycle Theory of Legal Theories," *University of Chicago Law Review* 83 (Fall 2016): 1819–92, esp. 1820–25, 1844–47.

13. On the divergence between academic and judicial or political originalism, see Segall, *Originalism as Faith*, 122–40; Chemerinsky, *Worse Than Nothing*, 139–65; Colby, "The Sacrifice of the New Originalism," 714–16, 771–73; Michael C. Dorf, "The Undead Constitution," *Harvard Law Review* 125 (June 2012): 2014, 2020–23; Jamal Greene, "The Case for Original Intent," *George Washington Law Review* 80 (Nov. 2012): 1683–1706; Balkin, *Memory and Authority*, 163–68; Richard H. Fallon, Jr., "Selective Originalism and Judicial Role Morality," *Texas Law Review* 102 (Dec. 2023): 221–304. When it suits them, academic originalists are quick to distinguish their work from that of originalist judges. But only up to a point, for what they gain in intellectual respectability they risk losing in broader impact. Often then, they are just as eager to identify what unites originalists in the academy with those on the bench. Colby, "The Sacrifice of the New Originalism," 776–78.

14. In attempting to bring the dominant originalist conception of the Constitution into focus, I have not tried to cite everything from the vast and ever-proliferating originalist literature but instead have tried to call attention to those arguments that best capture the kind of assumptions that I believe pervade originalist thinking. Any effort to bring the broader picture into focus is potentially vulnerable to the objection that it overlooks certain nuances or differences. Although originalists too often deflect criticism by hiding behind distinctions of their own making, there are meaningful differences distinguishing varieties of the theory. I remain convinced, nonetheless, that a set of common assumptions unite most originalists who might otherwise see themselves apart and that it is important to bring those less-appreciated commonalities into focus because of the foundational, and often unrecognized, work they perform.

15. See Andrew W. Coan, "The Irrelevance of Writtenness in Constitutional Interpretation," *University of Pennsylvania Law Review* 158 (Mar. 2010): 1025–46; Thomas B. Colby, "Originalism and Structural Argument," *Northwestern University Law Review* 113 (2019): 1297–98, 1303–06; George Thomas, *The (Un)Written Constitution* (New York: Oxford University Press, 2021), 35–55. The originalist Stephen Sachs, in suggesting that originalism need not be predicated on text, otherwise confirms the orthodoxy. See Stephen E. Sachs, "Originalism Without Text," *Yale Law Journal* 127 (Oct. 2017): 156–69.

16. Steven G. Calabresi and Saikrishna B. Prakash, "The President's Power to Execute the Laws," *Yale Law Journal* 104 (Dec. 1994): 551; Mitchell N. Berman, "The Tragedy of Justice Scalia," *Michigan Law Review* 115 (Apr. 2017): 790–91.

17. See, e.g., Akhil Reed Amar, "A Few Thoughts on Constitutionalism, Textualism, and Populism," *Fordham Law Review* 65 (Mar. 1997): 1657. The Constitution is described as something that can be put in one's pocket in Bernick and Green, "There Is Something That Our Constitution Just Is," 266–77, 303–07.

18. Solum, "The Fixation Thesis," 15, 25–26; Barnett, *Restoring the Lost Constitution*, 102–11; Green, *Equal Citizenship, Civil Rights, and the Constitution*, 7–8.

19. Sachs, "Originalism Without Text," 157.

20. Lawrence B. Solum, "Communicative Content and Legal Content," *Notre Dame Law Review* 89 (Dec. 2013): 484–507. "Constitutional interpretation" is "the activity that discerns the communicative content (linguistic meaning) of the constitutional text." Solum, "Originalist Methodology," 272.

21. Randy E. Barnett, "The Gravitational Force of Originalism," *Fordham Law Review* 82 (Nov. 2013): 413–17 (quote at 413).

22. Solum, "Originalist Methodology," 286–91; Barnett, "The Misconceived Assumption About Constitutional Assumptions," 617–26; Balkin, *Living Originalism*, 6–7, 14–16, 23–34, 256–73; Michael W. McConnell, "The Importance of Humility in Judicial Review: A Comment on Ronald Dworkin's 'Moral Reading' of the Constitution," *Fordham Law Review* 65 (Mar. 1997): 1280–81.

23. "Construction" is defined as the activity of giving the Constitution meaning where interpretation runs out, or when the text's meaning is sufficiently vague, ambiguous, or indeterminate that it cannot generate a constitutional rule. See Keith E. Whittington, "Constructing a New American Constitution," *Constitutional Commentary* 27 (Fall 2010): 119–38; Lawrence B. Solum, "Originalism and Constitutional Construction," *Fordham Law Review* 82 (Nov. 2013): 453–538; Randy E. Barnett and Evan D. Bernick, "The Letter and the Spirit: A Unified Theory of Originalism," *Georgetown Law Journal* 107 (Oct. 2018): 10–18.

24. Lawrence B. Solum, "Originalism and the Unwritten Constitution," *University of Illinois Law Review* 2013 (2013): 1935–84, esp. 1947–80. Solum's case for how extratextual sources beyond the written Constitution can be used in originalist interpretation underscores the presumed textual nature of the Constitution. He claims that extratextual sources can illuminate the text—by providing evidence of linguistic meaning or enriching the semantic meaning by providing context. Or such sources can supplement the text where its meaning runs out through constitutional constructions that are "bound to the text."

25. Randy E. Barnett, "Underlying Principles," *Constitutional Commentary* 24 (Summer 2007): 413.

26. Michael Stokes Paulsen, "The Text, the Whole Text, and Nothing but the Text, So Help Me God: Un-Writing Amar's Unwritten Constitution," *University of Chicago Law Review* 81 (Spring 2014): 1385.

27. This provides a constitutive theory of constitutional substance, related to the monist constitutive theory of law that Mitchell Berman has identified among originalists. Berman, "Our Principled Constitution," 1342–44.

28. For a revealing example, see Solum, "Originalist Methodology," 272.

29. For a comprehensive defense, see Lawrence B. Solum, "The Public Meaning Thesis: An Originalist Theory of Constitutional Meaning," *Boston University Law Review* 101 (Dec. 2021): 1953–2048.

30. Corpus linguistics studies the use and structure of language through the compilation and analysis of a large body of texts, promising to offer a big-data empirical approach to naturally occurring linguistic practice. Solum, "Originalist Methodology," 283–84; Lawrence B. Solum, "Triangulating Public Meaning: Linguistics, Immersion, and the Constitutional Record," *Brigham Young University Law Review* 6 (2017): 1643–49; James C. Phillips, Daniel M. Ortner, and Thomas R. Lee, "Corpus Linguistics & Original Public Meaning: A New Tool to Make Originalism More Empirical," *Yale Law Journal Forum* 126 (May 2016): 21–32; Thomas R. Lee and James C. Phillips, "Data-Driven Originalism," *University of Pennsylvania Law Review* 167 (Jan. 2019): 261–336; Jennifer L. Mascott, "Who Are 'Officers of the United States'?," *Stanford Law Review* 70 (Feb. 2018): 465–507; Max Crema and Lawrence B. Solum, "The Original Meaning of 'Due Process of Law' in the Fifth Amendment," *Virginia Law Review* 108 (Apr. 2022): 467–68, 485–92.

31. They did so in large measure to combat the Supreme Court's willingness to identify unenumerated constitutional rights. See Bork, "Neutral Principles and Some First Amendment Problems"; Edwin Meese III, "The Law of the Constitution," *Tulane Law Review* 61 (Apr. 1987): 986.

32. See Steven D. Smith, "That Old-Time Originalism," in Huscroft and Miller, *Challenge of Originalism*, 223–45, which laments originalism's turn toward overly refined, esoteric theorizing.

33. See for instance the important work of Michael McConnell, which eschews the highly theoretical linguistic approach to originalism and instead maintains a traditional commitment to the kind of historical analysis that has become less common among originalists. McConnell, *The President Who Would Not Be King*, esp. 13–14, 365n17.

34. Original methods originalists thus readily adopt the standard text-based public meaning originalist definition of "constitutional meaning." See John O. McGinnis and Michael B. Rappaport, *Originalism and the Good Constitution* (Cambridge, Mass.: Harvard University Press, 2013), 8.

35. Many have claimed that virtually all originalists agree on this point. See Lee and Phillips, "Data-Driven Originalism," 264–75; Stephen E. Sachs, "Originalism as a Theory of Legal Change," *Harvard Journal of Law & Public Policy* 38 (Summer 2015): 822, 828–29; Solum, "Triangulating Public Meaning," 1626–29; John O. McGinnis and Michael B. Rappaport, "Unifying Original Intent and Original Public Meaning," *Northwestern University Law Review* 113 (2019): 1373. An original intentions originalist might contend that the framers' or ratifiers' original constitutional preferences are the object of originalist interpretation, but the dominant pattern still holds. Public meaning originalists often argue, after all, that public meaning originalism and original intentions originalism are consistent. See Lawrence B. Solum, "Intellectual History as Constitutional Theory," *Virginia Law Review* 101 (June 2015): 1136.

36. For the earlier critiques, see Henry V. Jaffa, *Original Intent and the Framers of the Constitution: A Disputed Question* (Washington, D.C.: Regnery, 1994); for recent critiques, see Vermeule, *Common Good Constitutionalism*; Hadley Arkes, *Mere Natural Law: Originalism and the Anchoring Truths of the Constitution* (Washington, D.C.: Regnery, 2023). The influential legal philosopher Ronald Dworkin leveled a similar criticism against early originalism, specifically targeted at originalist Robert Bork, not in defense of reading natural law principles, but rather principles of political morality, into the Constitution. This critique was an offshoot of Dworkin's broader challenge to legal positivism as espoused by theorists like H. L. A. Hart. Law was a branch of political morality, Dworkin claimed. Legal interpretation and decision-making necessarily relied upon normative judgments, rather than merely semantic or logical assumptions. Originalists were thus mistaken in claiming that they could bracket morality or political values simply by following what the Constitution's framers or ratifiers had, as a positive matter, laid down, for that could not explain at what level of generality their pronouncements ought to be interpreted. See Ronald Dworkin, "Bork's Jurisprudence," *University of Chicago Law Review* 57 (Spring 1990): 657–78, esp. 663–64. For Dworkin's theory of law, see Ronald Dworkin, *Law's Empire* (Cambridge, Mass.: Harvard University Press, 1986); for his theory applied to the Constitution, see Dworkin, *Freedom's Law*.

37. Jeffrey A. Pojanowski and Kevin C. Walsh, "Enduring Originalism," *Georgetown Law Journal* 105 (Nov. 2016): 97–158; Lee J. Strang, *Originalism's Promise: A Natural Law Account of the American Constitution* (New York: Cambridge University Press, 2019); J. Joel Alicea, "The Moral Authority of Original Meaning," *Notre Dame Law Review* 98 (Nov. 2022): 1–60.

38. It could be said that some of these natural law originalists, especially Pojanowski and Walsh, suggest that moral facts can alter the positive law. Though, even then, their claim is not that natural law alters the content of the Constitution so much as that it suggests when the positive law of the Constitution might be legally deficient.

39. In this regard, these recent natural law defenses of originalism are similar to Randy Barnett's natural-rights-based justification of originalism. The Constitution is legitimate, he has argued, not because of how it was made, but because if interpreted in accordance with its original textual meaning, it suitably protects natural rights. The Constitution itself, though, is a positive construction, one whose content is a function of what its language empirically communicates. See Barnett, *Restoring the Lost Constitution*, 1–119.

40. Solum, "The Fixation Thesis," 36.

41. Steven D. Smith, "Reply to Koppelman: Originalism and the (Merely) Human Constitution," *Constitutional Commentary* 27 (Fall 2010): 192–93, 198–99.

42. See Scalia, *A Matter of Interpretation*, 3–47; Lawrence B. Solum, "Constitutional Texting," *San Diego Law Review* 44 (Feb.–Mar. 2007): 123–52; Kesavan and Paulsen, "The Interpretive Force of the Constitution's Secret Drafting History," 1127–33; Antonin Scalia and Bryan A. Garner, *Reading Law: The Interpretation of Legal Texts* (St. Paul, Minn.: West, 2012); Ilan Wurman, *A Debt Against the Living: An Introduction to Originalism* (New York: Cambridge University Press, 2017), 129–33.

43. Scalia, *A Matter of Interpretation*, 38.

44. See Strauss, *The Living Constitution*, 1–3; Solum, "Originalism Versus Living Constitutionalism," 1270–71, 1276–77, 1281.

45. Solum, "The Fixation Thesis," 1–2, 15–16, 76–78; Lawson, "On Reading Recipes . . . and Constitutions"; Saikrishna B. Prakash, "The Misunderstood Relationship Between Originalism and Popular Sovereignty," *Harvard Journal of Law & Public Policy* 31 (Spring 2008): 485–91; Scalia, *A Matter of Interpretation*, 40–41; Scalia and Garner, *Reading Law*, 78–90. Or the content of *any* communication is fixed at the time of its utterance. See Wurman, *A Debt Against the Living*, 30–35.

46. Whittington, *Constitutional Interpretation*, 47–61, 124–27; Gary L. McDowell, *The Language of Law and the Foundations of American Constitutionalism* (New York: Cambridge University Press, 2010), 48–54; Pojanowski and Walsh, "Enduring Originalism," 126–35.

47. See Barnett, *Restoring the Lost Constitution*, 102–11.

48. Solum, "The Fixation Thesis." The "fixation thesis" is "a thesis about the activity of discovering the communicative content of the constitutional text" that states that the Constitution's "communicative content" was "fixed at the time of origination." Solum, "The Fixation Thesis," 15.

49. For an example, see John O. McGinnis and Michael B. Rappaport, "The Constitution and the Language of the Law," *William & Mary Law Review* 59 (Mar. 2018): 1325.

50. Barnett and Solum, "Originalism After *Dobbs, Bruen,* and *Kennedy*," 479.

51. Just consider how Lawrence Solum describes the fixation thesis: It is "an obvious and banal truth" that is "uncontroversially true." Solum, "The Fixation Thesis," 78.

52. Balkin, *Living Originalism*, 6–7, 12–13, 100–04; Mark D. Greenberg and Harry Litman, "The Meaning of Original Meaning," *Georgetown Law Journal* 86 (Jan. 1998): 586–97; Christopher R. Green, "Originalism and the Sense-Reference Distinction," *St. Louis University Law Journal* 50 (Winter 2006): 555–628; Barnett, "The Misconceived Assumption About Constitutional Assumptions."

53. Balkin, *Living Originalism*. On how this blurs the differences between originalism and non-originalism, see Colby, "The Sacrifice of the New Originalism," 744–76; Segall, *Originalism as Faith*, 91–102.

54. Akhil Reed Amar, "The Document and the Doctrine," *Harvard Law Review* 114 (Nov. 2000): 45–48; Barnett, "The Misconceived Assumption About Constitutional Assumptions," 659–60; Solum, "Originalist Methodology," 272–76.

55. Gary Lawson and Guy Seidman, "Originalism as a Legal Enterprise," *Constitutional Commentary* 23 (Spring 2006): 47–80; McGinnis and Rappaport, "The Constitution and the Language of the Law," 1355–1400; McDowell, *The Language of Law*, 248–51; Pojanowski and Walsh, "Enduring Originalism." Though not all conceptions of law are the same. Original law originalism has a different sort in mind. See William Baude and Stephen E. Sachs, "Grounding Originalism," *Northwestern University Law Review* 113 (2019): 1455–92.

56. Scalia and Garner, *Reading Law*; William Baude and Stephen E. Sachs, "The Law of Interpretation," *Harvard Law Review* 130 (Feb. 2017): 1079–1147.

57. Scalia, "Originalism: The Lesser Evil," 854.

58. John O. McGinnis and Michael B. Rappaport, "Original Methods Originalism: A New Theory of Interpretation and the Case Against Construction," *Northwestern University Law Review* 103 (Spring 2009): 755–58; 765–72; McGinnis and Rappaport, *Originalism and the Good Constitution*, 116–38; Robert G. Natelson, "The Founders' Hermeneutic: The Real Original Understanding of Original Intent," *Ohio State Law Journal* 68 (2007): 1239–1306. Other originalists, meanwhile, have argued that there were clear default rules for interpreting a text like the Constitution when it first appeared. See Saikrishna B. Prakash, "Unoriginalism's Law Without Meaning," *Constitutional Commentary* 15 (Fall 1998): 540–46; Paulsen, "Does the Constitution Prescribe Rules for Its Own Interpretation?," 860–61, 872–73, 883; Anthony J. Bellia Jr. and Bradford R. Clark, "The Constitutional Law of Interpretation," *Notre Dame Law Review* 98 (Dec. 2022): 519–616.

59. McGinnis and Rappaport, "Unifying Original Intent and Original Public Meaning," 1396–99.

60. Lawson and Seidman, "Originalism as a Legal Enterprise," 80.

61. McGinnis and Rappaport, "The Constitution and the Language of the Law."

62. Solum, "The Public Meaning Thesis," 1975–82.

63. Saikrishna B. Prakash and John C. Yoo, "The Origins of Judicial Review," *University of Chicago Law Review* 70 (Summer 2003): 887–982.

64. John F. Manning, "Separation of Powers as Ordinary Interpretation," *Harvard Law Review* 124 (June 2011): 2025.

Chapter 2. Originalist Justifications

Epigraph: W. V. O. Quine, "Two Dogmas of Empiricism," in *From a Logical Point of View: Nine Logico-Philosophical Essays* (Cambridge, Mass.: Harvard University Press, 1953), 26.

1. For the most detailed discussion, see Coan, "The Irrelevance of Writtenness in Constitutional Interpretation," 1031–46. For a revealing example of this originalist claim, see Greenberg and Litman, "The Meaning of Original Meaning," 571.

2. Scalia and Garner, *Reading Law*, 78–92; Prakash, "Unoriginalism's Law Without Meaning," 540–46; Paulsen, "Does the Constitution Prescribe Rules for Its Own Interpretation?," 860–61, 872–73, 883.

3. For an extended discussion, see Berman, "Originalism Is Bunk."

4. Michael Stokes Paulsen, "How to Interpret the Constitution (and How Not To)," *Yale Law Journal* 115 (June 2006): 2049.

5. Kesavan and Paulsen, "The Interpretive Force of the Constitution's Secret Drafting History," 1128; Calabresi and Prakash, "The President's Power to Execute the Laws," 551; Barnett, "Underlying Principles," 413 (emphasis in original); Lawrence B. Solum, "Semantic Originalism" (Illinois Public Law and Legal Theory Research Papers Series No. 07-24, Nov. 2008), 28, https://papers.ssrn.com/sol3/papers.cfm?abstract_id=1120244.

6. Solum, "Semantic Originalism," 5.

7. Green, *Equal Citizenship, Civil Rights, and the Constitution*, 8.

8. See Solum, "Originalist Methodology," 272; Solum, "The Public Meaning Thesis," 1957, 1974.

9. See Richard Primus, "Unbundling Constitutionality," *University of Chicago Law Review* 80 (Summer 2013): 1081–82, 1090–91; and on the deeper roots of this attachment to written constitutionalism, see Levinson, *Constitutional Faith*, 27–37.

10. United States Constitution, art. VI; Barnett, "The Gravitational Force of Originalism," 417–18.

11. Green, " 'This Constitution,' " 1643–48; Kesavan and Paulsen, "The Interpretive Force of the Constitution's Secret Drafting History," 1127–28.

12. Kesavan and Paulsen, "The Interpretive Force of the Constitution's Secret Drafting History," 1127. See also Amar, "A Few Thoughts on Constitutionalism, Textualism, and Populism," 1657; Akhil Reed Amar, *America's Constitution: A Biography* (New York: Random House, 2005), 285.

13. Paulsen, "Does the Constitution Prescribe Rules for Its Own Interpretation?," 859–60, 864–69 (quotes at 859, 869).

14. For an argument that the practice of oath taking reveals that oath takers in U.S. constitutional culture have seen themselves pledging fidelity to a common Constitution created at the Founding, see Evan D. Bernick and Christopher R. Green, "What Is the Object of the Constitutional Oath?," *Penn State Law Review* 128 (Fall 2023): 1–68.

15. Green, " 'This Constitution,' " 1674, and see esp. 1624–28, 1637–57; Bernick and Green, "There Is Something That Our Constitution Just Is," 266–71.

16. Green's analysis of the Constitution's indexicals and time-specific language predominates, whereas his analysis of the Constitution's purported reference to itself as a text is brief. Green, " 'This Constitution,' " 1648–68. And the evidence he marshals does not support his argument. He underscores uses of "this Constitution" in various state constitutions, except most of his examples come from well after 1787, when constitutional assumptions had begun to change. Far more importantly, his one example from the Founding period (the New Hampshire Constitution of 1784) in fact points in the other direction on account of the much different way Founding-era Americans understood constitutionalism. More on this evidence in chapter 4.

17. See also Coan, "The Irrelevance of Writtenness in Constitutional Interpretation," 1029–30.

18. McGinnis and Rappaport, "The Constitution and the Language of the Law," 1355–62, 1369–83; Lawson and Seidman, "Originalism as a Legal Enterprise," 72–73; Manning, "Separation of Powers as Ordinary Interpretation," 2025–28.

19. Lawson and Seidman, "Originalism as a Legal Enterprise," 72.

20. McGinnis and Rappaport, "The Constitution and the Language of the Law," 1357.

21. Baude and Sachs, "The Law of Interpretation," 1099.

22. Whittington, *Constitutional Interpretation*, 50.

23. Whittington, *Constitutional Interpretation*, 47–61, 124–27; Richard S. Kay, "Constitutionalism," in *Constitutionalism: Philosophical Foundations*, ed. Larry Alexander (New York: Cambridge University Press, 1998), 27–39; Herman Belz, *A Living Constitution or Fundamental Law? American Constitutionalism in Historical Perspective* (Lanham, Md.: Rowman & Littlefield, 1998), 1–39; Kurt T. Lash, "Originalism,

Popular Sovereignty, and *Reverse* Stare Decisis," *Virginia Law Review* 93 (Oct. 2007): 1440–41; McDowell, *The Language of Law*, 48–54, 222–26; Akhil Reed Amar, *America's Unwritten Constitution: The Precedents and Principles We Live By* (New York: Basic Books, 2012), xii.

24. *Marbury v. Madison*, 5 U.S. (1 Cranch) 137, 176–78 (1803).
25. See Calabresi and Prakash, "The President's Power to Execute the Laws," 551–52; Prakash and Yoo, "The Origins of Judicial Review," 914–15, 976–77; Michael Stokes Paulsen, "The Irrepressible Myth of *Marbury*," *Michigan Law Review* 101 (Aug. 2003): 2739–42; Bernick and Green, "There Is Something That Our Constitution Just Is," 276–77.
26. McGinnis and Rappaport, "The Constitution and the Language of the Law," 1360–61.
27. Examples abound, but a recent exemplar is Bernick and Green, "There Is Something That Our Constitution Just Is." Even though the authors focus primarily on limning the original Constitution's true nature according to its putative properties, they cannot resist claiming that the Founding generation understood the Constitution's nature in just the way they describe.

Chapter 3. A Foreign Country

Epigraph: L. P. Hartley, *The Go-Between* (London: H. Hamilton, 1953), 10.
1. For valuable reflections, see Robert Darnton, *The Great Cat Massacre and Other Episodes in French Cultural History* (New York: Basic, 1984).
2. Sam Wineburg, *Historical Thinking and Other Unnatural Acts: Charting the Future of Teaching the Past* (Philadelphia: Temple University Press, 2001), 6.
3. On differences in conceptual language across time and how that shapes our understanding of what past people were talking about, see Quentin Skinner, "Meaning and Understanding in the History of Ideas," *History and Theory* 8 (1969): 3–53. On the "tension between the familiar and the strange" in historical study, see Wineburg, *Historical Thinking and Other Unnatural Acts*, 5–7.
4. See Bernard Bailyn, *The Ideological Origins of the American Revolution* (1967; Cambridge, Mass.: Harvard University Press, 1992); Gordon S. Wood, *The Creation of the American Republic, 1776–1787*, 2nd ed. (1969; Chapel Hill: University of North Carolina Press, 1998); Stanley Elkins and Eric McKitrick, *The Age of Federalism: The Early American Republic, 1788–1800* (New York: Oxford University Press, 1993); Daniel T. Rodgers, "Republicanism: The Career of a Concept," *Journal of American History* 79 (June 1992): 11–38.
5. Elkins and McKitrick, *The Age of Federalism*, 5. As Hendrik Hartog has put it, "the emotional energy that lies behind the original republican impulse is largely unknown to us." Hendrik Hartog, "Imposing Constitutional Traditions," *William & Mary Law Review* 29 (Fall 1987): 82.
6. Wood, *The Creation of the American Republic*, xvi. For more, see Jonathan Gienapp, "Beyond Republicanism, Back to Constitutionalism: *The Creation of the American Republic* at Fifty," *New England Quarterly* 93 (June 2020): 288–93.

7. As should go without saying, wide overlap is essential to understanding cultures and historical eras that otherwise differ. Emphasizing difference doesn't deny overlap but presupposes it in order to identify precisely those areas of divergence that are significant or pass unnoticed.

8. For discussion and documentation of this problem among legal academics, see H. Jefferson Powell, "Rules for Originalists," *Virginia Law Review* 73 (May 1987): 668–78; Flaherty, "History 'Lite' in Modern American Constitutionalism," 524–26, 561–67, 575–79; Kramer, "When Lawyers Do History," 394–401.

9. Wineburg, *Historical Thinking and Other Unnatural Acts*, 3–27 (quote at 7).

10. Drawing on concepts in philosophy, I have developed this point at length: Jonathan Gienapp, "Knowing How vs. Knowing That: Navigating the Past," *Process: A Blog for American History*, Mar. 20, 2017, www.processhistory.org/gienapp-knowing-how. On the distinction, see Robert B. Brandom, *Perspectives on Pragmatism: Classical, Recent, and Contemporary* (Cambridge, Mass.: Harvard University Press, 2011), 26–32, 67–70. More broadly, see Wittgenstein, *Philosophical Investigations*; Robert B. Brandom, *Making It Explicit: Reasoning, Representing, and Discursive Commitment* (Cambridge, Mass.: Harvard University Press, 1994); Donald Davidson, *Truth, Language, and History* (New York: Oxford University Press, 2005), 89–141; Richard Rorty, *Philosophical Papers*, vol. 4, *Philosophy as Cultural Politics* (New York: Cambridge University Press, 2007), 14–24, 156–59, 176–83.

11. Such historical immersion often resembles ethnography. See William Bouwmsa, "Intellectual History in the 1980s: From the History of Ideas to the History of Meaning," *Journal of Interdisciplinary History* 12 (Autumn 1981): 279–91; Darnton, *The Great Cat Massacre*, 3–7; Clifford Geertz, *The Interpretation of Cultures* (1973; New York: Basic, 2000), esp. 3–30, 412–53.

12. For a description of this process in the history of science, see Thomas S. Kuhn, *The Road Since Structure: Philosophical Essays, 1970–1993, with an Autobiographical Interview*, ed. James Conant and John Haugeland (Chicago: University of Chicago Press, 2000), 59–60.

13. Kuhn, *The Road Since Structure*, 15–20. On starting with the peculiar features of a historical text, see Thomas S. Kuhn, *The Essential Tension: Selected Studies in Scientific Tradition and Change* (Chicago: University of Chicago Press, 1977), xii.

14. For testimonials, see Bailyn, *The Ideological Origins*, v, x–xi; Wood, *The Creation of the American Republic*, xv–xvi.

15. Too often, in debates over interpretation in the human sciences, the focus has been on radical indeterminacy, incommensurability, or the impossibility of translation. Unfortunately, that is sometimes how originalists have greeted historicist arguments. Those who conflate historicism with relativism fail to understand it. For an illustration of this misunderstanding, see Wurman, *A Debt Against the Living*, 102–06. It is not an uncommon mistake. For discussions of these themes, see Spiegel, "The Task of the Historian"; Peter E. Gordon, "Agonies of the Real: Anti-Realism from Kuhn to Foucault," *Modern Intellectual History* 9 (Mar. 2012): 127–47. For rejoinders explaining why incommensurability does not entail relativism, see Kuhn, *The Road Since Structure*, 33–57; Richard Rorty, "The World Well Lost," in *Consequences of Pragmatism* (Minneapolis: University of Minnesota Press, 1982), 3–18;

Richard Rorty, *Philosophical Papers*, vol. 1, *Objectivity, Relativism, and Truth* (New York: Cambridge University Press, 1991), 1–18, 113–25; Donald Davidson, "On the Very Idea of a Conceptual Scheme," in *Inquiries into Truth and Interpretation* (New York: Oxford University Press, 2001), 183–98; Quentin Skinner, "A Reply to My Critics," in *Meaning and Context: Quentin Skinner and His Critics*, ed. James Tully (Princeton, N.J.: Princeton University Press, 1988), 231–88.

16. William Baude and Stephen E. Sachs, "Originalism and the Law of the Past," *Law and History Review* 37 (Aug. 2019): 809–20, esp. 814–15.

17. See, e.g., Randy E. Barnett, "Challenging the Priesthood of Professional Historians," *The Volokh Conspiracy* (blog), Mar. 28, 2017, https://reason.com/volokh/2017/03/28/challenging-the-priesthood-of/; Solum, "Communicative Content and Legal Content," 498; Wurman, *A Debt Against the Living*, 99–101; Scalia and Garner, *Reading Law*, 399–402. Sometimes, originalists dismiss the notion that the Founding sprang from a different conceptual universe without refuting the decades of detailed historical work documenting that fact. On originalists' failures to engage with historical difference, see Stephen M. Griffin, "Rebooting Originalism," *Illinois Law Review* 2008 (2008): 1205–09.

18. Gienapp, "Historicism and Holism," 942–44; Powell, "Rules for Originalists," 668–78.

19. Solum, "Communicative Content and Legal Content," 484–507; Green, "Originalism and the Sense-Reference Distinction."; McGinnis and Rappaport, "Original Methods Originalism"; Baude and Sachs, "The Law of Interpretation."

20. For originalists' focus on linguistic drift, see Solum, "Originalist Methodology," 279–85.

21. On historical translation, see Gienapp, "Historicism and Holism," 935–36; Powell, "Rules for Originalists," 672–74. This version of translation is distinct from, if in vital ways related to, the edifying alternative defended by Lawrence Lessig. He argues that, in the context of U.S. constitutional interpretation, translation consists of not merely recovering the Constitution's original meaning in its original context, but then carrying that original meaning into the modern, or target, context in which contemporary constitutional disputes arise. Thus, translation is not just about understanding an unfamiliar past but understanding how to carry that past into the present in order to preserve original meanings (often by changing them) as the world, or context, itself changes. While his main theme is identifying the interpretive practices needed to connect past to present, in so doing Lessig valuably underscores the essential importance of historical difference, change, and discontinuity in U.S. constitutionalism, which is the crucial point emphasized here. Lessig, *Fidelity and Constraint*, esp. 49–69.

22. As originalists have fixated on the Constitution's text, they have increasingly drawn on theories of language and meaning, often taken from philosophy of language and linguistics, to help elucidate the endeavor. See Solum, "Communicative Content and Legal Content," 484–507; Solum, "The Public Meaning Thesis," 1967–2001; Green, "Originalism and the Sense-Reference Distinction"; Barnett, "The Misconceived Assumption About Constitutional Assumptions," 619–22; Lawson,

"Reflections of an Empirical Reader," 1457–79; Bernick and Green, "There Is Something That Our Constitution Just Is."

23. No originalist has done more to advance a comprehensive linguistified version of the theory than Lawrence Solum. He calls it a neo-Gricean approach because it is built on the philosophy of Paul Grice. See Solum, "Originalist Methodology," 276–77; Solum, "The Public Meaning Thesis," 1967–71. Grice is important in the history of philosophy, but that does not mean that his framework for understanding communication is especially helpful for discovering the *original* meaning of the U.S. Constitution. For one, Grice's model presupposed two interlocutors observing a set of conversational maxims aimed at making communication maximally efficient. The United States Constitution and its readers, then or since, don't fit this model. Moreover, and more importantly, because it wasn't germane to the problems he addressed, Grice never tackled the phenomenon of historical difference in language use and thus offers few tools for translating historical artifacts like the original Constitution. His work does not assist us with the principal issue faced by any originalist interpreter, which is bridging conceptual difference between past and present.

24. This consideration helps explains why I have drawn on a particular group of pragmatist philosophers of language to better understand the interpretive problems raised by originalism, chief among them Ludwig Wittgenstein (the later version that is commonly associated with pragmatism), W. V. O. Quine, Wilfrid Sellars, Donald Davidson, Richard Rorty, and Robert Brandom. See Gienapp, "Historicism and Holism"; Gienapp, "Knowing How vs. Knowing That." In a recent critique of my work, the originalists Evan Bernick and Christopher Green failed to appreciate the point of this intervention. They worried that in emphasizing Wittgensteinian interpretive insights, I may have intended to advance a broad thesis about the philosophy of language itself, and particularly the indeterminacy of language. See Bernick and Green, "There Is Something That Our Constitution Just Is," 252–66. I implied no such thing. I drew on those philosophers not because of what they could teach us about language generally but instead because of what they could help us understand about Founding-era constitutionalism in particular. There are two interrelated reasons why this brand of pragmatist philosophy is so helpful to that task: first, because it helps us deal with the problem of historical distance and conceptual difference; second, because it's ideally suited to illuminate the kind of inferential claims-making inherent to the use and application of constitutional norms. I discuss the latter point later in this chapter in note 81. In the remainder of this note, I discuss the former point. I foreground the insights of these pragmatist philosophers because they have contributed to our understanding of historicism and provided helpful tools for understanding it. In blurring the lines between meaning and understanding and emphasizing the practical contexts in which language operates, these various thinkers underscored the idea that meaning is tethered to the broader cognitive modes through which speakers, readers, and interpreters navigate the world—the implicit background of practices and know-how upon which the successful application of norms depends—and thus implied that meaning changes over time as the intersubjective practices through which norms are made determinate themselves change. By embedding meaning in

a thick context of intersubjective practices, these philosophers suggest how meaning can change as those kinds of practices themselves change. Whether they were
right about linguistic meaning, they help us understand how to think about the
problem of historical distance, particularly in the context of U.S. constitutionalism.
If the application of anti-Wittgensteinian principles does a better job illuminating
the interpretation of the original Constitution, it will not be because those principles offer a better general account of language and communication, but because
they help us better understand eighteenth-century language users who thought differently than we do. Thus far, originalists who have drawn on the philosophy of
language have offered no such justification, even though that's the pertinent issue.

25. Gienapp, "Historicism and Holism." On contextualizing ideas and texts generated
by alien cultures, see Skinner, "Meaning and Understanding in the History of
Ideas"; Skinner, "A Reply to My Critics." On how historical meanings are embedded in broader contexts, see James T. Kloppenberg, "Thinking Historically: A Manifesto of Pragmatic Hermeneutics," *Journal of the History of Ideas* 9 (Apr. 2012):
205–07. On meaning holism in the study of history, see Mark Bevir, *The Logic of the
History of Ideas* (New York: Cambridge University Press, 1999).

26. On historical languages and their recovery, see Keith Michael Baker, *Inventing
the French Revolution: Essays on French Political Culture in the Eighteenth Century*
(New York: Cambridge University Press, 1990), 1–27; J. G. A. Pocock, *Virtue, Commerce, and History: Essays on Political Thought and History, Chiefly in the Eighteenth
Century* (New York: Cambridge University Press, 1985), 1–34. On conceptual
holism, or the idea that individual ideas take on meaning and force according to
how they function within a broader conceptual scheme, see Thomas S. Kuhn, *The
Structure of Scientific Revolutions* (1962; Chicago: University of Chicago Press,
2012); Quine, "Two Dogmas of Empiricism"; Davidson, *Truth, Language, and History*; Richard Rorty, "Holism and Historicism," in *Philosophy as Cultural Politics*,
175–83.

27. As Sam Wineburg has put it: "We discard or just ignore vast regions of the past that
either contradict our current needs or fail to align tidily with them. . . . The past
becomes clay in our hands. . . . [W]e contort the past to fit the predetermined
meanings we have already assigned it." Wineburg, *Historical Thinking and Other
Unnatural Acts*, 6.

28. The forms of contextualization that originalists defend—contextual disambiguation and contextual enrichment, which include implicature, impliciture, and pre-
supposition (technical terms for understanding basic things that are unsaid or
implied)—are comparatively narrow and otherwise assume modest differences between how people today and at the Founding thought. Accordingly, they fail to
reach the broader form of historical contextualization that is needed. On these
forms of originalist contextualization, see Solum, "Originalist Methodology," 286–
93; Solum, "Originalism and the Unwritten Constitution," 1954–58; Solum, "Intellectual History as Constitutional Theory," 1125–39; Barnett, "The Misconceived
Assumption About Constitutional Assumptions," 619–22; Bernick and Green,
"There Is Something That Our Constitution Just Is," 289–90.

29. Gienapp, "Historicism and Holism," 941, 954–55.

30. On this distinction, see Clifford Geertz, "The Way We Think Now: Toward an Ethnography of Modern Thought," in *Local Knowledge: Further Essays in Interpretive Anthropology* (New York: Basic, 1983), 152–53; Darnton, *The Great Cat Massacre*, 3.

31. Bailyn, *The Ideological Origins*, 22–23, 53–159; Bernard Bailyn, "The Central Themes of the American Revolution," in *Essays on the American Revolution*, ed. Stephen G. Kurtz and James H. Hutson (Chapel Hill: University of North Carolina Press, 1973), 7–12.

32. Bernard Bailyn, *Sometimes an Art: Nine Essays on History* (New York: Knopf, 2015), 22, 23.

33. For touchstones, see Solum, "The Public Meaning Thesis"; Scalia, "Address Before the Attorney General's Conference on Economic Liberties in Washington, D.C."; Kesavan and Paulsen, "The Interpretive Force of the Constitution's Secret Drafting History," 1134–48; Whittington, "The New Originalism," 609–10; Barnett and Bernick, "The Letter and the Spirit," 9–10.

34. Barnett and Bernick, *The Original Meaning of the Fourteenth Amendment*, 5.

35. The most important debate over original meaning is over what constitutes and determines, and thus is proof of, that meaning. Whatever difference ultimately hangs on the familiar distinctions drawn between original meaning and original intent or original meaning and original applications can be found there. That is because in almost all instances that matter, the Constitution's words fail to self-define, so originalist interpreters need to look beyond the bare text to concrete linguistic usage of the terms in question, and in most instances not only the best evidence but often the only evidence of usage available is found in the concrete debates surrounding the provision's framing or adoption, the earliest interpretations of it, or the earliest practice that took place under it. The crucial question becomes, then, not whether one should look to legislative history or early interpretation and practice—as it turns out everyone always does—but *when* certain usages that crop up in the framing, adoption, or early practice history is evidence of original meaning and when it is not. Because originalists have privileged the distinctions between meaning and intent or meaning and expected application, they have spent less time clarifying or defending their understanding of what counts as evidence of public meaning and why. Instead, cynics will stress, they freely pick and choose evidence from framing, adoption, and early practice history without much rhyme or reason. They declare that some of it is good evidence of original meaning while dismissing other evidence from that same framing, adoption, and early practice history as bad evidence, in the latter case because it is said to be evidence of original intent or expected application rather than the true target, original meaning itself, even though it's not obvious what credibly differentiates the evidence that is used from the evidence that is discarded. It often feels as though the working injunction is as follows: For evidence of original public meaning, look to the framers' goals and expected applications, the ratifiers' understandings, and early interpretations and practices; if you like what you find, declare it sound evidence of original meaning; and if you don't, neatly differentiate it from original meaning as a tidy means of dismissing it. This pervasive two-step dance, which captures the real interpretive action, receives less scrutiny than it should simply because of the continued

obsession over the supposedly fundamental distinction between original meaning and either original intent or original application.

36. On the possibilities and challenges of corpus linguistics, see Alison L. LaCroix, "Historical Semantics and the Meaning of the Second Amendment," *The Panorama*, Aug. 3, 2018, https://thepanorama.shear.org/2018/08/03/historical-semantics-and-the-meaning-of-the-second-amendment/; Dennis Baron, "Corpus Linguistics, Public Meaning, and the Second Amendment," *Duke Center for Firearms Law Second Thoughts Blog*, July 12, 2021, https://firearmslaw.duke.edu/2021/07/corpus-linguistics-public-meaning-and-the-second-amendment/. For citations of originalists' interest in corpus linguistics, see chapter 1, note 30.

37. Gienapp, "Knowing How vs. Knowing That." In delineating the different techniques for recovering original meaning, Lawrence Solum suggests that an interpreter should triangulate between, among other things, corpus linguistics and historical immersion. Solum, "Triangulating Public Meaning." Except he fails to grasp what historical immersion fully entails or aims to recover and therefore why it's such an essential technique (at least when it comes to understanding historical periods like the American Founding) and so qualitatively different in kind from corpus linguistics. Immersion is not yet another way to fix the definitions of words. It's the only way interpreters can understand alien modes of thought so that they might then be able to comprehend the kind of complex speech and text found in something like a constitution of government—the kind of historical speech that presupposes a dense network of interconnected concepts and understandings and thus is necessarily embedded in a particular kind of rationality.

38. Jonathan Gienapp, "The Foreign Founding: Rights, Fixity, and the Original Constitution," *Texas Law Review Online* 97 (2019): 118–26; Jud Campbell, "Fundamental Rights at the American Founding" in *The Cambridge History of Rights*, ed. Dan Edelstein and Jennifer Pitts, vol. 4 (New York: Cambridge University Press, forthcoming).

39. On the centrality of representation, see Gordon S. Wood, *Representation in the American Revolution*, rev. ed. (Charlottesville: University of Virginia Press, 2008); Eric Nelson, *The Royalist Revolution: Monarchy and the American Founding* (Cambridge, Mass.: Harvard University Press, 2014), 66–107, 187–88, 195–96, 209–13.

40. Moses Mather, *America's Appeal to the Impartial World* (Hartford, Conn.: Ebenezer Watson, 1775), 70.

41. On the distinct way in which English speakers tended to understand liberty in the seventeenth and eighteenth centuries—as the right to be governed according to one's will and happiness rather than the right to be left alone by the state—see Quentin Skinner, *Liberty Before Liberalism* (New York: Cambridge University Press, 1998); Philip Pettit, *Republicanism: A Theory of Freedom and Government* (New York: Oxford University Press, 1997), 17–50 (and for a theoretical elaboration of the ideas, 51–79); Annelien de Dijn, *Freedom: An Unruly History* (Cambridge, Mass.: Harvard University Press, 2020), esp. 1–5. On how this conception of liberty predominated at the American Founding, see Campbell, "Fundamental Rights at the American Founding," 7–11; John Phillip Reid, *The Concept of Liberty in the Age of the American Revolution* (Chicago: University of Chicago Press, 1988), 55–59; Barbara

Clark Smith, *The Freedoms We Lost: Consent and Resistance in Revolutionary America* (New York: New Press, 2010).

42. Levi Hart, *Liberty Described and Recommended: in a Sermon Preached to the Corpora-tion of Freemen in Farmington* (1775), in *American Political Writing During the Found-ing Era, 1760–1805*, ed. Charles S. Hyneman and Donald S. Lutz, 2 vols. (Indianapolis: Liberty Fund, 1983), 1:310.

43. Campbell, "Fundamental Rights at the American Founding," 5–6, 8–11; Jud Camp-bell, "Republicanism and Natural Rights at the Founding," *Constitutional Commen-tary* 32 (Winter 2017): 90–98; Jonathan Gienapp, "In Search of Nationhood at the Founding," *Fordham Law Review* 89 (Apr. 2021): 1788–91. For the mistaken view that the Founders conceived of rights as the inverse of government powers, see Philip Hamburger, "The Inversion of Rights and Power," *Buffalo Law Review* 63 (Aug. 2015): 738–52. For a critique of this view, see Jud Campbell, "Determining Rights," *Harvard Law Review* 138 (forthcoming): 54–56.

44. The Founding generation would not have easily recognized the distinction, so pop-ular among modern legal thinkers, between a so-called presumption of liberty and a presumption of democracy, which pits individual liberty against majoritarian gov-ernance. For accounts of the Founding that conceive of liberty in these terms, see Randy E. Barnett, *Our Republican Constitution: Securing the Liberty and Sovereignty of We the People* (New York: Harcourt, 2016), 31–82; Richard A. Epstein, *The Classical Liberal Constitution: The Uncertain Quest for Limited Government* (Cambridge, Mass.: Harvard University Press, 2014), 3–6, 17–25; Wurman, *A Debt Against the Living*, 87–91; Amul R. Thapar and Joe Masterman, "Fidelity and Construction," *Yale Law Journal* 129 (Jan. 2020): 793–96.

45. To be sure, rights were often understood as limits on government power. See Campbell, "Republicanism and Natural Rights at the Founding," 98–99. But these understandings varied depending on the kind of right in question and often hinged on the character of the entity seeking to regulate the right as well as the aim the entity had in view. And even in those few instances where those rights deemed "inalienable" appeared to operate like trumps, representative institutions still were expected to play an important role in determining the boundaries of those rights. See chapter 4, note 160 and accompanying text. Therefore, while it would be incor-rect to say that rights were never defined in opposition to government power at the Founding, it would be a far greater error to suggest the reverse. Such an under-standing cannot capture how eighteenth-century Americans broadly understood fundamental rights or the conditions of their protection. Liberty was not the ab-sence of government power but the basis by which the exercise of (often robust) governmental power could be judged legitimate or unlawful.

46. The classic study is William J. Novak, *The People's Welfare: Law and Regulation in Nineteenth-Century America* (Chapel Hill: University of North Carolina Press, 1996), esp. 1–2, 8–13, 19–50.

47. On *Heller*'s historical errors, see Cornell, "Originalism on Trial."

48. *District of Columbia v. Heller*, 554 U.S. 570 (2008). For defenses of the ruling that have presupposed the aptness of these questions, see Nelson Lund, "The Second Amendment, *Heller*, and Originalist Jurisprudence," *UCLA Law Review* 56 (June

2009): 1343–76; James Lindgren, "Forward: The Past and Future of Guns," *Journal of Criminal Law and Criminology* 104 (Fall 2014): 705–16; Barnett and Bernick, "The Letter and the Spirit," 38–41.

49. *New York State Rifle & Pistol Association v. Bruen*, 142 S. Ct. 2111 (2022). For a critique of its historical errors, which illustrate the broader anachronisms that infect Second Amendment originalism, see Saul Cornell, "Founding Fantasies vs. Historical Realities in the Second Amendment Debate," *Duke Center for Firearms Law Second Thoughts Blog*, July 27, 2023, https://firearmslaw.duke.edu/2023/07/founding-fantasies-vs-historical-realities-in-the-second-amendment-debate/; Saul Cornell, "Constitutional Mischiefs and Constitutional Remedies: Making Sense of Limits on the Right to Keep and Bear Arms in the Founding Era," *Fordham Urban Law Journal* 51 (2023): 25–55. For more on *Bruen*'s anachronisms, see chapter 9.

50. Jud Campbell, "Originalism and the Nature of Rights," *The Panorama*, Nov. 27, 2023, https://thepanorama.shear.org/2023/11/27/originalism-and-the-nature-of-rights/.

51. Campbell, "Originalism and the Nature of Rights."

52. Jack N. Rakove, "The Second Amendment: The Highest State of Originalism," *Chicago-Kent Law Review* 76 (2000): 103–66; Saul Cornell, " 'Half Cocked': The Persistence of Anachronism and Presentism in the Academic Debate over the Second Amendment," *Journal of Criminal Law and Criminology* 106 (Spring 2016): 203–18.

53. On how popular constitutionalism was the primary means of enforcing a constitution at the time of the Founding, see Larry D. Kramer, *The People Themselves: Popular Constitutionalism and Judicial Review* (New York: Oxford University Press, 2004). On how these assumptions worked in tandem with standard views on the legal determination of fundamental rights, see Campbell, "Determining Rights," 2–3, 6, 26–27, 35–43, 52–57. On how this thinking influenced the Second Amendment in particular, see Jud Campbell, "Natural Rights, Positive Rights, and the Right to Keep and Bear Arms," *Law and Contemporary Problems* 83 (2020): 34–39.

54. As Jud Campbell has put it: "Understanding how the Founders thought about the Second Amendment requires looking at the historical materials through a different lens, and recovering the central importance of republican self-governance to how they thought about the maintenance of fundamental rights." Campbell, "Originalism and the Nature of Rights."

55. Saul Cornell, *A Well-Regulated Militia: The Founding Fathers and the Origins of Gun Control in America* (New York: Oxford University Press, 2006); Campbell, "Originalism and the Nature of Rights."

56. Solum, "The Fixation Thesis," 1–2; Lawson, "Reflections of an Empirical Reader," 1458–59, 1460–64, 1478–79; Prakash, "The Misunderstood Relationship Between Originalism and Popular Sovereignty"; Scalia and Garner, *Reading Law*, 82; Wurman, *A Debt Against the Living*, 31–35.

57. Scalia and Garner, *Reading Law*, 82.

58. Originalists like to ask, Why would other texts, such as the one you're reading right now, have a fixed meaning but somehow not the U.S. Constitution? Putting aside

the notable reasons why it's problematic to treat the original Constitution like an ordinary text (the subject of the next two chapters), one response is that the Constitution is different in kind from other texts we often interpret. There are many distinguishing characteristics one might stress, but for now two will suffice. First, the Constitution is not a description or analysis of the world in which we live; it is a bundle of rules and principles that are to be applied to cases, and whose meaning is discovered principally through those applications. In various ways, originalists are fond of distinguishing between meaning and application—the text's meaning remains the same even if applications of that meaning change over time ("state" means now what it meant in 1787, even if it applies to states that didn't exist back then); or the text lays down rules that require subsequent implementing rules to take effect (the principle of state sovereign immunity is not part of the meaning of the Eleventh Amendment but is instead among the implementing rules that are needed to give it concrete legal effect). But the need to draw that kind of distinction, in and of itself, points to a major difference between the Constitution and other texts, whose meanings aren't deciphered along a similar meaning-application track. Even if we put applications to the side, the second distinctive thing to note about the Constitution is its open-textured language. While plenty of its commands are clear, most of the ones that matter are not. The ones at the center of constitutional debate are part of what Sanford Levinson calls the "Constitution of Conversation" (as opposed to what he calls the "Constitution of Settlement") precisely because they are open to competing interpretations. Levinson, *Constitutional Faith*, 246–54. While plenty of other texts we might interpret—paradigmatically literary texts, but not simply those—also invite creative interpretation, there are particular reasons why the U.S. Constitution took this form and sustains this kind of interpretive activity. Unlike the other kinds of texts originalists often compare the Constitution to (recipes, letters, works of history), the Constitution was the product of many hands. Not only that, but it was a quintessentially political document—its many Framers had to reconcile far more than their stylistic and substantive preferences; as representatives of distinct regions, ideologies, and interests, they had to overcome fundamental political and philosophical differences. That reality shaped the protracted drafting process, forcing the Framers to settle on open-ended phrasings that alone could attract broad consensus. See Roderick M. Hills, Jr., "Strategic Ambiguity and Article VII: Why the Framers Decided Not to Decide," *Journal of American Constitutional History* 1 (Summer 2023): 379–447. As a result, whereas it is easier to agree on what other texts are saying, if not their wider significance, when it comes to the Constitution, from the beginning its most significant provisions have sustained an array of competing readings. The key to understanding how to interpret the U.S. Constitution, therefore, ought to begin from appreciating how it essentially differs from most other interpretive objects rather than forcing inapt comparisons.

59. Richard Rorty, "The Historiography of Philosophy: Four Genres," in *Philosophy in History*, ed. Richard Rorty, J. B. Schneewind, and Quentin Skinner (New York: Cambridge University Press, 1984), 49–56.

60. For instance, consider Sanford Levinson's close reading of *The Federalist* from an openly presentist perspective: Sanford Levinson, *An Argument Open to All: Reading The Federalist in the 21st Century* (New Haven, Conn.: Yale University Press, 2015).

61. For extended discussions, see Gienapp, "Constitutional Originalism and History"; Balkin, *Memory and Authority*, 235–36, 240–53; Stephen M. Griffin, "Optimistic Originalism and the Reconstruction Amendments," *Tulane Law Review* 95 (Jan. 2021): 281–358; Gordon, *Taming the Past*, 364–71.

62. Michael McConnell has described his own method of originalism: "I regard this approach as a species of intellectual history, in which we do our best to understand past events as the actors would have understood them at the time." And on the debate between historians and many originalists: "To the extent there is a disagreement between historians, who seek to understand what actual people believed in the past, and a certain strand of 'New Originalists,' who seek either what they think is the best meaning or that dictated by philosophy of language, I side with the historians." McConnell, *The President Who Would Not Be King*, 13–14, 356n17. And his illuminating work on the original meaning of the Constitution has embodied this commitment to a fuller historical approach that is more sensitive to the sort of eighteenth-century constitutional context that historians deem essential. See, e.g., McConnell, *The President Who Would Not Be King*; Nathan S. Chapman and Michael W. McConnell, *Agreeing to Disagree: How the Establishment Clause Protects Religious Diversity and Freedom of Conscience* (New York: Oxford University Press, 2023). He is not alone. A handful of other originalists tend to be interested in replicating historians' approach to contextualizing the past, even if some of them surely maintain a legal bent; the list includes Keith Whittington, John Harrison, Caleb Nelson, and others.

63. Consider a representative statement from Lawrence Solum: "Intellectual history may produce knowledge that is relevant to constitutional interpretation. . . . But this role is supplementary and complementary to the methods employed by originalists and textualists." Solum, "Intellectual History as Constitutional Theory," 1155; Baude and Sachs, "Originalism and the Law of the Past"; Lawson and Seidman, "Originalism as a Legal Enterprise"; Gary Lawson, "No History, No Certainty, No Legitimacy, No Problem," *Florida Law Review* 64 (Dec. 2012): 1551–72, esp. 1558–59; Wurman, *A Debt Against the Living*, 99–107; Randy E. Barnett, "Can Lawyers Ascertain the Original Meaning of the Constitution?," *The Volokh Conspiracy* (blog), Aug. 19, 2013, http://volokh.com/2013/08/19/can-lawyers-ascertain-the-original-meaning-of-the-constitution/; Michael Rappaport, "Historians and Originalists Part I: The Context of the Debate," *Law & Liberty*, Apr. 11, 2017, https://lawliberty.org/historians-and-originalists-part-i-the-context-of-the-debate/; Michael Rappaport, "Historians and Originalists Part II: The Adequacy of Originalist Scholarship," *Law & Liberty*, Apr. 22, 2017, https://lawliberty.org/historians-and-originalists-part-ii-the-adequacy-of-originalist-scholarship/; John O. McGinnis, "Why Mary Sarah Bilder Gets Originalism Wrong," *Law & Liberty*, Feb. 11, 2021, https://lawliberty.org/why-mary-bilder-gets-originalism-wrong/. On why originalists are mistaken in this belief, see Balkin, *Memory and Authority*, 240–53; Griffin, "Optimistic Originalism," 282–85.

64. Solum, "Intellectual History as Constitutional Theory"; Solum, "Triangulating Public Meaning," 1649–54; Randy E. Barnett, "Whence Comes Section One? The Abolitionist Origins of the Fourteenth Amendment," *Journal of Legal Analysis* 3 (Spring 2011): 172–73; Rappaport, "Historians and Originalists Part I"; John O. McGinnis and Michael B. Rappaport, "The Finished Constitution," *Law & Liberty*, Sept. 28, 2023, https://lawliberty.org/book-review/the-finished-constitution/.

65. Akhil Reed Amar, *The Words That Made Us: America's Constitutional Conversation, 1760–1840* (New York: Basic Books, 2021), xi–xii; Baude and Sachs, "Originalism and the Law of the Past," 810–12, 820; Solum, "Triangulating Public Meaning," 1652–54.

66. Solum, "Intellectual History as Constitutional Theory"; McGinnis and Rappaport, "The Finished Constitution." On originalists' tendency to sidestep most historical work on the Founding, see Logan Everett Sawyer III, "Method and Dialogue in History and Originalism," *Law and History Review* 37 (Aug. 2019): 847–48.

67. Baude and Sachs, "Originalism and the Law of the Past," 810–12, 820.

68. Baude and Sachs, "Originalism and the Law of the Past," 813–15.

69. *New York State Rifle & Pistol Association v. Bruen*, 142 S. Ct. 2111, 2130n6 (2022).

70. Baude and Sachs, "Originalism and the Law of the Past," 814.

71. Baude and Sachs, "Originalism and the Law of the Past," 814.

72. In recovering original law, Baude and Sachs write, immersion into *"legal* culture" is often more pertinent than "broad immersion in the intellectual and political culture of the day." Baude and Sachs, "Originalism and the Law of the Past," 814–15. Given the lack of sharp intellectual distinctions at the time, however, it's hard to see how legal culture, at least as it impinged on constitutionalism, could be fully disentangled from broader political and intellectual currents.

73. Amar, *The Words That Made Us*, xi–xii.

74. Bailyn, *Sometimes an Art*, 22.

75. Mary Sarah Bilder, "Colonial Constitutionalism and Constitutional Law," in *Transformations in American Legal History: Essays in Honor of Professor Morton J. Horwitz*, ed. Daniel W. Hamilton and Alfred L. Brophy (Cambridge, Mass.: Harvard University Press, 2009), 28–57; Kramer, *The People Themselves*, 9–72; Daniel J. Hulsebosch, *Constituting Empire: New York and the Transformation of Constitutionalism in the Atlantic World, 1660–1830* (Chapel Hill: University of North Carolina Press, 2005), esp. 3–10, 203–06. Britons were struck by the continuity between American constitutionalism and British practice. See Linda Colley, "Empires of Writing: Britain, America and Constitutions, 1776–1848," *Law and History Review* 32 (May 2014): 243–44.

76. Wood, *The Creation of the American Republic.*

77. Bernard Bailyn, "Confessional Thoughts on Re-reading *The Ideological Origins*," *New England Quarterly* 91 (Mar. 2018): 12–15.

78. Wood, *The Creation of the American Republic*; Bailyn, *The Ideological Origins*, 160–319; Rakove, "Joe the Ploughman Reads the Constitution," 588–93; Gienapp, *The Second Creation*, esp. 1–74.

79. On constitutional liquidation, see James Madison, *The Federalist* 37, in *The Documentary History of the Ratification of the Constitution*, ed. John Kaminski, Gaspare

J. Saladino, Richard Leffler, Charles H. Schoenleber, and Margaret A. Hogan, 39 vols. to date (Madison: State Historical Society of Wisconsin, 1976–), 15:346 (hereafter cited as *DHRC*); Alexander Hamilton, *The Federalist* 82, in *DHRC*, 18:111.

80. Gienapp, *The Second Creation*, 42–49, 75–77, 81–95, 106–12; Rakove, "Joe the Ploughman Reads the Constitution," 588–95; John R. Howe, *Language and Political Meaning in Revolutionary America* (Amherst: University of Massachusetts Press, 2004), 206–09, 217–25; Saul Cornell, "Constitutional Meaning and Semantic Instability: Federalists and Anti-Federalists on the Nature of Constitutional Language," *American Journal of Legal History* 56 (Mar. 2016): 21–28.

81. This argument is developed at length in Gienapp, *The Second Creation*. Earlier in this chapter, in note 24, I said there were two distinct reasons why the particular strain of pragmatist philosophy (found in the writings of Wittgenstein, Quine, Davidson, Brandom, and others) on which I continue to draw is so useful for understanding Founding-era constitutionalism. In that prior note, I elaborated on the first reason why: that these philosophers offer helpful insights into the problems generated by historicism, especially the problem of conceptual difference across historical time. Here is the second reason: in helping us think about how authoritative norms that work like governing rules are stabilized and defined through the practice of using them, these philosophers help illuminate the dynamic discursive processes that proved so central to the early history of the U.S. Constitution. In general, constitutionalism and law turn on the articulation and application of rules to cases, which raises conceptual issues distinct from those raised by ordinary language use. Even more specifically, because the Constitution was such an unsettled source of authority at the Founding, appeals to it simultaneously drew on and defined authoritative norms. Here the central Wittgensteinian and Quinean point that rules and their application are, as Brandom has put it, "reciprocally dependent conceptions, and reciprocally dependent processes," since "norms explicit in the form of statable rules and principles are only intelligible . . . against a background of implicit practical norms" helps illuminate the distinctive context in which the Constitution developed in the Founding era. Robert B. Brandom, "A Hegelian Model of Legal Concept Determination: The Normative Fine Structure of the Judges' Chain Novel," in *Pragmatism, Law, and Language*, ed. Graham Hubbs and Douglas Lind (New York: Routledge, 2014), 23, 21. Whatever these pragmatist philosophers happen to teach us about language—and I believe they teach us a lot—their insights are especially valuable in grappling with the distinctive problems raised by the early history of the U.S. Constitution.

82. Gerald Leonard and Saul Cornell, *The Partisan Republic: Democracy, Exclusion, and the Fall of the Founders' Constitution, 1780s–1830s* (New York: Cambridge University Press, 2019), 42–114.

83. Gienapp, *The Second Creation*.

84. Leonard and Cornell, *The Partisan Republic*.

85. See the rich account of U.S. constitutional debate between 1815 and 1861 in Alison L. LaCroix, *The Interbellum Constitution: Union, Commerce, and Slavery in the Age of Federalisms* (New Haven, Conn.: Yale University Press, 2024).

86. Jonathan Gienapp, "Constitutional Conflict (Almost) All the Way Down," *Balkinization* (blog), May 3, 2020, https://balkin.blogspot.com/2020/05/constitutional-conflict-almost-all-way.html.

87. Gienapp, "The Myth of the Constitutional Given," 183–89.

Chapter 4. Written Constitutionalism at the Founding

Epigraph: Publicola [John Quincy Adams], Letters of Publicola III (originally published in the *Columbia Centinel*, June 15, 1791), in *Writings of John Quincy Adams*, ed. Worthington Chauncey Ford, 7 vols. (New York: Macmillan, 1913–1917), 1:74.

1. Skinner, "Meaning and Understanding in the History of Ideas," 7.

2. The critique is not that originalists are guilty of textual literalism, as Lawrence Solum has mistakenly taken me to be saying. Solum, "The Public Meaning Thesis," 2044–45. Originalists of course have long recognized that the Constitution's meaning is broader than the bare semantic meaning of its text. My critique turns instead on whether the Constitution's content is the set of propositions communicated by its text (however broad that meaning might be in context), or whether some of the Constitution's content is derived from non-textual sources that no amount of linguistic interpretation or enrichment could disclose. In an earlier discussion of the contribution that extratextual sources make to written constitutional meaning, Solum betrayed his own text-centric view of extratextual sources with one exception: his brief discussion of "extratextual fundamental law," which is "freestanding" from the text. But his description of this law was narrow, and he failed to consider how or why it might have mattered to the original Constitution at the time of its birth. Solum, "Originalism and the Unwritten Constitution," 1966–67.

3. See chapter 5.

4. Bernick and Green, "There Is Something That Our Constitution Just Is," 306.

5. Amar, *The Words That Made Us*, 152–56; Whittington, *Constitutional Interpretation*, 47–61. On how this perceived break was mythologized only later for ideological reasons, see Asheesh Kapur Siddique, "The Ideological Origins of 'Written' Constitutionalism," *Early American Studies* 21 (Fall 2023): 557–99.

6. Hulsebosch, *Constituting Empire*, esp. 3–10, 203–06; Bilder, "Colonial Constitutionalism and Constitutional Law"; Gienapp, *The Second Creation*, 23–35.

7. Wood, *The Creation of the American Republic*, 127–34, and generally 127–389.

8. Jack P. Greene, *The Constitutional Origins of the American Revolution* (New York: Cambridge University Press, 2011); John Phillip Reid, *Constitutional History of the American Revolution*, 4 vols. (Madison: University of Wisconsin Press, 1986–1993); Bailyn, *The Ideological Origins*, 67–77; Barbara A. Black, "The Constitution of Empire: The Case for the Colonists," *University of Pennsylvania Law Review* 124 (May 1976): 1157–1211, esp. 1198–1203; Gienapp, *The Second Creation*, 23–24, 31–35.

9. J. G. A Pocock, *The Ancient Constitution and the Feudal Law: A Study of English History Thought in the Seventeenth Century* (1957; New York: Cambridge University Press, 1987); John Phillip Reid, *The Ancient Constitution and the Origins of*

Anglo-American Liberty (Dekalb: University of Northern Illinois Press, 2005), 28–40; Kramer, *The People Themselves*, 9–34; Hulsebosch, *Constituting Empire*, 32–41. Other texts that enjoyed constitutional status included the Act of Toleration of 1689, the Triennial Act of 1694, the Act of Settlement of 1701, and the Septennial Act of 1716 (which supplanted the Triennial Act). On text and the imperial constitution, see Siddique, "The Ideological Origins of 'Written' Constitutionalism," 562–78.

10. John Adams's Diary Notes on the Right of Juries, Feb. 12, 1771, in *The Legal Papers of John Adams*, ed. Kinvin Wroth and Hiller B. Zobel, 3 vols. (Cambridge, Mass.: Harvard University Press, 1965), 1:230.

11. William E. Nelson, *The Common Law in Colonial America*, vol. 4, *Law and the Constitution on the Eve of Independence, 1735–1776* (New York: Oxford University Press, 2018), 6, 150–55.

12. On how these institutions laid a foundation that the state constitutions built on, see Pauline Maier, *From Resistance to Revolution: Colonial Radicals and the Development of American Opposition, 1765–1776* (1972; New York: W. W. Norton, 1991); Wood, *The Creation of the American Republic*, 312–18; Willi Paul Adams, *The First American Constitutions: Republican Ideology and the Making of the State Constitutions in the Revolutionary Era*, expanded ed. (1980; New York: Rowman and Littlefield, 2001), 25–60.

13. Adams, *The First American Constitutions*, 16–20; Donald S. Lutz, ed., *Colonial Origins of the American Constitution: A Documentary History* (Indianapolis: Liberty Fund, 1998), xxi–ii; Wood, *The Creation of the American Republic*, 268–69.

14. Bailyn, *The Ideological Origins*, 190–93; Bilder, "Colonial Constitutionalism and Constitutional Law," 31–36; Reid, *Constitutional History of the American Revolution*, vol. 1, *The Authority of Rights*, 159–68; Donald S. Lutz, *The Origins of American Constitutionalism* (Baton Rouge: Louisiana State University Press, 1988), 35–49, 58–63, 98–99; Nikolas Bowie, "Why the Constitution Was Written Down," *Stanford Law Review* 71 (June 2019): 1397–1492.

15. Suffolk Resolves, Sept. 9, 1774, in *The Journals of Each Provincial Congress of Massachusetts in 1774 and 1775* (Boston: Dutton and Wentworth, 1838), 602.

16. Connecticut Resolves, Oct. 25, 1765, in *The Public Records of the Colony of Connecticut*, ed. J. Hammon Trumbull and Charles J. Hoadly, 15 vols. (Hartford, Conn.: Lockwood and Brainard, 1881), 12:422.

17. Declaration of Independence, July 4, 1776.

18. Kramer, *The People Themselves*, 39–41; Hulsebosch, *Constituting Empire*, 170–71.

19. Bailyn, *The Ideological Origins*, 192–93; Wood, *The Creation of the American Republic*, 271; David Ciepley, "Is the U.S. Government a Corporation? The Corporate Origins of Modern Constitutionalism," *American Political Science Review* 111 (May 2017): 424–27; Bowie, "Why the Constitution Was Written Down," 1492–1508.

20. Colley, "Empires of Writing," 246–47.

21. Adams, *The First American Constitutions*, 64–65; Lutz, *The Origins of American Constitutionalism*, 46–49.

22. Zephaniah Swift, *A System of the Laws of the State of Connecticut: In Six Books*, 2 vols. (Windham: John Byrne, 1795), 1:58.

23. Many years ago, I set out to research how the adoption of written constitutions in Revolutionary America rapidly remade constitutional consciousness, assuming

that it had—that those at the Founding must have believed that they had altered the nature of constitutionalism by drawing up stand-alone constitutional texts. After over a year of reading through all the constitutional commentary I could locate from between 1776 and 1787, I had found but a handful of examples that even hinted at such a shift. At that point, my expectations thwarted, I started to appreciate that early U.S. constitutional thinking had followed a different course than many had supposed.

24. Mary Sarah Bilder, "Charter Constitutionalism: The Myth of Edward Coke and the Virginia Charter," *North Carolina Law Review* 94 (June 2016): 1552, 1590.

25. On fundamental law in the British constitutional tradition, see J. W. Gough, *Fundamental Law in English Constitutional History* (New York: Oxford University Press, 1955); Thomas C. Grey, "Origins of the Unwritten Constitution: Fundamental Law in American Revolutionary Thought," *Stanford Law Review* 30 (May 1978): 850–59.

26. Oct. 14, 1774, in *Journals of the Continental Congress, 1774–1789*, ed. Worthington C. Ford et al., 34 vols. (Washington, D.C.: Government Printing Office, 1904–1937), 1:67 (hereafter cited as *JCC*). See also John Adams's Notes of Debates, in *Letters of Delegates to Congress, 1774–1789*, ed. Paul H. Smith et al., 24 vols. (Washington, D.C.: Government Printing Office, 1976–2000), 1:46 (comments of John Jay, Sept. 8, 1774).

27. On how this worked in New York, see Hulsebosch, *Constituting Empire*, 170–202.

28. Wood, *The Creation of the American Republic*, 10–17; J. G. A. Pocock, *The Machiavellian Moment: Florentine Political Thought and the Atlantic Republican Tradition* (Princeton, N.J.: Princeton University Press, 1975), 77–80, 361–400.

29. Gienapp, *The Second Creation*, 27–28.

30. North Carolina Constitution of 1776.

31. Benjamin Rush, *Observations upon the Present State of the Government of Pennsylvania* (Philadelphia: Steiner and Cist, 1777), 3.

32. See Gerald Stourz, "*Constitution*: Changing Meaning of the Term from the Early Seventeenth to the Late Eighteenth Century," in *Conceptual Change and the Constitution*, ed. Terence Ball and J. G. A. Pocock (Lawrence: University Press of Kansas, 1988), 35–54; Jack Rakove, *Revolutionaries: A New History of the Invention of America* (Boston: Houghton Mifflin, 2010), 157–97.

33. New Hampshire Constitution of 1784.

34. Wood, *The Creation of the American Republic*, 259–68, 273–82.

35. [Thomas Paine], *Four Letters on Interesting Subjects* (Philadelphia: Styner and Cist, 1776), 18.

36. Philodemus [Thomas Tudor Tucker], *Conciliatory Hints* [. . .] (Charleston, S.C.: A. Timothy, 1784), 21, 25.

37. Thomas Jefferson, *Notes on the State of Virginia* (1785), ed. William Peden (Chapel Hill: University of North Carolina Press, 1982), 124 (emphasis in original).

38. Mary Sarah Bilder, "The *Ordeal* and the Constitution," *New England Quarterly* 91 (Mar. 2018): 136–43; Mary Sarah Bilder, "The Emerging Genre of *The Constitution*: Kent Newmyer and the Heroic Age," *Connecticut Law Review* 52 (Feb. 2021): 1267–68.

39. Noah Webster, *An American Dictionary of the English Language* (New York: S. Converse, 1828). The full definition read as follows:

    1. The act of constituting, enacting, establishing, or appointing.

    2. The state of being; that form of being or peculiar structure and connection of parts which makes or characterizes a system or body. Hence the particular frame or temperament of the human body is called its *constitution*. We speak of a robust or feeble *constitution*; a cold, phlegmatic, sanguine or irritable *constitution*. We speak of the *constitution* of the air, or other substance; the *constitution* of the solar system; the *constitution* of things.

    3. The frame or temper of mind, affections or passions.

    4. The established form of government in a state, kingdom or country; a system of fundamental rules, principles and ordinances for the government of a state or nation. In free states, the constitution is paramount to the statutes or laws enacted by the legislature, limiting and controlling its power; and in the United States, the legislature is created, and its powers designated, by the constitution.

    5. A particular law, ordinance, or regulation, made by the authority of any superior, civil or ecclesiastical; as the *constitutions* of the churches; the novel *constitutions* of Justinian and his successors.

    6. A system of fundamental principles for the government of rational and social beings.

    The New Testament is the moral constitution of modern society.

40. Webster, *An American Dictionary*. At the Federal Convention, delegates frequently likened the federal constitutional system to the solar system. See Gienapp, *The Second Creation*, 61–63.

41. Adams, *The First American Constitutions*, 40–90; Rakove, *Revolutionaries*, 81–82, 167–72.

42. Webster, *An American Dictionary*.

43. John Adams, "Reply to *A Friendly Address to All Reasonable Americans*," Nov. 17, 1774, in *The Papers of John Adams*, ed. Robert J. Taylor et al., 20 vols. to date (Cambridge, Mass.: Harvard University Press, 1977–), 2:195.

44. Scott J. Shapiro, "The 'Hart-Dworkin' Debate: A Short Guide for the Perplexed," in *Ronald Dworkin*, ed. Arthur Ripstein (New York: Cambridge University Press, 2012), 22–55.

45. Exclusive legal positivists think law is derived entirely from social facts, whereas inclusive legal positivists concede that moral facts sometimes contribute to law.

46. On law as a branch of political morality, see Ronald Dworkin, *Justice for Hedgehogs* (Cambridge, Mass.: Harvard University Press, 2011), 5, 405–15. For Dworkin's ideas, the key touchstones are Dworkin's initial criticisms of H. L. A. Hart's legal positivism: Ronald Dworkin, "The Model of Rules I," and Ronald Dworkin, "The Model of Rules II," in *Taking Rights Seriously* (Cambridge, Mass.: Harvard University Press, 1977), 14–80. But Dworkin elaborated on, and in many ways altered, his views in Dworkin, *Law's Empire*. Dworkin then further refined his views in *Justice for Hedgehogs*. Where previously Dworkin had accepted that law and morality picked out two distinct systems of norms, and he merely defended the view that they were entwined—that law included not only the rules enacted through legiti-

mate processes but also the principles that provide the best moral justification for those rules—he later came to reject this two-picture view (in which law and morality were sharply distinct) in favor of an integrated view that treated law as itself a branch of morality (specifically political morality, or what a political community as a collective owes each member when acting on behalf of that collective community). Dworkin, *Justice for Hedgehogs*, 327–38, 400–15.

47. Lon Fuller set out one of the most influential defenses. Lon L. Fuller, *The Law in Quest of Itself* (Boston: Beacon Press, 1940). The book triggered a famous debate with H. L. A. Hart over whether law and morality could be separated. See H. L. A. Hart, "Positivism and the Separation of Law and Morals," *Harvard Law Review* 71 (Feb. 1958): 593–629; Lon L. Fuller, "Positivism and Fidelity to Law—a Reply to Professor Hart," *Harvard Law Review* 71 (Feb. 1958): 630–72. For jurisprudential defenses of natural law, see John Finnis, *Natural Law and Natural Rights* (New York: Oxford University Press, 1980); Robert P. George, *In Defense of Natural Law* (New York: Oxford University Press, 1999); Vermeule, *Common Good Constitutionalism*. Dworkin insisted that he wasn't a natural law theorist before admitting that, if all that was meant by that label was somebody who thought that what the law was hinged partly on what it ought to be, then the label fit. Ronald A. Dworkin, "Natural Law Revisited," *University of Florida Law Review* 34 (Winter 1982): 165–88.

48. Ronald Dworkin has referred to this framework as the "orthodox two-systems picture," which begins by assuming that "law" and "morals" describe distinct sets of norms before asking the "classic jurisprudential question": "How are these two different collections of norms related or connected?" While Dworkin himself hoped to sharply revise the orthodox picture later in his career, he did so on the belief that the "two-systems picture" was how the issue "has traditionally been conceived by almost all legal philosophers." Dworkin, *Justice for Hedgehogs*, 400–02. Dworkin proposed a more integrated view of law and morality. Later in this chapter, I describe how the Founding generation presumed an integrated view of law. Despite these seeming similarities, the Founding generation conceived of and approached law in ways that were still notably different.

49. On differences between modern debates over legal positivism and earlier understandings of natural law, see Stuart Banner, *The Decline of Natural Law: How American Lawyers Once Used Natural Law and Why They Stopped* (New York: Oxford University Press, 2021), 228–31.

50. In a thoughtful treatment, James Whitman argued that Founding-era legal thought was confused and lacked an inner logic, in essence because the Revolutionary generation freely mingled custom, reason, and constitutionalism. James Q. Whitman, "Why Did the Revolutionary Lawyers Confuse Custom and Reason?," *University of Chicago Law Review* 58 (Fall 1991): 1321–68. Rather than exhibiting a lack of "clear thinking," the manner in which the Founding generation mingled custom and reason, British constitutionalism and natural law, reveals their own particular way of thinking about fundamental law—one that can seem confused from the perspective of our legal assumptions but made sense by a different logic. If we treat custom and reason as different and only then ask how the Founding generation related them to one another, we'll struggle to find coherence in their statements.

But if we resist the temptation to ask that kind of question and instead see how custom and reason naturally harmonized—as with Kuhn and Aristotle's physics—we can reconstruct an inner logic that was once there.

51. See James Wilson, "Lectures on Law," in *Collected Works of James Wilson*, ed. Kermit L. Hall and Mark David Hall, 2 vols. (Indianapolis: Liberty Fund, 2007); Nathaniel Chipman, *Sketches of the Principles of Government* (Rutland, Vt.: J. Lyon, 1793); Swift, *A System of the Laws of the State of Connecticut*.

52. For works emphasizing the Founding generation's commitment to natural law, see Banner, *The Decline of Natural Law*; R. H. Helmholz, *Natural Law in Court: A History of Legal Theory in Practice* (Cambridge, Mass.: Harvard University Press, 2015); Thomas G. West, *The Political Theory of the American Founding: Natural Rights, Public Policy, and the Moral Conditions of Freedom* (New York: Cambridge University Press, 2017); Arkes, *Mere Natural Law*. This work often treats natural law as a discrete source of law, minimizing how natural law integrated with other kinds of law.

53. John Mikhail broadly describes Founding-era legal elites as "natural lawyers," with an incomplete contextualization of their complex legal attitudes. See John Mikhail, "Does Originalism Have a Natural Law Problem?," *Law and History Review* 39 (May 2021): 361–67. Mikhail takes me to be arguing that Founding-era lawyers were natural lawyers rather than legal positivists, and suggests, in contrast, that they were both. But in so doing he has missed my point—developed further here—which has not been to classify eighteenth-century legal thinkers on a particular side of that divide but instead to put aside that distinction since it tends to obscure their integrated view of law.

54. This section restates and further develops an argument about Founding-era legal thinking that I previously advanced in greatly reduced form: Jonathan Gienapp, "Written Constitutionalism, Past and Present," *Law and History Review* 39 (May 2021): 321–60. Since appearing, it has been sharply criticized by several originalists—including in articles by Lawrence Solum and by Evan Bernick and Christopher Green. See Solum, "The Public Meaning Thesis," 2038–47; Bernick and Green, "There Is Something That Our Constitution Just Is," 264–66. To clear the ground for what follows, it's worth noting that these critiques suffer from the precise anachronisms I aim to emphasize. Rather than responding to my arguments about Founding-era law on their own terms, these critiques distorted my main claims. In taking for granted the terms and classifications of modern legal theory and evaluating my historical arguments on the basis of them, these critiques obscured the very point I was trying to make: that Founding-era views on fundamental law can't be easily understood on the terms of modern legal theory, in particular any view of law that draws a sharp distinction between positive and non-positive law. Instead of engaging with my central historical point, then, these critics incorrectly took me to be classifying the Founders according to a set of familiar modern legal categories, when I was in fact arguing against the applicability of that very classification. Little that followed their initial mistake was therefore responsive to what I argued. The account that follows will hopefully clear up earlier confusion and point the way toward a more productive line of discussion.

55. Wood, *The Creation of the American Republic*, 291–305.

56. *Independent Chronicle* (Boston), Sept. 4, 1777.

57. Publicola [Adams], Letters of Publicola II, in *Writings of John Quincy Adams*, 1:70.

58. For overviews, see Banner, *The Decline of Natural Law*, 11–18; Helmholz, *Natural Law in Court*, 2–4; Philip Hamburger, "Natural Rights, Natural Law, and American Constitutions," *Yale Law Journal* 102 (1993): 922–30.

59. Jacob Rush, *Charges, and Extracts of Charges, on Moral and Religious Subjects* (Philadelphia: D. Hogan, 1803), 14.

60. Wilson, "Lectures on Law," in *Collected Works of James Wilson*, 1:523.

61. *Robin v. Hardaway*, 1 Jeff. 109, 114 (Va. 1772), as quoted in Banner, *The Decline of Natural Law*, 18–19.

62. Banner, *The Decline of Natural Law*, 14–18.

63. Swift, *A System of the Laws of the State of Connecticut*, 1:39.

64. Wilson, "Lectures on Law," in *Collected Works of James Wilson*, 1:509. On how Wilson betrayed synthetic views of natural law that were continuous with the Christian natural law tradition, see Justin Buckley Dyer, "Reason, Revelation, and the Law of Nature in James Wilson's Lectures on Law," *American Political Thought* 9 (Spring 2020): 264–84.

65. Wilson, "Lectures on Law," in *Collected Works of James Wilson*, 1:523.

66. Banner, *The Decline of Natural Law*, 24–29.

67. Campbell, "Natural Rights and the First Amendment," 2291; Banner, *The Decline of Natural Law*, 14–15; Hamburger, "Natural Rights, Natural Law, and American Constitutions," 925–26.

68. Richard Tuck, *Natural Rights Theories: Their Origin and Development* (New York: Cambridge University Press, 1979); Knud Haakonssen, *Natural Law and Moral Philosophy: From Grotius to the Scottish Enlightenment* (New York: Cambridge University Press, 1996).

69. Rush, *Charges, and Extracts of Charges, on Moral and Religious Subjects*, 15.

70. Wilson, "Lectures on Law," in *Collected Works of James Wilson*, 1:498.

71. Wilson, "Lectures on Law," in *Collected Works of James Wilson*, 1:523, and generally 500–25.

72. Banner, *The Decline of Natural Law*, 19–20, 26–27.

73. *Ham v. McClaws*, 1 S.C.L. (1 Bay) 93, 95–96 (1789).

74. Banner, *The Decline of Natural Law*, 20–28.

75. Wilson, "Lectures on Law," in *Collected Works of James Wilson*, 2:777.

76. Peter Du Ponceau, *A Dissertation on the Nature and Extent of the Jurisdiction of the Courts of the United States* (Philadelphia: Abraham Small, 1824), 91.

77. On the differences, see Banner, *The Decline of Natural Law*, 46–68; Novak, *The People's Welfare*, 35–42; Caleb Nelson, "*Stare Decisis* and Demonstrably Erroneous Precedents," *Virginia Law Review* 87 (Mar. 2001): 23–27.

78. Pocock, *The Ancient Constitution and the Feudal Law*, 14–22, 30–69; Kunal M. Parker, *Common Law, History, and Democracy in America, 1790–1900: Legal Thought Before Modernism* (New York: Cambridge University Press, 2011), 25–66.

79. Swift, *A System of the Laws of the State of Connecticut*, 1:2.

80. *Blackwell v. Wilkinson*, Jeff. 73, 82 (Va. 1768).

81. William Blackstone, *Commentaries on the Laws of England*, 4 vols. (Oxford: Clarendon Press, 1765–1769), 1:63.

82. Blackstone, *Commentaries on the Laws of England*, 1:63–64.

83. Blackstone, *Commentaries on the Laws of England*, 1:67. On Blackstone's complex legal views, see David Lieberman, *The Province of Legislation Determined: Legal Theory in Eighteenth-Century Britain* (New York: Cambridge University Press, 1989), 31–67.

84. Banner, *The Decline of Natural Law*, 47–48.

85. Wilson, "Lectures on Law," in *Collected Works of James Wilson*, 2:773.

86. James R. Stoner, *Common Law and Liberal Theory: Coke, Hobbes, and the Origins of American Constitutionalism* (Lawrence: University Press of Kansas, 1992), 5–10.

87. On the melding of custom and republican consent, see Parker, *Common Law, History, and Democracy in America*, 87–92; Ellen Holmes Pearson, *Remaking Custom: Law and Identity in the Early American Republic* (Charlottesville: University of Virginia Press, 2011), 11–12, 23–26; Novak, *The People's Welfare*, 38–39.

88. On how Wilson conjoined common law and consent, see Stephen A. Conrad, "James Wilson's 'Assimilation of the Common-Law Mind,' " *Northwestern University Law Review* 84 (1989): 186–219, esp. 197–215.

89. Wilson, "Lectures on Law," in *Collected Works of James Wilson*, 1:494.

90. Wilson, "Lectures on Law," in *Collected Works of James Wilson*, 1:470.

91. Wilson, "Lectures on Law," in *Collected Works of James Wilson*, 1:494.

92. Wilson, "Lectures on Law," in *Collected Works of James Wilson*, 1:470.

93. Jesse Root, *Reports of Cases Adjudged in the Superior Court and Supreme Court of Errors*, 2 vols. (Hartford, Conn.: Hudson and Goodwin, 1798–1802), 1:xii.

94. Swift, *A System of the Laws of the State of Connecticut*, 1:42.

95. Bernadette Meyler, "Towards a Common Law Originalism," *Stanford Law Review* 59 (Dec. 2006): 581–84.

96. Wilson, "Lectures on Law," in *Collected Works of James Wilson*, 2:773. On how Wilson reconciled contemporaneous consent with customary consent, see Parker, *Common Law, History, and Democracy in America*, 89–92.

97. Lieberman, *The Province of Legislation Determined*.

98. On the artificial reason of the common law, often associated with Sir Edward Coke, and how it was reconciled with accumulated custom, see Lieberman, *The Province of Legislation Determined*, 36–49, 85–87.

99. Swift, *A System of the Laws of the State of Connecticut*, 1:41.

100. Root, *Reports of Cases*, 1:ix, xi.

101. Grey, "Origins of the Unwritten Constitution," 853–54.

102. Banner, *The Decline of Natural Law*, 64–65; William R. Casto, *The Supreme Court in the Early Republic: The Chief Justiceships of John Jay and Oliver Ellsworth* (Columbia: University of South Carolina Press, 1995), 34–35.

103. [William Barton], *Observations on the Trial by Jury* (Strasburg, Pa.: Brown and Bowman, 1803), 37.

104. Helmholz, *Natural Law in Court*, 89–93, 96–98; Campbell, "Natural Rights and the First Amendment," 290–93.

105. Wilson, "Lectures on Law," in *Collected Works of James Wilson*, 2:750.

106. Alexander Addison, *Analysis of the Report of the Committee of the Virginia Assembly, on the Proceedings of sundry of the other States in Answer to their Resolutions* (Philadelphia: Zachariah Poulson, Junior, 1800), 29.

107. [Barton], *Observations on the Trial by Jury*, 37–38.

108. Pocock, *The Ancient Constitution and the Feudal Law*; Novak, *The People's Welfare*, 39–41; Meyler, "Towards a Common Law Originalism," 584–92.

109. Wilson, "Lectures on Law," in *Collected Works of James Wilson*, 2:773–74. See also Swift, *A System of the Laws of the State of Connecticut*, 1:40.

110. Eighteenth-century common law is often anachronistically treated as positive law. For an example of this mistake, see Solum, "The Public Meaning Thesis," 2043.

111. Wilson, "Lectures on Law," in *Collected Works of James Wilson*, 2:1025.

112. This mentality has been called the "common-law mind." See Pocock, *The Ancient Constitution and the Feudal Law*, 30–69; Stephen A. Conrad, "The Constitutionalism of 'the Common-Law Mind,' " *Law and Social Inquiry* 13 (Summer 1988): 619–36; David Thomas Konig, "James Madison and Common-Law Constitutionalism," *Law and History Review* 28 (May 2010): 509–12.

113. Originalists often mistakenly treat the eighteenth-century common law as a set of static doctrines. See Scalia, *A Matter of Interpretation*, 3–47. On how this conception of the common law necessitates deleting the approach to law on which it was based, see Meyler, "Towards a Common Law Originalism," 559–67, 580–92.

114. For an example of how judicial adjudications were treated as a source of common law, albeit a lesser one, at the Founding, see Root, *Reports of Cases*, 1:ix–xiv.

115. Wilson, "Lectures on Law," in *Collected Works of James Wilson*, 2:777. On how Wilson conceived of the common law as a "progressive social science," see Charles Barzun, "James Wilson's Legal Science" (unpublished manuscript) (on file with author).

116. William E. Nelson, *Americanization of the Common Law: The Impact of Legal Change on Massachusetts Society, 1760–1830* (Cambridge, Mass.: Harvard University Press, 1975); Mary Sarah Bilder, *The Transatlantic Constitution: Colonial Legal Culture and the Empire* (Cambridge, Mass.: Harvard University Press, 2004); Meyler, "Towards a Common Law Originalism," 567–80.

117. Delaware Constitution of 1776, art. XXV; New Jersey Constitution of 1776, art. XXII; Ford W. Hall, "The Common Law: An Account of Its Reception in the United States," *Vanderbilt Law Review* 4 (June 1951): 798–800; Nelson, "*Stare Decisis* and Demonstrably Erroneous Precedents," 26–27.

118. Meyler, "Towards a Common Law Originalism," 571–75.

119. Banner, *The Decline of Natural Law*, 54–57.

120. Stewart Jay, "Origins of the Federal Common Law: Part One," *University of Pennsylvania Law Review* 133 (June 1985): 1003–1116; Stewart Jay, "Origins of the Federal Common Law: Part Two," *University of Pennsylvania Law Review* 133 (July 1985): 1231–1334.

121. These criticisms of common-law jurisprudence are discussed in chapter 7.

122. Pearson, *Remaking Custom*, 11–30, 181–87.

123. John Adams's Notes of Debates, in *Letters of Delegates*, 1:47 (comments of Roger Sherman, Sept. 8, 1774).

124. James Kent, *Commentaries on American Law*, 4 vols. (New York: O. Halsted, 1826–1830), 1:439; Hulsebosch, *Constituting Empire*, 274–302.

125. Hulsebosch, *Constituting Empire*, 23–24, 27–41.

126. Pocock, *The Ancient Constitution and the Feudal Law*, 38, 46–55.

127. Reid, *The Ancient Constitution and the Origins of Anglo-American Liberty*.

128. Declaration and Resolves of the First Continental Congress, Oct. 14, 1774, in *JCC*, 1:69.

129. See also Kramer, *The People Themselves*, 10–12.

130. *Terrett v. Taylor*, 13 U.S. (9 Cranch) 43, 52 (1815).

131. James Otis, "John Adams's Notes on the First Argument of the Case, Feb. 1761," in *Collected Political Writings of James Otis*, ed. Richard Samuelson (Indianapolis: Liberty Fund, 2015), 6.

132. Philanthropos, *Maryland Gazette*, Apr. 27, 1748, in *Exploring the Bounds of Liberty: Political Writings of Colonial British America from the Glorious Revolution to the American Revolution*, ed. Jack P. Greene and Craig B. Yirush, 3 vols. (Indianapolis: Liberty Fund, 2018), 2:1221–22; [Theophilus Parsons], *The Essex Result* (1778), in *American Political Writing During the Founding Era*, 1:487; Swift, *A System of the Laws of the State of Connecticut*, 1:50–51.

133. Wood, *The Creation of the American Republic*, 291–305; William E. Nelson, "The Eighteenth-Century Background of John Marshall's Constitutional Jurisprudence," *Michigan Law Review* 76 (May 1978): 928.

134. These aspects of the Constitution that detail the structure and composition of the national government are part of what Sanford Levinson has instructively called the "Constitution of Settlement"—or those clear features of the Constitution that resist creative interpretation. They are distinct from the other more open-textured features of the Constitution—what Levinson has termed the "Constitution of Conversation"—that have invited ongoing debate across the Constitution's life. Levinson, *Constitutional Faith*, 246–54.

135. James Madison, Aug. 10, 1787, in *The Records of the Federal Convention of 1787*, ed. Max Farrand, 4 vols. (New Haven, Conn.: Yale University Press, 1911–1937), 2:249–50.

136. James Madison, Aug. 7, 1787, in Farrand, *The Records of the Federal Convention*, 2:197–99.

137. Alexander Hamilton, Speech at the New York Ratifying Convention, June 28, 1788, in *DHRC*, 22:1984; Caleb Nelson, "Originalism and Interpretive Conventions," *University of Chicago Law Review* 70 (Spring 2003): 542–44; Philip A. Hamburger, "The Constitution's Accommodation of Social Change," *Michigan Law Review* 88 (Nov. 1989): 275–300. Though neither Nelson nor Hamburger quite seem to grasp the broader meaning that "constitution" had at this time.

138. See Samuel Johnston, Speech at the North Carolina Ratifying Convention, July 25, 1788, in *DHRC*, 30:284–85.

139. Philodemus [Tucker], *Conciliatory Hints*, 30.

140. For more, see Wood, *The Creation of the American Republic*, 273–305.

141. To again invoke Sanford Levinson's distinction between the "Constitution of Settlement" and the "Constitution of Conversation," when we look back to the

7

eighteenth century and make sense of the work that constitutional text was doing in early U.S. constitutions, we can add a wrinkle to Levinson's formulation. Not only was some text clear and other text open-textured, but, in addition, some text entrenched new, contingent constitutional rules, while other text effectuated or modified preexisting constitutional rules. Text was sometimes settling certain rules (creating those aspects of the federal Constitution we still regard as part of the "Constitution of Settlement") and sometimes working in concert with unwritten principles of fundamental law. The latter instances invited more creative interpretation, not because the text was open-textured, but because the text was in conversation with a robust conception of fundamental law (a "Constitution of Conversation" distinct from the one we tend to imagine). This eighteenth-century "Constitution of Conversation" could be found where constitutional text and general fundamental law were most tightly entwined—where constitutional text either reinforced or worked in concert with an underlying legal principle. But some constitutional rules were created and fixed solely through text—such as the creation of a single national executive and precise rules for selecting that executive through state electors. Levinson, *Constitutional Faith*, 246–54.

142. Publicola [Adams], Letters of Publicola III, in *Writings of John Quincy Adams*, 1:74. See also Letters of Publicola VI and XI, 1:86–87, 107–08. On the context of the Publicola letters and the debate it provoked, see James R. Zink, "The Publicola Debate and the Role of the French Revolution in American Constitutional Thought," *American Political Thought* 4 (Fall 2015): 557–87; Siddique, "The Ideological Origins of 'Written' Constitutionalism," 586–87. Recently, Evan Bernick and Christopher Green have distorted what Adams wrote in this essay. They claim that his definition of a constitution as a "system of fundamental laws" referred only to the British constitution and that, in fact, Adams agreed with Paine that the defining feature of American constitutions was their written character. See Bernick and Green, "There Is Something That Our Constitution Just Is," 274–76. Bernick and Green focus on Adams's description of Paine's argument: In claiming that constitutions needed to take "visible form," Adams wrote, Paine had "only the American Constitutions in his mind, for excepting them, I believe he would not find any in all history, a government which will come within his definition; and of course, there never was a people that had a Constitution, previous to the year 1776." Yet Bernick and Green fundamentally misconstrue Adams. To be sure, Adams acknowledged the obvious fact that American constitutions had a "visible form" *in some respects* and were thus distinct from the British constitution *in certain ways*. But he plainly did not accept Paine's narrow definition of a constitution. Quite the opposite. Adams was disputing Paine's definition and, from there, challenging Paine's claim that American constitutions were defined by Paine's restrictive criteria. These points are made clear in Adams's initial letter (Publicola III) and in a subsequent letter (Publicola XI). In the initial letter, Adams's definition of a constitution as a "system of fundamental laws" immediately followed a sentence about *American* constitutions. In that sentence, Adams stressed how American constitutions "adopted the whole body of the *common law*," which led him to ask, "[D]id they adopt nothing at all, because that law

cannot be produced in a visible form?" Here, Adams assumed that certain unwritten common-law rights and principles formed part of American constitutions, thus disproving the suitability of Paine's narrow definition *even in the American case.* That is among the reasons Adams was adamant that "the Constitution of a country" was a "system of fundamental laws" and "not the paper or parchment upon which the compact is written." Notice, Adams did not write that this description applied only to "the Constitution of *that* country" or "the Constitution of Great Britain," but instead wrote that it applied to "the Constitution of *a* country," that is, any country, including the United States, since neither American constitutions nor the British constitution could be wholly reduced to their visible form. In a later letter, Adams reiterated the contrast he had drawn from Paine's understanding of U.S. constitutionalism, writing that the entirety of his "Publicola" letters challenged "arguments contained in a late pamphlet of Mr. Paine's, which are supposed to be directly opposite to principles acknowledged by the *constitutions of our country*" (emphasis added). Publicola [Adams], Letters of Publicola III and XI, in *Writings of John Quincy Adams,* 1:73–74, 107–08.

143. Alexander Hamilton, *The Farmer Refuted: or, A more impartial and comprehensive view of the dispute between Great-Britain and the colonies* (New York: James Rivington, 1775), 38.

144. United States Constitution, amend. IX.

145. Campbell, "Determining Rights," 8.

146. [James Otis], *A Vindication of the British Colonies* [. . .] (Boston: Edes and Gill, 1765), 8.

147. James Otis, *The Rights of the British Colonists Asserted and Proved* (Boston: Edes and Gill, 1764), 33.

148. [John Dickinson], *An Address to the Committee of Correspondence in Barbados* (Philadelphia: William Bradford, 1766), 4.

149. [Silas Downer], *A Discourse at the Dedication of the Tree of Liberty* (1768), in *American Political Writing During the Founding Era,* 1:100. See also A Freeholder, *Maryland Gazette,* Mar. 16, 1748, in *Exploring the Bounds of Liberty,* 2:1195.

150. See chapter 3.

151. On the eclectic nature of Founding-era rights talk, see Rakove, *Original Meanings,* 291–93; Reid, *Constitutional History of the American Revolution,* vol. 1, *The Authority of Rights,* 65–73; Forrest McDonald, *Novus Ordo Seclorum: The Intellectual Origins of the Constitution* (Lawrence: University Press of Kansas, 1985), 9–55.

152. For arguments that the Revolutionaries privileged natural rights, see Michael P. Zuckert, *The Natural Rights Republic: Studies in the Foundations of the American Political Tradition* (South Bend, Ind.: University of Notre Dame Press, 1996); or customary rights, see John Phillip Reid, "The Irrelevance of the Declaration," in *Law in the American Revolution and the American Revolution in the Law,* ed. Hendrik Hartog (New York: New York University Press, 1981), 46–89. For the argument that they instead synthesized natural and customary rights, see Dan Edelstein, *On the Spirit of Rights* (Chicago: University of Chicago Press, 2019), 143–71.

153. Campbell, "Fundamental Rights at the American Founding"; Campbell, "Republicanism and Natural Rights at the Founding," 87–99; Campbell, "Natural Rights

and the First Amendment"; Jud Campbell, "Judicial Review and the Enumeration of Rights," *Georgetown Journal of Law & Public Policy* 15 (Summer 2017): 569–92; Campbell, "Natural Rights, Positive Rights, and the Right to Keep and Bear Arms," 34–41; Jud Campbell, "Constitutional Rights Before Realism," *University of Illinois Law Review* 2020 (2020): 1436–43.

154. Richard Bland, *An Inquiry into the Rights of the British Colonies* (Williamsburg, Va.: Alexander Purdie, 1766), 9.

155. Timothy Stone, *Election Sermon* (1792), in *American Political Writing During the Founding Era*, 2:847.

156. Campbell, "Republicanism and Natural Rights at the Founding," 87–90.

157. Bland, *An Inquiry into the Rights of the British Colonies*, 9–10.

158. Theodore Dwight, *An Oration, Spoken Before the Connecticut Society, for the Promotion of Freedom and the Relief of Persons Unlawfully Holden in Bondage* (Hartford, Conn.: Hudson and Goodwin, 1794), 11–12.

159. Campbell, "Fundamental Rights at the American Founding," 3.

160. Campbell, "Fundamental Rights at the American Founding," 4–5.

161. Campbell, "Fundamental Rights at the American Founding," 7–8.

162. Importantly, the government could still legislate with respect to even those rights considered "inalienable" because, even then, the people themselves were ultimately responsible for locating the boundaries of that right. In other words, "even for those rights that were not thought to be regulable in promotion of the public good, the people still had authority to determine their boundaries." Campbell, "Determining Rights," 51n317.

163. "So long as the people themselves maintained control over these rights through self-governance, their rights were 'retained.' " Campbell, "Originalism and the Nature of Rights."

164. Campbell, "Republicanism and Natural Rights at the Founding," 86–87, 92–98.

165. [Parsons], *The Essex Result* (1778), in *American Political Writing During the Founding Era*, 1:487 (emphasis added).

166. Campbell, "Fundamental Rights at the American Founding," 13–14.

167. James Madison, June 8, 1789, in *Documentary History of the First Federal Congress of the United States of America, 4 March 1789–3 March 1791*, ed. Linda Grant De Pauw, Charlene Bangs Bickford, Kenneth R. Bowling, and Helen E. Veit, 22 vols. (Baltimore: The Johns Hopkins University Press, 1972–2017), 11:822 (hereafter cited as *DHFFC*).

168. Campbell, "Fundamental Rights at the American Founding," 3.

169. Campbell, "Judicial Review and the Enumeration of Rights," 576–77; Campbell, "Natural Rights, Positive Rights, and the Right to Keep and Bear Arms," 35–36.

170. Kramer, *The People Themselves*, 9–34.

171. Rakove, *Original Meanings*, 306–08; Wood, *The Creation of the American Republic*, 271–73.

172. The following states included declarations of rights: Virginia (written before its constitution), Delaware (contained in a separate document), Pennsylvania, Maryland, North Carolina, Vermont, Massachusetts, and New Hampshire (not its 1776 constitution, but its revised one written in 1784).

173. Compare the sixteen articles in Virginia's or Pennsylvania's declarations with the forty-two in Maryland's. While many of the same core rights appear across the enumerations, significant differences remain. See Eric Slauter, "Written Constitutions and Unenumerated Rights," *Proceedings of the American Antiquarian Society* (2007): 283–84.

174. [Paine], *Four Letters on Interesting Subjects*, 15, 22.

175. Kramer, *The People Themselves*, 51.

176. Campbell, "Judicial Review and the Enumeration of Rights," 577–78.

177. Campbell, "Determining Rights," 4–5, 22–25.

178. This aim became especially important to James Madison amid debates over whether the federal Constitution should include a bill of rights. Rakove, *Original Meanings*, 332–36; Colleen A. Sheehan, *James Madison and the Spirit of Republican Government* (New York: Cambridge University Press, 2009), 108–09.

179. Virginia's declaration of rights came before its constitution and Delaware's was contained in a separate document.

180. Rush, *Observations upon the Present State of the Government of Pennsylvania*, 3.

181. Gienapp, *The Second Creation*, 55–57, 60–63, 104–05, 174–76; Jack N. Rakove, *A Politician Thinking: The Creative Mind of James Madison* (Norman: University of Oklahoma Press, 2017), 96–137, esp. 120–31. This point is worth emphasizing since several originalists have misunderstood it: Madison was not claiming that constitutional text was malleable but rather deflating the importance of constitutional text by emphasizing that constitutional structure and politics superseded it. It was further reminder that, as he saw it, a constitution was a *system* to be built, not a *legal text* to be drafted. In that regard, he was not denying that the Constitution had a fixed meaning so much as denying the importance of the question. Those who posed that question misunderstood the constitutional system that Americans were attempting to devise—both how it worked and what might account for its future success, or failure. For a penetrating discussion of this constitutional vision, as seen from *The Federalist*, see Connor M. Ewing, "Publius' Proleptic Constitution," *American Political Science Review*, published ahead of print Nov. 6, 2023, https://doi.org/10.1017/S0003055423001119.

182. On Madison's changing attitudes toward written constitutionalism, see Gienapp, *The Second Creation*, 200–01, 328–32.

183. This argument was popular among Federalists during ratification, though critics of the Constitution voiced it too. Gienapp, *The Second Creation*, 82–83, 104–07, 165–66; Mark A. Graber, "Enumeration and Other Constitutional Strategies for Protecting Rights: The View from 1787/1791," *University of Pennsylvania Journal of Constitutional Law* 9 (Jan. 2007): 361–72.

184. Publicola [William Paca], "To Aristides," *Maryland Gazette* (Annapolis), June 28, 1787, 2.

185. Fabius IV [John Dickinson], *Pennsylvania Mercury* (Philadelphia), Apr. 19, 1788, in *DHRC*, 17:183–84.

186. George Nicholas, Virginia Ratifying Convention, June 16, 1788, in *DHRC*, 10:1334.

187. This paragraph draws heavily on the argument developed in Campbell, "Determining Rights," esp. 26–43.

188. "[B]ills of rights could serve different functions. Under a *declaratory* approach, the drafters could identify existing rights (either natural rights or customary rights), with the text serving as a placeholder for underlying concepts. Or, using a *specificatory* approach, the drafters could try to determine rights by textually determining their content in some respect." Campbell, "Determining Rights," 8, see also 4–5.

189. Campbell, "Determining Rights," 26–32, 35–37. See especially Thomas Jefferson to James Madison, Mar. 15, 1789, in *The Papers of Thomas Jefferson*, ed. Julian P. Boyd et al., 45 vols. (Princeton, N.J.: Princeton University Press, 1950–2021), 14: 659–60. Jefferson's draft of a new constitution for Virginia from 1783 revealed a desire to determine rights with much greater specificity through carefully worded textual formulas. See "Jefferson's Draft of a Constitution for Virginia," in *The Papers of Thomas Jefferson*, 6:298, 304.

190. Campbell, "Determining Rights," 5, 32–43.

191. James Madison, June 8, 1789, in *DHFFC*, 11:808. On Madison's various motivations, see Gienapp, *The Second Creation*, 168–74.

192. James Madison, June 8, 1789, in *DHFFC*, 11:807.

193. Roger Sherman, Aug. 13, 1789, in *DHFFC*, 11:1230. On the dominance of this testimony, see Graber, "Enumeration and Other Constitutional Strategies for Protecting Rights," 380–90.

194. On how Madison defended rights declarations without claiming that enumeration was essential to the legal status of those rights, see Gienapp, *The Second Creation*, 174–76. Rights declarations could serve an educative function. They could also help check potential abuses of federal power, especially as the Constitution gave Congress the authority to exercise certain "discretionary powers with respect to the means" by way of the Necessary and Proper Clause. James Madison, June 8, 1789, in *DHFFC*, 11:823, and generally 823–24.

195. James Madison, June 8, 1789, in *DHFFC*, 11:824, 822. On the importance Madison attached to the pedagogical value of rights declarations, see Rakove, *Original Meanings*, 332–36.

196. James Madison, Aug. 15, 1789, in *DHFFC*, 11:1270.

197. United States Constitution, amend. VII. On those initial amendments that were specificatory in character, see Campbell, "Determining Rights," 40–42.

198. The idea of declaring preexisting fundamental rights was thus quite different from the idea of codifying those preexisting rights. In *District of Columbia v. Heller*, Justice Antonin Scalia failed to understand the distinction. In the Court's opinion, he stressed that the Second Amendment "was widely understood to codify a pre-existing right, rather than to fashion a new one," but at the same time made clear that this "pre-existing right" had gained constitutional force only through textual enumeration, that is, once it "was codified in a written Constitution." *District of Columbia v. Heller*, 554 U.S. 570, 581–92, 597–603 (2008) (quotes at 603, 599). As we've seen, the Founding generation had a much different understanding of preexisting fundamental rights and their constitutional enumeration. On Scalia's mistakes, see Campbell, "Determining Rights," 56–57. The early amendments were even more declaratory in character than they might have been once

the states rejected the first two of the twelve amendments proposed by Congress, each of which had been included in Madison's original proposal: one that set a formula for determining the ratio of representation in the House of Representatives as the population grew; another stipulating that any laws affecting congressional compensation would take delayed effect. *DHFFC*, 4:9–10, 46.

199. Campbell, "Determining Rights," 27, 58.

200. Ellsworth, Aug. 22, 1787, in Farrand, *The Records of the Federal Convention*, 2:376.

201. Wilson, Aug. 22, 1787, in Farrand, *The Records of the Federal Convention*, 2:376.

202. Madison's notes covering the waning weeks of the Convention must be approached with caution. As Mary Sarah Bilder has demonstrated, Madison's later Convention notes (covering the period from August 22 to September 17) were likely composed at least two years after the fact, and it seems doubtful—for at least these closing weeks—that he had detailed rough notes from which to work. See Bilder, *Madison's Hand*, 141–201. There is little reason to doubt the notes' portrayal of the exchange discussed here, however. In investigating the original meaning of "ex post facto law," John Mikhail has raised important questions about how Madison's notes characterize the Convention debates over this concept. See John Mikhail, "James Wilson, Early American Land Companies, and the Original Meaning of 'Ex Post Facto,' " *Georgetown Journal of Law & Public Policy* 17 (Winter 2019): 79–146, esp. 87–89. But while Mikhail focuses on whether prohibitions on ex post facto laws were originally believed to ban only retroactive criminal laws or also retroactive civil laws, I am interested in how delegates understood what these prohibitions (be they narrowly or widely construed) implied about the relationship between constitutional text and content, and thus see no reason to doubt that Wilson and Ellsworth reacted to the prohibition as Madison's notes suggest they did.

203. Founding-era Americans believed that venerable common-law rights (including prohibitions against ex post facto laws and rights to habeas corpus and jury trial) were already inherent to the social compact. It was precisely because prohibitions against bills of attainder were less familiar, and thus less obviously inviolable, that the delegates likely included such a prohibition in the Constitution without any debate. Campbell, "Judicial Review and the Enumeration of Rights," 579–80.

204. The Founding generation was steeped in a constitutional culture in which there was a much clearer sense of the customary baseline against which complementary constitutional text could be evaluated. What seems imprecise or inexplicit to us was far more obvious to them.

205. Prakash and Yoo, "The Origins of Judicial Review," 916–18.

206. Douglas E. Edlin, "Judicial Review Without a Constitution," *Polity* 38 (July 2006): 345–50; Kramer, *The People Themselves*, 50–52, 125–27.

207. Mary Sarah Bilder, "The Corporate Origins of Judicial Review," *Yale Law Journal* 116 (Dec. 2006): 502–67; Philip Hamburger, *Law and Judicial Duty* (Cambridge, Mass.: Harvard University Press, 2008).

208. William Michael Treanor, "Judicial Review Before *Marbury*," *Stanford Law Review* 58 (Nov. 2005): 455–562, esp. 473–97; William Michael Treanor, "Against Textualism," *Northwestern University Law Review* 103 (Spring 2009): 983–1006; Suzanna

Sherry, "The Founders' Unwritten Constitution," *University of Chicago Law Review* 54 (Fall 1987): 1134–46.

209. Wayne D. Moore, "Written and Unwritten Constitutional Law in the Founding Period: The Early New Jersey Cases," *Constitutional Commentary* 7 (Summer 1990): 352–58; Hulsebosch, *Constituting Empire*, 189–202.

210. As stressed earlier, a recurring mistake—even among scholars who have properly attended to the unfamiliar basis of early judicial reasoning—has been to assume that these putatively separate sources of law were sharply distinct. For a complementary take, see Edlin, "Judicial Review Without a Constitution," 356–58.

211. Austin Scott, "*Holmes vs. Walton*: The New Jersey Precedent," *American Historical Review* 4 (Apr. 1899): 456–69 (quote at 458). The court's opinion has not been found, but this was the argument made by the defendant's counsel, and the defendant prevailed. See Moore, "Written and Unwritten Constitutional Law in the Founding Period," esp. 352–58; though Moore problematically separates the various sources of law identified in the case.

212. James M. Varnum, *The Case, Trevett against Weeden* [. . .] (Providence, R.I.: John Carter, 1787), 11, 14, 23, 35; Bilder, *The Transatlantic Constitution*, 188–90.

213. Bilder, *The Transatlantic Constitution*, 190.

214. Peter Charles Hoffer, *Rutgers v. Waddington: Alexander Hamilton, the End of the War for Independence, and the Origins of Judicial Review* (Lawrence: University Press of Kansas, 2016); Hulsebosch, *Constituting Empire*, 194–202.

215. Along with other lawyers in the 1780s, Hamilton took on cases just like this one. Daniel J. Hulsebosch, "A Discrete and Cosmopolitan Minority: The Loyalists, the Atlantic World, and the Origins of Judicial Review," *Chicago-Kent Law Review* 81 (2006): 825–66.

216. Julius Goebel, Jr., ed., *The Law Practice of Alexander Hamilton: Documents and Commentary*, 5 vols. (New York: Columbia University Press, 1964–1981), 1:296–306; Hoffer, *Rutgers v. Waddington*, 65–71, 77–79.

217. Goebel, *The Law Practice of Hamilton*, 1:341, 363, 367–68 (emphasis in original).

218. New York Constitution of 1777, art. XXXV.

219. Goebel, *The Law Practice of Hamilton*, 1:340.

220. Goebel, *The Law Practice of Hamilton*, 1:306–12, 400–05, 418; Hulsebosch, *Constituting Empire*, 195–99; Hoffer, *Rutgers v. Waddington*, 77–81.

221. It is too often assumed that this was how judges used natural law in the eighteenth and nineteenth centuries: primarily as a narrow technique for disambiguating written law or interpreting it equitably. Those who conclude that natural law was most often used in this fashion typically have disputes over slavery in mind, where judges often broke with standard legal practice and drove a wedge between natural and positive law. More often, however, judges refused to draw such sharp distinctions, dynamically linking the stipulated requirements of statutory law to the imperatives of general fundamental law. On how cases over slavery compelled early U.S. judges to draw sharper distinctions between positive and natural law, see Robert M. Cover, *Justice Accused: Antislavery and the Judicial Process* (New Haven, Conn.: Yale University Press, 1975); Banner, *The Decline of Natural Law*, 149–60. On the deeper British common-law roots of early American slavery, and the

ways it had departed from other common-law tendencies, see Holly Brewer, "Creating a Common Law of Slavery for England and Its New World Empire," *Law and History Review* 39 (Nov. 2021): 765–834.

222. The most notable criticism directed at Duane's ruling came in a pamphlet likely written by Melancton Smith and signed by eight others. *To the People of the State of New-York*, in *The Anti-Federalist Writings of the Melancton Smith Circle*, ed. Michael P. Zuckert and Derek A. Webb (Indianapolis: Liberty Fund, 2009), 3–11.

223. David M. Golove and Daniel J. Hulsebosch, "The Law of Nations and the Constitution: An Early Modern Perspective," *Georgetown Law Journal* 106 (Aug. 2018): 1595–98, 1605–39; Hulsebosch, *Constituting Empire*, 196–99, 282–83; Casto, *The Supreme Court in the Early Republic*, 130–41; Robert J. Reinstein, "Executive Power and the Law of Nations in the Washington Administration," *University of Richmond Law Review* 46 (Jan. 2012): 373–456. Originalists have not ignored the law of nations at the Founding, but they have usually downplayed its relative legal legitimacy (as compared with the Constitution) or sought to cabin it (so that it was not binding on the political branches or courts). See Anthony Bellia, Jr., and Bradford Clark, *The Law of Nations and the United States Constitution* (New York: Oxford University Press, 2017); John Harrison, "The Constitution and the Law of Nations," *Georgetown Law Journal* 106 (Aug. 2018): 1659–1706. For a historical critique of these views, see Golove and Hulsebosch, "The Law of Nations and the Constitution."

224. Golove and Hulsebosch, "The Law of Nations and the Constitution," 1616–23.

225. John Jay's Charge to the Grand Jury of the Circuit Court for the District of New York, Apr. 12, 1790, in *The Documentary History of the Supreme Court of the United States, 1789–1800*, ed. Maeva Marcus et al., 7 vols. (New York: Columbia University Press, 1985–2007), 2:29 (hereafter cited as *DHSC*). See also James Wilson's Charge to the Grandy Jury of the Circuit Court for the District of Virginia, May 23, 1791, in *DHSC*, 2:179–80; John Jay's Charge to the Grand Jury of the Circuit Court for the District of Virginia, May 22, 1793, *DHSC*, 2:381–87; James Wilson's Charge to the Grand Jury of a Special Session of the Circuit Court for the District of Pennsylvania, July 22, 1793, *DHSC*, 2:417–18; James Iredell's Charge to the Grand Jury of the Circuit Court for the District of South Carolina, May 12, 1794, *DHSC*, 2:455–59, 467–70.

226. Casto, *The Supreme Court in the Early Republic*, 2, 34–35, 157–59, 192–93; Kramer, *The People Themselves*, 42–44.

227. Charles F. Hobson, *The Great Yazoo Lands Sale: The Case of* Fletcher v. Peck (Lawrence: University Press of Kansas, 2016), 10, 121–34, 153–56.

228. *Ware v. Hylton*, 3 U.S. (3 Dallas) 199, 255 (1796) (opinion of Paterson, J.).

229. *Fletcher v. Peck*, 10 U.S. (6 Cranch) 87, 143 (1810) (Johnson, J., concurring).

230. *Calder v. Bull*, 3 U.S. (3 Dallas), 386, 388 (1798) (opinion of Chase, J.).

231. Therefore, I disagree with Sherry, "The Founders' Unwritten Constitution," 1167–76. For a corrective, see Thomas, *The (Un)Written Constitution*, esp. 57–60.

232. *Ware*, 3 U.S. (3 Dallas) at 223 (opinion of Chase, J.).

233. Wood, *The Creation of the American Republic*, 453–63.

234. Jack N. Rakove, "The Origins of Judicial Review: A Plea for New Contexts," *Stanford Law Review* 49 (May 1997): 1051–64.

235. Kramer, *The People Themselves*, 44–49.

236. Richard Dobbs Spaight to James Iredell, Aug. 12, 1787, in *The Papers of James Iredell*, ed. Don Higginbotham, Donna Kelly, and Lang Baradell, 3 vols. (Raleigh: North Carolina Division of Archives and History, 1976–2003), 3:298.

237. Swift, *A System of the Laws of the State of Connecticut*, 1:53.

238. Campbell, "Judicial Review and the Enumeration of Rights," 570, 584–85.

239. Jefferson to Madison, Mar. 15, 1789, in *The Papers of Thomas Jefferson*, 14: 659.

240. See chapter 7.

241. Campbell, "Determining Rights," 28–31. Jefferson's commitment to textual constitutionalism stemmed from his commitment to popular sovereignty and must be understood in that context. First, his concern was primarily directed at the federal government. He was wary of federal power of all varieties and thus routinely demanded that its agents hew closely to the text of the U.S. Constitution. Comparatively, he had much greater confidence in state governments and thus was more comfortable with them exercising discretion. Second, he famously declared that all constitutions should be rewritten every generation so that those living were never subject to a constitutional order made by those long dead. The written constitution deserved respect, but only ever for a short time, after which point it ceased to enjoy legitimacy.

242. James Madison, June 8, 1789, in *DHFFC*, 11:825.

243. Campbell, "Judicial Review and the Enumeration of Rights," 586.

244. For an extended discussion, see Campbell, "Judicial Review and the Enumeration of Rights," 583–91.

245. For an extended discussion, see Campbell, "Judicial Review and the Enumeration of Rights," 586–87, 591–92.

246. This section draws heavily on Campbell, "Determining Rights," 47–49.

247. For more, see *DHSC*, 8:89–99.

248. *Calder v. Bull*, 3 U.S. (3 Dallas) 386, 388 (1798) (opinion of Chase, J.)

249. *Calder*, 3 U.S. (3 Dallas) at 398, 399 (opinion of Iredell, J.)

250. *Calder*, 3 U.S. (3 Dallas) at 398; Campbell, "Determining Rights," 47n299. At other times, it is important to note, Iredell seemingly denied the existence of customary constitutionalism. See James Iredell to Richard Dobbs Spaight, Aug. 26, 1787, in *The Papers of James Iredell*, 3:307–10. But at least in *Calder*, perhaps because the case focused on Connecticut's constitution, that was not the case.

251. Campbell, "Determining Rights," 48.

252. *Calder*, 3 U.S. (3 Dallas) at 399.

253. *Calder*, 3 U.S. (3 Dallas) at 399.

254. *Calder*, 3 U.S. (3 Dallas) at 399. For his most important earlier statement of this principle, see James Iredell to Richard Dobbs Spaight, Aug. 26, 1787, in *The Papers of James Iredell*, 3:310.

255. For originalists' understanding of communicative content, see Solum, "Communicative Content and Legal Content," 484–507; Barnett, "The Misconceived Assumption About Constitutional Assumptions," 622–26.

256. Massachusetts Constitution of 1780, ch. VI, art. XI; New Hampshire Constitution of 1784, part II, art. 101; Bernick and Green, "There Is Something That Our Constitution Just Is," 267.

257. Donald S. Lutz, "From Covenant to Constitution in American Political Thought," *Publius* 10 (Autumn 1980): 103–06.

258. Massachusetts Constitution of 1780, ch. VI, art. XI; New Hampshire Constitution of 1784, part II, art. 101.

259. Michael Warner, *The Letters of the Republic: Publication and the Public Sphere in Eighteenth-Century America* (Cambridge, Mass.: Harvard University Press, 1990), 97–117; Slauter, "Written Constitutions and Unenumerated Rights," 292–95.

260. Thomas Paine, *Rights of Man, Part the Second* (London: J. S. Jordan, 1792), 43–44.

261. Slauter, "Written Constitutions and Unenumerated Rights," 293–94.

262. Slauter, "Written Constitutions and Unenumerated Rights," 294n14. A duodecimo book is approximately 7 by 4.5 inches in size, or similar in size to a modern paperback book. An octavo book is approximately 9 by 6 inches in size, or similar to a modern hardback book.

263. "Resolutions of the Convention Recommending the Procedures for Ratification and for the Establishment of Governments Under the Constitution by the Confederation Congress," in *DHRC*, 1:317.

264. Bernick and Green, "There Is Something That Our Constitution Just Is," 271–74 (quotes at 271).

265. Charles Thomson to Thomas Jefferson, Nov. 20, 1779, in *The Papers of Thomas Jefferson*, 3:196.

266. Bernick and Green, "There Is Something That Our Constitution Just Is," 306.

Chapter 5. Federal Constitutionalism and the Nature of the United States

Epigraph: John Vining, Feb. 8, 1791, in *DHFFC*, 14:472.

1. Wood, *The Creation of the American Republic*; Stourz, "*Constitution*: Changing Meaning of the Term from the Early Seventeenth to the Late Eighteenth Century."

2. See Wood, *The Creation of the American Republic*, 306–89.

3. Wood, *The Creation of the American Republic*, 307–08; Adams, *The First American Constitutions*, 61–83; Marc W. Kruman, *Between Authority and Liberty: State Constitution Making in Revolutionary America* (Chapel Hill: University of North Carolina Press, 1997), 15–33. Of the eleven state constitutions written in 1776 and 1777, only two (Delaware's and Pennsylvania's) were created by conventions called for that express purpose. The other states relied on either their sitting legislatures or provincial congresses. While several states elected new assemblies, many of which called themselves conventions, to draft constitutions, these bodies continued as the state's sitting legislatures even after enacting the new constitutions. None of these early state constitutions, moreover, were popularly ratified; once completed, they were merely declared law.

4. Wood, *The Creation of the American Republic*, 328–43; Rakove, *Original Meanings*, 96–100; Donald S. Lutz, *Popular Consent and Popular Control: Whig Political Theory*

in the Early State Constitutions (Baton Rouge: Louisiana State University Press, 1980), 72–84.

5. Gienapp, *The Second Creation*, 38–39.

6. James Iredell to Richard Dobbs Spaight, Aug. 26, 1787, in *The Papers of James Iredell*, 3:307, 308–09. Iredell elaborated on the essay he had published the prior year: "To the Public," Aug. 17, 1786, in *The Papers of James Iredell*, 3:227–31. Among jurists of this period, Iredell was arguably the exception that proved the rule. His burgeoning positivism seems to stand in stark contrast to the general jurisprudence of his peers. As noted earlier, such a sharp portrayal overstates the matter. See chapter 4. Nonetheless, Iredell was certainly more eager to emphasize the written character of U.S. constitutions than some of his counterparts.

7. [Paine], *Four Letters on Interesting Subjects*, 15, 18.

8. Thomas Paine, *Rights of Man: Being an Answer to Mr. Burke's Attack on the French Revolution* (London: J. S. Jordan, 1791), 56–57.

9. Gienapp, *The Second Creation*, 81–102. Plebeian Anti-Federalists especially favored precise constitutional text. See Cornell, "Constitutional Meaning and Semantic Instability," 22, 26–27.

10. Patrick Henry, Virginia Ratifying Convention, June 20, 1788, in *DHRC*, 10:1422–23 (quote at 1423).

11. Jack N. Rakove, "The Dilemma of Declaring Rights," in *The Nature of Rights at the American Founding*, ed. Barry Alan Shain (Charlottesville: University of Virginia Press, 2007), 187–96; Campbell, "Fundamental Rights at the American Founding," 13, 15–16; Campbell, "Natural Rights and the First Amendment," 295–301; Graber, "Enumeration and Other Constitutional Strategies for Protecting Rights," 358–61, 366–72; Gienapp, *The Second Creation*, 98–102.

12. Federal Farmer, Letter XVI, in *DHRC*, 17:348, and see generally 342–48. While Anti-Federalists were eager to enumerate rights and spoke as if securing those rights depended on it, importantly, by and large they were still calling for a declaratory bill of rights, one that reaffirmed existing rights and one that was not necessarily so different in kind from the sort that was eventually added. Campbell, "Determining Rights," 32–34. That said, in placing such emphasis on textual enumeration, to the point of implying that rights effectively would not exist without this entrenchment, they were giving the traditional declaratory bill of rights a distinctive new flavor that broke with convention as much as it adhered to it.

13. It is often claimed that Federalists erred in neglecting to add a bill of rights to the federal Constitution and that Anti-Federalists had the decisively better argument on this score. It is easy to say that now, given how our constitutional culture has developed and the importance we have come to attach to enumerated constitutional rights. But from the perspective of 1787, Federalists' arguments justifying the omission were commonplace, whereas Anti-Federalists' novel argument that common-law rights (though apparently not natural rights) were not protected unless enumerated was peculiar.

14. Gienapp, *The Second Creation*, 133–36, 143–46.

15. Gienapp, *The Second Creation*, 225–32.

16. St. George Tucker, "Of the Several Forms of Government," in *View of the Constitution of the United States with Selected Writings* (Indianapolis: Liberty Fund, 1999), 32; Saul Cornell, *The Other Founders: Anti-Federalism and the Dissenting Tradition in America, 1788–1828* (Chapel Hill: University of North Carolina Press, 1999), 187–94, 243–45, 270–73.

17. *Eakin v. Raub*, 12 Serg. & Rawle 330, 355, 348 (Pa. 1825) (Gibson, J., dissenting).

18. James Madison to Thomas Ritchie, Sept. 15, 1821, in *The Papers of James Madison: Retirement Series*, 2:381.

19. *Vanhorne's Lessee v. Dorrance*, 2 U.S. (2 Dall.) 304, 308 (C.C.D. Pa. 1795) (opinion of Paterson, J.).

20. *Marbury v. Madison*, 5 U.S. (1 Cranch) 137, 177–78, 180 (1803).

21. Again, authoritative written constitutional texts predated independence in the form of colonial charters, so it was hardly a mechanical process by which the drafting of written constitutions inexorably awakened a new written constitutional consciousness. Things changed only as people began advancing novel arguments *about* the nature of written constitutions.

22. This is among the principal arguments advanced in Gienapp, *The Second Creation*.

23. Publicola [Adams], Letters of Publicola XI, in *Writings of John Quincy Adams*, 1:107–08 (emphasis added). See also Letters of Publicola III, 1:73–77. For more, see chapter 4, note 142.

24. Swift, *A System of the Laws of the State of Connecticut*, 1:55.

25. On how judges were engaged in cultural invention of this kind, see Siddique, "The Ideological Origins of 'Written' Constitutionalism," 590–92. On how confident judicial rhetoric was often issued during this period to mask institutional fragility, see Cornell and Leonard, *The Partisan Republic*, 89–92.

26. See *United States v. Fisher*, 6 U.S. (2 Cranch) 358, 390 (1805); *Fletcher v. Peck*, 10 U.S. (6 Cranch) 87 (1810); *Terrett v. Taylor*, 13 U.S. (9 Cranch) 43, 50–52 (1815); *Dartmouth College v. Woodward*, 17 U.S. (4 Wheat.) 518 (1819).

27. Gienapp, *The Second Creation*, 125–334.

28. On how long-standing habits endured, see Parker, *Common Law, History, and Democracy in America*, 67–116; Banner, *The Decline of Natural Law*, 71–221; Suzanna Sherry, "Natural Law in the States," *University of Cincinnati Law Review* 61 (1992): 171–222; Jud Campbell, "The Emergence of Neutrality," *Yale Law Journal* 131 (Jan. 2022): 861–947.

29. William Baude, Jud Campbell, and Stephen E. Sachs, "General Law and the Fourteenth Amendment," *Stanford Law Review* 76 (forthcoming).

30. Justice Oliver Wendell Holmes, Jr., famously declared: "The common law is not a brooding omnipresence in the sky, but the articulate voice of some sovereign or quasi-sovereign that can be identified." *Southern Pacific Co. v. Jensen*, 244 U.S. 205, 222 (1917) (Holmes, J., dissenting). Eventually, the Supreme Court entrenched this broader view of law in *Erie Railroad Co. v. Tompkins*, the 1938 ruling that denied the existence of general federal common law—"a transcendental body of law outside of any particular State but obligatory within it." *Erie Railroad Co. v. Tompkins*, 304 U.S. 64, 79 (1938).

31. Alison L. LaCroix, *The Ideological Origins of American Federalism* (Cambridge, Mass.: Harvard University Press, 2010); Samuel H. Beer, *To Make a Nation: The*

Rediscovery of American Federalism (Cambridge, Mass.: Harvard University Press, 1993); Rakove, *Original Meanings*, 161–202; Christian G. Fritz, *Monitoring American Federalism: The History of State Legislative Resistance* (New York: Cambridge University Press, 2023), 1–2, 11–25.

32. Madison declared that the "proposed Constitution therefore is in strictness neither a national nor a federal constitution; but a composition of both." James Madison, *The Federalist* 39, in *DHRC*, 15:385; Gienapp, "The Myth of the Constitutional Given."

33. Gienapp, "In Search of Nationhood at the Founding," 1783–1813.

34. As Jud Campbell has put it, "the Constitution could not settle the nature of the polity because that was by definition pre-constitutional." Jud Campbell, "The Nature of Constitutional Histories," *Balkinization* (blog), May 1, 2020, https://balkin.blogspot.com/2020/05/the-natures-of-constitutional-histories.html.

35. LaCroix, *The Interbellum Constitution*. Gregory Ablavsky has offered a different account of federalism, contending that an initial period of legal pluralism had, by the early nineteenth century, collapsed into the familiar federal-state binary of dual federalism as state governments welcomed the federal government's exertions of authority insofar as they swept away local competitors' claims to sovereignty. Gregory Ablavsky, "Empire States: The Coming of Dual Federalism," *Yale Law Journal* 128 (May 2019): 1792–1869. Whoever is right in this debate, their accounts share an appreciation for how messy and contested federalism initially was.

36. LaCroix, *The Interbellum Constitution*.

37. Randy Barnett has married a strong commitment to unenumerated rights and written constitutionalism. Randy E. Barnett, "Who's Afraid of Unenumerated Rights?," *University of Pennsylvania Journal of Constitutional Law* 9 (Oct. 2006): 1–22; Barnett, *Restoring the Lost Constitution*, 102–11. It follows from his justification for originalism—that it adequately protects natural rights. The people retain their rights only if government is textually circumscribed. He breaks from originalists who insist that only enumerated rights enjoy constitutional status. But in different ways he breaks from the Founding-era views we've been charting. Despite his support for unenumerated rights, he resolutely defines original meaning in terms of text, often focusing intently on the words of rights provisions and accessing unenumerated rights through textual hooks like the Ninth Amendment or the Due Process Clauses. The Founders, by contrast, often thought the words of rights provisions were non-constitutive of those rights. Because of that, determinations of those rights were often unfixed and left in the hands of the people's representatives who could robustly regulate those rights for the public good. Which brings us to powers and text. As we will see, many of the same reasons the Founders looked beneath text to limn rights was why they looked beneath text to limn powers. Identifying the legitimate ends and means of government was not principally a matter of interpreting constitutional text but rather interpreting the underlying constitution of union.

38. Kenneth Stampp, "The Idea of a Perpetual Union in American History," *Journal of American History* 65 (June 1978): 5–33; Christian G. Fritz, *American Sovereigns: The People and America's Constitutional Tradition Before the Civil War* (New York: Cambridge University Press, 2008).

39. Gienapp, "The Myth of the Constitutional Given," 188–89.

40. Gienapp, *The Second Creation.*

41. Jud Campbell, "Four Views of the Nature of the Union," *Harvard Journal of Law & Public Policy* 47 (Spring 2024): 13–37.

42. David S. Schwartz, "A Question Perpetually Arising: Implied Powers, Capable Federalism, and the Limits of Enumerationism," *Arizona Law Review* 59 (2017): 575–79, 581–84. For examples of this orthodoxy applied to the original Constitution, see, e.g., Kurt T. Lash, "The Sum of All Delegated Power: A Response to Richard Primus, 'The Limits of Enumeration,'" *Yale Law Journal Forum* 180 (Dec. 2014): 180–207; Barnett, *Restoring the Lost Constitution,* 277–80.

43. Those questioning the orthodox take on enumeration include: Mikhail, "The Necessary and Proper Clauses," 1045–1132; Primus, "The Limits of Enumeration"; Schwartz, "A Question Perpetually Arising"; Calvin H. Johnson, "The Dubious Enumerated Power Doctrine," *Constitutional Commentary* 22 (Spring 2005): 25–96.

44. Gienapp, "The Myth of the Constitutional Given"; Graber, "Enumeration and Other Constitutional Strategies for Protecting Rights," 373–77; Primus, "The Limits of Enumeration," 620–22.

45. On the underappreciated importance of nationalist constitutionalism at the Founding, see Symposium, "The Federalist Constitution," *Fordham Law Review* 89 (Apr. 2021): 1669–2112, in particular the foreword by David S. Schwartz, Jonathan Gienapp, John Mikhail, and Richard Primus, at 1669–75.

46. Campbell, "Republicanism and Natural Rights at the Founding," 87–90; Lutz, "From Covenant to Constitution," 103–06.

47. John Adams, *A Defence of the Constitutions of Government of the United States of America* (Philadelphia: Hall and Sellers, 1787), 6.

48. Wilson, "Lectures on Law," in *Collected Works of James Wilson,* 1:554.

49. Wilson, "Lectures on Law," in *Collected Works of James Wilson,* 1:556.

50. Gienapp, "In Search of Nationhood at the Founding," 1788–93; Campbell, "Republicanism and Natural Rights at the Founding," 101–03.

51. Wood, *The Creation of the American Republic,* 344–89, 445–46, 462–63.

52. Gienapp, "The Myth of the Constitutional Given," 193–94, 201–04.

53. James Wilson, *Considerations on the Bank of North-America* (Philadelphia: Hall and Sellers, 1785).

54. Articles of Confederation of 1781, art. II.

55. Wilson, *Considerations on the Bank of North-America,* 10.

56. Wilson, *Considerations on the Bank of North-America,* 10.

57. Wilson, *Considerations on the Bank of North-America,* 10.

58. Wilson, *Considerations on the Bank of North-America,* 10.

59. Wilson, *Considerations on the Bank of North-America,* 9–11.

60. Gienapp, "The Myth of the Constitutional Given," 202–03.

61. James Wilson, June 19, 1787, in Farrand, *The Records of the Federal Convention,* 1:324.

62. Mikhail, "The Necessary and Proper Clauses," 1096–1106; William Ewald, "The Committee of Detail," *Constitutional Commentary* 28 (Fall 2012): 197–286 (on Wilson's role on the committee, see 213–14, 242–46, 276–83).

63. United States Constitution, art. I, sec. 8; Mikhail, "The Necessary and Proper Clauses," 1099–1101, 1121–28.
64. William Michael Treanor, "The Case of the Dishonest Scrivener: Gouverneur Morris and the Creation of the Federalist Constitution," *Michigan Law Review* 120 (Oct. 2021): 48–51.
65. United States Constitution, preamble.
66. John Mikhail, "The Constitution and the Philosophy of Language: Entailment, Implicature, and Implied Powers," *Virginia Law Review* 101 (June 2015): 1097–1103.
67. Gienapp, "The Myth of the Constitutional Given," 198–201, 204–05.
68. Samuel Adams to Richard Henry Lee, Dec. 3, 1787, in *DHRC*, 4:349.
69. Robert Whitehill, Pennsylvania Ratifying Convention, Nov. 28, 1787, in *DHRC*, 2:393.
70. Brutus V, *New York Journal*, Dec. 13, 1787, in *DHRC*, 14:423.
71. An Old Whig II, *Philadelphia Independent Gazetteer*, Oct. 17, 1787, in *DHRC*, 13:402–03.
72. James Madison, *The Federalist* 45, in *DHRC*, 15:479.
73. James Wilson, Pennsylvania Ratifying Convention, Dec. 4, 1787, in *DHRC*, 2:470 (emphasis added).
74. Wilson, Pennsylvania Ratifying Convention, Dec. 4, 1787, in *DHRC*, 2:472.
75. A Citizen of New York [John Jay], *An Address to the People of the State of New York*, Apr. 15, 1788, in *DHRC*, 17:111.
76. Massachusettensis, *Massachusetts Gazette* (Boston), Jan. 29, 1788, in *DHRC*, 5:830.
77. Gienapp, "The Myth of the Constitutional Given," 205–11; Richard Primus, "The 'Essential Characteristic': Enumerated Powers and the Bank of the United States," *Michigan Law Review* 117 (Dec. 2018): 415–98.
78. John Vining, Feb. 8, 1791, in *DHFFC*, 14:472.
79. Fisher Ames, Feb. 3, 1791, in *DHFFC*, 14:386, 389.
80. *Chisholm v. Georgia*, 2 U.S. (2 Dall.) 419, 453, 465 (1793) (opinion of Wilson, J.).
81. *Chisholm*, 2 U.S. (2 Dall.) at 465, 470 (opinions of Wilson, J., and Jay, J.).
82. Gienapp, "In Search of Nationhood at the Founding," 1809–13. Some nationalists, most notably John Marshall, agreed that the U.S. was a nation but thought that its national polity had been created later, through the Constitution, rather than through independence. See Campbell, "Four Views of the Nature of the Union," 26–30.
83. James Madison, Feb. 2, 1791, in *DHFFC*, 14:371.
84. William Giles, Feb. 7, 1791, in *DHFFC*, 14:468.
85. On the first political parties, see Jeffrey L. Pasley, *The First Presidential Contest: 1796 and the Founding of American Democracy* (Lawrence: University Press of Kansas, 2013).
86. Gienapp, "In Search of Nationhood at the Founding," 1804–09.
87. [Thomas Jefferson], "Resolutions Adopted by the Kentucky General Assembly," Nov. 10, 1798, in *The Papers of Thomas Jefferson*, 30:550.
88. Clyde N. Wilson, foreword to Tucker, *View of the Constitution of the United States*, viii–x. On Tucker's constitutionalism more broadly, see Cornell, *The Other Founders*, 263–72.
89. Tucker, *View of the Constitution of the United States*, 91–106.

90. See James Madison, *The Federalist* 39, in *DHRC*, 15:380–86.

91. On the Virginia and Kentucky Resolutions and the *Report of 1800*, see Fritz, *Monitoring American Federalism*, 91–128.

92. [James Madison], "Virginia Resolutions," Dec. 21, 1798, in *The Papers of James Madison, Congressional Series*, ed. William T. Hutchinson, William M. E. Rachal, and Robert Allen Rutland, 17 vols. (Chicago: University of Chicago Press, 1977–1991), 17:189.

93. [Madison], "Virginia Resolutions," in *The Papers of James Madison, Congressional Series*, 17:189.

94. [Madison], *Report of 1800*, in *The Papers of James Madison, Congressional Series*, 17:309.

95. [Madison], *Report of 1800*, in *The Papers of James Madison, Congressional Series*, 17:315.

96. Some originalists have effectively chosen sides in these Founding-era debates, insisting that one particular account of the federal union gets at the truth of the matter, while either dismissing the robust forms of nationalist constitutionalism present at the time or flattening the diversity of anti-nationalist constitutionalism by privileging Madison or assuming that he represented positions he rejected. See Anthony J. Bellia, Jr., and Bradford R. Clark, "The International Law Origins of American Federalism," *Columbia Law Review* 120 (May 2020): 835–940, esp. 865–71; Kurt L. Lash, "The Original Meaning of an Omission: The Tenth Amendment, Popular Sovereignty, and 'Expressly' Delegated Power," *Notre Dame Law Review* 83 (July 2008): 1889–1956, esp. 1902–15, 1951–53.

97. On how this framework for debate persisted, see Jud Campbell, "General Citizenship Rights," *Yale Law Journal* 132 (Jan. 2023): 611–701.

Chapter 6. Fixing Fixity

Epigraph: James Madison, *The Federalist* 37, in *DHRC*, 15:346.

1. Gienapp, "The Foreign Founding," 132–35.

2. Henry St. John, Viscount Bolingbroke, "A Dissertation Upon Parties" (1733), in *The Works of Lord Bolingbroke*, 4 vols. (Philadelphia: Carey and Hart, 1841), 2:88, 112.

3. Otis, *The Rights of the British Colonists Asserted and Proved*, 37.

4. Joseph Galloway, "A Letter to the People of Pennsylvania," 1760, in *Exploring the Bounds of Liberty*, 3:1662.

5. A Native of Maryland, *Maryland Gazette*, May 11, 1748, in *Exploring the Bounds of Liberty*, 2:1235; Reid, *Constitutional History of the American Revolution*; Black, "The Constitution of Empire"; Charles A. McIlwain, *Constitutionalism, Ancient and Modern* (Ithaca, N.Y.: Cornell University Press, 1940); Adams, *The First American Constitutions*, 16–18; Gough, *Fundamental Law in English Constitutional History*, 198–200.

6. Resolution of Oct. 23, 1765, in *Speeches of the Governors of Massachusetts from 1765 to 1775* (Boston: Russell and Gardner, 1818), 45 (emphasis added).

7. Colley, "Empires of Writing," 241–42; Grey, "Origins of the Unwritten Constitution," 857–58; Wood, *The Creation of the American Republic*, 292.

8. Massachusetts Circular Letter to the Colonial Legislatures, Feb. 11, 1768, in *Speeches of the Governors of Massachusetts*, 134.

9. Bilder, "Charter Constitutionalism," 1551–52, 1590–91.

10. See chapter 4. See also Campbell, "Determining Rights," 5–6, 32–43, 55.

11. As Jud Campbell has put it, since "[a]t the Founding . . . bills of rights were usually thought to be *declaratory* . . . parsing the exact language of rights provisions was usually beside the point." Campbell, "Originalism and the Nature of Rights." The substance of an amendment's text can still be revealing. That is certainly the case if the enumerated rights provision did not simply declare but also in some sense specified the content of the right. But even the text of a declaratory amendment can prove important for decoding its meaning since both that text and the history of its drafting can provide valuable evidence of its underlying content. Whatever the case, what is clear is that historical interpreters need to be very careful not to anachronistically ascribe significance to certain textual choices found in the Constitution's early rights provisions. Campbell, "Determining Rights," 50–57.

12. Gienapp, *The Second Creation*, 32–34.

13. Sir Matthew Hale, *The History of the Common Law of England* (1713), ed. Charles M. Gray (Chicago: University of Chicago Press, 1971), 40.

14. Reid, *The Ancient Constitution and the Origins of Anglo-American Liberty*, 17–22; Reid, *Constitutional History of the American Revolution*, vol. 1, *The Authority of Rights*, 25–26.

15. Edward King, *An Essay on the English Constitution and Government* (London: Benjamin White, 1767), 3.

16. Aequus, "From the Craftsman," *Massachusetts Gazette*, or *Boston News-Letter*, Mar. 6, 1766, in *American Political Writing During the Founding Era*, 1:63–64.

17. Wood, *The Creation of the American Republic*, esp. 127–389; Gienapp, "Beyond Republicanism, Back to Constitutionalism."

18. Wood, *The Creation of the American Republic*, 328–43, 372–89, 599–602; Rakove, *Original Meanings*, 96–100; Warner, *The Letters of the Republic*, 97–117.

19. Jefferson, *Notes on the State of Virginia*, 123.

20. Jefferson, *Notes on the State of Virginia*, 125, 129.

21. David E. Kyvig, *Explicit and Authentic Acts: Amending the U.S. Constitution, 1776–1995* (Lawrence: University Press of Kansas, 1995), 30–41.

22. On constitution making in Massachusetts, see Oscar Handlin and Mary Handlin, eds., *The Popular Sources of Political Authority: Documents on the Massachusetts Constitution of 1780* (Cambridge, Mass.: Harvard University Press, 1966), 15–25; James F. Hrdlicka, "War and Constitution Making in Revolutionary Massachusetts, 1754–1788" (Ph.D. diss., University of Virginia, 2016).

23. For a recent example of this familiar account of ratification's development and significance, see Amar, *The Words That Made Us*, 191–92.

24. Anne Twitty, "The Rise and Fall and Rise of Ratification: State-Constitution Making in the Shadow of the Revolution, 1770s–1840s" (unpublished manuscript) (on file with author).

25. Oliver Ellsworth, July 23, 1787, in Farrand, *The Records of the Federal Convention*, 2:91.

26. Elbridge Gerry, July 23, 1787, in Farrand, *The Records of the Federal Convention*, 2:89.
27. Gerry, July 23, 1787, in Farrand, *The Records of the Federal Convention*, 2:89.
28. Twitty, "The Rise and Fall and Rise of Ratification."
29. Swift, *A System of the Laws of the State of Connecticut*, 1:55, 62, 58.
30. Richard Tuck, *The Sleeping Sovereign: The Invention of Modern Democracy* (New York: Cambridge University Press, 2015), x–xi, 181–212, 251–54.
31. Twitty, "The Rise and Fall and Rise of Ratification"; Mathew Steilen, "The Constitutional Convention and Constitutional Change: A Revisionist History," *Lewis & Clark Law Review* 24 (2020): 1–52; Fritz, *American Sovereigns*, 80–116, 153–276; Ablavsky, "Empire States," 1812–35, 1847–62.
32. Kramer, *The People Themselves*, 105–14, 170–213; Leonard and Cornell, *The Partisan Republic*, 57–60, 92–102, 106–13.
33. Campbell, "Determining Rights," 13–16, 30–32, 50–51, 58.
34. Leading originalists have often misunderstood what the Founding generation fixed, and what they left unfixed, by enumerating certain constitutional rights. These originalists have mistakenly claimed that by entrenching those rights in text the Founders fixed a balancing test between the right and its regulation. See, e.g., Scalia, *A Matter of Interpretation*, 3, 40, 133–37; *District of Columbia v. Heller*, 554 U.S. 570, 634–35 (2008).
35. Thus challenging those originalists who might claim to embrace subsequent, even dynamic, determinations of fixed constitutional provisions through their promotion of constitutional construction. As these originalists maintain, the activity of interpreting the meaning of fixed constitutional text should be distinguished from the activity of constructing doctrines that give that text legal effect, especially when that text's meaning is underdetermined. Whittington, "Constructing a New American Constitution"; Solum, "Originalism and Constitutional Construction"; Barnett and Bernick, "The Letter and the Spirit," 10–18. While this distinction can potentially square fixed constitutional meaning with the idea of subsequent determinations (the determinations need only be consistent with and constrained by the fixed meaning), where it falters regarding the original Constitution is in assuming that constitutional rights are fixed *in* text, when, as we have seen, in most instances at the Founding they were fixed before and independently of text. Because *what* was fixed and *how* it was fixed were so different, *how* it could be determined was different too. See Campbell, "Determining Rights," 7–8.
36. Gienapp, *The Second Creation*, esp. 287–90, 325–27, 332–34.
37. *Vanhorne's Lessee v. Dorrance*, 2 U.S. (2 Dall.) 304, 308 (C.C.D. Pa. 1795) (opinion of Paterson, J.).
38. William Baude, "Constitutional Liquidation," *Stanford Law Review* 71 (Jan. 2019): 1–70; Nelson, "*Stare Decisis* and Demonstrably Erroneous Precedents," 10–21; Nelson, "Originalism and Interpretive Conventions," 525–29; Caleb Nelson, "The Constitutionality of Civil Forfeiture," *Yale Law Journal* 125 (June 2016): 2452–53; Stephen E. Sachs, "The 'Unwritten Constitution' and Unwritten Law," *University of Illinois Law Review* 2013 (2013): 1806–08; Michael McConnell, "Time, Institutions, and Interpretation," *Boston University Law Review* 95 (Dec. 2015): 1773–76; Po-

janowski and Walsh, "Enduring Originalism," 142–46. The Supreme Court has begun to take interest as well, see *New York State Rifle & Pistol Association v. Bruen*, 142 S. Ct. 2111, 2162–63 (2022) (Barrett, J., concurring).

39. James Madison, *The Federalist* 37, in *DHRC*, 15:346; Alexander Hamilton, *The Federalist* 82, in *DHRC*, 18:111.

40. Madison, *The Federalist* 37, in *DHRC*, 15:346. On *Federalist* 37 and scholars' mounting interest in it, see Todd Estes, "The Emergence and Fundamental Centrality of James Madison's *Federalist* 37: Historians, Political Theorists, and the Recentering of Meaning in *The Federalist*," *American Political Thought* 12 (Summer 2023): 424–52.

41. James Madison to Spencer Roane, Sept. 2, 1819, *The Papers of James Madison: Retirement Series*, 1:502.

42. *Dobbs v. Jackson Women's Health Organization*, 142 S. Ct. 2228, 2253 (2022).

43. Balkin, *Memory and Authority*, 200–09; Rachel Reed, "Should the Supreme Court Care About Tradition?," *Harvard Law Today*, Nov. 18, 2022, https://hls.harvard.edu/today/should-the-supreme-court-care-about-tradition/.

44. Nelson, "*Stare Decisis* and Demonstrably Erroneous Precedents," 10–21; Nelson, "Originalism and Interpretive Conventions," 525–29.

45. Baude, "Constitutional Liquidation."

46. Baude, "Constitutional Liquidation," 13–21.

47. Baude, "Constitutional Liquidation," 21–29.

48. Originalists disagree about whether liquidation permanently fixes new meanings. Nelson suggests it does: Nelson, "Originalism and Interpretive Conventions," 525; Nelson, "The Constitutionality of Civil Forfeiture," 2453. Baude suggests it does not: Baude, "Constitutional Liquidation," 53–59.

49. David S. Schwartz, "Madison's Waiver: Can Constitutional Liquidation Be Liquidated?," *Stanford Law Review Online* 17 (Sept. 2019): 23.

50. Baude, "Constitutional Liquidation," 59; McConnell, "Time, Institutions, and Interpretation," 1774; Schwartz, "Madison's Waiver," 25–26. Michael McConnell has thoughtfully attempted to distinguish liquidation from living constitutionalism: "There is a similarity" between the two, he writes. "Both of them provide a means by which social change can be reflected in constitutional meaning. But the object of liquidation is to 'fix' the meaning of the Constitution through a course of deliberative decisions. Presumably, this 'fixing' is not irrevocable, but, as in the case of precedent, departures require substantial justification and a similar process of deliberation and widespread acceptance. Under a 'living constitution,'" by contrast, "constitutional meaning is never fixed. . . . [L]iquidation is a form of 'construction'—it is not a backdoor means of constitutional amendment." McConnell, "Time, Institutions, and Interpretation," 1774. It is unclear, however, how much ultimately hangs on this distinction, at least in practice anyway. Under both liquidation and living constitutionalism, lots of constitutional meaning is treated as settled and change occurs only when there is widespread recognition that some settled meanings ought to be rethought. Whether or not those meanings that are taken to be settled (either before or after this process of deliberative change) are

labeled "fixed" seems less important than the fact that those meanings can always be modified through further deliberation and debate.

51. For an account of how original interpretive techniques are part of the Founders' law, see Baude and Sachs, "The Law of Interpretation."

52. Baude, "Constitutional Liquidation," 32–35.

53. Pojanowski and Walsh, "Enduring Originalism," 143. See also Nelson, "Stare Decisis and Demonstrably Erroneous Precedents," 14–21; Nelson, "Originalism and Interpretive Conventions," 525–29.

54. Curtis A. Bradley and Neil S. Siegel, "Historical Gloss, Madisonian Liquidation, and the Originalism Debate," Virginia Law Review 106 (Mar. 2020): 1–72.

55. Saul Cornell, "President Madison's Living Constitution: Fixation, Liquidation, and Constitutional Politics in the Jeffersonian Era," Fordham Law Review 89 (Apr. 2021): 1776.

56. Bradley and Siegel, "Historical Gloss, Madisonian Liquidation, and the Originalism Debate," 59, 71.

57. Bradley and Siegel, "Historical Gloss, Madisonian Liquidation, and the Originalism Debate," 59–70; Cornell, "President Madison's Living Constitution," 1775–78.

58. Jonathan Gienapp, "How to Maintain a Constitution: The Virginia and Kentucky Resolutions and James Madison's Struggle with the Problem of Constitutional Maintenance," in Nullification and Secession in Modern Constitutional Thought, ed. Sanford Levinson (Lawrence: University Press of Kansas, 2016), 53–90.

59. Gienapp, "How to Maintain a Constitution," 88–90.

60. For treatments of Federalist 37 that emphasize that Madison had in mind a broader form of constitutional uncertainty and liquidation, see Gienapp, The Second Creation, 110–12; Rakove, A Politician Thinking, 138–45, 152–53; Bilder, Madison's Hand, 160–64; Jeremy D. Bailey, James Madison and Constitutional Imperfection (New York: Cambridge University Press, 2015), 28–36, 43–46. On how Madison, throughout much of his political career, presumed that a full-bodied brand of constitutional politics would settle constitutional disputes, see Leonard and Cornell, The Partisan Republic, 135–37; Larry D. Kramer, " 'The Interest of the Man': James Madison's Constitutional Politics," in The Cambridge Companion to the Federalist, eds. Jack N. Rakove and Colleen A. Sheehan (New York: Cambridge University Press, 2020), 330–69. Madison was not unusual in this regard. The Founding generation often had a more robust appreciation for constitutional politics and their essential relationship to the Constitution than tends to prevail in legal circles today.

61. James Madison, The Federalist 49, in DHRC, 16:16–17. On this enduring Madisonian commitment, see Gienapp, "How to Maintain a Constitution."

62. James Madison, June 17, 1789, in DHFFC, 11:926–27; Gienapp, "How to Maintain a Constitution," 66–69.

63. Ryan Nees, "Historical Gloss, Liquidation, and the Living Constitution" (unpublished manuscript) (on file with author). See also Thomas, The (Un)Written Constitution, 93–94.

64. See generally Kramer, The People Themselves; Leonard and Cornell, The Partisan Republic. Nor did this attitude toward judicial enforcement soon dissipate. It un-

dergirded the dominant forms of nineteenth-century constitutional politics, including most prominently leading Republicans' approach to reconstructing the union and the Constitution in the wake of the Civil War. See Graber, *Punish Treason, Reward Loyalty*. And when, over the course of the nineteenth century, the judiciary did, in fits and starts, begin to play a subordinate role in resolving various political disputes, they usually did so at the invitation of those in the other branches, therefore in lockstep with the reigning vision of constitutional politics rather than in opposition to it. See Mark A. Graber, "The Nonmajoritarian Difficulty: Legislative Deference to the Judiciary," *Studies in American Political Development* 7 (Spring 1993): 35–73; Keith E. Whittington, *Political Foundations of Judicial Supremacy: The President, the Supreme Court, and Constitutional Leadership in U.S. History* (Princeton, N.J.: Princeton University Press, 2007); Kevin Arlyck, "The Executive Branch and the Origins of Executive Independence," *Journal of American Constitutional History* 1 (Summer 2023): 343–77.

65. For this argument, see Gienapp, *Second Creation*, esp. 125–334.

Chapter 7. Before the Legalized Constitution

Epigraph: William Lenoir, North Carolina Ratifying Convention, July 30, 1788, in *DHRC*, 30:412.

1. See Lawson and Seidman, "Originalism as a Legal Enterprise"; Scalia and Garner, *Reading Law*.
2. McGinnis and Rappaport, "Original Methods Originalism."
3. McGinnis and Rappaport, *Originalism and the Good Constitution*, 121; McGinnis and Rappaport, "Unifying Original Intent and Original Public Meaning," 1375–76.
4. McGinnis and Rappaport, "The Constitution and the Language of the Law," 1355–1400.
5. McGinnis and Rappaport, *Originalism and the Good Constitution*, 116–38. William Baude and Stephen Sachs express similar confidence that there were known rules of legal construction at the Founding: Baude and Sachs, "The Law of Interpretation," 1140–42. Much more on Baude and Sachs's distinctive version of originalism to come in chapter 10. See also Bellia and Clark, "The Constitutional Law of Interpretation," 525–29, 579–87.
6. McGinnis and Rappaport, "Unifying Original Intent and Original Public Meaning," 1396–99.
7. Gary Lawson and Guy Seidman, *"A Great Power of Attorney": Understanding the Fiduciary Constitution* (Lawrence: University Press of Kansas, 2017).
8. Bellia and Clark, "The Constitutional Law of Interpretation," 529–51, 587–94.
9. Scalia and Garner, *Reading Law*; Prakash, "Unoriginalism's Law Without Meaning," 540–46; Natelson, "The Founders' Hermeneutic"; Paulsen, "Does the Constitution Prescribe Rules for Its Own Interpretation?," 860–61, 872–73, 883.
10. Leonard and Cornell, *The Partisan Republic*, 85. Christopher Tomlins describes a similar debate at this time between those who defended a discourse of police (a democratic ideology of communal good order and collective happiness) and those

who defended a discourse of law (a language of rule that disciplined and constrained certain forms of popular rule and regulation). See Christopher L. Tomlins, *Law, Labor, and Ideology in the Early American Republic* (New York: Cambridge University Press, 1993), 19–97.

11. Sylvia Snowiss, *Judicial Review and the Law of the Constitution* (New Haven, Conn.: Yale University Press, 1990), 1–3, 7–8; Gordon S. Wood, "The Origins of Judicial Review Revisited, or How the Marshall Court Made More out of Less," *Washington and Lee Law Review* 56 (Summer 1999): 794–99; Kramer, *The People Themselves*, 29–30.

12. Wood, *The Creation of the American Republic*, esp. 162–389, 532–36, 593–615.

13. Kramer, *The People Themselves*, 24–34, 44–57.

14. Cornell, *The Other Founders*, 81–120.

15. Saul Cornell, "The People's Constitution vs. The Lawyer's Constitution," *Yale Journal of Law & the Humanities* 23 (Summer 2011): 304–10.

16. Cornell, "The People's Constitution vs. The Lawyer's Constitution," 304–34; Gienapp, *The Second Creation*, 95–98.

17. Patrick Henry, Virginia Ratifying Convention, June 23, 1788, in *DHRC*, 10:1466.

18. Samuel Osgood to Samuel Adams, Jan. 5, 1788, in *DHRC*, 15:264.

19. Oliver Ellsworth, A Landholder V, in *DHRC*, 14:335.

20. James Madison, *The Federalist* 49, in *DHRC*, 16:16–17. On this enduring Madisonian commitment, see Gienapp, "How to Maintain a Constitution."

21. James Madison, "Observations on Jefferson's Draft Constitution of Virginia," Oct. 15, 1788, in *The Papers of James Madison, Congressional Series*, 11:293.

22. Leonard and Cornell, *The Partisan Republic*, 97–101.

23. Thomas Jefferson to William Charles Jarvis, Sept. 28, 1820, in *The Papers of Thomas Jefferson: Retirement Series*, ed. J. Jefferson Looney et al., 18 vols. (Princeton, N.J.: Princeton University Press, 2004–2021), 16:287–88.

24. Charles A. Lofgren, "The Original Understanding of Original Intent?," *Constitutional Commentary* 5 (Winter 1988): 82–85; Rakove, *Original Meanings*, 128–30.

25. Cornell, *The Other Founders*, 81–120; Todd Estes, *The Jay Treaty Debate, Public Opinion, and the Evolution of American Political Culture* (Amherst: University of Massachusetts Press, 2006).

26. Maier, *From Resistance to Revolution*; Pauline Maier, *Ratification: The People Debate the Constitution, 1787–1788* (New York: Simon and Schuster, 2010); Cornell, *The Other Founders*, 19–120; Todd Estes, "Perspectives, Points of Emphasis, and Lines of Analysis in the Narrative of the Ratification Debates" and "Power and Point of View in the Ratification Contest," *William and Mary Quarterly* 69 (Apr. 2012): 361–64, 398–400. Akhil Reed Amar has aptly described this period of American constitutional debate as a "constitutional conversation," though his own treatment of the period ends up focusing on a small group of well-known political elites at the expense of the thousands of others who participated in and shaped a much wider conversation. Amar, *The Words That Made Us*.

27. Jeffrey L. Pasley, Andrew W. Robertson, and David Waldstreicher, eds., *Beyond the Founders: New Approaches to the Political History of the Early Republic* (Chapel Hill:

University of North Carolina Press, 2004); David Waldstreicher, *In the Midst of Perpetual Fetes: The Making of American Nationalism, 1776–1820* (Chapel Hill: University of North Carolina Press, 1997); Jeffrey L. Pasley, *"The Tyranny of Printers": Newspaper Politics in the Early American Republic* (Charlottesville: University of Virginia Press, 2001); Estes, *The Jay Treaty Debate*; Marcus Daniel, *Scandal and Civility: Journalism and the Birth of American Democracy* (New York: Oxford University Press, 2009); Seth Cotlar, *Tom Paine's America: The Rise and Fall of Transatlantic Radicalism* (Charlottesville: University of Virginia Press, 2011); Saul Cornell, " 'To Assemble Together for Their Common Good': History, Ethnography, and the Original Meanings of the Rights of Assembly and Speech," *Fordham Law Review* 84 (Dec. 2015): 915–34; Matthew Rainbow Hale, "Regenerating the World: The French Revolution, Civic Festivals, and the Forging of Modern American Democracy, 1793–1795," *Journal of American History* 103 (Mar. 2017): 891–920.

28. Leonard and Cornell, *The Partisan Republic*, 84–85. For a comparable account of legal-political debate at the local level, see John Phillip Reid, *Controlling the Law: Legal Politics in Early National New Hampshire* (DeKalb: Northern Illinois University Press, 2004), 33–55.

29. Leonard and Cornell, *The Partisan Republic*, 105–13; Hobson, *The Great Yazoo Lands Sale*, 37–55.

30. Leonard and Cornell, *The Partisan Republic*, 91–92, 109–11.

31. Campbell, "Natural Rights and the First Amendment," 293–94; Jud Campbell, "The Invention of First Amendment Federalism," *Texas Law Review* 97 (Feb. 2019): 540–60.

32. Leonard and Cornell, *The Partisan Republic*, 87–101.

33. Jefferson to John Dickinson, Dec. 19, 1801, in *The Papers of Thomas Jefferson*, 36:165.

34. Morton J. Horwitz, *The Transformation of American Law, 1780–1860* (New York: Oxford University Press, 1977), 18–23; Parker, *Common Law, History, and Democracy in America*, 78–92.

35. Root, *Reports of Cases*, 1:xii.

36. Meyler, "Towards a Common Law Originalism," 575–80; Richard E. Ellis, *The Jeffersonian Crisis: Courts and Politics in the Young Republic* (New York: Oxford University Press, 1971), 111–16, 176–78; Reid, *Controlling the Law*, 33–55; Andrew Shankman, *Crucible of American Democracy: The Struggle to Fuse Egalitarianism and Capitalism in Jeffersonian Pennsylvania* (Lawrence: University Press of Kansas, 2004), 194–96.

37. James Sullivan, *The History of Land Titles in Massachusetts* (Boston: I. Thomas and E. T. Andrews, 1801), 13.

38. *Aurora General Advertiser* (Philadelphia), Dec. 21, 1807.

39. Charles M. Cook, *The American Codification Movement: A Study in Antebellum Legal Reform* (Westport, Conn.: Greenwood, 1981); Robert W. Gordon, "The American Codification Movement," *Vanderbilt Law Review* 36 (Mar. 1983): 431–58.

40. Sullivan, *The History of Land Titles in Massachusetts*, 13.

41. Jay, "Origins of the Federal Common Law: Part One"; Jay, "Origins of the Federal Common Law: Part Two."

42. G. Edward White, *The Marshall Court and Cultural Change, 1815–1835*, abr. ed. (New York: Oxford University Press, 1988), 79–95; Gordon S. Wood, *Empire of Liberty: A History of the Early Republic* (New York: Oxford University Press, 2009), 457–68.

43. Kramer, *The People Themselves*, 156–64; R. Kent Newmyer, "Harvard Law School, New England Legal Culture, and the Antebellum Origins of American Jurisprudence," *Journal of American History* 74 (Dec. 1987): 822–23.

44. Horwitz, *The Transformation of American Law, 1780–1860*, 253–59.

45. Snowiss, *Judicial Review and the Law of the Constitution*, 3–4; Stephen Griffin, *American Constitutionalism: From Theory to Politics* (Princeton, N.J.: Princeton University Press, 1996), 15–18. But see LaCroix, *The Interbellum Constitution* (suggesting that this portrait of the Marshall Court can be overdrawn).

46. Snowiss, *Judicial Review and the Law of the Constitution*, 121–61; Charles F. Hobson, *The Great Chief Justice: John Marshall and the Rule of Law* (Lawrence: University Press of Kansas, 1996), 172–99.

47. Wood, "The Origins of Judicial Review Revisited," 801–09.

48. White, *The Marshall Court and Cultural Change*, 119, 155; Kramer, *The People Themselves*, 149–50.

49. On the emergence of the genre of constitutional law, see Hulsebosch, *Constituting Empire*, 212–13, 239–40, 253–58; Bilder, "Colonial Constitutionalism and Constitutional Law," 36–44.

50. Newmyer, "Harvard Law School, New England Legal Culture, and the Antebellum Origins of American Jurisprudence," 828–33 (quote at 831); Hendrik Hartog, "The Constitution of Aspiration and 'The Rights That Belong to Us All,'" *Journal of American History* 74 (Dec. 1987): 1030.

51. James Wilson, Pennsylvania Ratifying Convention, Dec. 11, 1787, in *DHRC*, 2:556.

52. Gienapp, "The Myth of the Constitutional Given," 194–209.

53. James Wilson, Pennsylvania Ratifying Convention, Nov. 28, 1787, in *DHRC*, 2:383–84.

54. Joseph Story, *Commentaries on the Constitution of the United States*, 3 vols. (Boston: Hilliard, Gray, 1833), 1:443–45.

55. Kramer, *The People Themselves*, 196–213; Leonard and Cornell, *The Partisan Republic*, 113–14, 207–08, 212–20.

56. *Eakin v. Raub*, 12 Serg. & Rawle 330, 355, 348 (Pa. 1825) (Gibson, J., dissenting). For more, see Thomas, *The (Un)Written Constitution*, 6–8.

57. See Hendrik Hartog, "Pigs and Positivism," *Wisconsin Law Review* 899 (1985): 899–936; Laura F. Edwards, *The People and Their Peace: Legal Culture and the Transformation of Inequality in the Post-Revolutionary South* (Chapel Hill: University of North Carolina Press, 2009); Anne Twitty, *Before Dred Scott: Slavery and Legal Culture in the American Confluence, 1787–1857* (New York: Cambridge University Press, 2016); Masur, *Until Justice Be Done*; Mary Sarah Bilder, "Without Doors: Native Nations and the Convention," *Fordham Law Review* 89 (Apr. 2021): 1707–60; Gregory Ablavsky and W. Tanner Allread, "We the (Native) People?: How Indigenous Peoples Debated the U.S. Constitution," *Columbia Law Review* 123 (Mar. 2023): 243–318; Maggie Blackhawk, "Foreword: The Constitution of American Colonialism," *Harvard Law Review* 137 (Nov. 2023): 22–66; Farah Peterson, "Constitu-

tionalism in Unexpected Places," *Virginia Law Review* 106 (May 2020): 559–609; Tomlins, *Law, Labor, and Ideology in the Early American Republic*; Hartog, "The Constitution of Aspiration and 'The Rights That Belong to Us All.' " On this literature with further citations, see Gregory Ablavsky, "Akhil Amar's Unusable Past," *Michigan Law Review* 121 (Apr. 2023): 1119–46.

58. A handful of originalists have recognized the diversity of people who held constitutional views in the early United States. See Christina Mulligan, "Diverse Originalism," *University of Pennsylvania Journal of Constitutional Law* 21 (Dec. 2018): 379–438, esp. 412–28; Barnett and Bernick, *The Original Meaning of the Fourteenth Amendment*. While these are a valuable corrective, neither emphasizes the diverse ways in which these various groups of people not only interpreted constitutional provisions but understood law and constitutionalism more generally.

59. This is among the reasons I focused on Congress in my account of constitutional debate across the 1790s. See Gienapp, *The Second Creation*.

60. Thomas Jefferson's Opinion, Feb. 15, 1791, in *DHFFC*, 21:781.

61. Gienapp, *The Second Creation*, 116–23; Nelson, "Originalism and Interpretive Conventions," 563–78; Cornell, "The People's Constitution vs. The Lawyer's Constitution"; Larry D. Kramer, "Two (More) Problems with Originalism," *Harvard Journal of Law & Public Policy* 31 (Summer 2008): 911–13; Kurt T. Lash, "Originalism All the Way Down?," *Constitutional Commentary* 30 (Winter 2015): 149–66; Farah Peterson, "Expounding the Constitution," *Yale Law Journal* 130 (Oct. 2020): 2–85.

62. Nelson, "Originalism and Interpretive Conventions," 561–73.

63. For the argument that the Constitution is like a power of attorney, see Lawson and Seidman, *"A Great Power of Attorney."* For the counterargument that the Constitution was hardly ever likened to a power of attorney at the Founding, see Richard Primus, "The Elephant Problem," *Georgetown Journal of Law & Public Policy* 17 (Summer 2019): 373–406; John Mikhail, "Is the Constitution a Power of Attorney or a Corporate Charter?: A Commentary on *'A Great Power of Attorney': Understanding the Fiduciary Constitution*, by Gary Lawson and Guy Seidman," *Georgetown Journal of Law & Public Policy* 17 (Summer 2019): 407–40.

64. Interpreters often likened the United States government to a corporation and the Constitution to its corporate charter, though this analogue had its own limits. See Mikhail, "Is the Constitution a Power of Attorney or a Corporate Charter?," 421–29; Mikhail, "The Constitution and the Philosophy of Language," 1097–1103; Ciepley, "Is the U.S. Government a Corporation?"

65. Cornell, "The People's Constitution vs. The Lawyer's Constitution," 304–10; Kramer, *The People Themselves*.

66. Lofgren, "The Original Understanding of Original Intent?," 82–85; Snowiss, *Judicial Review and the Law of the Constitution*, 13–89.

67. Gienapp, *The Second Creation*, 118–21.

68. Original methods originalists contend that the original rules for interpreting the Constitution were essentially the rules for interpreting statutes. See McGinnis and Rappaport, "Unifying Original Intent and Original Public Meaning," 1396–99. In his influential article, H. Jefferson Powell argued that the framers expected the Constitution to be interpreted in accordance with familiar common-law methods

of statutory construction. It is important to stress two caveats. First, even if Powell incorrectly claimed that the statutory analogy was at first widely endorsed, he also claimed that the Founding generation divided sharply over how liberally or strictly to construct the Constitution, with many rejecting construction entirely. Second, Powell argued that the statutory analogy was soon replaced with a contract analogy, underscoring early flux. See H. Jefferson Powell, "The Original Understanding of Original Intent," *Harvard Law Review* 98 (Mar. 1985): 902–48. Even Powell, then, points toward early interpretive contestation and dynamism. In his telling, we find initial disagreement over the applicability of known rules of construction followed by concerted attempts to invent and entrench new ones.

69. On the contested nature of the eighteenth-century common law, see Meyler, "Towards a Common Law Originalism," 567–80; and on the diversity of common laws at the Founding, see Bernadette Meyler, "Common Law Confrontations," *Law and History Review* 37 (Aug. 2019): 763–86. On how Blackstone's *Commentaries* offered a polemical, rather than a descriptive, account of the common law, see Lieberman, *The Province of Legislation Determined*, 13–67. For a related point about common-law writers generally, see Holly Brewer, *By Birth or Consent: Children, Law, and the Anglo-American Revolution in Authority* (Chapel Hill: University of North Carolina Press, 2005), 10–11.

70. Edmund Randolph, Virginia Ratifying Convention, June 17, 1788, in *DHRC*, 10:1347.

71. In a creative account, Farah Peterson has argued that rules for interpreting public and private legislation shaped early interpretation of the Constitution. Peterson, "Expounding the Constitution." At least initially, however, both legal elites and non-legal elites often refused to think of the Constitution in narrow statutory terms.

72. Charles Hobson has suggested that the Supreme Court case *Fletcher v. Peck*, in 1810, marked a key interpretive transition away from general legal principles and toward a new emphasis on text. Hobson, *The Great Yazoo Lands Sale*, 9–10, 129–34, 149–57. The shift was likely more gradual and uneven, however.

73. Honestus [Benjamin Austin], *Observations on the Pernicious Practice of the Law* (Boston: Adams and Nourse, 1786), 12; Gienapp, *The Second Creation*, 119–20.

74. On the underdetermined character of the Articles of Confederation, see Jack N. Rakove, *The Beginnings of National Politics: An Interpretive History of the Continental Congress* (New York: Knopf, 1979), 135–91.

75. Wood, *The Creation of the American Republic*.

76. They claim that the Constitution was designed to transfer some sovereignty from the states to the federal government while maintaining the states as separate sovereign entities. Bellia and Clark, "The Constitutional Law of Interpretation," 522–23. See also Bellia and Clark, "The International Law Origins of American Federalism."

77. See David M. Golove and Daniel J. Hulsebosch, "A Civilized Nation: The Early American Constitution, the Law of Nations, and the Pursuit of International Recognition," *New York University Law Review* 85 (Oct. 2010): 932–1066; Golove and Hulsebosch, "The Law of Nations and the Constitution"; David M. Golove and Daniel J. Hulsebosch, "The Federalist Constitution as a Project in International Law," *Fordham Law Review* 89 (Apr. 2021): 1841–76.

78. Bellia and Clark's argument rests on several controversial premises pertaining to the nature of the American states, the character of the federal union, and how the Constitution transferred sovereignty that they claim are clear from the history of the early union or the use of key terms in Founding-era documents. Bellia and Clark, "The Constitutional Law of Interpretation," 536–51. However, the debate over the union, those key terms, and the documents that contained them suggest the opposite. For a critique, see David S. Schwartz, "The International Law Origins of Compact Theory: A Critique of Bellia & Clark on Federalism," *Journal of American Constitutional History* 1 (Fall 2023): 629–69. On the contested nature of the union, see chapter 5; Campbell, "Four Views of the Nature of the Union."

79. See debate at the Constitutional Convention: Luther Martin, June 19, 1787, in Farrand, *The Records of the Federal Convention*, 1:324; James Wilson, June 19, 1787, in Farrand, *The Records of the Federal Convention*, 1:324; Alexander Hamilton, June 19, 1787, in Farrand, *The Records of the Federal Convention*, 1:324. For a cogent discussion, see Rakove, *The Beginnings of National Politics*, 173–74.

80. The legal status of the states was initially ambiguous. See Mark A. Graber, "State Constitutions as National Constitutions," *Arkansas Law Review* 69 (2016): 373–78, 421–23. Much of Bellia and Clark's argument about interpretive rules depends on what they assume follows from the use of the word "States" in key early U.S. legal documents. Bellia and Clark, "The Constitutional Law of Interpretation," 521–22, 538, 541–42, 587–88, 603–04, 615–16 (quote at 521). But this formulation begs all the questions that were up for grabs at the Founding about the very nature of the states by stipulating as clear premise what was deeply disputed. The term "States" *could have* signaled that the American states were alike in kind to other sovereign states, but it need not have, as confirmed by the fact that so many eighteenth-century commentators expressly rejected that understanding of the legal status of the American states and attached a separate meaning to the term.

81. Wood, *The Creation of the American Republic*, 344–89.

82. Though some nationalists who strongly supported the U.S. Constitution nonetheless insisted that the United States had been a nation since independence and denied that the Articles had been a mere treaty among sovereign states. See Gienapp, "In Search of Nationhood at the Founding," 1793–97.

83. James Madison, July 23, 1787, in Farrand, *The Records of the Federal Convention*, 2:93. Max Edling has argued that the 1787 Constitution was akin to a federal treaty between the states, a curious claim given that Madison and most of the Constitution's leading architects and defenders were emphatic that it was not. See Max D. Edling, *Perfecting the Union: National and State Authority in the US Constitution* (New York: Oxford University Press, 2020).

84. In essence, Bellia and Clark (like Edling) take the position staked out by John C. Calhoun and other defenders of compact theory, drawing on the law of nations theorist Emmerich de Vattel to claim that the American states had originally entered into a confederacy with each other and transferred a limited share of their sovereignty to a new federal government through the express terms of the federal Constitution while retaining the vast remainder for themselves. Bellia and Clark, "The Constitutional Law of Interpretation," 536–51. Each of these propositions was

vigorously disputed in the early United States. On compact theory and the debates over it, see Fritz, *American Sovereigns*, 190–234.

85. Having passed off as historical what was, in effect, Calhoun's controversial account of the federal union, Bellia and Clark then claim early judicial decisions such as *Chisholm v. Georgia* and the landmark Marshall Court rulings in favor of their interpretation, which is hard to square, since in those cases Justices James Wilson, John Jay, and John Marshall expressly opposed the states'-rights reading of the Constitution. Bellia and Clark, "The Constitutional Law of Interpretation," 552–76. To square this circle, Bellia and Clark insist that what matters is not how the justices applied interpretive rules drawn from the law of nations, but the simple fact that the justices made use of them. But Wilson and Marshall appealed to the law of nations because they denied that the states were sovereign in the traditional sense. American interpreters could not use the law of nations to figure out how to interpret the U.S. Constitution without first figuring out the essential features of their constitutional system, which is why we find in Calhoun and Marshall not agreement over what the law of nations told them but bitter disagreement over the very thing one had to understand in order to clearly apply these interpretive principles to the matter at hand: the nature of sovereignty in the American federal union.

86. Gienapp, *The Second Creation*, 4–8.

87. Stephen Sachs has argued that the fact of interpretive pluralism at the Founding illustrates the different routes early interpreters took to locate an agreed-upon constitutional standard. Sachs, "Originalism: Standard and Procedure," 823–24. But interpretive disagreement in the early republic was fueled largely by disagreement over the nature of the underlying standard. There was broad agreement that the Constitution was the ultimate object of interpretive authority, but most efforts to thicken that standard by fleshing out what it was and what it required provoked debate, illustrating how thin that broader agreement in fact was. See Gienapp, *The Second Creation*; Campbell, "General Citizenship Rights," 695–99.

88. For an argument that there were default rules for interpreting a text like the Constitution when it first appeared, see Prakash, "Unoriginalism's Law Without Meaning," 540–46; Paulsen, "Does the Constitution Prescribe Rules for Its Own Interpretation?," 860–61, 872–73, 883; Bellia and Clark, "The Constitutional Law of Interpretation," 521–36, 587–94.

89. In a significant concession, McGinnis and Rappaport have finally acknowledged that there was disagreement over interpretive rules at the Founding but by way of advancing a new claim: that original disagreement over interpretive rules would have been resolved by appealing to what they call "meta rules," themselves drawn from familiar common-law rules and methods. McGinnis and Rappaport, "Unifying Original Intent and Original Public Meaning," 1391–95; 1399–1401. At the Founding, however, common-law rules and methods were diverse, conflicting, and multivocal. See Meyler, "Common Law Confrontations"; Meyler, "Towards a Common Law Originalism," 567–80. Not to mention, as we have already seen, the common law's very applicability to the Constitution was a steady source of dispute.

90. Baude and Sachs, "The Law of Interpretation," 1140–42; McGinnis and Rappaport, "The Constitution and the Language of the Law," 1396–1400.

91. Gienapp, *The Second Creation*.
92. For a complete account of the bank debate, see Gienapp, *The Second Creation*, 202–47.
93. James Madison, Feb. 2, 1791, in *DHFFC*, 14:371.
94. James Madison, Feb. 2, 1791, in *DHFFC*, 14:371.
95. Fisher Ames, Feb. 3, 1791, in *DHFFC*, 14:393.
96. James Madison, Feb. 8, 1791, in *DHFFC*, 14:474.
97. Fisher Ames, Feb. 3, 1791, in *DHFFC*, 14:389.
98. Gienapp, *The Second Creation*, 238–45; Elkins and McKitrick, *The Age of Federalism*, 229–32; Andrew Shankman, *Original Intents: Hamilton, Jefferson, Madison, and the American Founding* (New York: Oxford University Press, 2017), 93–112.

Chapter 8. Were the Founders Originalists?

Epigraph: Quentin Skinner, "Meaning and Understanding in the History of Ideas," 28.
1. Christopher Wolfe, *The Rise of Modern Judicial Review: From Constitutional Interpretation to Judge-Made Law* (New York: Basic, 1986); Raoul Berger, *Federalism: The Founders' Design* (Norman: University of Oklahoma Press, 1987); Bork, *The Tempting of America*, 22–24.
2. Powell, "The Original Understanding of Original Intent."
3. McGinnis and Rappaport, "Original Methods Originalism," 788–802; Pojanowski and Walsh, "Enduring Originalism," 130–35; Wurman, *A Debt Against the Living*, 40–42; Paulsen, "The Irrepressible Myth of *Marbury*," 2725; Scalia and Garner, *Reading Law*, 80–81, 403–05; Strang, *Originalism's Promise*, 9–17.
4. Ilan Wurman, "Stare Decisis in an Originalist Theory of Law," *Law & Liberty*, Sept. 9, 2020, https://lawliberty.org/forum/stare-decisis-in-an-originalist-theory-of-law/.
5. In addition to the prior citations, see Michael Rappaport, "Chief Justice Marshall's Textualist Originalism," *Law & Liberty*, Mar,. 21, 2019, https://lawliberty.org/chief-justice-marshalls-textualist-originalism/; Michael Rappaport, "How Old Is Originalism?," *Law & Liberty*, Apr. 25, 2019, https://lawliberty.org/how-old-is-originalism/; John O. McGinnis, "Originalism Protects the Timelessness of the Constitution," *Law & Liberty*, Apr. 26, 2019, https://lawliberty.org/originalism-protects-the-timelessness-of-the-constitution/.
6. Greene, "On the Origins of Originalism," 8–18, 62–64; Gordon, *Taming the Past*, 361–65.
7. Balkin, *Memory and Authority*, 34–53, 62–65, 82–85, 151–59; Jack M. Balkin, "The New Originalism and the Uses of History," *Fordham Law Review* 82 (Nov. 2013): 672–707; Greene, "The Case for Original Intent," esp. 1696–1701; Michael C. Dorf, "Integrating Normative and Descriptive Constitutional Theory: The Case of Original Meaning," *Georgetown Law Journal* 85 (June 1997): 1800–05; Reva B. Siegel, "The Politics of Constitutional Memory," *Georgetown Journal of Law & Public Policy* 20 (Winter 2022): 19–58, esp. 21–30.
8. See Gillman, "The Collapse of Constitutional Originalism and the Rise of the Notion of the 'Living Constitution,' " 203–13; Hartog, "The Constitution of Aspiration

and 'The Rights That Belong to Us All,' " 1013–14; Aaron R. Hall, " 'Plant Your-selves on Its Primal Granite': Slavery, History and the Antebellum Roots of Origi-nalism," *Law and History Review* 37 (Aug. 2019): 743–62; Simon J. Gilhooley, *The Antebellum Origins of the Modern Constitution: Slavery and the Spirit of the American Founding* (New York: Cambridge University Press, 2020); James Oakes, *The Crooked Path to Abolition: Abraham Lincoln and the Antislavery Constitution* (New York: W. W. Norton, 2021), xii–xiii, xvi, xviii–xx, xxiii–xxiv, 1–9, 48–50, 87; David P. Currie, *The Constitution in Congress: The Jeffersonians, 1801–1829* (Chicago: Univer-sity of Chicago Press, 2001); David P. Currie, *The Constitution in Congress: Demo-crats and Whigs, 1829–1861* (Chicago: University of Chicago Press, 2005).

9. James Madison to Henry Lee, June 25, 1824, *The Papers of James Madison: Retire-ment Series*, 3:339.

10. James Madison, Feb. 2, 1791, in *DHFFC*, 14:369.

11. James Madison, Apr. 6, 1796, in *Annals of Congress*, 42 vols. (Washington, D.C.: Gales and Seaton, 1834), 5:776. For more, see Gienapp, *The Second Creation*, 232–34, 313–22, 327–32.

12. *Gibbons v. Ogden*, 22 U.S. (9 Wheat.) 1, 188 (1824).

13. Skinner, "Meaning and Understanding in the History of Ideas."

14. Skinner, "Meaning and Understanding in the History of Ideas," 22–24.

15. I am indebted to Noah Rosenblum for help in generating these arguments.

16. Skinner, "Meaning and Understanding in the History of Ideas," 7–16.

17. Skinner, "Meaning and Understanding in the History of Ideas," 24–25.

18. These problems have surfaced especially in originalist debates over the meaning of "executive power," as it has been assumed that when the Founding generation de-bated executive power they must have been doing so within our modern paradigm. This has obscured both the substance of their thinking as well as the process by which that earlier paradigm slowly turned into something resembling our own. See Jonathan Gienapp, "Removal and the Changing Debate over Executive Power at the Founding," *American Journal of Legal History* 63 (Sept. 2023): 229–50.

19. McGinnis and Rappaport, "Original Methods Originalism," 788. See also Scalia and Garner, *Reading Law*, 80–82, 403–05.

20. On how living constitutionalism emerged only much later during the Progressive Era, see Gillman, "The Collapse of Constitutional Originalism and the Rise of the Notion of the 'Living Constitution.' "

21. On the necessity of these intellectual ingredients to living constitutionalism, see Kammen, *A Machine That Would Go of Itself*, 17–19; Morton J. Horwitz, "The Con-stitution of Change: Legal Fundamentality Without Fundamentalism," *Harvard Law Review* 107 (Nov. 1993): 32–34, 41–44; Gilman, "The Collapse of Constitutional Originalism and the Rise of the Notion of the 'Living Constitution,' " 193–94.

22. Some have located the origins of living constitutionalism in the antebellum era. See John W. Compton, *The Evangelical Origins of the Living Constitution* (Cambridge, Mass.: Harvard University Press, 2014). But we should be careful conflating earlier forms of flexible interpretation to living constitutionalism.

23. Jefferson to Roane, Sept. 6, 1819, in *The Papers of Thomas Jefferson: Retirement Se-ries*, 15:17.

24. Gillman, "The Collapse of Constitutional Originalism and the Rise of the Notion of the 'Living Constitution,' " 193–94, 204–05. On how it obscures Marshall's actual interpretive commitments, see D. A. Jeremy Telman, "John Marshall's Constitution: Methodological Pluralism and Second-Order *Ipse Dixit* in Constitutional Adjudication," *Lewis & Clark Law Review* 24 (2020): 1151–1218. For the argument applied more generally to the early Supreme Court, see D. A. Jeremy Telman, "Originalism and Second-Order *Ipse Dixit* Reasoning in *Chisholm v. Georgia,*" *Cleveland State Law Review* 67 (2019): 559–98.

25. Balkin, *Memory and Authority*, 10, 67–70, 86–88.

26. Balkin, *Memory and Authority*, 69–70.

27. Gienapp, *The Second Creation*; LaCroix, *The Interbellum Constitution*; Cornell and Leonard, *The Partisan Republic*.

28. *Ogden v. Saunders*, 25 U.S. (12 Wheat.) 213, 332 (1827) (opinion of Marshall, J.).

29. *McCulloch v. Maryland*, 17 U.S. (4 Wheat.) 316, 419 (1819).

30. Jefferson to William Johnson, June 12, 1823, *Founders Online*, National Archives, https://founders.archives.gov/documents/Jefferson/98-01-02-3562.

31. Jefferson to Thomas Ritchie, Dec. 25, 1820, in *The Papers of Thomas Jefferson: Retirement Series*, 16:483.

32. Aaron Hall has argued that, following the Missouri Crisis, American constitutional argument came to fixate on the idea of restoring the Founding. Hall, " 'Plant Yourself on Its Primal Granite,' " 748–60. The argument will soon be presented in fuller form in Aaron Hall, *The Founding Rules: Slavery and the Creation of American Constitutionalism, 1789–1889* (manuscript in progress). See also Gilhooley, *The Antebellum Origins of the Modern Constitution*. On how antebellum Americans conceived of constitutionalism in terms of preservation, see Hartog, "The Constitution of Aspiration and 'The Rights That Belong to Us All,' " 1013–14. Gesturing in a different direction, Alison LaCroix argues that during this era American constitutional interpreters were eager to embrace their own creativity and saw themselves as elaborating upon, if not breaking with, their constitutional inheritance. LaCroix, *The Interbellum Constitution*.

33. Alexander Hamilton, "Opinion on the Constitutionality of an Act to Establish a Bank," in *The Papers of Alexander Hamilton*, ed. Harold C. Syrett and Jacob E. Cooke, 27 vols. (New York: Columbia University Press, 1961–1987), 8:105.

34. See chapter 5.

35. [Thomas Jefferson], "Resolutions Adopted by the Kentucky General Assembly," Nov. 10, 1798, in *The Papers of Thomas Jefferson*, 30:553, and generally 550–55.

36. James Madison to Spencer Roane, Sept. 2, 1819, in *The Papers of James Madison: Retirement Series*, 1:503.

37. James Madison to Henry Lee, June 25, 1824, in *The Papers of James Madison: Retirement Series*, 3:339.

38. *McCulloch*, 17 U.S. (4 Wheat.) at 403–04; *Gibbons*, 22 U.S. (9 Wheat.) at 187.

39. *McCulloch*, 17 U.S. (4 Wheat.) at 407. On what divided Marshall and his opponents, see David S. Schwartz, *The Spirit of the Constitution: John Marshall and the 200-Year Odyssey of McCulloch v. Maryland* (New York: Oxford University Press, 2019), 24–58.

40. *McCulloch*, 17 U.S. (4 Wheat.) at 407, 415.
41. *Gibbons*, 22 U.S. (9 Wheat.) at 188.
42. *Gibbons v. Ogden*, 22 U.S. (9 Wheat.) at 190. See also *Dartmouth College v. Woodward*, 17 U.S. (4 Wheat.) 518, 625, 644 (1819).
43. Story, *Commentaries on the Constitution of the United States*, 1:407.
44. Story, *Commentaries on the Constitution of the United States*, 1:394.
45. *McCulloch*, 17 U.S. (4 Wheat.) at 404–05.
46. For the most famous originalist defense of *Brown v. Board of Education*, see McConnell, "Originalism and the Desegregation Decisions." For one of the more striking instances when Roosevelt used Founding-era history to defend the New Deal, see Franklin D. Roosevelt, "Constitution Day Address," Sept. 17, 1937, Gerhard Peters and John T. Woolley, The American Presidency Project, https://www.presidency.ucsb.edu/documents/address-constitution-day-washington-dc.
47. Rakove, *Original Meanings*, 339–65; Joseph M. Lynch, *Negotiating the Constitution: The Earliest Debates over Original Intent* (Ithaca, N.Y.: Cornell University Press, 1999), 82–85, 150–59, 221–22; Cornell, *The Other Founders*, 221–45; Hall, "'Plant Yourself on Its Primal Granite.'"
48. Gienapp, *The Second Creation*, esp. 287–334.
49. This is among the arguments mounted in Gienapp, *The Second Creation*.

Chapter 9. Making, Not Finding, the Constitution

Epigraph: Wittgenstein, *Philosophical Investigations*, sec. 118.
1. See Prakash, "The Misunderstood Relationship Between Originalism and Popular Sovereignty"; Lawrence B. Solum, "*District of Columbia v. Heller* and Originalism," *Northwestern University Law Review* 103 (Spring 2009): 941–44; Barnett, "The Gravitational Force of Originalism," 415–18; Lawson, "On Reading Recipes . . . and Constitutions," 1823–25; Lawson, "Reflections of an Empirical Reader," 1472–73; Wurman, *A Debt Against the Living*, 4–6, 35–38, 133; Barnett and Solum, "Originalism After *Dobbs, Bruen*, and *Kennedy*," 479. Originalists surely move too fast in drawing this distinction. The Constitution is not merely a historical artifact but the nation's fundamental law. How it should be interpreted today is at least partly a function of what accounts for its legitimacy. See Michael C. Dorf, "Recipe for Trouble: Some Thoughts on Meaning, Translation and Normative Theory," *Georgetown Law Journal* 85 (June 1997): 1858–61.
2. For defenses of originalism grounded on popular sovereignty, see Whittington, *Constitutional Interpretation*, 110–59; Lash, "Originalism, Popular Sovereignty, and Reverse Stare Decisis," 1444–46; Michael W. McConnell, "Textualism and the Dead Hand of the Past," *George Washington Law Review* 66 (Jun./Aug. 1998): 1127–42. On an individual-liberty account of justice, see Barnett, *Restoring the Lost Constitution*, 32–115. On natural law, see Pojanowski and Walsh, "Enduring Originalism"; Strang, *Originalism's Promise*; Alicea, "The Moral Authority of Original Meaning." On supermajoritarian rule, see McGinnis and Rappaport, *Originalism and the Good Constitution*, 1–18, 33–99. On the rule of law, see Solum, "The Constraint Principle," 54–78.

And on judicial constraint, see Scalia, *A Matter of Interpretation*, 3–47. For a summary of the most popular views, which are described as "mutually consistent and reinforcing," see Barnett and Solum, "Originalism After *Dobbs, Bruen,* and *Kennedy*," 479–80. Many of these defenses ultimately invoke popular sovereignty, which remains perhaps the most popular justification of the theory. See Daniel A. Farber, "The Originalism Debate: A Guide to the Perplexed," *Ohio State Law Journal* 49 (1989): 1097–1100; Berman, "Originalism Is Bunk," 69–75; Colby, "Originalism and Ratification of the Fourteenth Amendment," 1631–38.

3. Lash, "Originalism All the Way Down?"; Whittington, *Constitutional Interpretation*, 49–50.

4. Solum, "Triangulating Public Meaning," 1629–38; Whittington, "Originalism," 378–86; Balkin, *Living Originalism*, 6–7, 12–13, 100–04; Greenberg and Litman, "The Meaning of Original Meaning," 586–97; Green, "Originalism and the Sense-Reference Distinction"; Barnett, "The Misconceived Assumption About Constitutional Assumptions."

5. Bernick and Green, "There Is Something That Our Constitution Just Is," 289.

6. See Solum, "Semantic Originalism," 28–30, 36–37, 51; Lawrence B. Solum, "The Interpretation-Construction Distinction," *Constitutional Commentary* 27 (Fall 2010): 99–100; Solum, "Originalism and Constitutional Construction," 472, 479, 493; Solum, "The Fixation Thesis," 12; Solum, "Originalist Methodology," 278; Barnett, *Restoring the Lost Constitution*, 389–95; Barnett, "The Gravitational Force of Originalism," 415–17; Kesavan and Paulsen, "The Interpretive Force of the Constitution's Secret Drafting History," 1127–33; Paulsen, "Does the Constitution Prescribe Rules for Its Own Interpretation?," 873–75; Prakash, "The Misunderstood Relationship Between Originalism and Popular Sovereignty"; Lawson, "On Reading Recipes . . . and Constitutions"; Lawson, "Reflections of an Empirical Reader"; Wurman, *A Debt Against the Living*, 4–6, 35–38, 133; Barnett and Bernick, *The Original Meaning of the Fourteenth Amendment*, 5–6.

7. Barnett, *Restoring the Lost Constitution*, 393.

8. See Gary Lawson, "Proving the Law," *Northwestern University Law Review* 86 (1992): 875; Scalia, *A Matter of Interpretation*, 17, 38; Kesavan and Paulsen, "The Interpretive Force of the Constitution's Secret Drafting History," 1134–48; Barnett, *Restoring the Lost Constitution*, 94–95, 389–93; Solum, "*District of Columbia v. Heller* and Originalism," 934–37.

9. For a standard originalist picture of constitutional communication, see Solum, "The Public Meaning Thesis," 1967–2001.

10. On communicative content, see Solum, "Communicative Content and Legal Content," 484–507; Barnett, "The Misconceived Assumption About Constitutional Assumptions," 622–26.

11. Scalia, *A Matter of Interpretation*, 3–47; Solum, "Constitutional Texting"; Kesavan and Paulsen, "The Interpretive Force of the Constitution's Secret Drafting History," 1127–33; Wurman, *A Debt Against the Living*, 129–33.

12. Solum, "Communicative Content and Legal Content," 484–507; Solum, "The Public Meaning Thesis," 1967–2001; Green, "Originalism and the Sense-Reference Distinction"; Barnett, "The Misconceived Assumption About Constitutional

Assumptions," 619–22; Lawson, "Reflections of an Empirical Reader," 1457–79; Bernick and Green, "There Is Something That Our Constitution Just Is."

13. See Solum, "Originalist Methodology," 286–93; Solum, "Intellectual History as Constitutional Theory," 1125–39; Green, "Originalism and the Sense-Reference Distinction"; Bernick and Green, "There Is Something That Our Constitution Just Is," 289–91.

14. *McCulloch v. Maryland*, 17 U.S. (4 Wheat.) 316, 407.

15. Gienapp, "Historicism and Holism," 945–51; Ian Bartrum, "Two Dogmas of Originalism," *Washington University Jurisprudence Review* 7 (2015): 157–94; Brandom, "A Hegelian Model of Legal Concept Determination." For more on alternative approaches in the philosophy of language, see generally Brandom, *Perspectives on Pragmatism.* On why they're better suited for understanding the specific problems posed by U.S. constitutionalism, see chapter 3, notes 24 and 81.

16. Barnett, "The Misconceived Assumption About Constitutional Assumptions," 659.

17. Solum, "Intellectual History as Constitutional Theory," 1115–16.

18. A theory of language isn't a substitute for a theory of constitutionalism unless we blur the distinction between these two kinds of theories by following Donald Davidson in "eras[ing] the boundary between knowing a language and knowing our way around in the world generally." That would call for a holistic approach to Founding-era written constitutionalism, which would encourage us to see the interconnected conceptual world in which American constitution making originally took shape. That, in essence, would amount to the same thing as saying that constitutionalism cannot be reduced to linguistic analysis, for it would necessitate confronting Founding-era attitudes toward constitutionalism head on, rather than putting them to the side, as originalists who fetishize language are wont to do. Donald Davidson, "A Nice Derangement of Epitaphs," in *Truth, Language, and History,* 107.

19. While this objection undermines the most popular versions of originalism, it reinforces what original law originalists have begun arguing. See Baude and Sachs, "The Law of Interpretation," 1082–1120; Sachs, "Originalism Without Text," 161–62, 166–67. More on their theory in chapter 10.

20. Solum, "The Public Meaning Thesis," 1969, see also 1960–64.

21. Solum, "The Public Meaning Thesis," 2042; Bernick and Green, "There Is Something That Our Constitution Just Is," 277–80, 289–90.

22. For related discussions, see Campbell, "Determining Rights"; Campbell "General Citizenship Rights," 695–99. On how understandings of the nature of law were entwined with understandings of the content of law, see Lessig, *Fidelity and Constraint,* 228–32; Lawrence Lessig, "The Brilliance in *Slaughterhouse*: A Judicially Restrained and Original Understanding of 'Privileges or Immunities,'" *University of Pennsylvania Journal of Constitutional Law* 26 (Dec. 2023): 14–17, 35–42.

23. Oliver Ellsworth, Aug. 22, 1787, in Farrand, *The Records of the Federal Convention,* 2:376.

24. See, e.g., Barnett and Solum, "Originalism After *Dobbs, Bruen,* and *Kennedy,*" 479–80; Whittington, *Constitutional Interpretation,* 110–59; Solum, "The Constraint Principle," 66–72.

25. Solum, "The Public Meaning Thesis," 2042; Green, "Constitutional Truthmakers," 12–15.

26. But see William P. Deringer, *Calculated Values: Finance, Politics, and the Quantitative Age* (Cambridge, Mass.: Harvard University Press, 2018), which, in historicizing quantitative reasoning, illustrates the social and political practices that often undergird even the most prosaic of factual observations.

27. Bernick and Green, "There Is Something That Our Constitution Just Is"; Solum, "The Public Meaning Thesis," 2042.

28. Of course, though, as pioneering work in the philosophy of science, mind, and language has long suggested, there are profound reasons to doubt that this is even true of so-called natural objects. See Kuhn, *The Structure of Scientific Revolutions*; Wilfrid Sellars, *Empiricism and the Philosophy of Mind* (1956; Cambridge, Mass.: Harvard University Press, 1997); Quine, "Two Dogmas of Empiricism"; Richard Rorty, *Philosophy and the Mirror of Nature* (1979; Princeton, N.J.: Princeton University Press, 2009).

29. On the irreducible relationship between intersubjective practices and public objects, which applies especially well to constitutionalism, see Brandom, *Making It Explicit*; Davidson, *Truth, Language, and History*, 89–141; Rorty, *Philosophical Papers*, vol. 4, *Philosophy as Cultural Politics*, 14–24, 156–59, 176–83; Brandom, *Perspectives on Pragmatism*, 26–32, 67–70.

30. Campbell, "Originalism and the Nature of Rights."

31. Campbell, "Originalism and the Nature of Rights."

32. *New York State Rifle & Pistol Association v. Bruen*, 142 S. Ct. 2111 (2022); Campbell, "Originalism and the Nature of Rights."

33. See chapter 3.

34. Campbell, "Originalism and the Nature of Rights."

35. Gienapp, "The Foreign Founding," 118–26; Kramer, *The People Themselves*.

36. Campbell, "Originalism and the Nature of Rights."

37. Darrell A. H. Miller and Joseph Blocher, "Manufacturing Outliers," *Supreme Court Review* 2022 (2023): 49–79.

38. *New York State Rifle & Pistol Association*, 142 S. Ct. 2111 (2022).

39. Especially see Laura Edwards and Mandy Cooper, "The Sounds of Silence: An Examination of Local Legal Records Reveals Robust Historical Regulation of the Public Peace," *Duke Center for Firearms Law Second Thoughts Blog*, Aug. 18, 2023, https://firearmslaw.duke.edu/2023/08/the-sounds-of-silence-an-examination-of-local-legal-records-reveals-robust-historical-regulation-of-the-public-peace/; Laura Edwards, " 'The Peace,' Domestic Violence, and Firearms in the New Republic," *Fordham Urban Law Journal* 51 (2023): 1–24. For a valuable meditation on how precedential legal thinking often prefigures and distorts the very historical archive it appeals to for authority, see Paul D. Halliday, "Authority in the Archives," *Critical Analysis of Law* 1 (2014): 110–42.

40. Campbell, "Originalism and the Nature of Rights."

41. Randy E. Barnett, "The Original Meaning of the Commerce Clause," *University of Chicago Law Review* 68 (Winter 2021): 101–48; Randy E. Barnett, "New Evidence of the Original Meaning of the Commerce Clause," *Arkansas Law Review* 55 (2003):

847–900; Steven G. Calabresi, " 'A Government of Limited and Enumerated Powers': In Defense of *United States v. Lopez*," *Michigan Law Review* 94 (Dec. 1996), 752–831; Richard A. Epstein, "The Proper Scope of the Commerce Power," *Virginia Law Review* 73 (Nov. 1987): 1388–99.

42. Barnett, "The Original Meaning of the Commerce Clause"; Barnett, "New Evidence of the Original Meaning of the Commerce Clause."

43. *United States v. Lopez*, 514 U.S. 549 (1995); *National Federation of Independent Business v. Sebelius*, 567 U.S. 519 (2012).

44. See chapter 5.

45. LaCroix, *The Interbellum Constitution*.

46. See chapter 5; Campbell, "Four Views of the Nature of the Union"; Campbell, "General Citizenship Rights," 695–99.

47. I draw inspiration here from the philosopher of mind Wilfrid Sellars, who famously targeted the "Myth of the Given" in philosophical empiricism. How leading originalists are guilty of a distinct, if comparable, myth, see Gienapp, "The Myth of the Constitutional Given," 183–89, 211.

48. Tara Smith, "Why Originalism Won't Die—Common Mistakes in Competing Theories of Constitutional Interpretation," *Duke Journal of Constitutional Law & Public Policy* 2 (2007): 161.

49. Scalia and Garner, *Reading Law*, 89.

50. Whittington, *Constitutional Interpretation*, 15.

51. Barnett and Solum, "Originalism After *Dobbs*, *Bruen*, and *Kennedy*," 492.

Chapter 10. Imposing the Modern on the Past

Epigraph: Rorty, "The Historiography of Philosophy," 52–53.

1. H. L. A. Hart, *The Concept of Law*, 3rd ed. (1961; New York: Oxford University Press, 2012).

2. This distinction is spelled out in William Baude and Stephen E. Sachs, "The 'Common-Good' Manifesto," *Harvard Law Review* 136 (Jan. 2023): 884.

3. William Baude, "Is Originalism Our Law?," *Columbia Law Review* 115 (Dec. 2015): 2349–2408; Sachs, "Originalism as a Theory of Legal Change," 818–19, 835–39, 844–58, 864–68; Baude and Sachs, "Grounding Originalism," 1457–58, 1491.

4. Baude and Sachs, "Originalism and the Law of the Past," 817.

5. Baude and Sachs, "Originalism and the Law of the Past," 809–11.

6. Others appreciate the advantages of this move while offering their own modifications. Jeffrey Pojanowski and Kevin Walsh argue that the positive turn points in the proper direction but that it ought to rest on a conceptual and normative account derived from classical natural law. See Pojanowski and Walsh, "Enduring Originalism."

7. For criticisms of their positivist account, see Charles L. Barzun, "The Positive U-Turn," *Stanford Law Review* 69 (May 2017): 1323–88; Richard Primus, "Is Theocracy Our Politics?," *Columbia Law Review Online* 116 (May 2016): 44–60; Berman, "Our Principled Constitution," 1354n104; Mark Greenberg, "What Makes a Method

of Legal Interpretation Correct? Legal Standards vs. Fundamental Determinants," *Harvard Law Review Forum* 130 (Feb. 2017): 105–26.

8. This returns us to the liquidation debate. Baude's notion of liquidation seems to accept the possibility that significant and potentially sweeping constitutional change can be derived from the Founders' law. Baude, "Constitutional Liquidation." On why this kind of emphasis on post-ratification practice undermines originalism, see Bradley and Siegel, "Historical Gloss, Madisonian Liquidation, and the Originalism Debate." This need not be considered a flaw, however, but merely an acknowledgment that originalism serves radically different purposes than previously assumed. That is assuredly the upshot of Jack Balkin's influential work. See Balkin, *Living Originalism.*

9. Quine, "Two Dogmas of Empiricism," 45–46.

10. They have addressed this issue by insisting that their originalism "is catholic in theory but exacting in application. It might look tame, but it has bite." William Baude and Stephen E. Sachs, "Originalism's Bite," *Green Bag* 20 (2016): 103–08 (quote at 104). By which they seem to mean that an implicit commitment to a kind of originalism—a tacit acceptance that there have been no constitutional revolutions since the Founding and the Founders' law remains our law today—creates *criteria* for falsifying some of the interpretations that violate the Founders' law (and upon which the authority of the Founders' law is positively based). But that merely redirects argument. The point of the positive turn has been to ground originalism in social practice, but if most people who sanction originalism through social practice actually just turn out to be bad originalists, then we are back where we started. The point of emphasizing the ubiquity of originalist-sounding argument is to convince people who don't think they are originalists that they in fact are. But once they have been shown that originalism is our law because *their own practices* legitimize that criterion, they are asked to believe that the criterion they were initially skeptical of in fact nullifies their own understanding of the valid application of law. Surely at that point they would be convinced of what they initially thought: that originalism is not our law. Shifting focus from substantive disagreement to rhetorical agreement is not, ultimately, going to resolve substantive disagreement. On how the shared topics of constitutional culture are consistent with a variety of constitutional theories, see Jack M. Balkin, "Arguing About the Constitution: The Topics in Constitutional Interpretation," *Constitutional Commentary* 33 (Summer 2018): 244–60.

11. Sachs, "Originalism as a Theory of Legal Change," 875, 882–83; Baude and Sachs, "The Law of Interpretation," 1131, 1135. Though, in certain ways, they do explicitly differentiate the two approaches, see 1134–36. McGinnis and Rappaport acknowledge this disagreement. See McGinnis and Rappaport, "The Constitution and the Language of the Law," 1353–55.

12. Sachs, "Originalism as a Theory of Legal Change," 883–85; Baude and Sachs, "The Law of Interpretation," 1140–42.

13. Baude and Sachs, "The 'Common-Good' Manifesto," 884.

14. Baude and Sachs, "The Law of Interpretation," 1088–92; Baude and Sachs, "The 'Common-Good' Manifesto," 884, 887–88.

15. Sachs, "Originalism Without Text."
16. Baude and Sachs, "The Law of Interpretation," 1097–99; Stephen E. Sachs, "Finding Law," *California Law Review* 107 (Apr. 2019): 578.
17. For their account of the positive-posited distinction, see Baude and Sachs, "The 'Common-Good' Manifesto," 884–85.
18. Sachs, "Finding Law," 530–31.
19. Baude and Sachs, "The Law of Interpretation," 1097–20; Stephen E. Sachs, "Constitutional Backdrops," *George Washington Law Review* 80 (Nov. 2012): 1813–88; Sachs, "The 'Unwritten Constitution' and Unwritten Law," 1800–01, 1803–05; Baude and Sachs, "The 'Common-Good' Manifesto," 887–89.
20. Sachs, "Originalism as a Theory of Legal Change," 855–58; Baude and Sachs, "The Law of Interpretation," 1133–38; Baude and Sachs, "Grounding Originalism," 1458, 1483, 1491; Baude, "Constitutional Liquidation."
21. Baude and Sachs, "The Law of Interpretation," 1083, 1104–20; Sachs, "Constitutional Backdrops."
22. McGinnis and Rappaport, "Unifying Original Intent and Original Public Meaning," 1399–1401.
23. This is among the fundamental reasons original law originalism is so different from original methods originalism. Aspects of this disagreement are touched on in Baude and Sachs, "The Law of Interpretation," 1134–40; McGinnis and Rappaport, "The Constitution and the Language of the Law," 1353–55; McGinnis and Rappaport, "Unifying Original Intent and Original Public Meaning," 1396n78.
24. Baude and Sachs, "The Law of Interpretation," 1118–20; Sachs, "Constitutional Backdrops"; Sachs, "The 'Unwritten Constitution' and Unwritten Law," 1800–01, 1803–05.
25. Baude and Sachs, "The Law of Interpretation," 1137–38; William Baude and Stephen E. Sachs, "The Misunderstood Eleventh Amendment," *University of Pennsylvania Law Review* 169 (Feb. 2021): 613–17; Baude and Sachs, "The 'Common-Good' Manifesto," 883–87; Sachs, "Constitutional Backdrops," 1819–38, 1868–75; Sachs, "Originalism as a Theory of Legal Change," 873–74, 878–79; Sachs, "Finding Law," 878–81; William Baude, "Sovereign Immunity and the Constitutional Text," *Virginia Law Review* 103 (Mar. 2017): 4–12. Here, the differences between Baude and Sachs's approach to customary law and the approach of most other originalists become especially clear. In discussing the common law and its relationship to the Constitution, most (though not all) originalists presuppose a decidedly modern understanding of it unknown at the Founding (or before the twentieth century) that primarily equates the common law with judge-made law. For examples of this error, see Scalia, *A Matter of Interpretation*, 3–47; McGinnis and Rappaport, "Unifying Original Intent and Original Public Meaning," 1396n78. By contrast, Baude and Sachs recognize that in an earlier era, the common law was more akin to preexisting unwritten law. See Baude and Sachs, "The 'Common-Good' Manifesto," 889–90, esp. n146. For an illuminating discussion of these issues—what differentiates the modern view of law from the view of law that predominated from the Founding through the nineteenth century, as well as originalists' peculiar unwillingness to embrace the latter or justify their departure from it—see Lessig, *Fidelity and Constraint*, 223–32, esp. 228–32.

26. Sachs, "Finding Law"; *Southern Pacific Co. v. Jensen*, 244 U.S. 205, 222 (1917) (Holmes, J., dissenting).

27. For their part, Baude and Sachs have acknowledged, however modestly, the differences between themselves and other originalists. "To be sure, there are familiar versions of originalism that do focus exclusively on text and that have a harder time addressing customary law." "To be sure, some originalists have made the mistake [of not leaving room for general background principles]." Baude and Sachs, "The 'Common-Good' Manifesto," 886, 884. See also Sachs, "Originalism Without Text." The differences are far sharper than even Baude and Sachs are yet willing to admit. They claim that "many" originalists appeal to "general background principles" and "use these background principles just as well as anybody else." Baude and Sachs, "The 'Common-Good' Manifesto," 884. But appealing to background principles of the common law because the Constitution's text seems to instruct one to do so is markedly different than appealing to those principles because the Constitution, as a legal matter, left general law in place.

28. For their avowed legalism, see Baude and Sachs, "The Law of Interpretation," 1118–20, 1140–42.

29. On the diverse voices that shaped early constitutionalism, see Ablavsky and Allread, "We the (Native) People?"; Bilder, "Without Doors"; Peterson, "Constitutionalism in Unexpected Places"; Twitty, *Before* Dred Scott; Masur, *Until Justice Be Done*.

30. *Chisholm v. Georgia*, 2 U.S. (2 Dall.) 419, 453–66, 469–79 (1793) (opinions of Wilson, J., and Jay, J.). The case exposed deep internal legal disagreement as the issue of state suability raised larger questions about American sovereignty.

31. Baude and Sachs, "Originalism and the Law of the Past," 814–15. On Baude and Sachs's narrow approach to history, see Balkin, *Memory and Authority*, 245–53.

32. Baude and Sachs, "Originalism and the Law of the Past," 814–15.

33. For more, see the exchange between Rick Hills and Baude and Sachs: Rick Hills, "What Makes History Constitutionally Relevant? Some Reservations About Baude and Sachs' View of the Past," *PrawfsBlawg*, July 20, 2019, https://prawfsblawg. blogs.com/prawfsblawg/2019/07/what-makes-history-constitutionally-relevant-some-reservations-about-baude-and-sachs-view-of-the-pas.html. See also Christian R. Burset, "The Messy History of the Federal Eminent Domain Power: A Response to William Baude," *California Law Review Circuit* 4 (Dec. 2013): 187–208.

34. Sachs, "Originalism as a Theory of Legal Change," 855–58; Baude and Sachs, "The Law of Interpretation," 1133–38; Baude and Sachs, "Grounding Originalism," 1458, 1483, 1491; Baude, "Constitutional Liquidation."

35. The growth of legal positivism and the turn away from the "brooding omnipresence" view of law across the nineteenth century was intricate, brought about by writings and debates in Britain, the European continent, and the United States, and driven by intellectual exchange across many nations. It also owed a great deal to cultural developments and political movements, not to mention the necessity, felt in all modern legal systems, of organizing the law and making it more precise.

36. Thomas Kuhn famously argued that science developed not by linear progress but through conceptual revolutions in which one scientific paradigm was supplanted by

another whose terms were largely incompatible with its predecessor. Kuhn, *The Structure of Scientific Revolutions*.

37. Lessig, *Fidelity and Constraint*, 228.

38. Campbell, "The Emergence of Neutrality," 873–74, 892–96, 923.

39. Campbell, "The Emergence of Neutrality," 923–43.

40. Baude and Sachs, "The Law of Interpretation"; Baude and Sachs, "Originalism and the Law of the Past." On how different earlier general law reasoning was from legal thinking today—how lawyers back then "lived in a different conceptual universe"—and how Baude and Sachs fail to appreciate the depth of this difference, see Lessig, "The Brilliance in *Slaughterhouse*," 14–17, 35–42 (quote at 36).

41. Jack M. Balkin, "The Construction of Original Public Meaning," *Constitutional Commentary* 31 (Spring 2016): 78–92; Jack Balkin, "The Second Creation and Originalist Theory," *Balkinization* (blog), Oct. 15, 2018, https://balkin.blogspot.com/2018/10/the-second-creation-and-originalist.html.

42. Sachs, "Constitutional Backdrops"; Baude and Sachs, "The Law of Interpretation."

43. For hints of these commitments, see Baude and Sachs, "Grounding Originalism," 1482–83; Baude and Sachs, "The Law of Interpretation," 1136–40; Sachs, "Originalism Without Text"; Sachs, "Constitutional Backdrops."

44. On how the "official story" of American constitutional law presumes legal continuity between the Founding and today, see Sachs, "Originalism as a Theory of Legal Change," 869–71; William Baude and Stephen E. Sachs, "The Official Story of the Law," *Oxford Journal of Legal Studies* 43 (Spring 2023): 178–201.

45. Baude and Sachs, "Grounding Originalism," 1457–58; Baude and Sachs, "Originalism and the Law of the Past," 810.

46. See also Alfred H. Kelly, "Clio and the Court: An Illicit Love Affair," *Supreme Court Review* 1965 (1965): 156–57.

47. These ways of engaging the Founding again strongly parallel Quentin Skinner's mythologies in the history of ideas. Skinner, "Meaning and Understanding in the History of Ideas," 24.

48. See Baude and Sachs, "Originalism and the Law of the Past," 811 (calling this activity perhaps "anachronistic"), 814 (conceding that "law often handles historical evidence in an artificially limited way"), 820 (acknowledging that lawyers operate by way of "necessary fictions" in ways that historians do not).

49. Jack Balkin—the only self-identified originalist who seems to embrace the character of this activity—calls it a "theoretical reconstruction" of the past from the perspective of legal theory, in which those theories "filter, shape, and configure the history" that is ultimately deployed in modern legal argument. Balkin, "The Construction of Original Public Meaning," 78, 89.

50. Baude and Sachs, "Grounding Originalism," 1475. On how these cultural and legal practices tend to work and often reinforce one another, see Balkin, "The New Originalism and the Uses of History," 672–717.

51. On the difference between historicizing the original Constitution and privileging continuous links with the Founders, see Primus, "Is Theocracy Our Politics?," 58–60.

52. On the importance of this substitution, see Skinner, "Meaning and Understanding in the History of Ideas," 7–16, 24–25; Gordon S. Wood, "The Fundamentalists and the Constitution," *New York Review of Books* 35 (1988): 33–40. On how modern legal scholars often impose their terms on an unsuspecting past, see Powell, "Rules for Originalists"; Flaherty, "History 'Lite' in Modern American Constitutionalism," 561–67, 575–79; Kramer, "When Lawyers Do History," 394–401.

53. Rorty, "The Historiography of Philosophy," 49–56.

54. Morton J. Horwitz, "The Conservative Tradition in the Writing of American Legal History," *American Journal of Legal History* 17 (July 1973): 275–76; William E. Nelson and John Phillip Reid, *The Literature of American Legal History* (Dobbs Ferry, N.Y.: Oceana Publications, 1985), 235–37; Laura Kalman, "Border Patrol: Reflections on the Turn to History in Legal Scholarship," *Fordham Law Review* 66 (Oct. 1997): 114–15; Balkin, *Memory and Authority*, 4–6, 17–26, 238–68.

55. What Rorty wrote about the study of philosophy could just as easily be said about the activity of enlisting the Founders as participants in our constitutional debates: "Such enterprises in commensuration are, of course, anachronistic. But if they are conducted in full knowledge of their anachronism, they are unobjectionable." Rorty, "The Historiography of Philosophy," 53.

56. Kalman, "Border Patrol," 95–109. See also Laura Kalman, *The Strange Career of Legal Liberalism* (New Haven, Conn.: Yale University Press, 1996).

57. Baude and Sachs, "Grounding Originalism," 1477–78; Baude, "Is Originalism Our Law?," 2363–91; Sachs, "Originalism as a Theory of Legal Change," 837–38, 864–71.

58. Powell, *A Community Built on Words*, 7.

59. Baude and Sachs, "Originalism and the Law of the Past."

60. See chapter 3.

61. Campbell, "Determining Rights," 58 (emphasis in original).

62. This point is stressed in various ways in Balkin, *Memory and Authority*, 90–93, 121–22, 170–72, 241–42; Siegel, "Memory Games," 1130–36, 1169–76, 1180–93; Reva B. Siegel, "Dead or Alive: Originalism as Popular Constitutionalism in *Heller*," *Harvard Law Review* 122 (Nov. 2008): 191–245, esp. 191–201, 236–45.

63. Balkin, *Living Originalism*.

64. Balkin, "The Construction of Original Public Meaning," 78, 89. As Balkin adds: "All legal theories reconfigure history to theory in varying degrees. All legal theories beat the past into shape. . . . Theories of original public meaning," therefore, "construct the past so that it can serve the needs and values of the present." Ultimately, however, "there is nothing wrong with this," he notes, "as long as . . . people are candid about the nature of the enterprise." Balkin, *Memory and Authority*, 242. Undoubtedly, few originalists would be willing to concede that they are artificially distorting the historical past.

65. Lessig, *Fidelity and Constraint*, 63–64.

66. Lessig, *Fidelity and Constraint*, 57.

67. Lessig, *Fidelity and Constraint*, 445.

68. Lessig, *Fidelity and Constraint*, esp. 49–69. Lessig is not tracking the interpretation-construction distinction embraced by leading originalists. His account of

interpretation as translation diverges from theirs, partly because it defines interpretation as far more than the activity of decoding original textual meaning, but
also because it doesn't pivot on textual ambiguity, vagueness, or indeterminacy, but
rather on converting original meaning (indeterminate or not) into a new kind of
meaning fit for a new context when constitutional fidelity demands that. His aim
is preserving meaning by fitting it into new contexts, not fleshing out provisions
that happened to be indeterminate when first written. Lessig thus bridges past to
present in a much different way.

69. For additional reflections on the costs of this concession, see Cary C. Franklin,
    "The Construction of an Originalist Constitution," *Jotwell*, Dec. 20, 2021, https://
    conlaw.jotwell.com/the-construction-of-an-originalist-constitution/.

70. Barnett, "The Misconceived Assumption About Constitutional Assumptions,"
    660.

71. *District of Columbia v. Heller*, 554 U.S. 570 (2008).

Conclusion

Epigraph: John Adams to Benjamin Rush, Sept. 8, 1808, *Founders Online*, National
Archives, https://founders.archives.gov/documents/Adams/99-02-02-5252.

1. For a comparable version of this argument, see Skinner, "Meaning and Understanding in the History of Ideas," 52–53.

2. Balkin, *Living Originalism*, 6–7, 14–16.

3. For a fuller elaboration of this insightful understanding of U.S. constitutionalism,
   see Lessig, *Fidelity and Constraint*.

4. Gienapp, *The Second Creation*.

5. Rorty, *Philosophical Papers*, vol. 4, *Philosophy as Cultural Politics*; John Dewey, *The
   Public and Its Problems* (New York: Holt, 1927); Louis Menand, *The Metaphysical
   Club: A Story of Ideas in America* (New York: Farrar, Straus and Giroux, 2001), esp.
   440–442; James T. Kloppenberg, *Toward Democracy: The Struggle for Self-Rule in
   European and American Thought* (New York: Oxford University Press, 2016), 1–18.

ACKNOWLEDGMENTS

This book benefited from the help and support of a great many people, and it is a pleasure to acknowledge their assistance and offer them my sincere thanks. As a historian who chose to write on a topic that falls at the intersection of law and history, I spent considerable time—sometimes bewildering, but always edifying—outside my home discipline. In the process, I have been warmly embraced by true intellectual companions from other corners of the academy who have helped broaden my intellectual horizons and have allowed me to better appreciate what historical thinking has to offer.

Yale University Press has proved an ideal home for this book. That is largely thanks to Bill Frucht, a patient and supportive editor who has been invested in what I was trying to accomplish from the beginning. Thanks to the rest of the editorial team at the press, especially Amanda Gerstenfeld, who diligently shepherded the manuscript through the publication process. Special thanks to Karen Schoen for exceptionally careful and helpful copyediting. When the book was in its incipient stages, Emily Silk took the time to helpfully discuss it, and proposed the eventual title.

Portions of the book draw from a previously published article: "Written Constitutionalism, Past and Present," *Law and History Review* 39 (Summer 2021): 321–60. Thanks to the journal and Cambridge University Press for allowing me to publish a revised version of those arguments here. Thanks especially to the journal's editor, Gautham Rao, for his confidence in my work, and his patience, as I prepared what turned out to be an early preview of this book.

This book was shaped by my experiences teaching my seminar "Originalism and the American Constitution: History and Interpretation" and the amazingly talented students who have taken it, primarily at Stanford University, over the past several years. Their enthusiasm for the subject and the issues it raised was matched only by the depth of their engagement.

During the Covid-19 pandemic, I had the good fortune of being invited to join what became weekly Zoom discussions on constitutional history, theory, and interpretation with Jack Balkin, Sandy Levinson, Mark Graber, Steve Griffin, and a rotating cast of scholars. It proved a steady source of intellectual sustenance, camaraderie, and friendship. It also proved decisive in producing this book. I originally set out to write something shorter, and after the manuscript ballooned in length because I had far more to say than I realized, it was Jack who enthusiastically told me that I should embrace the fact that I had written a book. After taking his advice, I shared the first draft with my Zoom compatriots and was treated to probing feedback and indispensable encouragement. Over the ensuing months and years, my project continued to be a source of conversation during our weekly meetings, prompting subsequent discussions that did every bit as much to shape the final result. During the process, Jack again proved tremendously helpful in connecting me with my eventual editor and publisher.

I benefited enormously from a manuscript workshop funded by the Salvatori Center for Individual Freedom at Claremont-McKenna College and hosted by the Kinder Institute on Constitutional Democracy at the University of Missouri in the spring of 2022. My deepest thanks to George Thomas, the director of the Salvatori Center, for proposing and then executing the idea, and Justin Dyer, then the director of the Kinder Institute, for agreeing to host the workshop. George and Justin joined the terrific group of participants they helped bring together to discuss my book: Tom Colby, Ken Kersch, Julian Mortenson, Saul Cornell, Haley Proctor, Tommy Bennett, Alan Gibson, Jeff Pasley, and Anne Twitty. Collectively, they provided incisive commentary, valuable criticism, helpful feedback, and genuine encouragement that have made it a much better book.

I was also afforded the opportunity to preview some of the ideas in this book at the University of Chicago, Georgetown University Law Center, Northwestern Law School, Penn State, Yale Law School, and the annual meeting of the American Society for Legal History.

As this book entered production, it was featured as part of the Law and Interpretation Section panel at the Association of American Law Schools annual meeting. My deepest thanks to Jim Fleming and John Kang, the section co-chairs, for extending this invitation, and to Jack Balkin for suggesting the idea to them. Charles Barzun, Jud Campbell, and Alison LaCroix, extraordinary scholars all, were invited to comment, and each offered penetrating reflections on what I had written.

In addition to those already thanked, a number of friends and colleagues read portions or full drafts of the book and provided helpful feedback: Greg Ablavsky, Nora Barakat, Mary Bilder, Lindsay Chervinsky, Liz Covart, Rowan Dorin, Todd Estes, Bill Ewald, John Mikhail, Kathryn Olivarius, Steven Press, Jack Rakove, Arjun Ramamurti, Rachel Shelden, Partha Shill, Emily Sneff, and Calvin TerBeek. For the press, I received generous and helpful reader's reports from Eric Segall, Saul Cornell, Mark Graber, and one anonymous referee. Still other scholars provided valuable engagement, feedback, and confidence boosters along the way: Keith Baker, Jim Banner, Randy Barnett, Dennis Baron, Will Baude, Mitch Berman, Holly Brewer, Zach Brown, Christian Burset, Austin Clements, David Como, Jennifer Depew, John Donohue, Dan Edelstein, Laura Edwards, Martin Flaherty, Cary Franklin, Bob Gordon, Aaron Hall, Ben Halom, Dirk Hartog, Jim Hrdlicka, Henry Ishitani, Pam Karlan, Andrea Katz, Andrew Kent, Amalia Kessler, Jim Kloppenberg, Andy Koppelman, Larry Kramer, Adam Lebovitz, Larry Lessig, Jane Manners, Kate Masur, Michael McConnell, Alison McQueen, Bernie Meyler, Darrell Miller, Johann Neem, Ryan Nees, Eric Nelson, Nicholas Parrillo, Jim Pfander, Robert Post, Richard Primus, David Rabban, Dan Rodgers, Noah Rosenblum, David Schwartz, Andy Shankman, Jed Shugerman, Asheesh Siddique, Reva Siegel, Quentin Skinner, David Sklansky, Aaron Spikol, Austin Steelman, Matthew Steilen, Rebecca Talbott, Amanda Tyler, Derek Webb, Morgan Weiland, Keith Whittington, John Witt, Tom Wolf, Gordon Wood, and Rosie Zagarri. My colleagues in the Stanford History Department, at Stanford Law School, and across the university were also a steady source of support. Thanks to Austin Clements for help checking citations. And thanks to Elizabeth Hoff for help making the index.

A handful of interlocutors deserve special mention. A few years ago, recognizing our deep intellectual affinities, Charles Barzun and I began regularly sharing and discussing work, and through those enriching exchanges, he did as much as anyone to stimulate and clarify my thinking as well as improve the book's largest interventions. The same goes for Jud Campbell, now happily a colleague here at Stanford, who read multiple drafts of the book, spoke with me at length about each of its historical and theoretical arguments, and helped improve the final product beyond measure. Anyone who reads the book carefully will note the enormous intellectual debt I owe to his work. I owe a similar debt for the assistance he offered as a reader, editor, and above all, interlocutor. John Mikhail and I have been exchanging ideas and interpretations on Founding-era history and originalism for years now, and I've come to value his friendship as much as his vast knowledge and penetrating observations. Bill Ewald possesses masterful knowledge of Founding-era constitutional history, philosophy, and legal theory, and generously offered me the gift of his wisdom across each. Saul Cornell, a veteran of originalist battle, has made me the lucky beneficiary of his expertise and, more importantly, legendary sense of humor. Jack Rakove and I have shared an interest in constitutional history and its use by modern legal scholars for as long as I've known him. Once again, he volunteered his precious time to comment in great detail on what I had written, sharpening my claims, improving my style, and elevating my ambitions. Michael McConnell has been a valued colleague and loyal friend during my time at Stanford. When it comes to history and constitutional interpretation, we agree on a great deal, but where we disagree, he has always been a model of serious, good-faith exchange, and his critical reflections have consistently sharpened my thinking.

My family has always been a vital source of support. My brother, Bill Gienapp, has provided camaraderie, kept things in perspective, and been a steady source of the best kind of humor. The book is dedicated to my parents, Erica Gienapp and the late William Gienapp, who did so much to nurture my scholarly spirit and support me along the way.

Finally, my deepest thanks is reserved, as ever, to my wife, Annie Twitty—my true partner in every conceivable way. She has become an expert in the debate over constitutional originalism merely from being forced to endure years of conversation on the subject. I've proven the true beneficiary of her forced education as she sharpened my ideas and pushed my arguments in helpful directions. She also lent her unparalleled gift for clear and evocative writing by serving yet again as my best and toughest editor. Above all, she afforded me her resolute love and support, which is not something words could possibly repay.

INDEX